Intentions

(things to learn, ideas to ponder, ways it can help, please list below)

~~~~
~~~~

LIFE LESSONS FROM DAD

101 Ways to Get More from Life
(From Someone Who Loves You)

By Chip Franks

ISBN-13: 978-1-64316-917-0 (Kindle Version)
ISBN-13: 978-1-64316-916-3 (Paperback Version)

Interior design by Sandeep Likhar

Go to LifeLessonsBonus.com
for Reports, Resources, and
Your Free ($100 Value) Training,
"*Design and Execute Your Ideal Week.*"

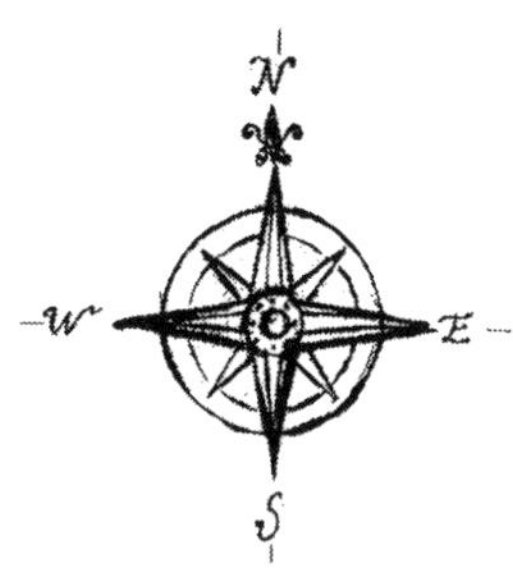

The Foreword
by Hal Elrod

I am a bit of a Chip Franks Facebook stalker. I admit it. The man writes well, I can usually get a good bit of inspiration from his posts, and I love seeing the unbridled love that he has for his family.

We know each other from a few professional masterminds and have gotten to know each other better this year. One of the most profound posts I read from him was about the things that he learned from having a stroke at age forty-four, which was very profound. I shared it with 125,000+ members in The Miracle Morning Community on Facebook and appreciated the positive reactions and shares from the group that resulted. To say that a lot of people took inspiration from that post would be an understatement.

It took on special meaning for me, as I was in my own battle with a rare form of cancer at the time. The things that he learned from his stroke really hit home. The superficial falls away very quickly when something like this happens to your health. Chip's advice (in his words), "Don't Friggin' WAIT," was profound. So many people are just coasting in life and haven't had a wakeup call like this.

One of the lessons from Chip's post really stuck with me. It was, "It is So Important to Leave Something of Yourself for Others." As a dad with two perfect children, I felt this so deeply. I faced the very real possibility that I was done on this Earth, and when you face that possibility, you just wonder if you've done enough to teach and guide your children in life. I appreciated what Chip had to say.

That's why I was excited to hear Chip was writing a book, and I can say that it has exceeded my already high expectations. It is a masterpiece wrapped in love from a father to his adult children on how to live a better life. It's inspired me to write again and leave even more for my kids—although I plan on being around for a very long and healthy time!

Life Lessons from Dad: 101 Ways to Get More from Life (From Someone Who Loves You) is a *fantastic* book.

Chip has done something that I've termed "the Book 2.0." One of the many exceptional things about this book is that it gives many, many wonderful ideas. I love these and agree with almost every piece of wisdom that he lovingly doles out to his children. However, the thing that is really great about these lessons is his insistence on the importance of actually *applying* the wisdom in our everyday lives.

Many books give great information. If you think about it, smart minds gathering useful information—sometimes over the course of years—are already available in books. Books are such a bargain. But almost every book you pick up will simply leave you with the good information. It's almost as if the authors are saying, "Here's something to know," and then leaving the reader at that point.

What I tried to do with *The Miracle Morning: The Not-So-Obvious Secret to Transforming Your Life before 8AM* is to help change *behavior* for those that read it. It wasn't the *knowledge* of The Miracle Morning that changed my life for the better. It was actually *doing* The Miracle Morning that was a game-changer. It was the daily practice of it, day in and day out, that changed everything.

Jim Rohn, a mentor of Chip and mine, said it best:

"Nothing changes until you change. But when you change, everything changes for you."

I think we all know this, but it bears repeating: Knowledge isn't really power. It's potential power if acted upon. That's why I was excited to see that one of the very first Life Lessons from Dad is the idea, "Schedule to Make It Real." I also love that each letter has a section of theory and then a section on actual application of the knowledge in the life of the reader.

I highly encourage you to read this. Very valuable life lessons are contained in this book. But what I really want you to do is the "Advice in Practice" at the end of each lesson. This is where the magic actually happens. It's where you put the knowledge into action to make change real.

When a book comes along, it can change your thinking. This is a great thing, but then the next book comes along and changes your thinking again . . . and the change from the first book is lowered tremendously, if not all but forgotten. That's why it is the rare books like this one that help to change *behavior* which are so much more valuable.

Given a chance, *Life Lessons from Dad: 101 Ways to Get More from Life (From Someone Who Loves You)*, is the rare kind of book that will change your behavior. Many of the principles and strategies are timeless, and you can come back to them again and again.

Some of the lessons that cover things like how to get every job you've ever wanted, or how to outsource everything that doesn't bring you joy (I can use that!), are so practical and easily worth the price of the book. The lessons that really can change the trajectory of a life are found in the Heart and Soul sections. Learning to love yourself, to do a kind act every day, and "Releasing the Result," are profound and presented in such a way as to make it all a real possibility for the reader.

I am honored to write the Foreword and be associated with this book. Chip has given us something to learn from and to keep close as the inevitable slings and arrows of life attempt to knock us down.

In fact, I'm going to give this book you're about to read the ultimate compliment:

I'm going to get it for my kids when they're ready for it.

Thank you, Chip, for writing this. I am certain that it will help many, many families. Congratulations to you, the reader, for getting a copy of this as well. You are going to be blessed by taking in this wisdom and then putting it into practice.

With love,
Hal Elrod
April 2018

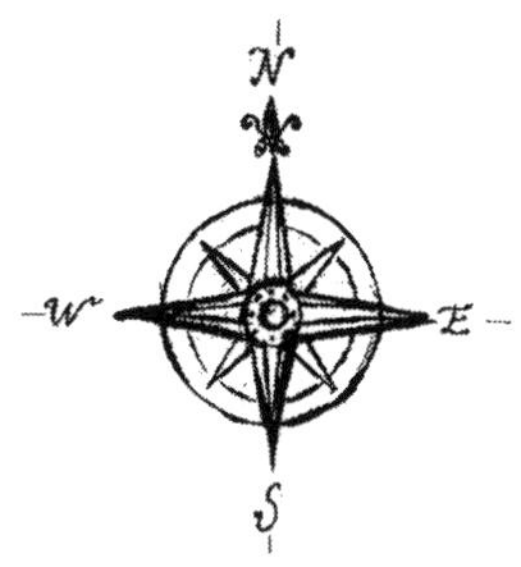

Dedication.

In Birth Order: Mandy, Aly, (My Godson) Cristian, and The Amazing Alec.

Mandy.

My precious girl-beebie. You gave me the world's most wonderful gift by making me a Daddy. You amaze me with your wit, your humor, your work ethic, and your giant heart. I love you, and your sweet, funny, sometimes neurotic ways more than I can say (and I'm generally good with words). Now, please get me a Venti iced water with fifty-six ice cubes.

Aly.

You are my Partner in Crime. We "get" each other because we're on the same wavelength. You are another me (sorry about that!), but a much better version. Your sweet emotional heart, your quirky talent, and genius fill me with pride. Just remember that I will send a fully armed battalion to remind you of my love.

Cristian.

We haven't spent a lot of time together due to distance, but you are never far from my thoughts. I am trying to help with giving you some 'Godfatherly' advice with this book. I hope it helps you. You are smart. You are kind. You have SUCH a bright future ahead of you. Your Godfather loves you and will always be ready to help you in all matters of life!

The Amazing Alec.

Oh, my sweet, precious, wonderful gift from God. You arrived, and you were not like we thought you'd be. It turns out that you're even more loving, kind, smart, funny, and PERFECT than we ever could have known. You expanded all of our hearts, and you make a better person of everyone that you meet. I love you, and am able to love more BECAUSE of you.

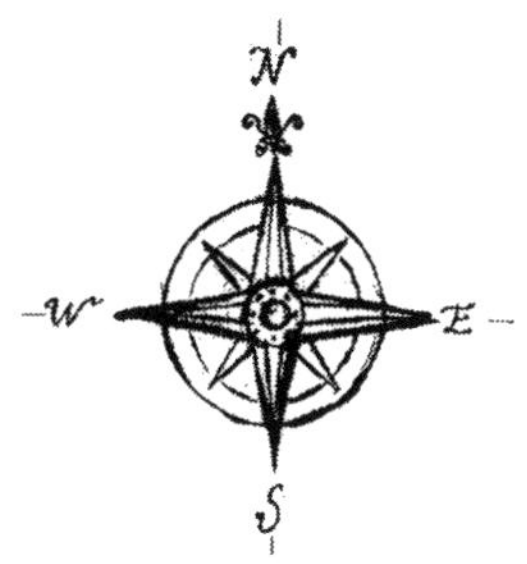

Where It All Is.
(The Table of Contents.)

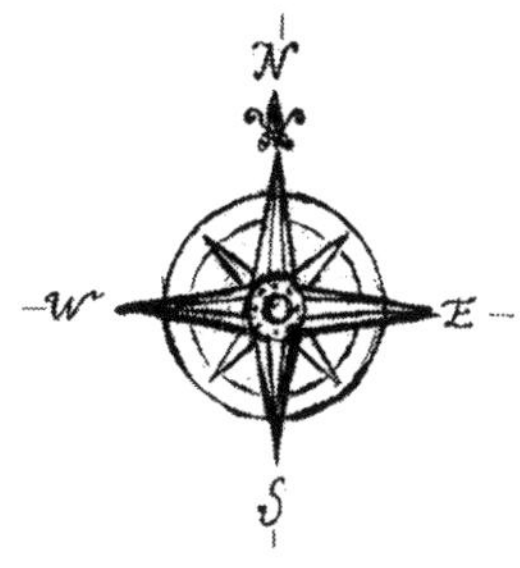

A Note to the Reader.

Have you ever had a big wake-up call in life?

Mine happened when I was forty-four years old at the Langham Huntington Resort in Pasadena, California, 1,392 miles from home.

I was talking to my friend Josh before going back into the ballroom where our business conference of big-hearted entrepreneurs who want to change the world was being held.

I was suffering horribly from the worst flu of my life, and I had to miss much of the morning session to try to sleep it off. I asked Josh who the speakers were that morning.

Or, at least I tried to ask him.

The words coming out of my mouth were gibberish. And the strange thing was, I knew in my mind exactly what I wanted to say. I just couldn't form the words.

I couldn't communicate *at all*.

The strange thing was, I was lucid the entire time, trying to make sense of what was happening. Why couldn't I speak? Was it just the flu? Dehydration, no... I drink entirely too much water for that to happen.

Two doctor friends attended to me right there in the lobby and tested me as the paramedics were called.

I had a stroke.

Technically, it was called an Ischemic Thrombotic Stroke causing aphasia.

Someone contacted my wife Laura, who was in staying in our room with our three children. I could see the anguish on her face, and I tried to reassure her.

"I'm fine. It's all going to be okay."

They wheeled me out of the front of the hotel on that stretcher. I remember passing my friend Steve who was on the phone looking at the parade of paramedics rolling past.

They say your life flashes before your eyes. But for me, there were just burning questions in my mind:

Did I do enough for my children? Did I tell them what I wanted to tell them about life? Did I leave anything for them?

This book you're now holding is the answer to that. It's most everything I'd want them to know in my absence.

These are the lessons on life I want to pass on to them, written specifically to them, but also recorded for your benefit.

This book was written for an audience of three.

It's a set of lessons—lots and lots of them—to my children:

Mandy: eighteen years old, in college and currently working as a barista at Starbucks; hilarious, sentimental, kind, brilliant, responsible, and ridiculously mature.

Aly: fourteen years old and in a special "unschooling" school; quirky, introspective, as well as hilarious, artsy, unconventional, affectionate, and an absolute genius of her own unique variety.

And—last but not least—**The Amazing Alec**: six years old and with Down Syndrome in special education and Kindergarten at our local school; intuitive, empathetic, crazy-affectionate, opinionated, dancing (!), independent, very bright, and adored by the masses.

These lessons are written directly to my children (so when you read "My sweethearts," don't be offended when you realize I'm not calling *you* a sweetheart). They are a compendium of what I want my children to know in life, specifically as they become adults. This book is the accumulation and distillation of wisdom that I've picked up over the forty-five years of my life. I wrote these with a picture of my children before me. You will see that throughout this book I address Mandy, Aly, and Alec—that is because I held them in my mind and heart while writing out all that I know.

But here's the thing: I didn't hold anything back because I also wrote with the hope that others might read this as well. These lessons contain what I want my children to know and to remember about me whether I am with them or not. They contain what I believe all of us should know.

As a reader, you may find flaws with this. There may be pieces of life advice with which you disagree—that's fine. In fact, I *want* you to question everything and see what's true for you. I want to start a conversation about what's best in life. You can (and should) question everything in the pages to follow.

But you cannot doubt my love for my children and my deeply held intention of sharing the *very best* of everything I have with them.

These lessons are pure, genuine, and from the heart. So much thought and emotion have been put into these. I know that this is my legacy with my children—and now with the world—so I left it all out on the table and gave everything that I have.

Although it was written for a very small audience, I want you to get something from the lessons shared here, too. Something else I was hoping to accomplish with this is to encourage other parents to write to their own children and leave a legacy for generations to follow. My grandfather was a very wise man, as was my father, and I would love to know their thoughts about life. I'd love to know what they thought about, what was important to them, and to read what they wrote for me.

But that's not usually how things are done in this day and age.

This book is my attempt to change that.

Enjoy this, but more importantly, *take something* from it. Write your own notes, consider your thoughts on all I have to say, and then actually *do* the Advice in Practice. Schedule some of these exercises with your journal, and change up your daily routine to help make your life better.

After all, making life better is really what we're all here to do.

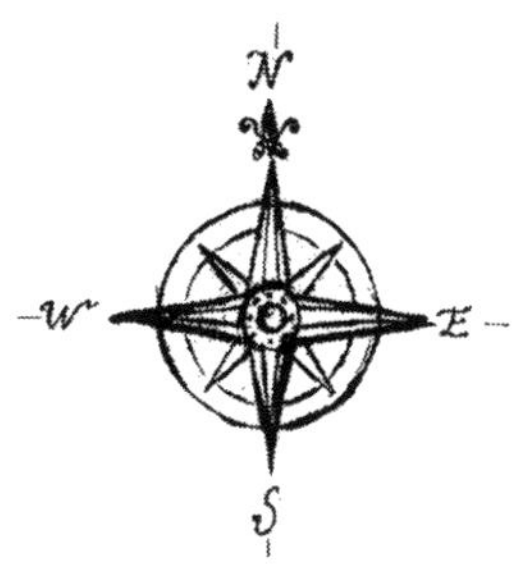

What Are These Lessons All About?
(The Introduction.)

My sweethearts,

I think you know this, but I'll say it again: I love you. Deeply and truly and with all of my heart. That's really the reason behind everything that I'm sharing with you. I want you to know so much more as you enter adulthood. More than I ever did. It's my duty to get this information to you, and to do everything in my power to get you ready for life. That's maybe the most important thing in my entire life.

You already know this, but school doesn't teach you the things that you *really* need to know in life. Sure, you may be able to recite the state capitals (at least on the day of the test) or learn how to calculate the area of a parabola . . .

BUT . . . things like how to love yourself, how to start your own hero's journey, how to truly ask for what you want in life, how to set worthy goals, how to get *every* job you ever apply for, and even how to optimize your sleeping, eating, and moving each day . . .

Yeah. Those types of subjects—arguably *the* most important things—are hardly ever mentioned in school.

That's not good enough for my children.

I DON'T WANT MY KIDS LEFT TO THAT. I want you to know these types of things at *least* as well as I do, and hopefully more. Yet there never seems to be a great time to go over these with you. If and when I do, these lessons are accompanied by a heavy sigh, an eye-roll, and a reply something along the lines of, "I *know*, Dad," or "Not *now*, Dad."

But I want—and I bet you do, too—my precious, wonderful kids to know these types of things. I want you to take all of my knowledge, the things that I've learned from living my forty-five years on this Earth (so far), and STAND ON MY SHOULDERS. I want you to have a solid foundation to stand on while blossoming into fully grown adults. I want you to have access to all of this and more. So, inside these pages I've done just that—wisdom from your Dad, whether I'm with you or not.

You should know about Earl Nightingale's *The Strangest Secret*; you should learn the principles of *The Richest Man in Babylon*; you should understand Joseph Campbell's Hero's Journey; and I want to share Tim Ferriss's thoughts on the "deferred life plan."

The lessons in this book have taken me many decades to collect . . . and I want you to know all of it in less time.

In a world of instant answers and endless information at the touch of a button, the curation of that information and those lessons become more and more important.

That started this whole project—and that's what you are about to read.

Who am I—besides the person who (arguably) loves you most in the world—to be giving advice? I'm an entrepreneur. I just successfully sold my real estate business of twenty-plus years (after being involved in a few thousand transactions) and started on my own Hero's Journey. I've studied marketing. I've worked in sales. I've donated time and money to taking care of others (and I'm not just talking about you).

Totaling it up in my head, I've read nearly 1,000 books on life, business, health, spirituality, self-development, finance, productivity . . . and, of course, a lot of fiction, too, which has its own lessons. I've been blessed to speak onstage at Harvard and in the U.S. and Canada, and have shared the stage with people like Tony Robbins, Daymond John, and Peter Diamandis.

I'm also a bona fide podcast and audiobook *junkie*. I've turned my car into its own university of real life lessons from the masters. I've successfully knocked on doors for eighty hours a week selling books door-to-door. I've stared down depression and despair and overcome them both. I've learned gratitude and unusual kindness—and am generally pretty humble about it, haha! I'm an insatiable learner, and I've practiced techniques on how to remember and put those lessons into action.

Don't get me wrong—I'm an imperfect person and messenger. However, if I was forced to hire someone to talk with you about the "big rocks" (more on that term later) in life, I'd feel very confident in hiring myself. I'm betting and hoping that when you get a chance to read some of these lessons yourself, you'll feel confident in using this advice and even passing it onto *your* kids too.

Do you want advice on how to crush that voice inside your head that says you're not enough? Those pearls of wisdom can be found in the chapter "Kick Your Inner Critic to the Curb," which can be found in the lessons on the Heart.

Want to know about Tony Robbins's time-management thought process? Flip to the chapter "Learn What the Heck an OPOA Is, and Start Using It," in the Mind lessons.

Would it be good for you to know the quickest, easiest way to eliminate brain fog and maintain energy? (The answer is an emphatic *yes*.) That's in the lessons on the Body.

Do you want to know about Jim Rohn's (and Jesus's) principle on how to become great in life? That's in the chapter "Become Great by Finding a Way to Serve the Many," with the lessons on the Soul.

I've gotten every available job that I've ever applied for in my life (about ten of them throughout the years), and to do so, I used a method that I learned from an obscure book written for college grads back in the '80s. Do you think that would be some valuable advice? Of course!

I've tried to pack as much useful information and life-changing advice as I could into this collection of knowledge for you and those with whom you share. Is there more? Yes.

But I guarantee that this is an excellent start, and it's something you can't get from a sterile, state-run classroom.

I say this with every bit of modesty I can muster:

READING THESE LESSONS AND TAKING ACTION ON THE ADVICE CONTAINED INSIDE WILL MAKE YOU A BETTER PERSON.

Even if you learn *one* piece of advice from this book—like starting a "green shake" practice, or building a pipeline versus carrying buckets, how to do your own bucket list, or scheduling family dinners—it will change your life for the better. That's my promise. But even better than that, if you keep this for a reference, it can help with nearly every area of your life: heart, mind, body, and soul!

My mentor said it best:

"What's easy to do, is also easy NOT to do."

Don't let this opportunity to get this distilled wisdom pass you by. Even if you disagree with what I say (and remember, I encourage you to question *everything*), the conversation it starts in your head will be well worth undergoing this journey.

Here are my heart and soul poured out on the pages for you. I invite you to start reading along now . . . let's begin this discussion.

Love,
Dad
a.k.a. Chip Franks
May 2018

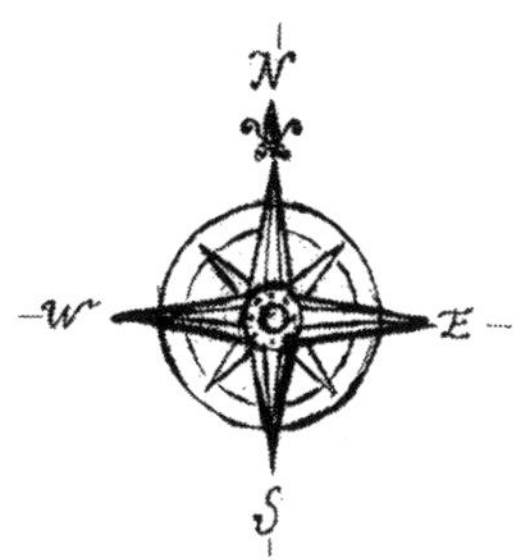

1. Learn The Five Big Steps. (If You Read Nothing Else, Read This.)

"Appreciate and love your ideal daily hero." More on what this means in a bit.

I was talking with a dear friend of mine, James, who happens to own a publishing company, and he told me something disturbing: the vast majority of people don't read past the first part of a nonfiction book.

That's astonishing.

I think it's partly because we expect immediate gratification in most everything we do . . . and books (or, in this case, a collection of lessons) don't necessarily give that *instant* feel-good boost. They're more of a slow-burn kind of experience that you need to pore over for a while before you can get the goodies out of them.

But I also think it's the fault of the authors. If what they're saying isn't compelling, if it doesn't keep you *wanting* to come back for more, then the problem is often with the teacher rather than the student. So to help in this regard, I want to give you the absolute best information right up front.

If I had nothing else to tell you, what would I say were the biggest things I'd want to go over with you? What are the pieces of advice, in order, I'd give you if it were with my dying breaths? I've struggled to make this list, but I have them all now. I feel confident about them, and have experienced the *profound* difference each of these has made in my life—and now I get to share them with you.

Are you ready?

Here they are:

1. **Get into the habit of ACTIVE APPRECIATION**. This absolutely has to be first. It's the difference between happiness and despair. It's the way to start looking at everything as if it's a miracle (it is), and get out of the trap of *entitlement* thinking. I was talking to my pal Hal (you met him in the Foreword) the other day, and he said something so profound yet so simple.

   "People's happiness is determined by how much gratitude they have in their lives."

   Wow. Short and sweet, and so achingly true. You'll find out much more about how to get into active appreciation on page 521. When you get into this habit, you're going to experience life on a whole new level, and I'm excited for you.

2. **LOVE YOURSELF like everything in your world depends on it (because it does).** After an appreciative heart, the thing I would wish most for you in the world is to *actually LOVE yourself*. I want you to realize the spectacular creation you are, and how you deserve the best in life. You really, really do. The thing that's so profound about this is that when you love yourself, you'll start to really treat yourself right. You'll want to make the improvements, and to treat your heart, mind, body, and soul the way you should. It's the foundation for caring enough to do the other things in these lessons.

   I can't wait to share this with you. I want it for you so very much.

3. **Create and follow your own IDEAL SCHEDULE**. Wow, this one is such a biggie—and it may take a while to get it right, and even then it will constantly be revised. But done well, it's going to set you up for an *incredible* life! An Ideal Schedule encompasses your Miracle Morning (ever heard of that book?)—time to exercise, to plan, to do some deep-thought work, to spend quality time with your loved ones, do your Daily Practice, and have your weekly check-in, where you can ponder some of life's biggest questions. This is about self-improvement. *Such* a big deal.

4. **Define and start your very own DAILY PRACTICE**. This is where you do something *every single day* that invigorates you, replenishes your soul, and makes you better. My mentor in this believes that you should do something good for yourself mentally, spiritually,

emotionally, and physically every single day. Picking something to do for each of these areas and committing to do them every day is what we call a "Daily Practice." Mine includes doing Idea Lists (more on those later), doing something I enjoy each day, something good for my body, and, maybe most importantly, something kind for someone else each day.

You'll need to figure out what your Daily Practice looks like, and then start it. You'll find that it makes you a better, happier, and constantly improving person.

The quality of your life is determined by how you spend your time.

This is the best way to get a handle on that. When this starts to fall into place, everything in your life will start to click for you. You'll feel purposeful, like you're gaining momentum in your life . . . because you will be.

5. **Begin your Hero's Journey**. This could be defined as your purpose in life, or the reason that you feel that you were put on Earth. It's the calling that tugs at your soul and makes your heart beat a little faster when you discover it. It's, as Joseph Campbell (the author of this concept) says, "following your bliss." It's what you feel like you *have* to do. The big thing about this is that most don't ever even *look* for it, or have their ears perked up to listen to the soft sound of the call to adventure.

   There is a lot on the Hero's Journey and making an extraordinary life for yourself and others in the lessons to follow. I am so honored to share this with you, my sweethearts.

I'm hoping that these items are at least a *little* intriguing to you. If you do just one of them—if you're not already doing them—your life will improve. If you are able to do all of these, your life will be *revolutionized*. You'll have a very solid foundation for everything in your life, and you'll improve every single day. That's something I want for you—and hopefully you want for yourselves, too.

It's in your grasp. You just need to take it.

Advice in Practice:

- Get out your journal—you're going to need one as you read these lessons! Before you get started in reading these, write out each of these steps. See if you can commit them to memory. It's tough to make them an acronym, but I'd like you to remember them. I use this sentence to help me: "Appreciate and love your ideal daily heroes." Hopefully that's enough to do it.

  Whenever you're struggling in life, come back to this. Taking each of these steps in your life will help in returning to a more fulfilling state of equanimity.

- Go look at each section in these lessons. The best way is to refer to that Where It All Is table of contents in the front of the book. Browse through them now—get an idea about what they each contain, and then come back to the journal and write out what you think about each.
  - Where are you now?
  - Are you actively appreciating every day?

- Do you love (or even like) yourself, honestly? It's okay for *now* if you don't—you'll get better at this with practice.
    - Do you have a Daily Practice, or maybe rules for yourself?
    - Are you spending your time wisely? Consistently?
    - Are you living your own Hero's Journey right now? Have you ever? Do you want to?

- Get it all out on the page, and do it now. What we're going to do with these lessons and the Advice in Practice is to get these thoughts out of the deep, dark recesses of your beautiful mind and out onto paper, where you can examine them, keep what works, and discard what doesn't.

Notes, thoughts, and intentions.

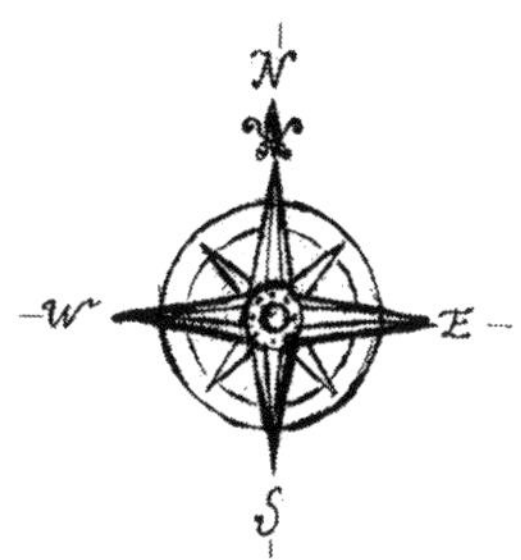

2. Build on a Foundation Instead of a Hobo Shack.

Obviously, you're holding an entire BOOK of *Life Lessons from Dad* right now. And the temptation might be to just flip through and pick and choose different pieces of advice that you (hopefully) find relevant and/or interesting.

Well, hold on just for a bit—because before you get into the rest of this book I want to talk to you about the concept of a hobo shack versus a strong foundation. I got this concept from the book *The Millionaire Real Estate Agent* by Gary Keller.

Keller said that if you go to a real estate seminar and get some business-building ideas, and you decide to use a random tactic here and another there, another, then another, and if you do that without first having a *structure* for your business, a *foundation*, and you just start adding all of this creativity . . .

Pretty soon your business will end up looking like a hobo shack.

Instead, he said (and I paraphrase), you should first build a solid foundation, create a set system, and *then* you can add creativity as needed.

So one of the first pieces of advice that I'd like to talk with you about is getting your FUNDAMENTALS right before I start dispensing somewhat random—though hopefully very valuable—advice to you that you can actually implement into your life.

You definitely need to work on the fundamentals first. Have them pretty much solidified to help live successfully and meaningfully, before really digging deep on the other advice I'm dishing.

So, what are the fundamentals?

I've been thinking about this, and I believe they should be best divided between *physical* and *character* fundamentals.

The Physical Fundamentals (or "Fundies") are easier to define: eating, hydrating, moving, and sleeping. We'll talk about those later in the pages to come about the Body. It's easier to quantify these. You instantly know if you're doing them right or if you're not. They're a little easier to get straight, usually.

The Character Fundies are a little more complex. But they're just as important—probably more so—as the Physical Fundies in leading a quality life.

I've tried to distill them for you by breaking the Character Fundies into three parts. Benjamin Franklin had thirteen virtues, so maybe I should add more . . . but I think these three cover the "big rocks" in life:

- Gratitude/Appreciation.
- Self-Development/Getting Better.
- Kindness/Contribution.

I've been thinking over these a lot, and I think they cover pretty much all the bases of someone with good character. If you have these, then you're doing well in life. Regardless of money, relationships, or circumstances, these are the things that can't be taken from you. They are a part of you, and they're all great attributes to cultivate.

If you *don't* have these (please understand, my children, that I think you *do*), then at some level I think this grand experience of life will be unfulfilling for you.

And you deserve to have a fulfilling life. A life full of love, of grand experiences, of contribution, of unusual kindness, and open-mouthed wonder!

Now, don't get me wrong: I'm not *mandating* any of this. I'm not saying you have to do any of this. No matter what happens, you'll be loved unconditionally. That's your birthright. It's *all* of our birthrights. But I'm definitely suggesting that these are important—when you cultivate these traits and you use them in your life, it will take on a rich vibrancy that few people truly experience.

And that's what I want for you.

I love you so much, and you deserve this.

Advice in Practice:

I also use the word *practice* very deliberately. This grand tapestry of life is always a chance to practice. We'll never reach perfection (at least not in our actions, but you're all perfect now, just as God created you), but we can always *practice*. Practice is *doing*, and far superior to just theory on a subject.

- Take stock of where you are with the fundamentals of Gratitude, Self-Development, and Kindness. I'd suggest pulling out your journal and writing it out on paper. Try to be honest, but not unnecessarily harsh (that's good advice in itself—yay, me!). Do you feel like you're pretty good on these attributes? Do you think you need to improve? Does it concern you?

  The good news is that all of these can be developed and improved. ALL of them.

  The best way is to begin with the one you feel you're worst at initially. Is it the self-development, the gratitude, or the kindness part? Truly?

  Some may say that we're either born with these or we're not, but I don't find that belief useful in the slightest. You absolutely *can* improve just about anything you set your mind on. That's an awesome thing about life. Maybe one of the best. Can I get your agreement on this?

- Write out or commit this quote to memory. It's so, so good:

"I know of no more encouraging fact than the unquestionable ability of man to elevate his life by a conscious endeavor."
— Henry David Thoreau.

(There will be much more of Mr. Thoreau's wisdom throughout these lessons!)

- Come back to revisit this chapter during and after you read all of these lessons. It's good to think about the whole of what we're trying to accomplish when going through each part.

  Before we get on to advice about each of these fundamentals . . . I'll pause again and let you know:

  You are loved.

Notes, thoughts, and intentions.

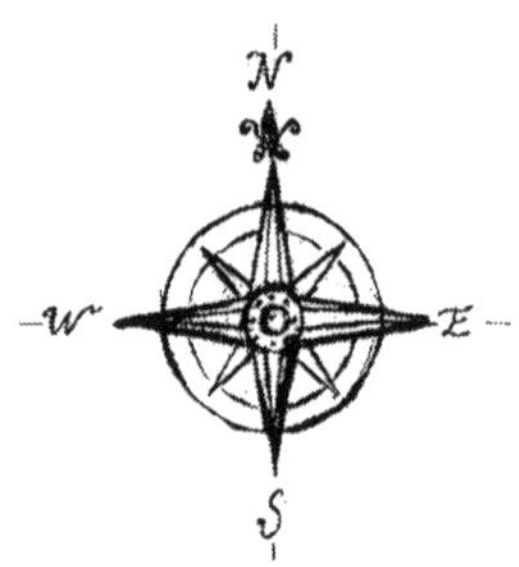

3. Remember the Parable of the Big Rocks, and First Things First.

My precious loves,

You're almost to the meat of these lessons, I promise . . . but I want to explain one of the most important concepts before we get into talking about your Heart, Mind, Body, and Soul. That's the concept of "big rocks."

We'll go over a story first, and then the meaning behind it. When I first heard the term "big rocks," it had such a profound effect on me that it has been a part of my everyday vocabulary since. I read about this in the book The *7 Habits of Highly Effective People: Powerful Lessons in Personal Change*, by Stephen R. Covey, while I was in college (a book not mandated by college, as that would've been far too useful for school).

The Parable:

> A professor stands in front of her class at a table. On the table she has a huge jar, and next to it a container of good-size rocks.

Starting the lesson, she pours all of the rocks into the jar, filling it to the top. Looking at it and then the class, she asks, "Is the jar full?"

The class looks and answers "Yes!" because it's filled to the brim.

"Oh, really?" the professor asks. She pulls a container of pebbles from under the table and proceeds to pour all of them into the big jar, too.

"Now," she asks when finished, "is it full?"

The students agree that it's now full.

Then the professor pulls a container of sand from under the table, and the class groans as she pours all of it into the giant jar.

"Is it full now?" she asks.

"No," they respond. "You can put water in it now." They are catching on.

The professor pulls out a pitcher of water and is able to pour it into the giant jar, as well. All of it fit.

Then a question: "Now, would all of this have fit if I had poured the sand and water in first?"

The class answers "No!"

The wise teacher explains that everything only fits when the big rocks go in first, then the smaller rocks, the pebbles, sand, and finally the water.

> The professor teaches what this all means: "Imagine that this big jar represents your life, and all of the items put into it are the things of life—the appointments, the work, the calls, the vacations, the good times and bad. The big rocks are the most important things in life—the family, a sense of mission or purpose. The next smaller rocks might be your job, or taking care of things at work. The pebbles are the incessant emails, texts, and phone calls . . . and the sand and water could be some of the more frivolous things in life. They can still be fun, but maybe won't lead to something more.

Now the principle is this:

You will only have enough time and room in your life if you put the big rocks—the most important things in life—first.

You can't try to put them into the end of the an already-stuffed appointment book. *For everything to work, do the most important things first.*

It's a powerful lesson, and just being able to put it into a parable-like form helps to make the story stick. A quote from the late Mr. Covey puts this very eloquently:

"The key is not to prioritize what's on your schedule, but to schedule your priorities."
— Stephen Covey

So, the question is—what are the BIG ROCKS in your life? This is maybe, just maybe, the most important question that exists for us. Time spent contemplating this, thinking about it, deciding on it, refining it—and then, of course, doing something about it—is probably the most precious and valuable thing that we can do in life.

What are your big rocks?

This will be different for each of us, at least somewhat. But like the above, I hope and think that family, the important relationships in life, and your Hero's Journey are all part of your big rocks.

We'll talk about this a *lot* in the upcoming pages, but I'm strongly convinced that we are here to do something in this world. I believe we're made to serve others in some capacity, to live beyond ourselves. And I think that a big rock is and should be your *mission*, or your own Hero's Journey.

That mission or purpose or Hero's Journey is absolutely key to a life well-lived.

What are other big rocks? Relationships (especially with your dad, amiright?!), actually spending time with your loved ones, listening to them, and helping them, appreciating them . . . that's obviously so important.

Lastly, I'd say that self-development and rejuvenation time are important, and should be considered as big rocks. There's not a lot of urgency to self-development, because not too many people are looking over your shoulder, setting deadlines, and checking progress for you. That's why they call it "self" development, I guess. But the fact is, a commitment to it—to learning, to implementing, to staying curious, to trying new things, to contemplating what worked and didn't, to self-reflection, meditation, working out, and all of those types of things—will make your life better in every way.

BUT.

I don't want to decide what your big rocks are for you. That's something you should do for yourself. And if you do it, and really think about—and most importantly, keep them in mind and actually form your life around those priorities—you'll live an even more amazing life.

Advice in Practice:

(Lots for this . . . it's a *really* important concept!)

- Look up the Parable of the Big Rocks on YouTube to get a better understanding of it, and to see it presented in a much better fashion than I've been able to present to you.
- Journal this. Write out the question at the top: "What are my big rocks? What's most important to me in life?" And just go about answering that. Write it all out. Get it out of your soul and onto paper so that you can look at it objectively. You can think about it, rearrange it, see what's been lurking under the surface, and expose it to the light of day.
- Then examine your big rocks. Which are most important? Clarify, clarify, clarify. Get them clear and write them down, and then perhaps commit them to memory (maybe the order of them).

- Examine your calendar. What have you been spending your time on lately? For the last week? Month? Years? Have you been spending the actual time honoring those big rocks? Honestly? Is most of your life right now spent on making a living, without a lot of regard to those big rocks? That's okay—for a while, but not indefinitely. You're better than that, and your time is worth more.

- Brainstorm and make an Idea List (if you don't know how to do that yet, go check out the section on Idea Lists on page 200) on ways that you can integrate your big rocks more in your life. If you're working ten-plus hours a day to make ends meet, these ways may look like bringing your children to work occasionally, or studying a book on self-development while you're on your lunch break. I don't know your circumstances now, but you do, so take a little time and make that list.

- See how you're spending your money (get the Mint app—very helpful). These are probably your priorities now, but are they in line with what you've determined your big rocks to be? If not, try to correct that. Write out another Idea List on how you can change your spending to be more in line with what you've determined is most important.

- Lastly, consider the Regular Check-In (there's advice on that in this book for your convenience on page 505) and include your big rocks on that list. How are you doing on them? My friend Brian says the most important things (his big rocks) are the "Five F's"—Faith, Family, Friends, Fitness, and Finance. Sounds good to me . . .

but whatever your big rocks are, actually *schedule* the time in your calendar to check in and see how you're doing with each of them.

- Call your dad. Tell him that you love him after reading this.
- (And if you're not my kid . . . call your dad anyway.)

I love each of you so, so very much. I want this to land for you, and for you to understand it all for yourselves. Life can be so very wonderful for you!

Notes, thoughts, and intentions.

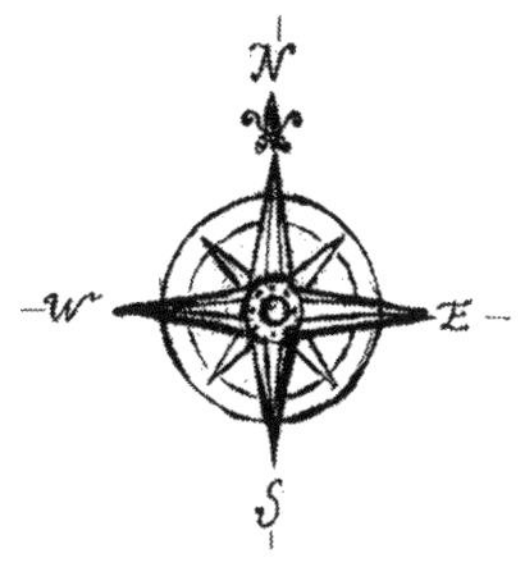

4. Schedule It to Make It Real.

My beauties!

This is so important, because—despite what you've heard—knowledge is not power. It's only *potential* power, if you use it. None of this that I'm writing to you in these lessons will make any difference at all unless you act on it. That's what this letter is all about.

Schedule it to make it real.

This is a fundamental fact that I want you to know. It's the reason I include this topic in the introductory lessons, because it is of universal importance.

> ***Nothing changes until it becomes a part of your schedule. If you learn a new skill, if you have a brilliant idea, this is not going to make a difference for you until it's part of your everyday life.***

There's a quote that I love by Anthony Robbins, who says:

> ***"If you talk about it, it's a dream; if you envision it, it's possible; but when you schedule it, it's real."***

And that's what this is all about—it's actually where the rubber meets the road. When you take your big ideas, your big dreams, or your big plans and you actually put them down on your calendar to know *exactly when* you're doing them.

Education and knowledge are fairly useless if you don't put any of it into action somehow. Therefore, you must turn your thoughts and your ideas into clear, concrete actions. Actions that you can see, that you can do, and that actually make a difference in your life.

One of the biggest common denominators of successful people is that they will take action immediately. A lot of times, it's *imperfect* action. Action that is more along the lines of "ready, fire, aim." These people just get started with something, rather than waiting for the perfect plan to come along later, and they iterate and optimize as they go.

Another one of my favorite quotes by Tim Ferriss on this subject goes like this:

> ***"The stars will never align and the traffic lights of life will never all be green at the same time. The universe doesn't conspire against you, but it doesn't go out of its way to line up the pins either. Conditions are never perfect. 'Someday' is a disease that will take your dreams to the grave with you."***

Putting something into your schedule to work on your plan, to work on your business, to work on a relationship—*that* is where the change actually starts.

One of the things I'd like to impart to you—and this is again something that Tony Robbins talks about—is to never leave the scene of a good idea without taking an immediate first step toward its completion.

If you have an idea that strikes your soul, that you *have to* accomplish right then and there, you need to do something to make it *real*. That could be as little as scheduling a phone call or just taking the time to think about it. The important thing is that you do *something* to start it *immediately*, or it will be lost forever to what Jim Rohn called "the Law of Diminishing Intent."

The same thing happens when you're reading a book. I don't want you just to think, "This is the most *amazing* collection of lessons in a book by a brilliant and freakishly handsome dad!" Instead, think of how you're going to *use* this information, and then implement it into your life.

Have a way to put that piece of knowledge into a place where you can reference and use it again and again. It can be notes that you take on Evernote or it can be your journal, but it needs to be a place where you can retrieve it when it's needed. My friend Ari calls this "the external brain."

So let me ask you now . . . have you *scheduled* your ideas?

Advice in Practice:

- Get a calendar and use the heck out of it! It can be digital on your phone/computer, or a dry-erase board, or even a yellow notepad. The key is to use one and only one calendar. If you use more than that, things will get jumbled and meetings will get lost. If you use that one calendar and schedule in your time for working *on* your life, there's a much better chance that you'll actually do it.

- I want you to get into the habit of doing one tangible action toward the accomplishment of your goal the *moment* that you set it. Make a call, schedule a meeting, order the thing you need to do it, or write that specific time you're going to do it in your calendar. Actually stick to it. Something I like to do is use my phone to set alarms for the time I've scheduled to work on my ideas and life.

- Set up your "external brain." You need a place to reference your ideas and grand plans for the future. Compare Evernote, your journal, your planner, Trello on the computer, or whatever it is you can carry—what works for you?

- My last piece of practice for this is that when you get a *great* idea—something you *have* to follow, something you have to actually put out into the world, something that "sings that siren song"—write an Idea List of at least ten things you can do to immediately *breathe life* into it.

  I'm a great starter, but not necessarily a great finisher. So, for me to finish something in the past, I've had to have a spectacular start. I'd need to get a good 50 to 75 percent of it done on the initial push, or I'd fall prey to the law of diminishing intent and not finish things. The Idea List has to be a list of ways you can get a lot done on this very quickly and to make it happen. Get into the habit of doing Idea Lists to make your dreams, your goals, your projects, or your relationships flourish quickly.

- I love you so much, my sweethearts, and I can't wait to get the rest of these lessons to you.

Notes, thoughts, and intentions.

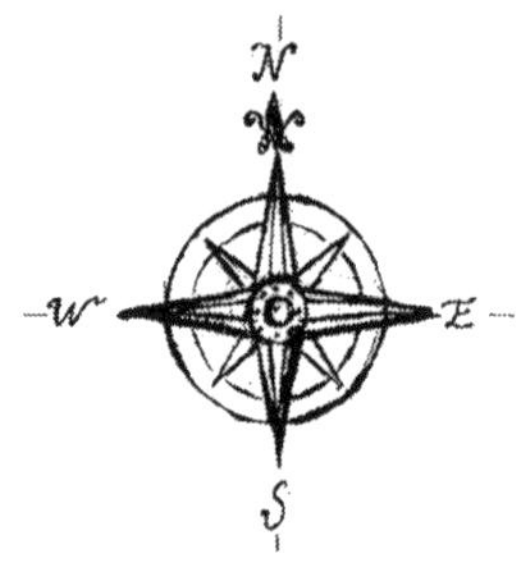

5. Don't Be Holier than Thou.

(Or, Messages from an Imperfect Messenger.)

Something I wanted to get out there right away is that I don't want to come off as "holier than thou." To act like I have it all together when I don't would directly contradict some of the advice dispensed in the lessons to follow.

We fight. We have disagreements. We don't keep as clean of a house as we should. Our weeks can be chaotic, and our patience can sometimes wear thin. We don't always put big rocks first, or schedule things we want in our life immediately.

But, of course, that doesn't stop the love. In fact, perhaps it even *enhances* it—because we see one another, warts and all, and we still accept each and every one. It's one of the greatest gifts in life to completely, totally be *yourself* and still know you're loved and supported.

So please know that this advice isn't meant to come from a pedestal. It's more from the day-to-day trenches—and, of course, from the heart.

It's important to keep in mind that *everyone* struggles. No matter who it is, how successful they seem, they have their bad moments, and their life is usually *vastly* different than it appears from the outside looking in. This is especially true in the Facebook age, when the highlights are shouted from the rooftops, and often the lowlights are barely whispered and left out of public view.

So please know that our family is always a work in progress. All families are.

And *thank you* for reading these lessons. Really, I'm overwhelmed that you want to hear what I have to say.

Go to LifeLessonsBonus.com
for Reports, Resources, and
Your Free ($100 Value) Training,
"*Design and Execute Your Ideal Week.*"

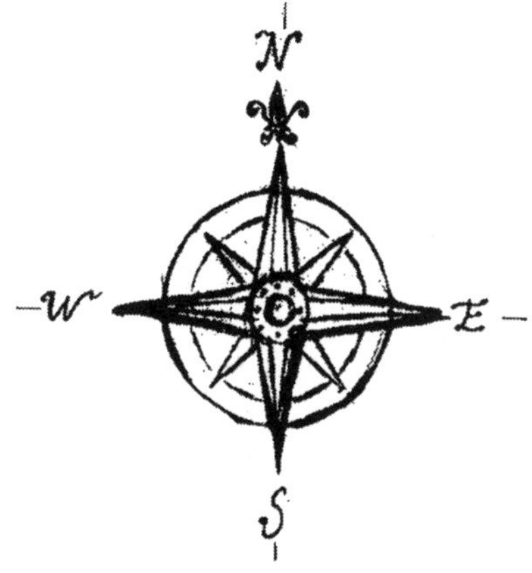

THE HEART.

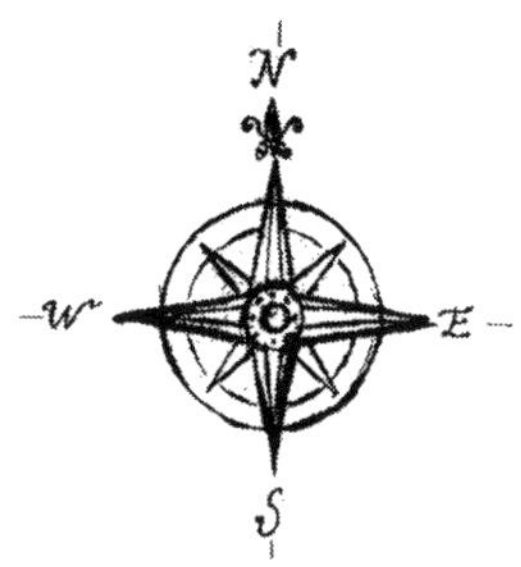

Introduction to The Heart.

My children . . . mis tesoros (which is Spanish for *my treasures*, but I hope you knew that already, mis amigos) . . . We begin the bulk of this book with matters of the heart.

This is the section where all of my advice revolves around LOVE. Loving yourself. Loving others. Loving what you're doing every day. That kind of thing. Which is really, really important.

But it also has to do with COURAGE. It's funny, because we actually had this talk in the car yesterday. Where does the word "courage" come from? Do you remember? Well, this part of the book gives it away. The word courage comes from "heart."

From the great sage, Google: from Middle English *corage* and early French *curage* (denoting the heart, as the seat of feelings); and from Latin *cor*, literally "heart."

Courage is the one virtue that makes all of the other virtues possible.

It takes *courage* to do the right thing, to ask questions, to do something different in life when the crowd might be doing something else entirely.

The big problem with all matters of the heart and courage? We rarely talk about it. Think about this: in traditional education, how often does your teacher mention courage or heart (outside of biology class, which is more literal)? As I mentioned in the introduction—school doesn't talk about it.

And it often doesn't come up at home, either, when we sit at the dinner table or we talk in the car. Yes, I try to broach these subjects . . . but they're often squashed by whatever is happening that day, or the music we listen to in order to pump us up for the day. It's always the tyranny of the mundane that hides the more important things.

The advice in this section is what the great, late Stephen R. Covey would call the IMPORTANT but not URGENT things that we should all know and talk about.

It's advice as simple as, "Say please and thank you"—showing care to others.

It's how to maintain courage (practice everyday acts of courage).

It's caring for what enters your heart (a.k.a. avoiding gossip and news).

It's maintaining love, such as with a practice that's so simple and life-changing yet so easy not to do—making regular dates with your loved ones.

It's *showing* love better (i.e., don't keep compliments to yourself!).

It's even how to set your heart free through experiences versus buying stuff.

Some—or perhaps *all*—of these pieces of advice can have a profound impact on your everyday life. They can change the way that you look at life and at yourself, and help you to have more love in your life. Love for yourself, and through that, love for others. In fact, I would argue that self-love is NECESSARY for the proper loving of others in your life. That's why we begin with "The Self-Love Manifesto."

The promise I make to you: if you can take even some of these pieces of advice, and put them into regular practice in your life, you'll live a much fuller, much richer life. And that's what I want for you more than anything.

I love you, and it's an honor to have this conversation with you.

Notes, thoughts, and intentions.

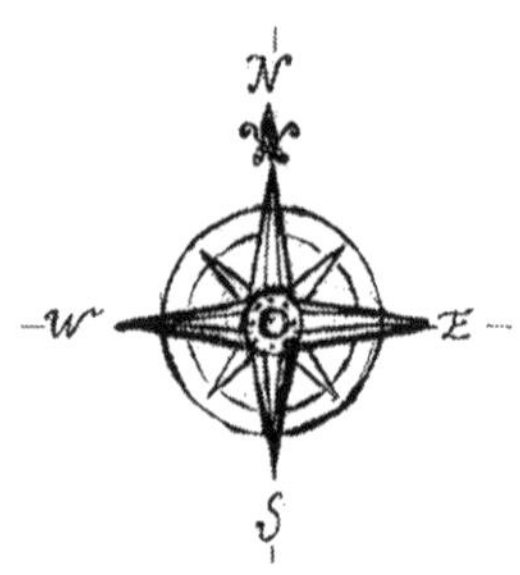

6. Love Yourself.
(The Self-Love Manifesto.)

The Supreme Importance of Self-Love, and How to Achieve It: A Manifesto.

Let me ask you a question, in all seriousness.

DO YOU LOVE YOURSELF?

Can you look in the mirror and truly love who it is that's looking back at you?

It sounds so strange, a little weird . . . but maybe that's because it's something that's not talked about nearly enough in today's society.

Being able to stop and ponder something like this is actually a fairly recent phenomenon in human evolution. Our ancestors were probably too busy running from saber-toothed tigers and scrounging for food for most of their waking hours.

But we are now blessed to be part of a prosperous place where our physical needs are met (for the most part), and we have the luxury—often taken for granted by all of us, myself included—of exploring how we feel about ourselves and everything in our lives.

Self-love is a topic that sits heavily on my heart. Several people very close to me have confided in me that this has been a serious issue for them. I have friends that by all outward appearances are the very definition of "success," yet they still carry this hollow feeling inside—and some have even been plagued with thoughts of suicide.

I don't know exactly what these folks are thinking. I don't know that I've ever gotten so down as to think about ending it all. However, I *have* been extremely down and depressed, so I can empathize with the feeling that life isn't going to get better. I've dug out of that since then. I've clawed and scratched, and eventually cruised, to feeling very much better—on top of the world, even.

I can say with all honesty that I've gotten to the point of LOVING MYSELF.

And having done this, I've discovered some things that are true for me which I would like to share with you:

A truly beautiful life is only possible with self-love.

You must first love yourself to truly love others.

If you don't feel worthy to love yourself, your love for others will be diminished.

The amount of joy you feel in life is limited by what you think you deserve.

The things you strive for in life—the pursuit of grand dreams and your Hero's Journey—are directly related to how much you care for and love yourself.

You will only attempt that which you believe you deserve . . . and what you believe you deserve is determined by the amount of love you have for yourself.

If you truly love yourself, you'll be less likely to be depressed or contemplate hurting yourself.

Paradoxically, it's not a selfish act to love yourself—in fact, it's the most selfless thing you can do. When you love yourself more, you are then able to love others more.

It ALL comes back to SELF-LOVE.

Let me ask you: do these statements ring true for you? Honestly? Take the time to examine them. Hold them up to the light, twist them, turn them, and see if they are incontrovertible. Anything that is an incontrovertible truth should be able to be inspected closely.

These are all true for me, and again, having come from a place where I did *not* love myself and where I hated who I was, it's easier for me to look back and see how true these statements are.

Don't get me wrong. It's not all sunshine, unicorns, and rainbows all of the time. I only maintain my attitude daily through *practice*. I have rituals, things I do to maintain my frame of mind. Sometimes I slip, and when I do I can feel the darkness of those thoughts fighting to invade my mind.

As my mentor would say, "Left unattended, the weeds will take the garden."

But, having come from that place, I can now tell you the actions and the thought processes that helped to bring me out of that place. And if you're there now, maybe, just *maybe*, these can work for you too.

It would be such an honor to know that this would have helped even one person.

***

Two years ago, I didn't like myself.

I wasn't really happy with what I was doing.

I was terribly overweight, constantly *tired* . . . and *tired* of being tired. I didn't want to get out of bed. I didn't feel like I was making any difference in the world.

And yet, I had a beautiful, wonderful family. I had a business that helped in living a great lifestyle.

So why was I so unfulfilled, feeling like I wasn't living up to my potential?

Deep down, I knew that I wasn't doing what I was meant to do. And I felt so guilty for having these feelings after all that God had given me. I wasn't honoring Him/Her/It.

I get it. I understand not loving yourself. And I'm wondering if maybe *you're* feeling some of that, too.

I mean, don't get me wrong: There are still some good times. You laugh once in a while, and you still have some good times with friends. You watch movies and TV, maybe listen to podcasts . . . but you turn it up to drown out the crying you're feeling deep inside.

Or maybe it's a lot more subtle for you. You're just going along with things and life is just *happening*. The days are going slowly and the years are going fast, but you just haven't truly felt connected to true joy. Obviously, I don't know your situation . . . but it just may come back to a lack of self-love.

Does any of this ring true for you?

***

Yesterday, I had this realization as I was working out: doing something good for myself wasn't about building discipline.

It may feel like that. Like you need more *discipline* in order to pull out of this low rut and make progress in your life. But it's really about this:

You need to love yourself enough to want to do it.

If you value yourself enough, you'll want to eat right, take care of yourself, take a course, read a book, go to a conference to improve yourself.

So maybe the biggest self-development "hack" of all is to *learn to love yourself* completely.

To know that you are a part of some divinity, that unconditional love is your birthright, and that you are worthy of all of God's blessings.

If and when you truly feel that, then everything else gets better—and I mean *everything*: your life *and* the lives you're able to touch from that place of self-love.

It's being able to look at yourself in the mirror and honestly, truly, genuinely *liking* that person you see staring back at you. Remember that saying, "I may love you, but I don't *like* you right now"? It all flows from there.

Loving yourself is of supreme importance. And if you *don't*, that's the first and only thing you need to improve in your life. It's not getting in shape or taking a course in [insert here]. It's LOVING YOURSELF enough to do those things to improve your life.

This is a universal truth:

Your life experience will never exceed the amount of love you have for yourself.

If you really ask yourself whether or not you agree with this, and you do (and I hope you do), then it's time to start loving yourself. It's not something that I think happens overnight, even when all of this makes sense. It's something you need to feel like you deserve.

But the funny thing is, loving yourself is not something you need to deserve. You've already earned it just by existing. Just by *being*.

You are a child of God (Universe or Source or whatever you subscribe to). His divinity runs through your veins, my friend. When you were formed in the womb, you were already worthy of the greatest blessings. You didn't need to make good grades or be the perfect son or daughter. You were made to be loved.

One of my friends was talking with me about this when I was having some trouble thinking that I "deserved" true success. Maybe this will resonate with you like it did me:

He asked, "When your son was born, did he deserve love?"

Of course.

"But wait," he asked, "did he *do* anything to deserve this love?"

No.

"But he's still loved? He deserved that?"

Yes.

We all do.

Here is a fundamental fact of life: YOU DESERVE TO BE LOVED . . . just for the fact that you were made and you occupy this world.

And it doesn't matter if you're just scraping by, living on the streets, or if the world whispers your name in hushed reverence. You're not different in that regard. You are worthy of love just for who you are. You're not the exception to this rule—no one can break this universal law.

Think about yourself as a child, and maybe some of the hurts or disappointments that little human being faced. Really imagine what you looked like and the thoughts you had back then, and ask if you deserved complete and unconditional support, encouragement, and love then . . . did you?

(Your answer should be an unequivocal YES!)

You deserve it now, too.

Are you starting to see this? Is it sinking in?

You deserve to love yourself. But the fact that you still may not is because it's a process(or it certainly was for me).

***

How to love yourself (again).

I'm telling you what it took for me—maybe it will work for you. If it doesn't, I invite you to try other ways. It's the most important thing you can do for yourself, and it's the most important thing you can do for others as well.

I was lucky or blessed enough to have a book cross my path which gave me a way to start feeling better about myself. I followed the process it outlined only slowly at first, and just like a muscle, my self-worth grew stronger as I exercised it.

The book was called Choose *Yourself! Be Happy, Make Millions, Live the Dream*, by James Altucher, and the process he describes in it is called the "Daily Practice." It's where you do something good for yourself physically, emotionally, mentally, and spiritually every day. Starting to take a daily walk, doing something just for me that I enjoyed each day, doing Idea Lists and becoming an Idea Machine . . . and, most importantly, taking care of my soul.

I wrote down what I was grateful for every day in a Gratitude Journal. And I made a decision then that really affected me: I resolved to do a KIND ACT for another human being every single day.

And when I felt like I didn't want to get out of bed, thinking I wasn't going to make a difference to anyone, I remembered that self-promise of a kind act, and I knew that I'd make a difference in the life of *at least one* other person that day.

And I got better.

The longer I did this, the better I felt—and the more I loved myself.

In fact, Altucher recommends another book called *Love Yourself Like Your Life Depends On It*, by Kamal Ravikant. I read that, too, and did those exercises. I said "I love myself" several *thousand* times during those months of healing . . . and I started to experience a renaissance in my life. I started to feel like I deserved some of the good things that started happening in my life. And that helped *more* good things happen.

I learned about something called the "Miracle Morning," from Hal Elrod—heard of *him*? It had me waking up each morning (enthusiastically, I might add, and it had been quite a while since that had happened) to pray and meditate, say affirmations, visualize myself doing the things to make my life better, exercising, and journaling. I know I mention these in some of the very first chapters of this book, but the ideas behind the Miracle Morning are important enough to reiterate over and over again.

I was suddenly loving myself enough to take action on improving my life. That's made such a difference for me, and I'm betting and hoping that doing something similar will help you feel better about yourself, too.

I don't ever want this to sound like I'm speaking from a place of superiority, or that I have everything figured out (recall the intro chapter, "Don't Be Holier than Thou"). I assure you that I do not. But I want to share this in case you're meant to hear it. I would absolutely love to know that my journey to self-love can happen for others, too.

So, if this helps, or if you think that someone you know may get some benefit from this, please share this with others.

Also, if you're feeling overwhelmed and beaten down by life, and you need someone to talk to—PLEASE reach out to me or someone you trust. It can make all the difference in the world, and remember—you *deserve* it.

The world and the people in your life need you.

Do you love yourself?

Advice in Practice:

- I'd like you to write yourself a love letter—or, even better, a "Self-Love Manifesto." It's a great exercise. I want you to write out why *you* think you should love yourself, and some reasons that you *do* love yourself.

- Revisit what you've written occasionally, and update it. Keep it handy—in a journal you keep with you, or printed out in your own planner, or on your bathroom mirror. Read it especially when you've had rough days or are feeling down on yourself. Maybe even write above it as a reminder: I DESERVE TO FEEL LOVED.

- Create an Idea List of powerful self-love affirmations that you can go over during your Miracle Morning practice. Add to it, amend them, and change them as you go so that you feel they will always resonate with you.

- Lastly, one of the best things I can tell you is to read the book *Love Yourself Like Your Life Depends On It*, by Kamal Ravikant. It's a small book that can literally be read in an hour or two (unlike this behemoth), but it can really change your life. Get in the habit of saying, "I love myself."

- Call your dad and let him tell you how much you are loved!

Notes, thoughts, and intentions.

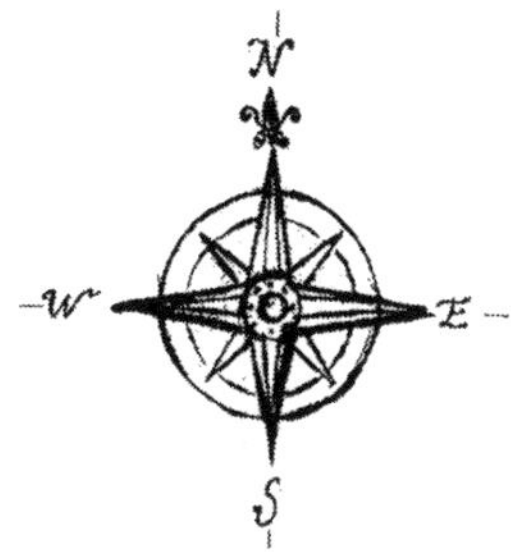

7. Kick Your Inner Critic to the Curb.

Now, my girls and my sweet boy, this is another very, very important topic. I was introduced to this last year—not as a new concept, but as something to think of this way—by a good friend named Billy Anderson. I need to give him a lot of credit for this, for both the work I've done on it myself and for now having the opportunity to share with you this piece of advice.

This is one of the most important pieces of advice that you'll ever receive, and it can have a dramatic impact on your life. Once again, it's something that's never taught in school or college or throughout the normal everyday life we all go through, yet it's of supreme importance. I ask that you really pay attention to this letter and consider its implications in your own life.

The inner critic is that voice—and I think most of us have this voice and understand it—that tells you something is wrong with you. Usually it's a specific something. Perhaps you're not worthy or you're not beautiful or you're not smart, or maybe you're too young or you'll never amount to anything. It's the ugly voice that speaks in your head and tells you the absolute worst things about yourself.

Unfortunately, we often believe exactly what the inner critic says. We don't pull it out into the light of day and examine it—we just accept its negativity as truth.

That's just a tragedy.

Understanding this, getting a good idea of what we feel and how we feel and actually dealing with it can make a massive difference in our lives.

There are lots of different inner critics. I don't know what yours might be, but I can tell you what mine was. This is something I've dealt with and I've worked on extensively, but it still rears its ugly head from time to time.

My inner critic says to me, *You aren't deserving of success.*

Maybe this is an issue of self-worth, or something that was drilled into me as I grew up. In fact, as I examined my own inner critic, I discovered that someone very close to me said these exact words to me—*You aren't deserving of success*—sometime after college and as I was experiencing my first semblance of success.

The *horrible, terrible, no good, very bad* thing about the inner critic is that we often believe it, even though it's not true.

I was fortunate enough to be friends with someone who walked me through this problem of an inner critic. You'll recall him from the previous chapter, when he asked whether or not I loved my son. After coming to the realization that I believed my son unequivocally deserving of my love, I listened as my friend asked:

"Now, do you think you're any different? Do you think *you're* not worthy?"

Examining this intellectually, I'd say of course I'm worthy—but the idea that I don't deserve success is still a deep-seated belief, and it's something that needs to be dealt with and thought about, wrestled with, and changed.

To change, I thought about my inner critic and what it was telling me, and I examined it.

The truth of the matter concerning your inner critic is that the *opposite* of what your inner critic tells you is the truth. This is very important.

For me, *I am not worthy of success* becomes *I am as deserving of every blessing from God as anyone else and it is my birthright.* I was born to deserve that.

It's the same thing with your inner critic. If you think you're not beautiful or you're ugly, I can tell you specifically (I'm talking to you, girls), I *know* you—and you are such beautiful, wonderful, precious, made-in-the-perfect-image-of-God human beings. I mean that both physically—which you may not feel, but you *are* absolutely beautiful—and, more importantly, internally. Your personalities, your hearts, and your kindness make both of you absolutely beautiful. As beautiful as anyone in the world. I don't know if that's an inner critic that plagues you or not, but that's an example of how the opposite of what your inner critic says is the absolute truth.

Think again about my story of Alec and whether or not he's deserving of love and deserving of God's greatest blessings. Now think to your inner critic and what it tells you. Would you ever talk to a child of yours that way? Would you allow a child of yours to go on believing that if you had the chance or the opportunity to help change their self-perception?

If you wouldn't treat a friend that way and you wouldn't treat a child that way, the question remains . . . why do you allow yourself to treat you this way?

So all that remains is how we actually get *rid* of the inner critic.

Advice in Practice.

- I talk about this elsewhere, but writing things down and actually being able to examine your thoughts outside of your head is one of the most profound things you can do. So pull out a journal and write out what your inner critic tells you and what you think it is saying. Be as specific as possible. If it comes to you easily, then you have it. If it doesn't come to you easily, then one of the things you might need to do is talk with a friend or a loved one or perhaps even your dad (hint-hint) about what *they* think your inner critic is. Really work hard to identify it, then write it out.

- After you've done that, I want you to write out what the *opposite* is. Be as specific and detailed as you can.

  Tony Robbins teaches something he calls the "Dickens Process." In it, you write out exactly what a negative belief or behavior will cost you in your life if you allow it to continue indefinitely. This is so powerful. For me, thinking I'm not worthy of life's greatest blessings could cause me not to try for my dreams, not to write this book or to change the world in some form or fashion. It could have me living a life far below my potential—and actually, I think it was. Not only that, but it could affect my children and give them a lower sense of self-worth if I believed that I wasn't worthy. Whether or not that's what it would cost you, I want you to be as specific as you can and write out how this will affect you if you allow it to go on. Then, after getting it completely out of your system by writing it all down, I want you to write out what your *new* belief is. If your inner critic is telling you that you're not beautiful, then write out the ways you *are* beautiful. If, for some reason, your inner critic says you'll always be poor, write out the reasons why you're *not* poor and the blessings you have that make you rich.

- Make sure you revisit this from time to time. Think about it and make sure that your inner critic's old beliefs aren't creeping back in. Actually set a time in your calendar—it can be when you do your quarterly or yearly planning—to go through these exercises again.

Lastly, I want you to think of someone, a friend or a family member you think is struggling with an inner critic, and without judgment, without making them feel badly about it, I want you to use all of this knowledge and this thought process to try and help them deal with their inner critic.

Often, it's our parent's voice that talks to us as our inner critic. I try to do my very best, as you know, but if you have these critical thoughts, I am so sorry if I contributed in any way. I hope that through this advice you are able to feel the amount of love I'm putting forth. Please understand that I want only the best for you.

Notes, thoughts, and intentions.

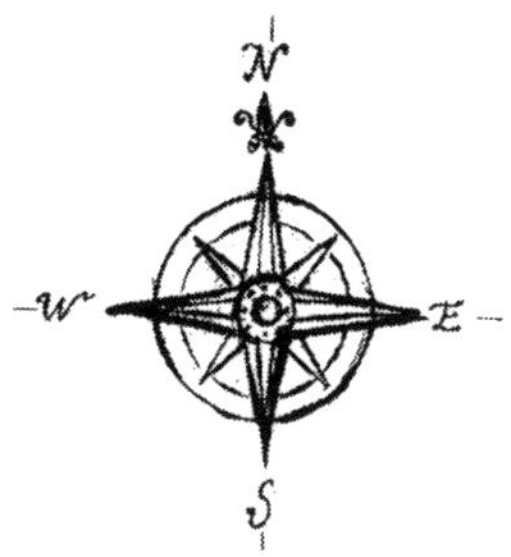

8. Keep the Darkness Away. (Dealing with Depression.)

I think I've talked to you about this. I'm pretty open about this, but here it is again.

About two years ago, I was in a depression for many months. I was in horrible shape, I didn't want to get out of bed in the mornings, I resented my job and didn't want to help more people in my real estate career, I was tired all the time . . . and, maybe the biggest thing of all, I knew I wasn't living up to my potential. I knew I wasn't doing something with my life that I loved and was proud to do.

Depression/Darkness can run in the family, and it's not so easily described as just a chemical imbalance. I read this from a Harvard study: "Research suggests that depression doesn't spring from simply having too much or too little of certain brain chemicals. Rather, there are many possible causes of depression, including faulty mood regulation by the brain, *genetic vulnerability*, stressful life events, medications, and medical problems. It's believed that several of these forces interact to bring on depression."[1]

So because it's happened to me, it's very possible that this can happen to you as well. On top of that, I've noticed amongst many of my quite brilliant entrepreneur friends that depression and darkness seem to be a bit more frequent. I know how sharp you are, my children, and that makes me think you may be susceptible to it all the more.

Wow. When I think that this can happen to you, my heart breaks a little. I love you so much, and I don't want you to go through that—but sometimes it's necessary.

My friend Dr. Law says that if there's a devil, and this devil wanted to keep good things from happening, he would attack the minds of people with a lot of potential to do something great in the world. That makes a lot of sense.

Let me tell you something—YOU HAVE SO MUCH POTENTIAL.

You are capable of doing such great things, and I think that darkness may attack you because of this. You see it in artists and great talents all of the time.

So be especially vigilant, my sweethearts.

What helped me get out of the funk and really start thriving was something I explained in my Self-Love Manifesto, from

---

[1] Harvard Health Publishing, "What causes depression?" https://www.health.harvard.edu/mind-and-mood/what-causes-depression (April 11, 2017)

the book *Choose Yourself!* by James Altucher, called the Daily Practice.

The Daily Practice is simply doing something good for yourself every day, physically, emotionally, mentally, and spiritually (sometimes I'll cheat a little and combine the emotional and spiritual, because I think they're deeply connected).

So, for instance, for the physical practice, I'd take a walk (that was about all I could do initially) or I'd eat at least one healthy thing that day or skip having a Coke Zero and have water instead.

Just doing something small like that will help you feel much better . . .

. . . and several days of feeling better can help get you out of that funk.

For the emotional practice, I made an effort to stop hanging around emotional vampires. These are the people who walk into a room and you think, "Ugh . . ." and know that your energy is sapped just being around them. Don't be mean about it (especially if they're family members or some dude you call "Dad"), but consciously stop spending as much time around them.

For the mental practice, I made Idea Lists. There's a lot about this in the Mind section of this tome (check out the chapter "Revolutionize Your Life with Idea Lists"). It made a big difference.

I believe I made the most progress in the spiritual practice. For my spirit, I started journaling and writing down my gratitude (but more on that later). The advanced practitioners of life can find something to "actively appreciate," even in the bad, terrible, no good, awful things that happen in the world. If you can do that, my children, you're at the post-graduate level of keeping darkness away.

The MOST POWERFUL thing that I did to keep darkness away and get out of my depression was *this* spiritual practice: I resolved to do a Kind Act for another human being.

EVERY. SINGLE. DAY.

Wow. This is so very life-changing.

(There's an entire piece of advice about it in this very section, so keep your eyes peeled.)

You feel SO GOOD helping other people. And it's not about them appreciating you. It's just a cosmic chord in your soul that makes such a sweet sound to your spirit. I think it's why we're here on this planet, having this physical experience as spiritual beings. You *know* it deep in your heart, gut, and soul simply because of how good you feel when you help someone else.

If I could "check off," doing a Kind Act for someone, I felt so much better—specifically, better about MYSELF. There were some days when I was lying in bed in the morning, not wanting to get up, and literally thinking, *What am I doing with my life? What difference will I make?* The thought of helping someone and doing my Kind Act got me out of bed, to make a difference for at least one person, and it was magical.

The only side effect to the Daily Practice and Kind Acts is having a great life, so my advice to you—my precious, beautiful loved ones—is to do the Kind Act especially, and the Daily Practice every day that you can.

If you keep doing it, it will help in making sure that the depression doesn't stick.

As I write this, I hope this helps you with your life as much as it did mine. I love you SO, SO freaking much!

Advice in Practice:

This whole piece of advice was *about* practicing! But here this goes:

- Read *Choose Yourself!* by James Altucher at some point, and then read it again at some other point. It's a good read. It's interesting and it has a lot more goodness in it than just the Daily Practice. It's a manifesto on choosing a better life. It's one of my favorite books, and I hope it can bless you like it has me.

- Make the Daily Practice a habit. Resolve that you'll do it for a month. Mentally—or, even better, *physically*—check off each of the boxes every day: physical, emotional, mental, and spiritual. But *especially* do this if you're fighting the darkness.

- Come back to this often. The Daily Practice may not "stick" the first time or the first few times that you try it . . . but don't let that stop you. Keep at it.
- When it comes to the darkness, PLEASE, PLEASE, PLEASE reach out and get some help if you're feeling depression take you. I want to help, and it's the most important thing that I can ever do as your daddy.

*****If you are someone else other than my children reading this, please reach out to someone who cares for you—and if you don't have that person, reach out to me.**

Please know that you are loved, my children, despite any faults you may believe you possess. Knowing EVERYTHING about you, I can tell you that you are still loved, and you're loved dearly.

Notes, thoughts, and intentions.

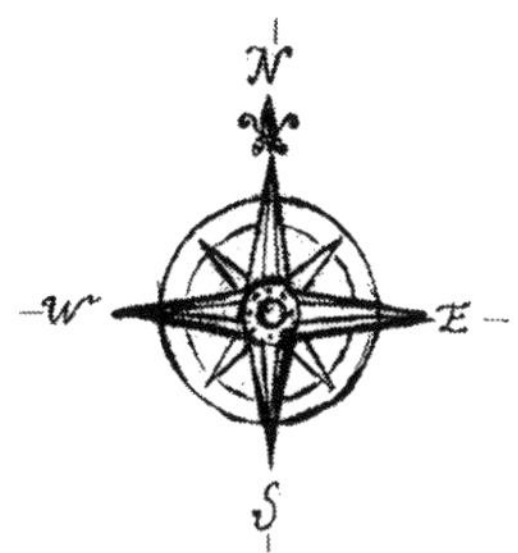

9. Learn to Love Your Own Company and Being by Yourself.

"I find it wholesome to be alone the greater part of the time. To be in company, even with the best, is soon wearisome and dissipating. I love to be alone. I never found the companion that was so companionable as solitude."
—Henry David Thoreau

Learn to enjoy some "alone time" now and again.

If you enjoy your own company, you'll never feel too alone. If you like yourself, you shouldn't have any problem with hanging out with such a cool person!

Now, I'm betting you know I love you at this point. Oh my goodness. My heart hurts (in a good way) when I think of how much I love you . . . but, with that said, I don't want to be around you *all* the time.

I'm an introvert by nature. That may surprise you a bit, because I can get up and speak to a bunch of people, do karaoke, or dance like a man possessed . . . but it's true. The way you know if you're an introvert or extrovert is to know how you get your energy. Do you need to "recover" after being around people for a while? Then you're an introvert. Do you actually get energy from being around people, and need to find someone after you've been alone for a while? Yep, you guessed it: you're an extrovert.

Regardless of whether you're an introvert, in which case you *need* to be alone, or if you're an extrovert, where you may not want to be alone . . . learning to love your own company will bring tremendous benefits.

If you enjoy being by yourself, you won't ever fear being alone. It won't have a grip on you. In that case, you're not going to be worried as much about others' opinions of you. If you're shunned by a group for some reason, it won't affect you as much because you just don't *mind* being alone. When you're comfortable in your own skin, you're not as affected by things that happen outside of that skin—does that make sense?

Here's a quick example: One of the biggest fears people have is public speaking. In terms of natural selection, this was built into us as humans because when we were cut off from our tribes, it usually meant death in the wilderness. Thus, even today, people are worried about being embarrassed or made to look foolish.

But times have changed. We don't die when we're cut off from a group today. There's really no reason to fear what people think of you. I think cultivating the love of solitude helps to eliminate irrational fears like this in your life.

Here's something else about the ability to be alone: it nurtures the soul. It's a time to get right with God. It's a chance to do the things *you* want to do, without having to run it by any kind of committee. It's been said that the most adjusted human beings are completely fine with spending time by themselves.

I get strange looks from people when I say that I want to eat alone for lunch. But it's one of the only times that I'm by myself during the workday. It gives me a chance to clear my head and prepare for the rest of the day.

I cherish my alone time at the beginning of the day during my Miracle Morning process. I also like to go to the lake to plan for the week/month/year and to soak in the silence. It's the best place in the world for me to read. It's also great to have some silence, because this is often the time when you can hear God whisper to you.

One of the things I put on "Chip's Fantastical Birthday List" and "Chip's Fantastical Christmas List" (both trademarked, although I just realized that I used "fantastical" on both of them) every year is an entire weekend spent at the lake. This is my "Thoreau" time, when I can "live deliberately" and "suck the marrow out of life."

It never seems to work out because I'm so dang needed—hahahaha! I might stick to my guns this Christmas, though. Just me, the lake, a few pens, and a journal. Ahhhh . . . just thinking about that makes me happy. Weird, I know.

I think some folks are so eager to be with others most of the time because they're afraid of their own thoughts. I could be wrong about that, as I'm not one of those people . . . but even if you're an extrovert, I'd encourage you to become more and more comfortable with spending that time alone. Even if it makes you uncomfortable or you're scared of it. *Especially* if you're scared of it—then you *know* it's the right thing to do.

Also, while I meant this as actually spending time alone, I also want it to mean being alone in relationships, too. I hope that you don't *need* someone in your life romantically to make you feel complete. I mean, I love romance, and it's a great thing—one of the best things—but you should never feel like you *have* to have someone there in your life. I think we all know people like this . . . and I think it's a good idea to pause and reflect on who you'd actually like in your life. Or even better—give yourself such amazing standards that someone who would become a boy- or girlfriend had better be a spectacular person.

So, now you know. There's your advice for this. But just remember . . . if you ever get tired of being alone and don't have anyone . . . call your daddy!

Advice in Practice:

- When you do your weekly schedule, hopefully your "Ideal Schedule" (more on that later on page 270), try to include some alone time—some time reading, journaling, creating your version of the Miracle Morning . . . time for the fun stuff you like to do alone . . . all of it.

- If this is a little harder for you, it's time to pull out that journal and do the Idea List. Write out all the things you could enjoy doing by yourself. Try for a good twenty of those bad boys. There will be some that stick and that you can put into the schedule mentioned above. If this is hard for you, it's all the more important that you do it.

- Plan your own Thoreau "*Walden* Weekend." Go to a place where you won't be disturbed. Turn off that dang phone. DISCONNECT. Get to the root of life. Listen to silence for a while. No music. No talkie shows, podcasts . . . not even the audiobook version of this fine tome! Especially if that makes you uncomfortable—then you know that you need to do it.

I love you!

Notes, thoughts, and intentions.

10. Find a Way to Serve the Many.

Your success—in every part of your life—is directly determined by your *service*. It's also one of the best ways to show love for others, and to feel more love for yourself. By serving others, you're practicing some of the greatest love a person can show.

In business, or in any job, you can see this easily: the more value you provide to more people, the more you are paid.

But it works for almost everything. The more service you give others, the richer your life will be. Always find ways to provide more service to a greater number of people.

There's an amazing quote I've asked you to memorize before, kiddos, but I haven't quizzed you on it enough:

"You can have anything you want in life if you'll just help enough people get what they want." — Zig Ziglar.

If you're ever unhappy with something, see if there's a way you can provide some service to the situation, and your rewards will follow. You will reap what you sow.

Jim Rohn put it this way while paraphrasing Jesus:

"Find a way to serve the many."

This leads to greatness. You are great, and you'll become even greater as you find ways to serve others in a greater capacity.

This may sound like a lot of work, or something that may be difficult, but if you truly do this, you'll find not just greatness, but a fulfillment reserved only for the charitable few.

Advice in Practice:

- If you're at your job, always ask yourself, "Is there a way that I can provide more value to my Customer?" (We always capitalize "Customer" and "Client" in our home to emphasize their importance.) The Customer in this case can be the actual Customer, of course—but it's probably also your boss and/or the company for which you work.
    - Of course, if you own the company (something I hope you give serious thought to doing in your future), then the question is, "What are the ways that I can provide more value to my Customers and Team?"
    - More value means being better priced, offering a higher level of service, solving their problems more eloquently and thoroughly, making them feel special and important, saving them time and effort, etc. Think through all of this.

- Create an Idea List of ways you can better serve. We'll talk about this more later, but asking that question can lead to some GREAT Idea Lists that can absolutely revolutionize your life!

I love you! (Have I told you that in the last few pages?)

Notes, thoughts, and intentions.

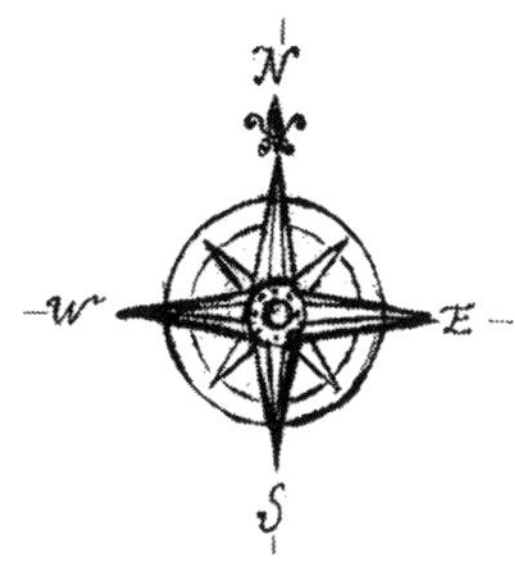

11. Rest If You Must, But Just Don't Quit.

"Never give up on something that you can't go a day without thinking about."
— Winston Churchill

This is some important advice, so keep it close at hand. I know I say that a lot, but I mean it each and every time.

In your life—in your relationships, in your job/career/mission, etc.—you're going to feel like quitting. It will happen. If it hasn't already happened, it will in the future. You've got to know that. You've got to understand this and prepare for it. Because if you don't know it's going to come, it can be so overwhelming that you'll feel as if you have no choice but to succumb to it. You'll throw in the towel and call it a day.

When I decided to go after JoeVolunteer, my project to spread kindness throughout the world, I was filled with an innocent, maybe even naïve belief that it was going to change the world, it was destined to happen, and that I was the person to make it happen. I still believe it's going to change the world—but the whole endeavor, which was completely new to me, was so, so much harder than I'd imagined. Many days, I let that defeat me; there were many sleepless nights during which I thought, *How am I going to make this happen?*

But know this: I will not quit. It is too important, and it's a part of me.

In smaller matters, things that aren't close to your heart, it's completely okay to stop. The advice "If it's not a 'Hell yes!,' it's a 'No' " applies to this. It's okay to do that, and even noble to focus your time, energy, heart, and efforts on the *meaningful few* rather than the trivial many.

BUT. That big goal. The one that's in your heart and that you *have* to do, have to get out to the world. The one that's burning a hole in your soul. With *that*, you're going to want to quit. But you can't.

My advice is to rest, but just don't quit.

Take a break. Regroup. Find and stir those deep emotions that caused you to begin this grand endeavor in the first place. There is no shame in that.

For the idea to succeed, you absolutely *have* to look out for its champion—that's YOU. If you're feeling too stressed about it, if it's causing you sleepless nights and dominating all of your thoughts in a negative way, then a rest is in order.

I suggest taking some time away. Allow yourself to breathe . . . pause . . . reflect. Find yourself some space in order to disassociate from the problem for a while, and can start to think rationally about it again—later. It's okay to do this. I imagine that, like it is with me, the desire to quit and the subsequent benefits of taking a moment to reflect will always happen when something is so close to your heart and soul.

As I mentioned in the Thoreau chapter, my refuge has always been the lake, miles away from other human souls. If you have a place you can retreat to, think about going there for a while . . . just to be.

Bring a journal and write it out. When the time comes and it feels right, get that insidious thinking and all the worries, anxieties, problems, and such associated with it OUT OF YOUR HEAD and onto paper. Examine it in the light of day. If you've taken enough time, everything will become clear.

But here's the big thing: Don't stop whatever it is that you're doing. Revisit it with fresh eyes and renewed vigor. Don't let it die on the vine and then fill you with regret. Part of the reason you should be able to step back and rest is that you *know* you'll return to the fight soon to make it happen.

I just heard this the other day from one of my mentors, and it's so, so true: on your Hero's Journey, you're not fighting lizards . . . you're fighting DRAGONS! And fighting dragons is hard work. If it weren't hard work, if you weren't being stretched by what you were doing, there wouldn't be much point in it. Pursuing your dream, and following the Hero's Journey, makes you the person you're meant to become.

You will need to face those dragons. You will need to muster the courage to face whatever it is that's scaring you. That's why you can't quit. When you quit, that fear becomes a part of you. You're missing out on the growth that happens when you face down those dragons and keep coming back to fight again and again.

Show that courage. Charge forward when you're really scared. *That* is when the magic happens—and I want that so much for you.

So know that it's going to happen. Prepare for it. Rest if you must . . . but just don't quit.

Advice in Practice:

- Take a self-assessment. Are you exhausted and beat down? Get out your journal, of course, and write about it—right now. What are you feeling? What's the obstacle? Are you able to get over it? If you're feeling great and energized, if you're waking up excited about what you're doing every day (yay, you!), then this advice isn't for you—yet. Just take note and come back to it when it is relevant to you.

- If you *are* feeling beaten up and that maybe you can't go on longer, then first and foremost do this:

  SWEAR TO YOURSELF (and maybe to others) THAT YOU JUST WON'T QUIT! This is important, because if you know this one simple fact, and if you can trust yourself with that promise, it gives you the ability to step back from it, consciously, and rest. This step back is what allows you to take the necessary break.

- Your time off resting will probably depend on your feelings and the enormity of the project/quest you're tackling. I think the first part of your rest should be a complete shut-down for bit. Escape. Create some space, and as much as you're able, push it from your mind.

- Talk with someone trusted about this, (like maybe your good ole' dad!) and get their perspective.

- When the time is right (and you'll know when it is), break out that journal and get all those worries and things that need to be done—that incredibly long "to-do" list—out of your head and onto paper. I'd recommend doing something called the "Focus Finder," something I learned from my friend Dean Jackson. Look for Dean's video, "Focus Finder," online and do it with your project. Get *everything* down on paper. You'll notice that the first thing you feel when doing this is a sense of relief.

- Now, put down the actions you can take that will make the biggest difference. We're talking the smallest things that can make the most impact on your project. You'll need to get a few under your belt to create momentum.

- Work on that momentum and keep going. Pat yourself on the back, because you're in the race again, and get back to changing the world. You DESERVE THAT.

I love you.

Notes, thoughts, and intentions.

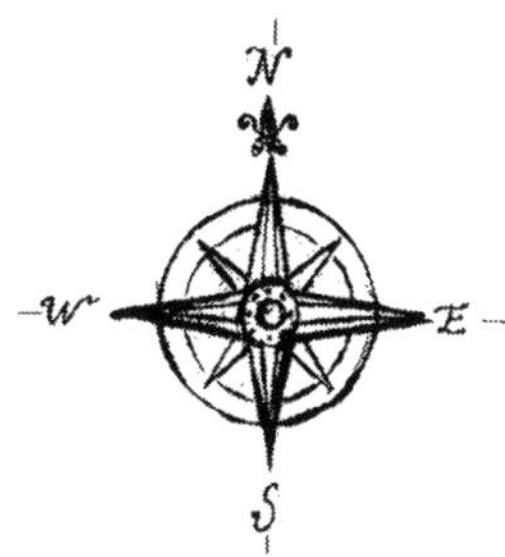

12. Take Imperfect Action.

It is so, so important to actually *do* something. Most of the world just waits, and they only take action to change their lives when it's forced upon them, or maybe after some life-changing event.

Here's my favorite quote on the subject:

> ***"For all of the most important things, the timing always sucks. Waiting for a good time to quit your job? The stars will never align and the traffic lights of life will never all be green at the same time. The universe doesn't conspire against you, but it doesn't go out of its way to line up the pins either. Conditions are never perfect. 'Someday' is a disease that will take your dreams to the grave with you. Pro and con lists are just as bad. If it's important to you and you want to do it 'eventually,' just do it and correct course along the way."***
> ***— Tim Ferriss in The 4-Hour Work Week***

The traffic lights of life will never be all green at the same time. BOOM. The thought of that is so beautiful. It's *never* going to be perfect. So, if you really want to take the trip, my precious children, you just need to *book* it, and then make other things work around it.

Most people will wait and think about it rather than taking an "imperfect" action. The imperfect action is taking the chance, taking the little risk, and stepping out of your comfort zone to actually *do* it . . . even if it scares the bejeezus out of you. In fact, I believe the more it scares you, the more you *need* to do it. That's where the growth is. That's where you become a stronger person than you are now.

Tim Ferriss has also said that people would rather choose unhappiness than uncertainty. We can be so scared of what's going to happen on the other side of that uncomfortable conversation that we never even open our mouths. We can live years in the shadow of our own fear.

I know that most of this book is just me talking to you, like starting a business . . . but at some point, you have to start. That's SO, SO much more important than "getting it exactly right."

It's so much easier to correct course if you're actually *moving*. If you're standing still, it's pretty much impossible to turn the steering wheel.

I respect the person who has tried and failed much more than the person who's never even started . . . but, even more, I respect the person who's failed, changed course a few times, and finally succeeded. In fact, I'll say that I reserve the most respect for that person who's hit a wall and had to readjust over and over and *finally* succeeded. I think that struggle forges character—and if it's too easy, we start to believe our own hype and can become arrogant.

I know this is all theoretical at this point, but let me use an example in your life, one you may actually face, and we can talk about how to physically take your imperfect action.

You want a new job—and it's a little "out there." Maybe they're asking for someone with more experience than you have. Perhaps they want a skill or familiarity with a certain computer program you just don't have.

At this point, most people would actually give up, and NOT EVEN START.

But here's the concept I'm trying to teach you: the worst that can happen is trying for it and failing—and you're no worse off than if you had never tried. I'd say you're *better*, because at the VERY LEAST you've exercised your courage.

Some would say, "I can't get that job." Of course, we know that, as Franks, we never say "can't." Instead we ask, "How can I?"

So how can we get that job?

Immediately, the following pops into my head: first, set the appointment; then highlight the things you *are* good at. "I'm honest. I show up to work early. I don't give up when things are hard. And that's why I'm sitting in front of you now. I'm a highly proactive, goal-accomplishing person—and even though I don't know how to _____ (e.g., program JavaScript, do budgeting reports, run a focus group, etc.), I promise you that I can learn that, learn it well, and even do it on my time, so you're not paying me to learn it. In fact, Ms. Interviewer, I will work for FREE for the first six weeks while I'm learning to be proficient at this, and if I don't knock it out of the park for you, then we can part ways and you won't owe me a dime."

Think about something like that. It's possible they could say "No," but if you deliver that passionately, and you show how you'd be a huge asset to them . . . there's a huge chance that they'd say "Yes."

And remember, the whole theory behind this letter is that nearly *every* person would've never attempted to get their dream job when they came up against that obstacle. Therefore, they would fail 100 percent of the time. So your odds are already better just by having put yourself out there via imperfect action.

That's just one example. But it applies if you want to write a book, make a movie, develop a career in the arts, or start your business of taking care of special needs children . . . just take that first, shaky, unsure step. If it fails, you're better off for having dared where others won't.

I'm reminded of my favorite quote ever. I'm literally typing this from memory, so I'll probably get some of it wrong . . . but I'm just going to take imperfect action and get it "out there," anyway (see what I did there?). Here it is:

> ***"The credit belongs to the man actually in the arena ... whose face is marred by dust, and sweat, and blood ... who spends himself in a worthy cause ... who knows the great convictions, the great***

devotions ... who at best knows of triumph and high achievement ... and if he fails, he fails while daring greatly, so that his place shall never be with those cold and timid souls that know neither victory nor defeat." — Teddy Roosevelt

I taped that quote to the dashboard of my car and read it several times a day while I was selling books door-to-door in college. It was ragged, and had holes in it, and that imperfection inspired me to keep going while doing something very, very difficult.

Seth Godin, the marketing expert, said something at a conference I went to back in September. I'm paraphrasing a bit. He said:

"Don't tell me that you're unable to do it—*show* me where you've tried two hundred times to do it. Because *that* we can work with."

The principles are having the idea to start, the courage to fail, and the resilience to adjust and keep going. It's never going to be perfect, but don't let that stop you. Give yourself permission for it to be ugly, and improve from that point.

The perfect thing to do is to take the first imperfect action.

I already love you, but if and when I see you striving, trying, and going for something you don't know you can get . . . wow. That will make me so proud as your daddy.

I love you, and I always will.

Advice in Practice:

- Do an Idea List of twenty-plus things you want to try/do/experience but you've always been too scared to try. Be exhaustive. Get a little crazy. Write it out. Then pick the one idea from your list—you know, the one that makes you catch your breath when you think about it. I think it'll be kind of evident. *That's* the one we'll start with in doing.

- Do the Tim Ferriss practice of "Fear Setting." There's a great video of him explaining how it's done, so go find it, kiddos. But the basic principle is that you turn a sheet of paper on its side, and at the top you write what it is that you want, but you're scared of . . . let's say taking a month off to travel outside the country (I want to do this). Then, make three columns underneath it. In the first column, you write in detail the bad stuff that could happen. Get really specific. List ten things that can go wrong. In the second column, write out how you can minimize those bad things. Then, in the third column, write how you can get back to where you are now if it did go all wrong. Chances are, the consequences are nowhere near as bad as you think they are when they're just hanging out in your brain.

- Next, figure out what the FIRST, ATTAINABLE step is. Then the next step, and the next. Filter these through another Idea List (e.g., "15 Easily Done Steps to Make an Extended Out-of-Country Walkabout Possible and Doable!") The first step should be a ridiculously easy thing to do. You want the barrier of entry to your task to be small, then get momentum and keep going from there.

- Be sure to follow the Tony Robbins principle: DO NOT leave the scene of setting a goal without doing at least *something* toward getting it done.

- Set up someone or something to actually hold you accountable to doing what you set out to do. You can get a buddy that cares, your sister—or, even better, get your DAD to check up on you. (You know I'll do it!)

- Write a letter now from your future self on the other side of your fear to your current, scared self. Talk about what happened (get imaginative). Explain what you overcame, and why you're glad you did it. This can be in a morning journaling session. This is surprisingly powerful.

- Keep a list of the things you'd like to do, but are scared to do in your journal—and make sure that you read it every once in a while. I'd even suggest taking a picture of it, posting it in Evernote, and setting a reminder for that note to pop up every month or so, so it crosses your path on a regular basis. Otherwise, it's too easy to fall into a comfortable life and realize, with horror, that a decade or two has passed with you never trying something great. Don't let that happen, sweethearts!

I'm always proud of you, but I will always hope you dare greatly rather than playing it safe.

I love you!

Notes, thoughts, and intentions.

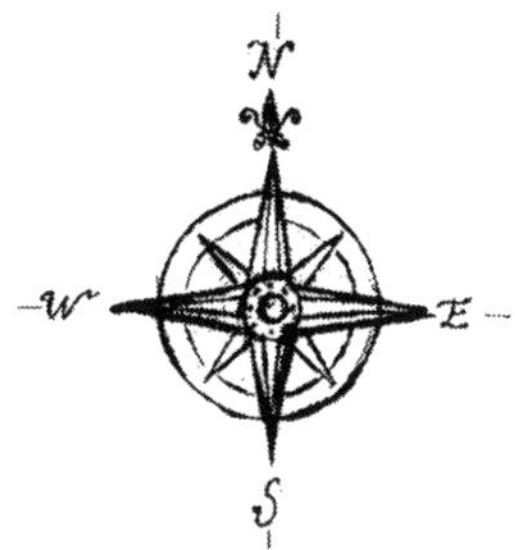

13. Teach People How to Treat You.

You teach people how they should treat you, kiddos, so *do not* let anyone treat you poorly.

Let others know that you'll treat them with respect—and that you expect the same treatment from them.

If they don't treat you right, get away from them if you have to do so, and don't feel guilty about it.

I've learned throughout my life that people will tend to treat you how you expect them to do so. It never fails—well, *almost* never. I'll get a call at work from someone demanding to talk to me and only me right away. My team will explain that they are being unreasonable, and the customer will then cuss . . . and just like that, they've shown that they are an ugly person because of how they treated my team at the real estate office.

But when they finally get to me, I call and let them know who I am, that I want to resolve this, and hear their side of the case.

And guess what? To a person, they'll treat me nicely. Now, some of that may be because I'm the owner and they don't have anywhere to go after that, but they all treat me with the same respect I'm showing them.

I know there are exceptions to this, and some folks are inherently unreasonable . . . but I think this is the case with almost everyone. You show them how you should be treated with how you treat them.

This goes in your relationships, too—*especially* those. One of my favorite lines from Tony Robbins (dang, I'm mentioning him a lot . . . but hey, he's got a lot of wisdom to curate for you) is, "You get what you tolerate."

Do NOT tolerate anyone treating you badly. Ever.

It's not justified, it's not deserved, and it doesn't get better if you allow it to continue.

If you find yourself being treated badly and you allow it to happen without doing anything to change it, this probably stems from a lack of love or respect for yourself. That's something we also need to examine. (Remember the first few lessons in this section? Go read them again!)

If someone is verbally abusive, *stay away from them*. Plain and simple. Do everything you can to limit your time with them. If it's at a job, you can have a talk with them—but remember that you never have to put up with it, even if it's a good job. It's just not worth it, sweethearts!

If someone is PHYSICALLY abusive—hmmm. Obviously, stay away from them, but TELL SOMEONE too. Tell me, for certain. I will talk to them and we'll have an attitude adjustment for sure. I don't care how much of a "badass" they think they are—physical abuse is never okay in any capacity. We'll have words, and we'll bring the police if need be. This is important for you, and there's a very good chance that they could be hurting others as well.

(To be honest, I'm getting mad just thinking of that scenario . . . so let's move on.)

I believe a big part of making sure someone treats you right is *how good you feel about yourself*. It all stems back to self-love and actually *liking* yourself. (Again—go revisit those earlier lessons.)

I know that we've been over this so many times, both in person and in this book, but one of the biggest things I can leave you with is that you are so, so WORTHY of all the good things. You deserve the best. You have the blood of the divine running through your veins (and I'm not talking about me). You, my children, are created in the image of God, and are just as deserving of all of His blessings as anyone on the entire planet. I don't know how to get that drilled into your skull more than I have in these pages, but it's one of the most sacred, important things that I can ever impart to you.

This is such a big deal, because when you believe this, when you *know* it, you won't settle for people treating you badly . . . nor will you settle for treating others badly yourself.

Advice in Practice:

- Is there a relationship now in which you're not treated as well as you should be? Well, that's got to stop. Think on it. It may take some courage, as you'll likely feel some fear going into this—but you absolutely *must* have that conversation.

- Write out some of the ways in which they treat you poorly. They'll ask incredulously, "When have I ever . . . ?!" And you'll be prepared.

- List out the consequences of the continued poor behavior. Tell them why and how it can be better. This isn't about confrontation. It's about having respect for yourself.

- Get their agreement. If they don't see things the way you do, and they continue to treat you in any way that makes you uncomfortable, it's time to avoid them . . . even if they're family. You don't need to take anyone's abuse, even if it's done "in love." In their twisted way of thinking, maybe it is done in love. But that doesn't mean you need to put up with it, because *that* wouldn't be done in *self*-love.

- In business relationships, something that I've found is that people will have as much respect for your time and schedule as you do. Meaning, you teach them how to work with you. If someone intrudes on your time without an appointment, then unless it's an extreme emergency, stand up, walk them to the door, and tell them you're in the middle of something; tell them how to make an appointment with you. More often than not, they won't even schedule it. And when and if they do, it will be on *your* schedule, you'll be prepared for it, and maybe—most importantly—they'll have the respect for your time (and you) that they should.

You deserve to be treated like the king and queens that you are, my precious children!

Notes, thoughts, and intentions.

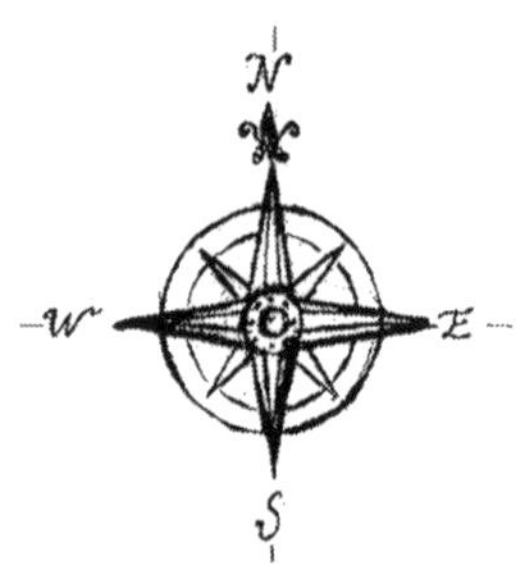

14. Know the Difference Between Love and Approval.

Your parents' love is unconditional. *Always*. Remember that.

Our approval, however, is not unconditional, and we will tell you when/if you're going down the wrong path. Some people call this "tough love," but I personally believe there's no difference between that and straight-up *love*.

We love you entirely too much to simply allow you to do anything—there will be a time for you to do that later in life, but for now you're under our care and protection.

We want the best for you, and we want you to grow up into a human who wants the best for yourself too. We'll allow you to explore and to test the edges, because that's how you learn . . . but we will reserve the right to say, "No."

The maxim that comes to mind is, "Love the sinner, hate the sin."

Or, something that I've said to you many, many times:

"I love you too much to let you act like this."

Hey, your parents are human (yes, yes, I know it's tough to believe). We screw up just like everyone else. But something we'll never mess up is loving you. Everything we do is for your best interest, even if what we do is flawed.

(You'll understand a lot of this as you have children of your own and think, "Ohhhh, *now* I know what Dad meant!")

Do I need to end a post on unconditional love with another "I love you"? Nah. But I will.

I LOVE YOU!

Advice in Practice:

- If there's something that you should be doing because it's the best thing for you, or something you're doing that you should NOT be doing . . . well, let's get that straightened out right away.
- This is an exercise for you and you alone, so don't hold back. Pull out your journal and write out some of the changes you need to make in your life. If you have a debilitating habit, write it out. Get it out of your soul, and let's start thinking about how to change that so we get love *and* approval.
- If there's something eating at your soul, something you know your parents or other loved ones wouldn't approve of, come and talk to a loved one about it. Get help when and where you can. You're loved, and it would be an honor to help you.

- With your friends and loved ones, keep the maxim in mind that love doesn't equal approval. Remember, you can love the sinner and hate the sin. If you see them doing something you know is debilitating, you can have that conversation with them. "I love you, but I don't like what you're doing . . . and you deserve more."

Notes, thoughts, and intentions.

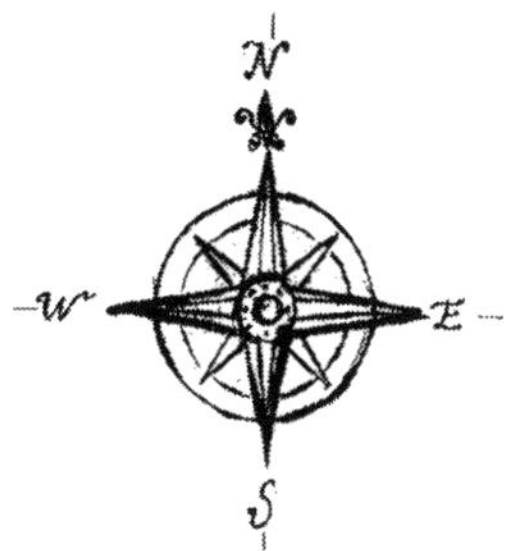

15. Treat People with the Daddy Rule.

I didn't always know how to treat people. I don't always treat people the right way—please remember that your dad's human just like everyone else—and I know there have been some things that I could've handled a lot better . . . but I certainly try each and every day.

I'm still haunted by the way I acted in the third grade: I was mean to a girl named Angela. I called her names and such. If I remember correctly, she was mean *back* to me, but I'm still ashamed of my behavior. You're older than I was then (except Alec), but I want to save you that personal shame if I can.

I can also remember some times when I let my temper get the best of me in stressful real estate transactions, or when talking to government officials (usually when they wanted to take money away from me).

I always regret treating people poorly, and there's never an excuse for it.

When it comes to treating people right, some people will say that the Golden Rule applies in most everything:

"Treat others as you would want to be treated."

I think that's merely a good start, and not at all the best way to treat others. The "Platinum Rule," is better:

"Treat others as THEY want to be treated."

That's good . . . but still, there's an even *better* way to treat people. I haven't come up with a clever name for it, so I'll call it the "Daddy Rule."

"Treat others better than they would hope."

Here's the thing—and this gets right down to the very fabric of what life, in my opinion is: **we were made to be of service to others**.

A lot goes into that. Of course, you really need to love and take care of yourself when you're serving others, or you'll be trying to pour from an empty cup. But that leads me to my favorite—and I think the most important—human attribute: kindness.

Specifically, *unusual* kindness.

That is, being one of those lights in the world that helps others joyfully, that shows care and concern not just for those you know and love but for *everyone* . . . even for the ones who have wronged you in some way.

This is a biblical idea (Matthew 5:44 and Luke 6:27), but if you can have enough love in your heart to share even with your enemies, you've really got something special going in your life. I know I strive for that and sometimes fail . . . but the more you work at it, the more you'll get it right as the years pass.

So again, the rule is:

"Treat people better than they would hope."

Before we get to the details involved in practicing the Daddy Rule, here's something that makes a lot of sense. Remember these words when trying to follow these rules:

"Be kind, for everyone you meet is fighting a hard battle." — attributed to Ian MacLaren

Further, this appeared in the Chicago *Tribune*:

> *Most of us are acutely aware of our own struggles and we are preoccupied with our own problems. We sympathize with ourselves because we see our own difficulties so clearly. But Ian MacLaren noted wisely, "Let us be kind to one another, for most of us are fighting a hard battle."*

If you can remember this, as you go about your day-to-day interactions, the rules below will be easier to follow and will make more sense. Also, for the Advanced Practitioner of the Daddy Rule: Think and actually *say to yourself* (warning: if said out loud, awkwardness will ensue), "I love you"—in fact, say it to everyone you meet. It takes some practice. I do it when I'm really on my game of being a "light" . . . but I *know* you can do it better than I can.

Now, some of the tenets to the Daddy Rule:

Engage with people when given a chance, strangers and friends alike. You be the one to initiate conversation. It's your duty—and it's not okay to sit passively and hope they'll be the ones to initiate a friendly word or two.

"If it's to be, it's up to me."

Others may say it's a shared responsibility, but I say it all falls on you. Other folks are woefully behind, still practicing the Golden Rule. Make it your mini-mission to improve their day. It usually takes so little! It's easy to do (and thus also easy *not* to do).

One of the things I really like to do is look them in the eye—in a friendly and not psycho way—and ask, "How are you doing today?" or "Are you doing okay today?" And I like to pause and actually listen to the answer. It takes a little practice, but you get better at it. Hopefully, while you're reading this, you can remember lots of times when I've done this and can do as I do, rather than just what I say.

When you meet someone, think and ask, "How can I serve you/help you/be of value to you?"

Part of this is the Stephen R. Covey Habit—seek first to understand, then be understood. You can serve people by truly listening to them, and if you're good, you can peel the onion of what they're saying to get to what's *behind* what they're saying.

That's practicing the Daddy Rule!

If they say, "I don't like it here now," what they might mean is that they feel uncomfortable, or threatened, or worse. If you can help with that, you're certainly treating them better than they could have hoped!

Remember the previous letter and be sure to attack the sins, never the sinner. Love is unconditional but approval is not. This is a big deal. No one likes getting criticized, and it often creates a lot of animosity or gives ammunition to the Inner Critic of the person in question. Here's the thing: everyone has the potential to be better, and they will be more inspired and capable of that if you feed them your love and appreciation instead of feeding their Critic with ammunition.

So, keep these rules in mind when dealing with others! If you do, the basics like telling the truth, being on time, and doing what you say you'll do should become second nature. Those are just some of the principles of treating people better than they could hope.

I think you'll find—we intuitively already know this—that when you are unusually kind to others, *you* will feel better. I've said it many times, and will repeat it again: it's an awesome quirk of human nature that you feel better by helping others to feel better. That's not the reason to do this, of course—but you have to admit that it's a pretty nice side benefit to what we're trying to do.

Advice in Practice:

- In your Miracle Morning practice, if you do affirmations (and you should!), please include some of the following (or whatever equivalent that feels right to you):

  - *I treat people better than they could hope.*
  - *I treat and greet people with love.*
  - *I always ask how I can be of service to others.*
  - *God shows through my actions.*

- Let's experiment! Make it a goal to consciously practice this every day for the next ten days to at least one other person. Write it down as a goal in your journal. Tell other friends about it. Post it on your social media so you can be held accountable.

- If it feels right, and you appreciate the wisdom in this advice, continue it!

- Lastly, if this appeals to you and you agree with what I advise (it's okay to disagree, and challenge this, after all—refer to the letter "Question Everything!"), see about teaching it to someone else, as that's usually the surest way to learn something like this.

I hope this has helped you, my precious, beautiful human beings! You are so, so loved, and my favorite human beings on this planet.

Notes, thoughts, and intentions.

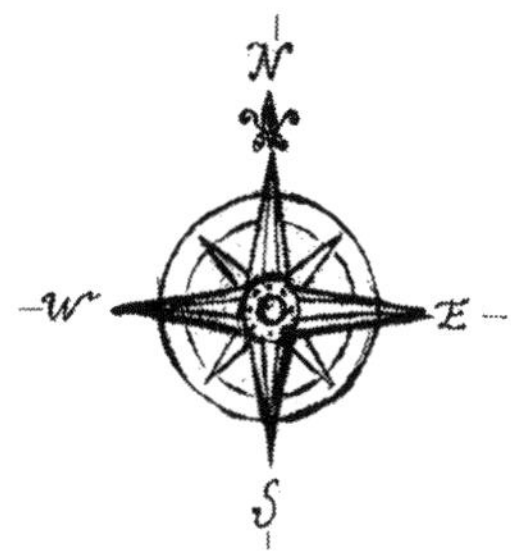

16. Say "Please" and "Thank You."

Say "Please" and "Thank you."

Always.

Or else.

Please.

Thank you.

When you say, "thank you," you are honoring the time, effort and thought that someone has given in doing something for you. When you don't say it, you are effectively dishonoring their effort.

There's not a whole lot more that needs to be said about this, other than it's inexcusable to not do it. I think all of you are pretty dang good about this, so I'm not going to spend a lot of time on it.

Just remember it, okay? Always.

Please. And thank you.

Advice in Practice:

- Just say "Please" and "Thank you." And make sure your brother and sister(s) do it, too, please. Thank you.
- Oh, and open doors for people following you, please. Thank you.
- And if they forget to say "Thank you," you're justified in saying, "You're welcome, Your Highness." I always get a kick out of doing that.

Notes, thoughts, and intentions.

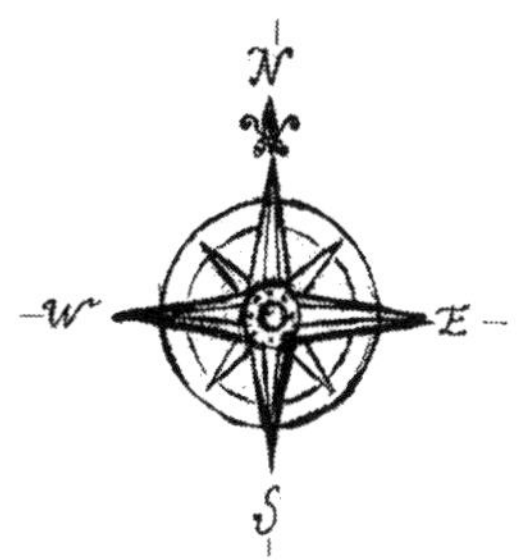

17. Don't Keep Compliments and Gratitude to Yourself.

The title of this letter says it all—show love and appreciation to others! But since I have you here, I'll say a bit more on the topic. You don't mind, right?

My precious human beings, this is a quick and easy piece of advice. And just as many quick and easy pieces of advice can do, this one will change your life and—maybe more importantly—change many lives around you.

And the advice is simple. Share compliments. Share your gratitude. Even share prayers that you have for others. Make sure they know you're thinking about them.

It's that simple.

And it's very easy to do. But, just like all simple and easy things, it's also easy not to do.

When you feel appreciation and gratitude for others, it makes you a much happier person. Those feelings of fear, anxiety, unworthiness . . . none of that can live in the same head at the same time as gratitude and active appreciation.

A wonderful, incredible part of life is the simple fact that you can *appreciate* and pray for things. What's even more wonderful than that, though, is taking that appreciation and gratitude—all of those wonderful feelings—and giving them to somebody else.

I know you've seen me do this many times—when I receive wonderful service, or an exceptional product, I'll take time to find the manager and brag on the person, service, or product. I'll let them know that what they do is appreciated. Doing this makes us all feel wonderful—they feel great to receive praise, and we feel great for giving it.

Two things will happen when you share gratitude:

1. People feel better when you share gratitude for them, let them know you're thinking of them, or if you tell them, "I remember when you helped me out and I appreciate it to this day, so thank you." They will feel better, and you will feel better. Win-win!
2. And something else: if you pray for or wish someone else well, or you think of a certain person and say, "I hope Such-and-such has a great day. I hope they are blessed today," or "I hope they feel abundance in their life right now" . . . *you* feel better about yourself.

Try it out right now. While you're reading this, pause for a second and think of two people specifically whom you love, you appreciate, and you want to have a great day. Are you doing it? How is it making you feel? Do you feel better after having thought of those folks?

And of course, the answer is *Yes!*

Now, let's go to work on making this a practice in our everyday lives.

Advice in Practice:

- Think of two people you know right now. Wish them well and say a prayer for them. Pray for their well-being and pray that they feel loved. If you don't pray, hold positive thoughts for them. Really—do it. I can wait for you.
- Now, I want you to pause and consider how that makes you feel right now. Do you feel better for having done this? Write it in your journal.
- Now the next step: send a text to those people right now. Let them know they were on your mind and that you prayed for them. If you're uncomfortable sharing that, just say you wish them well.
- Now consider their feelings and how they feel right now. Gratitude and appreciation multiply when shared with others.
- Try a ten-day experiment. Set an alarm on your phone to be grateful at a set time. Then promise to share your gratitude with someone. This is just for you, but do it for the next week and a half. How does it make you feel?
- Once the week and a half is over, post about your ten-day experiment on the social media of your choice. See if you can get at least one other person to join you in doing this experiment. I think you'll find that if even one person does it, you're going to feel great about that, too.

- The next time you receive exceptional service, ask to talk to the manager. It's pretty funny because they will always assume the worst—so when they come in, make sure you're within earshot of the person that provided the exceptional service. Then go on and on and extoll the virtues about the person giving the service, and be specific about how they did it. This may be very tough for an introvert, but it's so worth it.

- Have some courage and actually do this. The great feelings you get from this are so much more important than the slight discomfort you feel in doing it. As a side note, I try and do this with you all in my presence so you can learn from it.

- Teach this concept and principle to at least one other person.

- Finally, text and tell your daddy that you're grateful for and appreciate him—because he does love you, after all. (See what I did there?)

Notes, thoughts, and intentions.

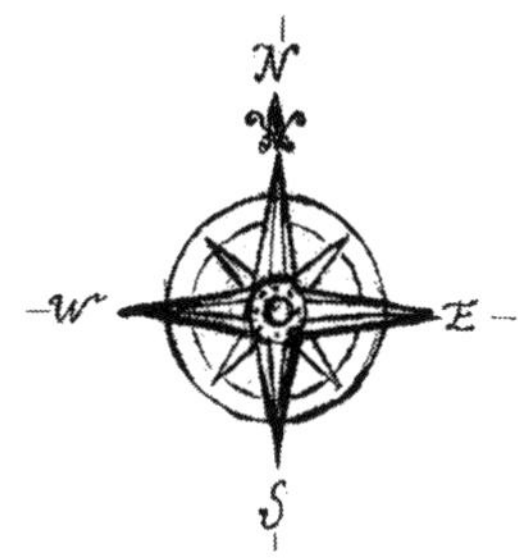

18. Praise the Hard Work, Not the Brilliance.

Here's the thing:

You're brilliant. Your mind is spectacular. The way you think is completely unique to you and you alone among everyone who has or ever will walk this planet.

BUT. You can't count on brilliance in everything you do. Because brilliance is fickle. It can (and will) sometimes lie, or leave you completely gutted when someone else comes along and does something better than you.

You'll think, *Well, that person must be more brilliant than me*, throw up your hands, and give up on being the "best" at whatever it is you want to do.

But where brilliance fails, hard work can often work: Practice, training, effort, conscious thought, and study. The 10,000 hours of plugging away at something, always consciously trying to get better.

Now, *that's* where it's at. That is where you can succeed and be able to do pretty much anything you ever want to do. It's paying your dues and taking the long road. It's learning from someone better than you, putting their advice and instructions into practice, and refining it yourself. *That* will pay off more than anything.

And that ability to work hard and diligently is *not* fickle.

It won't abandon you and leave you in tears and despair when something doesn't work out your way. Because you'll know in your heart that if someone is better than you at something, they probably worked at it more than you have. And you can remedy that.

So the thought process is:

I work hard at it, so I become good.

Full disclosure: I'm working at this one myself. I'm trying to hone my craft and get better at this writing gig. I've wanted to be a writer since the third grade. But I always kind of thought it was something you just *had* or *didn't have*.

The fact is . . . I'm getting better at it by conscious endeavor, or at least I think I am—and my editor agrees! I'm starting to feel like I'm okay at it. This book of ideas now in your hands is good, right? Right?!

This book isn't a product of *talent*. Talent didn't write the book—my *imperfect action* did. It's looking at what other people do, reading up on it, listening to Audible books . . . and just getting after it.

You have to have the COURAGE to do something you may not be great at doing. Then you have to show heart by keeping at it long enough to get better through the work.

I have to get better at this, too. Your mom gets after me because she tells me that I don't like to play certain card games I'm not good at playing. She's right. It shatters the precarious illusion that I'm brilliant at everything! Hahaha!

There's a story involved in this:

When a kindergarten teacher asks a class if they can sing and dance, they all say, "Yes! Of course!"

When a third-grade teacher asks a class if they can sing and dance, about half of them would say "Yes," and maybe not with much enthusiasm.

When a high school teacher asks a class if they can sing and dance, only a precious few hands will ever go up. And those are just the confident students who feel safe in bucking the system.

Of course, we can *all* sing and dance. We may not be great at it (unless you're me . . . heh, heh), but each of us can do it and get better at it through conscious endeavor.

If you go through life just doing the things for which you have a natural talent, you're shortchanging yourself. Have the courage to step out, fail if you must, and get better. All through hard work, and not just brilliance.

Remember: hard work trumps brilliance . . . but both together can change the world.

Advice in Practice:

- Pull out your trusted, worn (hopefully by now) journal and list some of the things which you believe you're not good at doing but would like to do better. Make it into an Idea List.

- Make a second Idea List of just one of those items, and list out ways you can get better at it. Even if it's something minor—there are always ways you can improve.
- Take one of those ways to get better and actually *schedule* it. Don't leave the scene of a good idea without doing something about it! You do remember that letter, right?
- Never, ever say "I can't" when describing a capability. If you haven't done it, you can always try—and if you've tried and failed, just add the word "yet" to your vocabulary. "I haven't sung for a play . . . *yet*."

Notes, thoughts, and intentions.

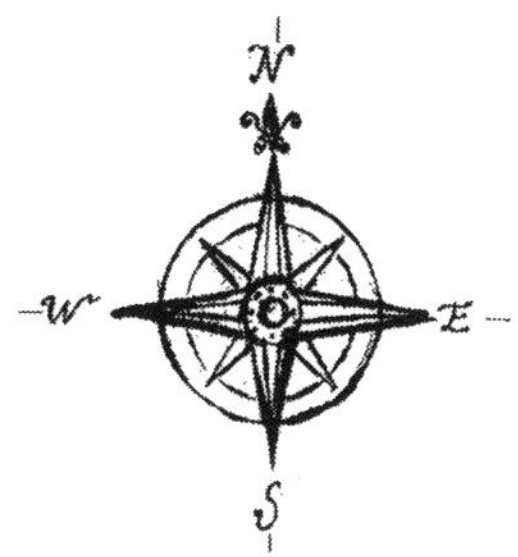

19. Avoid Gossip and the News Like the Plague They Are.

Avoid gossip and the people who partake in it. Gossip may feel good or fun at the time, but you'll feel badly afterward. It's not nice. Try to only say things the person you're speaking of could hear without you feeling awful over what you've said. Otherwise, it will cloud your heart.

Gossip is defined as talking badly about other people, what they've done, what they're doing, or what they may do.

My children . . . that's the lowest form of connecting with other people.

A quote attributed to Eleanor Roosevelt touched on this:

> ***"Great minds discuss ideas, average minds discuss events, small minds discuss people."***

I think there's a lot of truth to that.

There are a few reasons why I think it's not a good idea for you to engage in gossip. The first is that when you take part in and spread negativity via gossip, YOU are harmed.

Remember the fundamental law of humanity discussed in the previous letter about compliments and gratitude: you can't help others feel better without helping yourself feel better.

But the inverse is also true. Harming others—and I consider talking badly about others as harmful to them, even if they don't actually hear you—will do some damage to you, your spirit, and your self-love. And gossip not only negatively affects you and the person you're gossiping about, but it also spreads the infection of bad thought to those who are engaging in the gossip with you.

Instead, I ask that if you find yourself within earshot of gossip, you not participate. Instead, leave and/or (maybe even the best) when they engage with you, make it clear you don't want to participate. You don't have to be mean, but you can say you don't like to talk badly about people. They will get the message.

In fact, I believe that when you see bullying it's not enough to simply avoid it—you actually have an *obligation* to help put a stop to it and comfort the bullied person.

"If you are neutral in situations of injustice, you have chosen the side of the oppressor."
— Desmond Tutu

Well, gossip is a kind of bullying . . . and thinking about it that way means that it's not enough for you to just avoid it. If you can make it stop—at least on your watch—I strongly believe you should do that.

If you avoid it, choose not to engage in it, or actively put a stop to it in your presence—you will be blessed. To feel as if you are on the "good" side is the sweetest of feelings. That feeling is a great indicator that you're meant to do just that. So, I ask you to do it.

Now, sweethearts . . . let's turn to the news.

You know your daddy's given up the news, and it's been a good two to three years since that's happened. Let me tell you: it's like a weight has been lifted off my shoulders. The change in my mindset each day is incredible, and now I'm at the point where hearing the news—perhaps it's on wherever I am at the moment—is like nails on a chalkboard.

Today's news affects our mind and attitude so much that we barely even know that it's happening when we're glued to the TV, radio, or glowing screen on our phones and computers.

Think about it this way: most mainstream news outlets are paid by advertisers to literally scare you into continuing to watch them. Their objective isn't to inform you; it's to make money by selling ad space to companies that want their message in front of a lot of people.

The way the news gets people to watch and listen is to be sensationalistic. The phrase I've heard mentioned is, "If it bleeds, it leads." They are showing you the negative because we humans keep an eye out for negativity as a survival mechanism. Our brains are meant to look for the tiger in the bush—or in this case, what could cause pain or death.

Sadness or fear is a misfiring byproduct of this survival mechanism, and the news preys on that.

The fact is, life is much better now than it ever has been. Unfortunately, that means the bad can be amplified so much more easily than ever in history. There is less violence, less conflicts, and more freedom and opportunity than ever—but you wouldn't know that if you just watch the TV.

My sweet children! *Please* guard your mind with care. Be vigilant about what enters that beautiful brain of yours. Turn off the news. Don't participate in the gossip. Keep the negative out, and allow the goodness of appreciation, love, and nearly limitless opportunity occupy your mind instead.

Advice in Practice:

- If you watch the news on TV, quit cold turkey. It's usually best to replace a habit rather than just quitting one; so if you need something to fill that time, listen to positive podcasts or books you enjoy on Audible, or maybe even look up comedians. I like to have the computer nearby at home while making dinner or breakfast, watching something motivating, educational, or sometimes escapist in nature when the news would normally be on. Now the news is never part of my lifestyle . . . and that's so, so much better.
- The next time you hear people talking badly about someone, I hope a little alarm goes off in your head: *DANGER! DANGER!* Just say, "I don't want to talk badly about someone," and walk away . . . or, at the very least,

put a little distance between you and the bad vibes being spread near you. If you can defend them in an honorable way, try to do that, too. Remember that people who gossip about others in your presence will gossip about *you* in the presence of others, too. Make a mental note of that, and treat what you share with them accordingly. Or, as explained in "Teach People How to Treat You," cut those vampires out of your life.

This is a BIG tip, easy to do, and it made a *huge* difference for me: take the news feed off your phone. I have an iPhone, and it took a little bit of doing to completely eradicate the news (they're adamant about getting it to you, because even Apple is reporting the news or getting paid from the content). The difference of not seeing "4 Dead in Fiery Wreck" on your phone as you're preparing for your day is amazing. Please take the time to do this now. Google "How to remove the news feed from my phone" now, and don't keep reading this book until you do this simple act. I promise it will improve your daily mindset. If it doesn't, you can put it back on—but I bet you'll be like me, and the difference will astound you.

- Remember that you're loved!

Notes, thoughts, and intentions.

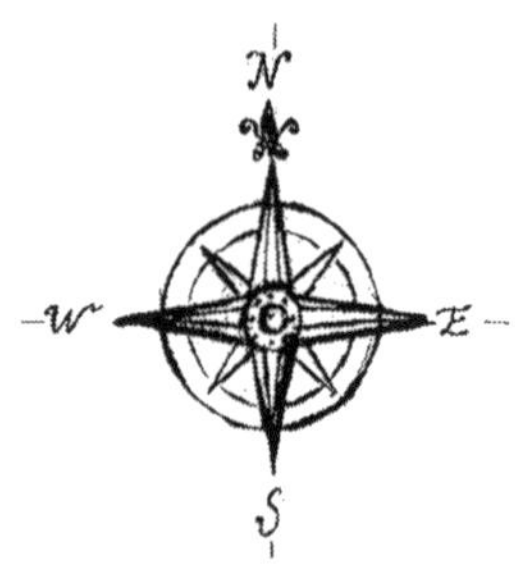

20. Make and Keep Regular Dates with Your Loved Ones.

This. Is. Important! One-on-one time can't be replaced by anything in the world.

No matter how many kids or siblings or parents or loved ones you have, spend some time alone with each and listen to them. Have fun doing something they want to do.

The most important date time will be with your spouse. Get away from the kids (no offense, kiddos) and keep romance alive at all costs. This, coincidentally, is one of the best things you can do for your children! Love their other parent with all of your heart, mind, body, and soul.

I'm hoping, as you read this, you'll recognize that I did this with you and you'll remember that time fondly. I'm also hoping it meant/means a lot to you, and you'll consequentially want to do this with your children and spouse as you go through life . . . and that this tradition will continue with your children. I want this to be a chain reaction of love and goodness that extends through several generations of our family.

I really believe in this, have done a lot of thinking on it, and even invested in "board meetings" with each of you, where we go someplace that you want, do things that you want to do—sans phones or electronics—for four hours or more at a stretch.

But I need to give credit to my mom—your Mona, Brenda Franks—for having these dates with me while I was growing up, especially as a teenager. She was a single mom, had a bit of a tough time sometimes in making ends meet, and yet she *still* always found time for me. We had two regular weekly dates. The first was stopping to watch *L.A. Law*, a legal drama on TV on Thursdays, and the second was our Saturday lunches with each other at Taiwan Dragon in Killeen, Texas. No matter what was going on that week, we always had those dates . . . and due mainly to that, I always felt I was an important part of her life.

Here's the thing: you're still young enough (as I write this) to go on dates with me and Mom. Actually, come to think of it, you'll *always* be young enough to have dates with us! I'm hoping we do this when I'm one hundred and you're seventy-two, sixty-eight, and sixty (respectively)! That means one-on-one time . . . asking important questions (and the nonsense ones, too) . . . looking into the other's eyes and truly connecting on a deep, soul level.

We should always, always have these times.

A dying person's biggest regret is that they didn't live a life true to themselves.

The second biggest regret?

That they didn't spend enough time with their loved ones.

DON'T WAIT TO DO THIS. Honestly, we hustle more every day. We concern ourselves with building businesses, or trying to get a promotion, or making money . . . however we plan to create an impact.

But WHAT FOR?

I'd suggest at least one of the reasons is to spend time with those we love.

But we don't have to go through all of that to make this happen. We can just do it. And it doesn't have to be expensive. It doesn't need to be a big production. It can be a simple meal, one you'd eat anyway. It can be watching a movie together at home while touching our feet together. It can be volunteering (yay!) and sharing that experience of helping others together.

It's just so very important. So DO IT!

And as I've said, as important as it is to spend time with your parents/children . . . it's even more important to spend time with your spouse. That time and the relationship built benefits everyone. It shows your children time with their spouse is important. It shows them you value their father or mother. And it trains you—the kids—to know what a healthy, romantic relationship looks like . . . which is another gift of great importance to give your children.

I'm actually writing this letter while looking at you, Mandy. It's not a daddy/daughter date per se, but it's still so very special. I love that we get to spend time together. It makes me happy.

And when we get to spend quality time with each other, that's about the best use of time that there is.

Advice in Practice:

- Consider having an *actual* board meeting, run by our friends Jim Shiels and Brian Scrone at Board Meetings International (www.boardmeetings.com) at the beach or the mountains with their group. For those who don't know, this is an event for one parent and one child, and it's set up to help bonding. A once-in-a-lifetime experience for both the parent and child.
- Have Board Meeting dates with your children (or parents). I got this from Jim Sheils who wrote a great book about it. The rules are (I mentioned this in the advice): one parent, one child, the child picks what is done, and the parent goes along with it, NO ELECTRONICS, pure bonding, and for four hours, plus. If the idea of not having a phone for that long scares you—then you definitely need to do it!
- Pick up the phone now, as you're reading this, and SCHEDULE your date. If it's early in the morning—thank you for reading this in the still quiet—just send a text that hopefully won't wake them up. Set the time and date, but no pressure on the *what* to do yet. That can be brainstormed, or the kids can think on it to make it their kind of date.

- If you're a married adult (or with a steady girl-/boyfriend), take this time and a little inspiration to make a date with your romantic partner—and pull out all the stops. It doesn't have to be for any particular reason at all. In fact, it takes on special meaning when it's just *because*.
- Lastly, put this on your Ideal Schedule (see the "Create Your Very Own Ideal Schedule," lesson in the Mind section of this book) to do this regularly. I'd suggest once a week. If you have a lot of kids, it may be tough to do it often with one parent/one child, but it is oh, so worthwhile. If it's a recurring thing (go ahead and add that recurring function on your phone calendar while you're there), it will remind you to keep setting those dates and sticking to them. The power of this ritual will transform your relationships.

As always, I love you . . . and I can't wait for our next date(s)!

Notes, thoughts, and intentions.

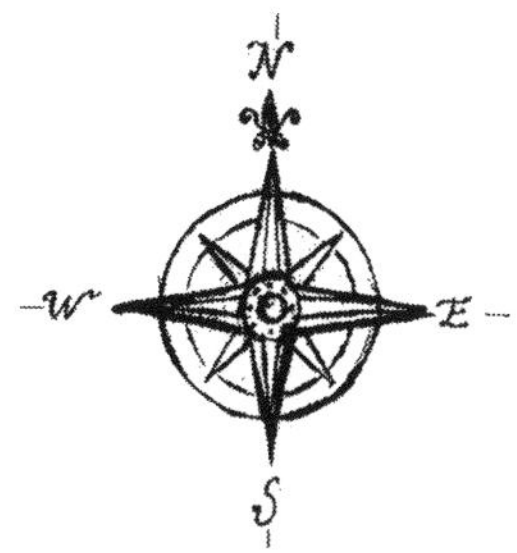

21. Strive to Have Family Dinners Together.

Family is important.

One of the best ways to keep the family unit close is to commit to have family dinners together. In fact, I think a lot of the decline in the closeness of families in general can be linked to this. In decades past it was a staple of life, but it's definitely more rare now (at least in my observation).

It's important for a few reasons. The obvious thing is that it gives the family a regular chance to check in with each other. If you do it several times a week, you can find out how each other's days went, what the day-to-day triumphs and challenges were, and generally be more involved with the lives of your loved ones. This makes it easier for you to help each other when you need it. If there's not a regular time to talk with each other, there's a really good chance that everyone will essentially live their own lives—and that feeling of camaraderie will be lost.

It's also generally a lot better for you, health-wise, to eat a family-prepared meal instead of something fast, convenient, and (probably) processed. If you make good meals, you can have "planned-overs" (a much better term than "left-overs") for lunch the next day. Just get in a good green shake for breakfast before that, and your meals are golden.

The final reason why family dinnertime is important is because it makes for good memories. It's a touchstone for the family, which strengthens your ability to touch base with everyone in the near future.

The biggest rule at dinner? To find out about each other and our lives. Don't criticize, don't find blame—just truly enjoy each other's company. What we want to create more than anything is a safe haven for the family—when you can discuss everything, warts and all, with the people who love you most.

We haven't been great about setting these times. I'm writing this after a week of two meals together as a family, where we all happened to be home and sat down together. That's a good week for us. A lot of the time the mundane takes charge. Mom is late to get home from work, and we all eat different meals, at different times. Even when we do get family dinnertime, a lot of the times at least one or more of us is missing.

That's certainly not the way to do it.

Even though we haven't done this as often as we should, I think it's very important. I'm hoping that the ways we mess up can also be used as examples of better ways to do things. I should have made a bigger emphasis on this as you were growing up. (To be fair, we used to be a lot better at it when you were younger. I think being teenagers and having very strong feelings about what you want to eat plays into that changing. That, and not having a set schedule due to your mom and I working for ourselves.)

So. When you have your own family, even with just you and your spouse, start the habit sooner rather than later, and vow to each other to keep that time as sacred. Time together laughing, loving, and helping each other is the glue that keeps a family strong.

On the same token, family meetings offer the same chance to be close, and with everyone on the same sheet of music. You can use it to talk over some of the "magic moments" of the week, or your current biggest challenge in life, or to coordinate schedules, calendars, vacations, events, and the like. We've had our family meetings very sporadically (as you know, kiddos). I think that's a mistake. These days you tend to roll your eyes now and let out a loud "*SIGH!*" whenever I even mention a family meeting. That's on me as family leader to be more assertive in getting them done. The importance lies in whether we are working together as a family, or off on our own separate paths.

Something else on this: make at the very least a good-hearted *attempt* to leave all glowing screens off and/or away from the table during your family meetings. There was a study done in 2015 by Elon University that found that over 25 percent of connection is lost if you only have a phone in your line of sight! You don't even have to be on your phone talking to someone else (over the chance to talk to your *family*—wouldn't that be cooler anyway?!) for the phone to wreak its havoc on your dinner/meeting.

It's also just plain rude to the rest of us if you're fiddling with your phone or talking to someone else instead of paying attention to the people you're currently with. I think we've all felt that feeling in our chest—that feeling of disappointment when someone leaves your conversation to answer the phone and talk to someone else. I know I have.

The last thing is the TV. Turn it off—unless you're enjoying something together as a family . . . but how often does that occur, really? Not a lot. It's the same principle as the phone: it detracts from the personal family connection you're trying to establish.

I hope this is helpful. It's rare that we as a family discuss these types of things, so I hope reading about it now makes a difference in the future. But even now, as you're a part of our household, don't let all of the responsibility lie with just your parents. You can make these dinners and meetings happen, too. You don't need to wait to be anointed to help. You and everyone in this family has an obligation to speak up to make things better—always.

Okay, I'll stop harping on you about this—but I hope you understand and realize its importance. If you can get this right now, I think it will make a huge difference with your own family in the future.

Advice in Practice:

- After you read this, schedule your next family dinner. Just do a group text with the whole family (like I'm about to do right now). Just be assumptive and do it—

don't wait for someone else to have the inspiration. It's up to you. Go ahead and do it now. I'll wait.

- Think about some of the things you'd like to talk about during the dinner and/or meeting. You can jot them down or just keep them in mind. Bring them up. ASK QUESTIONS of everyone else. Be more interested in everyone else than you are about getting your story in (although that's important, too).

- Help with dinner. Again, take some of the responsibility on your shoulders. Plan it, help get the ingredients, or remind someone else to get what's needed when they're out shopping. Dinner prep and the dishes afterward can be a continued time of togetherness. (And those chores help build character, too.)

- Create an agenda for a family meeting, then call one together. Just schedule it like you did the dinner. Get everyone's agreement on a meeting time, and hold them to it. Once you're there, you can ask what everyone would like in the meeting.

Notes, thoughts, and intentions.

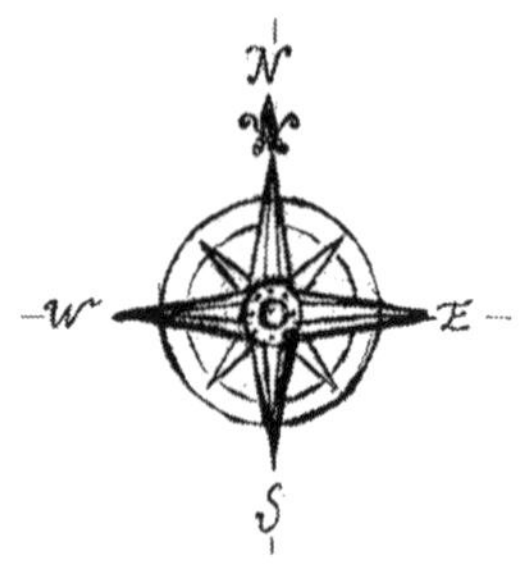

22. Pick Your Spouse Extremely Carefully.

I know it's right there in the title, but I'm gonna' say it again:

PICK YOUR SPOUSE EXTREMELY CAREFULLY!

I hope that sticks. Now let's get into the why.

You'll know when you're in love, but just love might not be enough.

Don't be in a rush to find "the one" . . . but don't be so certain your current love is the one until it's so blindingly obvious that you can't wait to make them yours forever.

If it's real, then it's going to last. So please don't pull an Anna from *Frozen* and get engaged in a day . . . or a year . . . or maybe even two.

I've heard this—and I don't know if it's the absolute truth, but it rings true: most people aren't fully "grown," personality-wise, until after age twenty-five or so. A 2013 study published in Cerebral Cortex shows that men in particular take longer to "act their age". The point being, you won't even know how this person will be for the rest of their lives. Their demeanor is still malleable. It can change—and probably will—and if you're super in love with who they are right now, then any change from that needs to be greeted with a little skepticism.

Also, it may (and probably will) be at least a year or two for the "honeymoon" period, when you're both putting your best foot forward all of the time. You won't necessarily know the real person until quite a bit later. Conversely, they may not know the real *you* for that time, either . . . you may change, and they may not, so that you're not as enamored with them anymore. If you're dedicated to growth and positive change, and they're not, then you'll definitely have some growing pains ahead that can turn into real cracks in the relationship.

I'm giving you a lot of reasons to wait—and they're valid—but the big point (I've told you this before, but it's worth repeating) is this:

If it's real, then it's going to last.

If you accept that, then there's NO REASON to be in a hurry when selecting the person you're (at least in theory) going to spend the rest of your life with.

Your spouse is going to color every part of your life. I won't go so far as to say that they help to determine *everything*, but it's pretty dang close. If you don't pick the "right" one, you're looking at a lot of possible hurt and even an entire life broken—or at the very least a decade or two.

This is the person that's going to be closer to you than any other human on Earth—including your dad.

You will be completely and totally vulnerable with them. They will see you at your best and at your worst. They'll be your best friend (if you do it right). You'll be partners in growth. You'll want to spend your waking hours with them, and they should be able to make you smile even twenty or thirty years after you first connected.

What are the things you should look for? Good question. The answer is going to be different for everyone . . . but here are some of the qualities on *my* list:

Attraction.

That's first on the list because if romantic attraction isn't there, it's just not going to work. I know you don't want to hear this, kids, but it's true: I find your mom sexy. And I suggest you find the same in your future spouse, from the very beginning. Because this spark will need to last a very, very long time.

Kindness.

We talk about this a lot, but I would submit that this is the most important quality in a human being. You'd better not fall for the "bad boy" in a serious way—because if they're not good-hearted people, they do NOT belong with my treasures! There are some good ways to tell this listed in the advice below.

Willingness to get better.

I hope neither you nor your future spouse "settles." Self-improvement is one of the key aspects to life, and most folks either have this desire to improve or don't. This is so important.

Friends.

You need to really enjoy spending time together in a friend capacity. This will really affect the longevity of a relationship. (My friend Shari on Facebook just suggested that people meet for first dates to run errands together. You'll see if you really like each other then, and if it doesn't work out, at least you have your errands done!)

Good parent potential.

Really, really *great* parent potential. This criterion will eventually determine the quality of the daddy to my grandchildren. (If you choose to have kids, of course. But if not, it's still a good quality to seek.)

They love you as you are and don't try to change you.

That's a recipe for a miserable relationship down the line. Be careful on this one, as people put their best fronts on early—and there may not be cases where they specifically criticize you that are overt. Keep your eyes open, though . . . because it will be magnified after marriage.

Advice in Practice:

- If you're dating someone new, or if you're with someone now—run them through the above criteria. How do they stack up on each of them? If even one of these is off, really consider whether or not they're "the one." Any of these can (and probably should) be a deal-breaker.

- If the person you're with now isn't "the one," and you know it, it's better to end it sooner rather than later. This is more fair to you both.
- If you truly agree with this advice (you don't *have* to agree, but I want you to think about it), please pass it on to others. It can save a lifetime of grief when a mistake is made.

Notes, thoughts, and intentions.

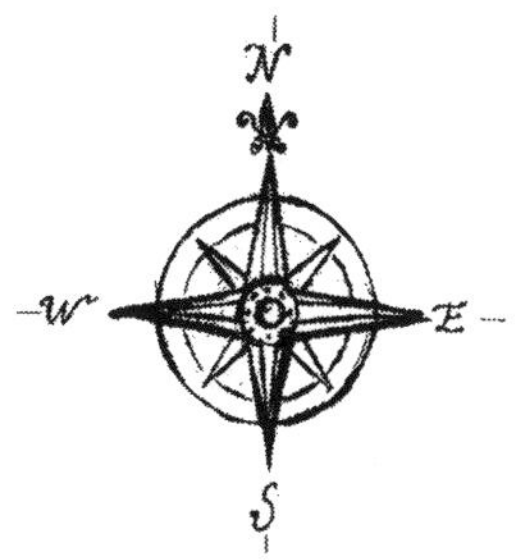

23. Be Wary of Marrying a Giver, Taker, or Matcher. (Get This Right!)

This one could end up being a big piece of advice, and I hope I'm on target with this, as it can make a significant and profound difference in your life.

When—or if (you don't *have* to get married)—you get married, or even have a serious long-term relationship with someone, here's one of the biggest personality traits you need to look for in them:

You need to decide whether that person is a Giver, a Taker, or a Matcher.

I learned about this concept through the book *Give and Take: A Revolutionary Approach to Success* by Adam Grant. Here's the low-down.

Giver.

This is someone who tends to give first and not need much of a reason to do it (a great quality). Grant gives some insights:

"Givers are a relatively rare breed. They tilt reciprocity in the other direction, preferring to give more than they get."

"Givers and Takers differ in their attitudes and actions toward other people. If you're a Taker, you help others strategically, when the benefits to you outweigh the personal costs. If you're a Giver, you might use a different cost-benefit analysis: you help whenever the benefits to others exceed the personal costs."

Taker.

Takers basically think, "If I don't look out for myself, no one will." Here's what Grant says about these:

"Takers have a distinctive signature: they like to get more than they give. They tilt reciprocity in their own favor, putting their own interests ahead of others' needs. Takers believe that the world is a competitive, dog-eat-dog place. They feel that to succeed, they need to be better than others."

Matcher.

And finally, here's what Grant says about these:

"Matchers strive to preserve an equal balance of giving and getting. Matchers operate on the principle of fairness: when they help others, they protect themselves by seeking reciprocity. If you're a Matcher, you believe in tit-for-tat, and your relationships are governed by even exchanges of favors."

Now, *Give and Take* generally talks about the workplace . . . but I want you to think about it on the personal level. A

Giver will give of themselves without looking for a return, a Taker is more strategic and tends to put their own needs first, and a Matcher will give if given to first.

To be happier in life, I whole-heartedly give the advice to look for a Giver. If you're both Givers you'll have a much happier life, and if you're a Giver while your spouse/significant other is a Taker or Matcher you'll spend a lot of time and energy trying to please them. Your needs will be sacrificed for theirs—and my dears . . . you're far too important for that to happen.

Honestly, I'd try to establish this personality trait of a potential partner as early on as possible. If they don't have the trait of a Giver, I'd quite literally not take the next step with them. Of course, that may be hard when attraction and matters of the heart are involved—but I think it's very important.

That's why I'm giving this advice, after all. So please take it to heart. Again, I believe it'll make a very big difference in your life.

And with that, please know that, once again, I love you dearly.

Advice in Practice:

- Take a good read of the book *Give and Take: A Revolutionary Approach to Success* by Adam Grant. Listen to it on Audible, or get the Philosopher's Note from Optimize.me, or however you like to read. And take it to heart.

- Figure out the tell-tale signs of Givers versus Takers and Matchers. Watch carefully how someone treats a waiter or waitress. See if they do things for you unexpectedly, without expecting something in return. That's key. Someone trying to court you may want something in return, and often it's physical. Watch that carefully, please.
- Does the person of interest seem to have a lot of empathy? Are they kind? (You already know this, as I've mentioned it here a lot, but that to me is the most important quality in a human being.) Do they return things they borrow? Have they ever stolen something? (If they have, you're probably dealing with a Taker.)
- Work on this list yourself and see if you can categorize some of your family members and friends as practice. Then check out the people you date. For real!
- If you're in a relationship with a Matcher—or worse, a Taker—please realize that they're probably not going to change. If you try to change them, that's honorable, but probably a little fruitless. Look at the things that tip you off about their behavior, and maybe use them as fuel to make your escape. It hurts, it really does, especially because you're probably a Giver yourself . . . but it will be much better for you to end it sooner rather than later.
- If they *are* a Giver, please know that's only one criterion of a potential spouse. It's not gospel. They need other traits too! But if they're a Taker, that's a red flag. Don't marry them.

As for yourself, realize that it's okay to be a Giver, and feel free to cultivate it in your life! You are perfect, and so very deserving.

Notes, thoughts, and intentions.

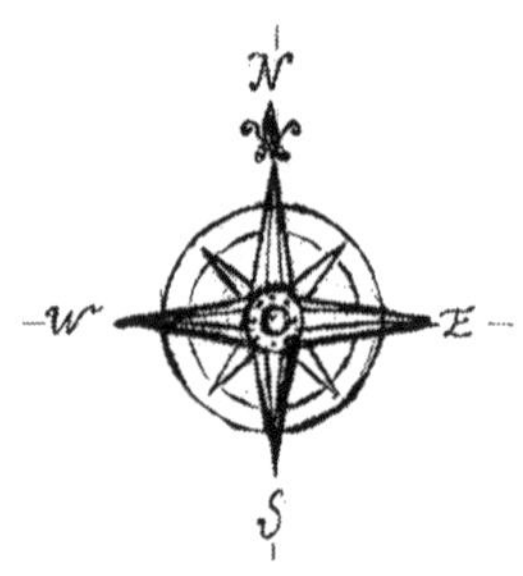

24. Plan—and Work—to Keep Romance Thriving.

My sweethearts. This one is close to my heart. I can't write a collection of lessons to you without talking about and giving some advice on romance. It's so important to life. It's the wonderful marinade that makes everything better.

You may or may not know (but I'm pretty sure you do) that your dad is an incurable romantic. I love LOVE. I love holding your mom's hand, and I love knowing that I get to surprise and delight her at times.

I've done some wonderfully romantic, sometimes over-the-top gestures, like our twentieth anniversary "movie showing," or whisking your mom away for some pre-planned (but still surprising) weekends away.

You see that, and you've experienced it.

In fact, as I write this, your beautiful mom and I just got back from our anniversary trip through Venice, Florence, and Rome, Italy. It was absolutely magical. We spent more time together, laughing and holding hands, than we have in many years. We needed it, and it will always remain one of the greatest memories of my life.

But I also feel like I haven't always done enough. There have been times in my life when I feel that I've flat-out taken your mom and our love for granted. That pains me, but it's good because it motivates me to do more now—and also to share this advice with you.

The title of this lesson begins with the words "plan" and "work." That's intentional. The thing is, romance doesn't always come easily. There's a life cycle to love and romance, and I want you to experience this in all its vivid hues, sounds, and exquisite feelings.

It can begin with a cosmic ***BOOM***. Your whole world is turned inside out—but in the best of ways. You feel like every breath needs to be spent living for your beloved. The rush of new love makes everything brighter—you can literally hear birds chirping almost everywhere. Every breath is exhilarating. In fact, remember the last chapter? Add this paragraph to the advice on attraction. It's so important to have this kind of blissful attraction and experience. It's life-giving, life-affirming, and it makes everything in the world worthwhile.

I remember, over twenty-two years ago now, thinking that if I had your mom, this exquisite, extraordinary, beautiful woman, as my wife . . . it wouldn't matter what else happened in my life—I would always be happy and fulfilled. It was such a strong feeling, and I believed it intensely. I can still feel that powerful pull on my heart today.

I remember talking to your Aunt Laura, my sweet Seefa, about marriage and love and planning to make a life with your mom. She said something to me that I still remember: that white-hot, fiery passion fades over time. When she told me this, I didn't believe it.

No, no, I thought, *not for me! I'm Mr. Romance! I'll always feel this passion!*

But . . .

As it turns out, your aunt was right. That white-hot passion does wane some over the years. The dirty dishes pile up . . . the monotony of life creeps into the cracks and crevices of a loving relationship . . . and the fire dims.

Aunt Laura was saying this to emphasize to me that a true relationship and marriage should be based on a lot more than passion. You need to be friends. You need to talk and communicate. You need to be on the same team and support each other—because life can be hard. You will experience some tragedy. Death and depression will touch us all.

To face this, you need a true partner, not just a lover.

But there still needs to be a spark, an attraction, and romance in life. I'm reminded of one of my favorite lines in the movie *Dead Poets Society*.

> ***"We don't read and write poetry because it's cute. We read and write poetry because we are members of the human race. And the human race is filled with passion. And medicine, law, business,***

engineering—these are noble pursuits and necessary to sustain life. But poetry, beauty, romance, love ... these are what we stay alive for."
— Robin Williams as John Keating

Love and romance. Showing your person in life that they are wonderful, that they are special to you . . . this too is a noble pursuit.

The fact is, this person is picking YOU. They're spending their time, their efforts, and their love on you. And they should be rewarded for that. You should do almost everything in your power, in your creativity and in your love, to make it special to be with you.

It will make them feel better—but as we discuss throughout this book, when you do something good for someone else, it will make *you* feel better, too.

So make romance a priority in your life. Plan and work to make it happen. Sometimes you may not even feel like it . . . but it's too important to let slide. You need to make the time for dates with your loved one.

Something I've learned is that when your relationship with your love isn't right . . . nothing in your world is right.

So, then, the question is how do we do it? What if you're telling me, "I'm not particularly romantic"?

That's not good enough.

Romance is a skill. It can be learned, developed, practiced, and honed. If you don't practice it and try it, then your life will lose that beautiful technicolor brightness that makes everything so sweet.

What matters is that initial effort and decision that you're going to do something magnificent and loving for your partner. *Decide* to be romantic, recognize its value, and feel that you want to show romance for your partner. Uncover the reasons *why* this should be important to you. Then, as Rohn says, "When the why gets big enough, the how gets easy."

HOW DO WE BE ROMANTIC?

In the simplest terms, you're romantic by showing love to your partner. Displays of romance are really best when you enact them in a way that's meaningful to your partner. You want them to know you think about them, that they're important to you, and that you'll do anything for them. You can show them that in words, of course, but I think it's more impactful if you show it in deeds.

You need to *plan* to be romantic!

If you do a regular "check-in" like I advise, that can even be one of the roles in your life that you examine on a fairly frequent basis. Tony Robbins has his COIs, or "Categories of Improvement," and one of those categories can be given a name like "Sorcerer of Sensuality," or "Pioneer of Passion." (Of course, it could just be a boring category name like "Romance.")

The thing is, if you regularly ask yourself how you're doing in that area of life, it will spur you to do more romantic things. It will keep the idea of romance alive for you and place it on the pedestal in life where it belongs.

You need a trigger, something that reminds you to show romance. Even if you have a regular date night, that can turn into a too-comfortable, ho-hum experience unless you bring some romance into it. I have a few ideas about that, and I'll share them in the Advice in Practice section of this lesson, but it's something you need to think about for yourself. How do you remind yourself to be romantic when a lot of life seems to get in the way?

After you've decided romance is important and you've set up a system to remind you to do it . . . it's time to actually show some love!

This is the fun part for me, as it's a chance to truly delight your mom. It lets my creativity out to play, and a noble pursuit is engaged: romance!

Can you guess what I'm going to say about how to do this?

[pausing . . . pausing . . . pausing]

That's right: MAKE AN IDEA LIST! An Idea List of ways to surprise and delight your sweetheart. To me, these are the most fun. I've done it several times, and I've gotten many, many ideas socked away on my Evernote.

But wait—I'm getting ahead of myself.

An Idea List is important, but it's even better if you use OPOA first.

That is, figure out the ideal Outcome of what you'd like to have happen (i.e., my partner feels overwhelmingly loved, appreciated, supported, and celebrated when they see what I've made happen for them).

Then you think about the Purpose of what you're doing (i.e., romance is important, so I'm keeping our love alive and celebrating this very special person).

Think about any Obstacles that may be in your way—maybe you have kids who need to be babysat, maybe you're struggling financially, or maybe work schedules clash. Think about those upfront, and start to devise ways around, over, under, and through them to make this happen.

. . . and then you get ready for ACTION.

The Action is the all-powerful Idea List. Brainstorm at least ten (I prefer fifteen to twenty) ideas of how to make that Outcome happen. Use Google if you need to, or you can ask help from your friends (or your dad, for that matter). Come up with ways to show romance and make your partner feel special.

They deserve it, and so do you.

One last thing I'll say about this all-important subject of romance: don't wait for your partner to show it. It's *your* responsibility to make it happen. Don't feel entitled and think they should be doing it for you instead. That kind of thinking chokes a relationship and sows bitterness.

Instead, appreciate the fact that YOU have the ability to make it happen, and that a lifetime of romance is well within your grasp.

I love you so dearly, and I want so much for you to be able to experience a life of romance and love like the one I share with your mother.

Advice in Practice:

- If you're in a relationship (or, heck, even if you're not, as it can still be fun and instructive), do a Romance OPOA now. Go over and write out your Outcome, Purpose, Obstacles, and then brainstorm your Actions through an Idea List. Get creative, think about it, meld your ideas and refine them. Experience the thrill of turning these intangible thoughts into something real in our world!

- Do an OPOA and Idea List on *how* you will keep romance very much alive and a part of your life. Why is romance important to you? What's your Purpose in doing this? What is the outcome of having romance be a part of your life? What are some of the things that will get in the way of it? What's going to keep you from allowing a year or two or *ten* go by without you creating a grand gesture of love for your partner? Do the Idea List with fervor. Really dig deep and think of how you want to make romance happen in your life.

- Keep an Evernote of these romantic ideas. I've done several Idea Lists of "How to Make Laura Feel Cherished, Loved, and Appreciated." I'll do different ones at different times to make them fresh. Some ideas overlap, but none are ever exactly the same. Think on it and make it fun. These are some of my favorite Idea Lists. Google or Pinterest and clip some pictures that spark your imagination, and use this as a resource when it's time for romance.

- Make a "Love" playlist. Put all of your favorite love songs on it. Take some time and effort to really get it right. You can share the list with your love, or just keep it for yourself and play it on dates or when you're thinking about them. Some songs I'd definitely include (but remember: it's *your* list) include "Let's Stay Together" by Al Green, "These Arms of Mine" by Otis Redding, and "Cry to Me" by Solomon Burke. Mmm, mmm! I love these songs! (Ooh, listen to and include "Nothing Can Change This Love" by Sam Cooke. I just started listening to it now.)

- Read *The 5 Love Languages: The Secret to Love That Lasts* by Gary Chapman. This book is so useful because it's important to make sure you're speaking a language your partner understands.

- There's a book called *Light Her Fire: How to Ignite Passion and Excitement in the Woman You Love*, by Ellen Kreidman, that I read a long time ago (back when I was courting your mom), and it really helped refine my romantic impulses. If you're male (I'm looking at you, Alec!) and you're reading these words . . . read that! She also has a book I assume is just as good called *Light His Fire: How to Keep Your Man Passionately and Hopelessly In Love with You.* Read these, and more importantly, make a study of this extraordinarily important aspect of life. Again, you and they deserve it.

- Lastly, I've included this in the letter "Make and Keep Regular Dates with Your Loved Ones," but having a regular time that's scheduled with your loved one is so, so important. I'd recommend scheduling it with them, and take some turns—have them plan a night, and then you plan one. Some will just be a movie and dinner, but those can be changed up. Something cool and unexpected might even happen, too. That's the beauty of romance!

<3

Notes, thoughts, and intentions.

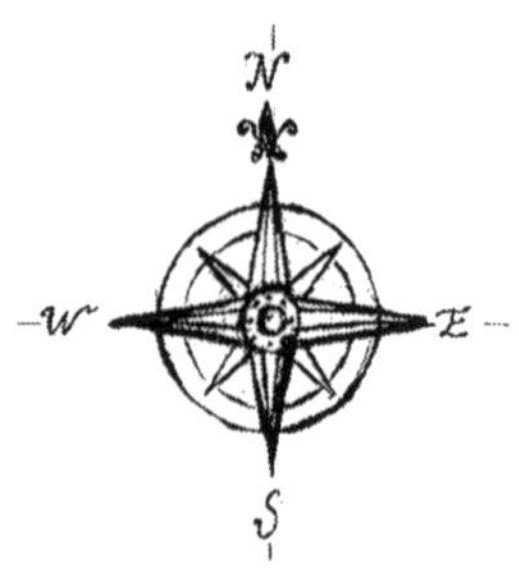

25. Tickle Your Daddy's Back. (Go a Little Out of Your Way to Do the Little Things)

Tickle your dad's back when he asks—you'll never know how much this means to him.

This was included in my original list of advice for you as somewhat of a joke—maybe, I thought, it would really get one of you to take some time out to actually run your hand across my back. But then it stayed and grew in importance.

Here's what it means in a real sense:

Go a little out of your way to do the little things that make a difference to people.

Having my back tickled is something I enjoy. I've loved it since I was a baby. My first word was literally "Baaaack," and I said it whenever I wanted my mom or dad to tickle it. For real. I'm not making this up!

So when you—Aly (usually) or Mandy (very occasionally) or Alec (I'm working on training you!)—actually take the time to do that for me, it really means a lot. It makes me feel loved and important.

Seem silly? It isn't. It's proof that just a little act goes a long way.

There are tons of little acts that can go a long way for a lot of people. In "Learn the Five Big Steps (If You Read Nothing Else, Read This)," I described the Daily Practice of doing something kind for another human every day. It's one of the best things anyone can decide to do. These little things can mean a whole lot to other people, even if you don't realize it at the time.

Just a quick text to someone saying you're grateful for them or that you're thinking of them today and hope they're well—just a little something like that can have a profound influence on someone's entire *life!* Remember my letter entitled "Don't Keep Compliments and Gratitude to Yourself"? Go read it again!

THIS IS SO, SO EASY TO DO.

But as Jim Rohn points out, what's easy to do is also easy *not* to do.

So think about that and add the thought of doing something nice for someone else to your daily routine. Or, better yet, add the *Action* of doing something nice for someone else.

Like tickling your daddy's back (wink, wink).

Advice in Practice:

Break out your ubiquitous cell phone. I know you have it right there next to you. Once you have it, send a quick message to two people you like or admire, letting them know you're thinking of them and you hope they're well or that you believe in them. Make sure it's honest—and go ahead and do it.

- Think of something you could do for someone that's the equivalent of tickling your daddy's back. Do a little digging. Find out what really does it for them, and then do that little something for them. But you better not be doing it just to get something out of it. That's disingenuous at best, and manipulative at worst. Just do it to make them happy!

- Here's some repetitive advice (first advised in my letter entitled "Plan—and Work—to Keep Romance Thriving") that's worth doing twice: read *The 5 Love Languages: The Secret to Love That Lasts* by Gary Chapman. As I've said, it talks about how people really want to be shown love—physical touch, gifts, quality time, words of affirmation, and acts of service. Use that to help decide what the important people in your life really need.

- If you happen to be in my vicinity when you're reading this, then find me and tickle my back (for a timed five minutes). Wow, you don't know or understand how much I like that. I think that when I'm really wealthy, I'm going to have a professional back-tickler follow me everywhere. Weird? Yes. Of course. (Your mom may freak out about this, too—hahaha!)

I love you so, so, SO much!

Notes, thoughts, and intentions.

26. Practice Everyday Acts of Courage.

My sweethearts. This is a big one. This is one of those lessons, where if you do what we talk about, your life will be so much more rich and wonderful. . . and if you don't do them, your quality of life will suffer.

Practicing everyday acts of courage means doing at least one thing every day that makes you feel uncomfortable.

It's facing the fear, knowing it scares you, and doing it anyways. It's the conscious act of getting out of your comfort zone.

You know this on an intuitive level and it sounds a little cliché, but all of the growth in life occurs when you're outside of your comfort zone. If you're doing things that are easy for you, that are just habitual then you're in danger of becoming complacent. You can get fat, dumb, and happy. Or at least happy *in the moment*. Because it feels *good* to sit and binge watch TV. It feels good to eat the junk food scientifically designed to increase cravings. At least in the moment.

But the results of that behavior do not feel good. The hours turn into days, those turn into weeks, months, years...and then you're wondering where those dreams of your childhood went at some point in your life--but you'll have enjoyed the time.

A cure for that kind of thinking is to practice everyday acts of courage.

It's the mindset of this that's important. My mentor Dan Sullivan says that the difference between courage and confidence is that courage feels horrible while confidence feels great. He also points out that competence and confidence never get to happen without the initial commitment and courage to get good at something. So, it all starts with that first shaky, imperfect action where you're scared to do something, but still do it.

The magic of what happens with that is that—just like a physical muscle—your courage gets greater and you become a better person each and every time that you take action. Knowing you're going to be uncomfortable and scared, and you do it anyways.

The thing is, this courage will get easier over time. Not because the act is any different, but because YOU are different. You're literally better each time you've performed an act of courage. You've improved your character through stepping out and doing the thing that scares you.

When we think of courage, we often think of the great big things: having the courage to end a relationship that's not working, or switching careers, or moving to a place where you don't know anyone. These are all acts of courage, and they're often defining moments in a great life.

However, these moments are usually far and few between. They don't usually happen often, so you can't use these times to *develop* your courage. You need to practice building your courage each and every day, and you do it by consciously putting yourself in a situation that makes you uncomfortable. Then you take action in the face of fear.

I'm going to give you some tools to help with this in a bit, but let's talk about some examples we may have to show courage. For me, I used to make sales prospecting calls for real estate every day at the office. I never enjoyed them. There was always a little apprehension over making that first call, but I picked up the phone more often than not and started dialing. Usually when I didn't feel like it. If you *feel* like doing it, then you're not exercising much courage.

I'll brag right now, because I'm writing this at 6am-ish on a Saturday. I've been up for a while, and I'm thinking I want to go lay down and get comfortable. But alas, no! I'm practicing a bit of everyday courage by writing this to you now. I want to help you, and I'm also concerned about my character. If I keep doing what's easy all of the time, instead of what's right then that will invade my life, become a habit, and be cancerous to my character and the things I want to accomplish for myself and others. So, I'm going to keep writing for both of us!

These days, the things that are making me uncomfortable are mostly physical. They can include eating the right way even when you and mom leave cake on the counter. It is especially my burpees in the morning. Burpees just aren't fun, and there is literally a little fear every single morning before I do them. But—I always feel better when they're done. Out of breath, and breaking a little sweat, yes, but I feel like a total badass for having exercised that extra bit of courage.

And now—I've started to end my showers in the morning with turning the knob all the way to cold for a few *minutes* (it's supposed to be three). Whew! That just doesn't feel good. I can talk myself up, I can put on music that I love while doing it, but it still takes some courage to do it. Every. Single. Time.

There is a lot of science to show that the cold shower has a lot of health benefits. They help you boost your immunity, wake you up more completely, and can increase metabolism by using energy to warm you up again, helps circulation…and more. [2] BUT—the thing that I appreciate most about them, although I pretty much hate it—is that it gives me a chance to exercise my daily courage.

When you take daily cold showers, and do burpees, and pick up the phone when you don't feel like it, and do it consistently. . . it leads to confidence. That gets you feeling pretty good about yourself. It develops that courage muscle so that when those big decisions come that require intestinal fortitude—you'll be prepared. You can do it.

---

[2] Karen Reed, "9 Scientifically Proven Benefits of Cold Showers," https://www.positivehealthwellness.com, (July 28, 2017)

Another one of my virtual mentors and all around badass human (maybe the toughest man on the planet), David Goggins has a saying that can be applicable:

"Embrace the suck."

Just know it's going to be horrible and lean into it. Yell at it, curse at it if you want to, mentally or actually out loud...and then do it.

Form the habit of practicing every day courage, and then watch as that habit forms *you*.

The Advice in Practice:

- Decide on something that makes you uncomfortable. Even if it's mildly so at first (you will get better as you practice this). Here are some suggestions:
    - Burpees. Start with just a single one if you need to, and build up to more.
    - The cold shower end we mentioned above, even if it's for a few seconds to begin.
    - Writing out an idea list first thing in the morning.
    - Doing the hardest thing first on your daily "to-do" or outcome list.
    - Starting a conversation with a stranger when you're an introvert.
    - Any kind of sales. If you're already doing the sale, then doing an upsell.
    - Pressing "post" on something that scares you a bit.

- Do an Idea List in your journal about things that make you uncomfortable if these aren't doing it for you. It's a good idea to do it, regardless.

- Commit and decide to do it for a minimum of a week, or more if you're feeling brave in the moment. Write down that promise to yourself (don't underestimate putting it in writing, it's important).

- Then *do* it. Mark it down in your journal each day to start and keep a streak going.

- Look for and study the "5 Second Rule" from Mel Robbins. It's basically where you feel and know that you're about to do something beneficial (like burpees for instance), and your brain starts to try to talk you out of it. We're REALLY good at talking ourselves out of things, especially when they're uncomfortable.

  When you even start to get an inkling of that self-talk starting, you count down out loud, "Five, four, three, two, one," and TAKE ACTION before that brilliant mind of yours can list the 3,827 reasons you shouldn't be doing this. There is a lot online about the rule, and Mel has actually written an entire book about it which I recommend. This tool for everyday courage has been invaluable to me in the past few months.

- Get two accountability buddies to do this with you. The reason you need two is that one will always flake out. The rule in the Army is about redundancy. They often say, "If you have two, you have one and if you have one, you have none." So get two buddies for this, and replace one whenever one flakes out and stops being accountable.

Let me know you're doing the uncomfortable thing! I want to know. I love you, you know.

Notes, thoughts, and intentions.

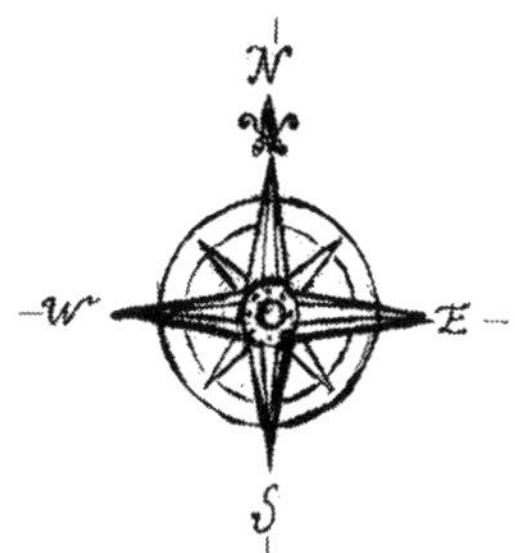

27. Don't Let Your Circumstance Define Your Self-Worth.

My sweethearts.

I sincerely hope this lesson isn't needed, or needed often. . . but I imagine that it is, and it will be many times in life.

As your dad, I am trying my best to help fill you with confidence. I'm doing everything I can to give you that inner fortitude to know that you're as worthy and deserving as anyone to ever walk the planet. Have I been successful in this? I don't know, but I'm holding out hope! I'm also including this little lesson to break out and read when you may need a little boost to your confidence.

Your self-worth is how you feel about yourself. A good self-worth is characterized by understanding and loving yourself, warts and all. It's knowing that you're a good person, and a person who is deserving and worthy of blessings in life.

It means that you don't define yourself by external forces. It means that no matter what happens, you have a deep soul contentment knowing that you are just fine. If you fail, the self worth will help you to get up, dust yourself off, iterate, and attempt it again until you succeed.

Self-worth is confidence in yourself, and valuing yourself.

But sometimes it's HARD to have self-worth like this. Especially if life circumstance is also hard at the time. It's difficult to have confidence after things in your life have fallen apart. Hard times in life can conspire to undermine the feeling that you're worthy.

In my own life, there have been times when I've been horribly out of shape. There have been times when I've been broke (never poor, but just out of money). And there have been lots of times when I've doubted myself and the path I've been on in life.

The history books are full of people who have overcome all kinds of adversity, crippling handicaps, extreme poverty, nervous breakdowns and the like to achieve stunning success in life. In fact, this is just anecdotal for me, but I think that *most* great lives had very hard moments and situations that had to be overcome. It is the exception rather than the rule that people haven't had those seemingly bad, no good, horrible, terrible times in life on their way up the ladder to a life of meaning.

I have the fortune of talking with a lot of highly successful entrepreneurs these days, and almost to a person they've overcome a ton in their lives. They almost always STILL experience doubt and self-worth issues. Many (sometimes including myself) are going through that currently. There seems to be a nearly manic personality in many of them, where there are elevated "highs," and very depressive "lows," in their lives.

So, here is the first real lesson with this:

It's completely normal to doubt your self worth.

When you're at a tough time in your life:

- When the money won't seem to cover the bills.
- When relationships fall apart.
- When you don't seem to be making progress.
- When you're not treating yourself as well as you should.
- When there are health problems.
- When you're facing an identity crisis.
- When you're feeling like an imposter even though things are going well.
- When you feel defeated, tired, and lost.
- When you don't love the person in the mirror.

Here are some ideas I'd ask you to consider:

You are a SPECTACULAR CREATION OF GOD (please see that chapter in the SOUL section of this book). There is divinity running through your veins, and you were created by the Almighty as a unique and valuable soul.

Every human life (including yours) is precious. When you look at people you love, do you ever think that they don't deserve a life of abundance and happiness? Of course not! Yet that feeling can often sneak in with us when we're not careful. Especially when we are experiencing hard times.

But, the hard times *can* truly make you better. The darkness helps you appreciate the light. Being hungry helps to bring value to the food we often take for granted. The times of self-doubt that you may be experiencing can help in the future to keep you humble and gracious for when you do conquer your personal world.

Your hard times will make for a great, inspirational story for others at some time. My friend Philip McKernan says your gift lies right next to your wound. Your wounds include these tough times, and your gift lies in overcoming them so that you can help others along the path, too.

Circumstance can be used to fuel your fire towards something greater. Just like a forest fire uses trees in its way to make itself stronger, you can use the obstacles of life to become a better person. When your self-worth and confidence are high, there is NOTHING that can stop you.

Remind yourself often that it's all going to be okay in the end—and if it's not okay, it's not the end. I heard that from the billionaire John Paul DeJoria who was twice homeless, and at one point lived in his car with his child.

You need some self-compassion, to a point. Love yourself enough to give yourself a hug, or a kick in the buttocks as needed.

That self-compassion needs to be a springboard to some action to make things better. At some point, you have got to get going to improve your circumstances.

Improving Your Self-Worth

There are two types of self-worth.

The first type of self-worth is an intrinsic one of being a human being. It's knowing that we are living, breathing creations of God. It's knowing that there has never been another human just like us, and there never will be. It's in the recognition that all life is precious, and that we all have a level of dignity, no matter what happens.

The second type is self-worth based on confidence and competence, most often preceded by accomplishment. It's that self-assured feeling of knowing that you're a badass.

To improve your self-worth as a human being, here are some ideas:

I touch on this in other areas of these lessons, but I feel it's important enough to repeat. Ask yourself if new human life has value. Does it? I believe it does, but do you? Does a baby deserve love? Does it deserve to eat, to be happy, to have the things of a good life? Of course! They are God's gift to the world. So precious and wonderful! Omigosh, I love babies. If you have children, do they deserve to feel self-worth? Should they be told that they're spectacular creations of God? The answer, at least to me, is an *emphatic* yes.

Now, ask yourself—are you any different? Has it changed along the way that you now *don't* deserve love and well-being?

You deserve it. You are worthy. You are not your current circumstance.

Now, here are some definite steps to move just beyond that basic self-worth towards some kickass self-confidence.

My mentor Dan Sullivan talks about this in his 4C Framework. In it, he explains that confidence is preceded by capability. Then he goes on to say that capability only happens after you have the courage to actually follow through on a commitment.

So the formula is: Commitment => Courage => Capability => Confidence.

You won't have the true, earned confidence in your life until you've committed to something. Then you've had the courage to do it (especially when you don't feel it) and then developed your skill and mindset to eventually get the confidence you're seeking.

He also points out that courage doesn't feel good, and confidence does. So if you're not feeling good about certain things, if you don't feel a lot of self-worth in your profession, for instance—then you have to know that it's built as a result of your actions. It's done by you deciding what you're after, and making a true commitment to get there. Then, it's the daily, sometimes repetitive acts of courage to do what it takes to get there. Through that courage, that trying, failing, getting better, and continuing to move forward you will get better. When you're better, you will feel good about yourself.

The best way to feel confidence towards something is to know you've done it again and again.

That's where the kick in the buttocks I mentioned above comes in handy. You've got to *take action* to get yourself out of the circumstance.

For example: if you feel like crap that your home is cluttered and disorganized, the first thing you have to know is that your level of cleanliness doesn't lower your worth as a human being.

Next, you've got to get out of that circumstance. It's time to make a commitment to clear things out and make your environment one that supports you and your life vision. Then, the part that often feels horrible—you've got to have the courage to take action on cleaning it. This leads to you getting better, and knowing you can do it...because you *have* done it. Congratulations, you have achieved confidence in keeping a tidy environment.

This is the formula for feeling better about yourself and rising above your current circumstance. In truth, it's how you change your circumstance.

Advice in Practice:

- It's time to get out the journal. Oh, yeah. Start off by writing how you're feeling. Do you feel unworthy? Are you associating your circumstance with how valuable you are as a person? What is it that really has you down?

Please get all of these ambiguous feelings out of your head, and make them clear and tangible on paper.

- Next, write down WHY you feel that way. If you don't know, then write why you *think* you feel that way. This provides some objectivity on it and helps to diagnose the problem for a cure.
- If the WHY is based on self-worth as a human being:

  Then please take the time to read, take notes on, and do the advice in the chapters "Love Yourself," and "Kick Your Inner Critic to the Curb," in this HEART section and "Remember That You Are a Spectacular Creation of God," in the SOUL section of this book. Tony Robbins says that repetition is the mother of skill. Just bathe in this material and get to a better mindset. The more you get in front of this feeling and deal with it, the better you'll be at it.

  Add affirmations to your morning routine that help with this.

  Also, take the time to talk to a loved and trusted person about this. Like your dad, for instance.
- If the WHY is based on a confidence issue:

  Write out the commitment you are making to get better. The actual act of writing that helps to imprint it on your beautiful brain.

  Write out WHY you're doing this, and the intentions you have for it. In the example of the clearing the clutter above, write out how you'll feel when it's done. Write out how the days will be different, or what will happen if you don't do it.

Set up your environment to win. Set alarms on the phone to remind you to take those little acts of courage. Write down progress each day in your journaling. Use the 5-second rule discussed in the "Practice Everyday Acts of Courage," to actually do what it is you need to do to create capability.

Keep at it, assess your results and see how it's working. Then iterate and keep going until you feel confidence in your abilities and what you've accomplished.

What you'll feel is a sense of well-being while you're pursuing a worthwhile goal.

- Create an Accomplishment List as discussed in the, "Learn Calmfidence," chapter in the MIND section. Refer to it often, and add to it often. Even make reading it as part of your morning routine when you're not feeling the self-worth.

- Reach out to help someone else in some way, form or fashion. When you help others, you help yourself. It's a metaphysical certainty.

Notes, thoughts, and intentions.

Go to LifeLessonsBonus.com
for Reports, Resources, and
Your Free ($100 Value) Training,
"*Design and Execute Your Ideal Week.*"

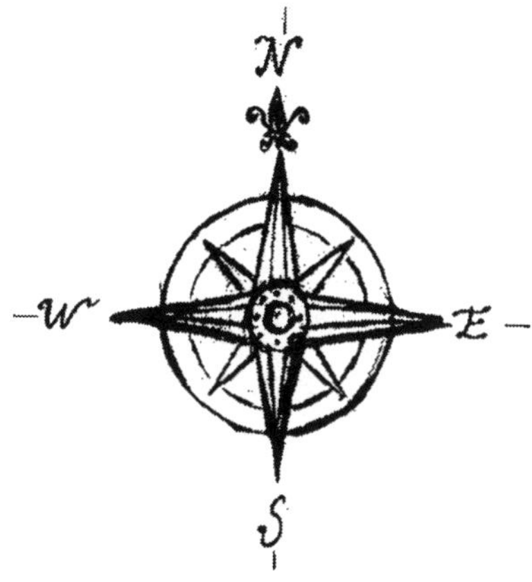

THE MIND.

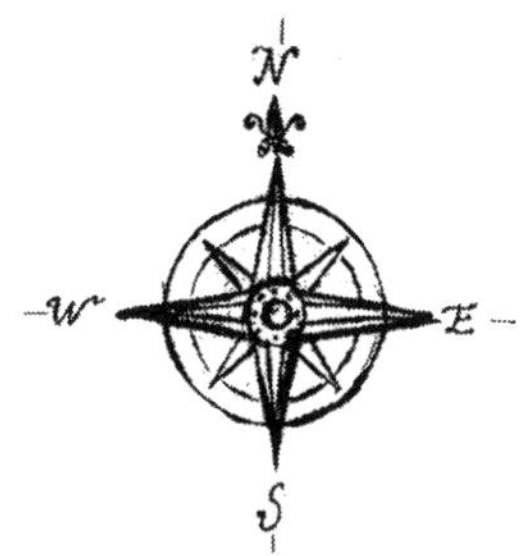

Introduction to The Mind.

My precious human beings!

As I have said and will continue to say (probably too often in these pages), I'm excited about getting this section of advice to you. I humbly suggest that there are many ways in here to lead a much better life, to do things better than most—or at least better for yourself.

Our world is filled with so much groupthink and often it's easy to just allow yourself to be led by conventional thought. We do what was done before us and what's always been done. There isn't a whole lot of critical thought between stimulus and reaction.

The problem with that? We don't ask "Why?" enough anymore. Do you remember when you were kids? (I do!) You'd ask "Why?" for nearly everything. *Everything*, from the cliché "Why is the sky blue?" to "Why do you have to work?"

Man! Kids are so curious. They want to know everything!

Coincidentally, childhood is the time in life when we learn the most, by far. The learning curve flattens out eventually, and we never learn enough after childhood. That goes especially for post-college/university. I think that's partly because our school system has made it a "job" to learn. Kids end up doing so reluctantly, instead of embracing it as a part of a life richly lived.

So, in this section, we're looking at the results of thinking *differently*. Of actually asking the "Whys?" We're taking a critical look at doing things *better*. From the concepts of money (Don't Let Money be a Bully), looking for a job (How to Get Any Job), ways to think critically (What the Heck is an OPOA? The All-Important Idea Lists), learning from others (The Incredible Power of Shadowing), and how not to spend your time (How to Outsource Everything in Your Life that You Don't Like).

I'm biased, but this information is just GOLD. You don't learn these nuggets in school, and most folks don't ever think about them in the everyday 9-to-5 existence.

I've always avoided groupthink. I'd like to think that I never stopped asking "Why?" *especially* if it's doing something that I don't want to do. If there's a better, more effective way to do something, I'm ALL OVER IT. I hate exerting effort that just doesn't need to be spent, unless I really enjoy it or it does a lot of good for me (then you could say that it needs to be done). I was often called "lazy" as a kid, sometimes by those close to me (yikes!); but the truth was I was just different in that I didn't blindly accept things, even back then.

I wouldn't have been able to articulate it at that time, but a phrase from Peter Drucker comes to mind:

"There is nothing quite so useless as doing with great efficiency something that should not be done at all."

Who knew I was already thinking like Drucker as a kid?!

So, reading these—and, more importantly, *making use* of this advice—will lead to a better life. That sounds a little arrogant, and I'm sorry—but I at least invite you to read these and think critically yourself: *Does this make sense? Should I do this? Is it worth the time and effort? Is there a way to make this better?*

Then get after it. Your life will be blessed just by considering some of these gems. I guarantee my life has been improved quite a bit since using them in my life. I've written a book, I've gotten a lot more done daily with less effort per task, and I've generally been more effective.

Don't try to incorporate all of these at once. As Bruce Lee (do you even know who he is? Google that, kiddos!) preached, *use what works and discard the rest.*

Let's get started by turning that page!

28. Partake in the Phenomenal Power of Journaling.

Journaling—the phenomenal power of dumping your brain and thoughts out onto paper.

I feel like I'm saying this with almost every piece of advice, but dang it—if it's true, it's true! Because this can make such a gigantic difference in your day-to-day life. The trajectory of the entire course of your life can be changed by implementing just this one habit.

The quickest way to better yourself is journaling. Why? I think it makes everything objective—you're stepping outside of yourself to take a look at your life in ways you just can't perceive from the inside looking out. Writing about your life almost as a third person looking at your life creates a process, something you're working toward. It allows you to be a sort of bystander and work on your life again, rather than working *in* it.

It also helps us to articulate our thoughts and feelings. In our life, we're often creatures of emotion and reaction.

Journaling allows us a better way to diagnose what's really happening in our lives and allows things to be more clear.

The best way to journal is to be consistent with it—no matter what kind of journaling you do. The fact that it helps make you a better person is something I can't really emphasize enough, because—just like most everything else we do in life—the most value we get out of it is the person we become while doing it.

To start, just set aside five minutes for journaling each night, without fail. I prefer night, but you're going to get benefits regardless of the time of day you choose to do it.

Making it a small goal of five minutes is important. Let me explain with a story I heard recently that goes like this:

Two teams set off to go to the South Pole. One team decided that they were going to cover twenty miles every single day, no matter what. The second team had decided that they would cover more ground when it was nice outside; they'd be able to do forty miles, sixty miles, maybe even more on a clear day, and hunker down and take it easier when the weather was bad or when things didn't line up or agree with them.

The first group—that group of the twenty-miles-a-day goal—actually reached the Pole and returned intact; they were able to do that while the other team that just did it according to the weather, or how they felt on a particular day, perished.

There's a little more to the story, but the point is this: You're a lot more likely to continue with a smaller, more manageable goal that you do consistently, no matter what, than with a bigger goal where you stall and then binge.

Therefore, set a very small goal to get into the habit of journaling for just five minutes a day.

I like to journal at night because it makes my brain work magic while I'm asleep. It also allows me to set the tone for the next day the night before. If I journal about the things that I'm thinking about, some questions I have, current problems, etc., what I find is that subconsciously my mind seems to go to work on it when I sleep. By the morning, I know and understand what the solutions are.

The mind is an amazing tool, and I'm pretty convinced that most of us are not using most of it.

My friend Jesse taught me an effective little trick: write down how you want to wake up the next day. He suggested just one word—it could be *energetic*, or *abundant*, or *loving*, or anything. (In fact, "How would I like to wake up most days?" is a good Idea List for you to work on—even something as simple as this can make a big difference for you.)

Jesse says to then write it out and put it under your pillow—which sounds silly, but it works like magic. You see, the last thought you have as you go to sleep is often the first thought that you have when you wake up in the morning. You wake up and you actually feel abundant, or energetic, or loving, or whatever word you chose. It just seems to work.

I have the same theory about journaling at night: it helps you feel better the next day. You begin the day with many of the problems from the previous night seemingly solved for you.

Another technique I got from Jesse: if you journal at night, you can "save your progress." You keep track of your wins—your accomplishments of that day—and doing that builds confidence and allows some reflection time. Saving progress means that you can build on that the next day, rather than forgetting about it when you don't journal—which often leads to taking two steps forward and one step back.

Advice in Practice:

- One of the easiest and quickest ways to get into journaling is to use *The Five Minute Journal: A Happier You in 5 Minutes a Day*, created in part by my friend UJ Ramdas.

  (Quick story: I happened to meet him at the exact week I ordered my first Five Minute Journal. He gave me a signed copy. When I came home from the event, the Five Minute Journal I ordered beforehand was waiting for me. I had no idea that I would meet him, but I think it was God's way of telling me that I needed to be using one of these bad boys.)

  You can get the physical book from their site, IntelligentChange.com; or you can download the app, which doesn't have the same tangible feel—but there aren't any special limits to what you can write, and you can add pictures. I have both, but prefer the actual book.

- Google "Jim Rohn how to use a journal." There's a good video on YouTube that walks you through his process. The journal he sells is one of the first ones I filled completely in my mid-twenties that started me on this practice.

- Set a thirty-day challenge to do five minutes of journaling every single day, and I promise you—just that five-minutes-a-day commitment will change your life.

- Another book to read is *Morning Pages* by Julia Cameron. What she recommends is three pages a day of stream-of-consciousness journaling, where you write down whatever comes to mind without pause. That's generally how I do my journaling these days, and I highly recommend taking a look at that and getting some methods and ideas from her as you become a serious student of the art of journaling.

- Listen to the interview with Tim Ferriss and Robert Rodriguez.[3] The good stuff is at about five minutes into the interview. I love to hear about how other people journal—and this method is pretty amazing.

- Lastly, find an accountability buddy, someone who is committed to doing this as well. Doing this for thirty

---

[3] Tim Ferriss, "The Wizard of Hollywood, Robert Rodriguez," https://tim.blog/2015/08/23/the-wizard-of-hollywood-robert-rodriguez (August 23, 2015).

days will revolutionize your life, so it's important to be held accountable. (And you can also tell me how it's going, kiddos!)

My children, I love you. It is such an honor to be able to pass on this information to you. I thank you from the bottom of my soul for actually reading this to know what your dad has to say to you. Thank you.

Notes, thoughts, and intentions.

29. Revolutionize Your Life With Idea Lists.

My children, you already know about this, but I want to make sure that we really, really underscore the importance of this *single practice* that can revolutionize your life. Here it is:

Do an Idea List every single day to make your brain sweat, to get your brain working and in top condition, to improve your life, and to turn you into an Idea Machine.

A few years back, I was in somewhat of a depression. I had a very good business, I had a fantastic family (as you know!) . . . life should have been good, but I was definitely in a funk. I think the reason why is that I felt like I wasn't living up to my potential. And personally, I think if you're not living up to your potential, or at least trying to, then you're doing a disservice to yourself and to God.

Along that time, I ran across a book called *Choose Yourself! Be Happy, Make Millions, Live the Dream* by James Altucher. And I know you've heard me talk about this, but I wanted to make sure to get this in print so you can refer to this again and again—because if you do, it will have a big impact for you. And I would love to see that.

Anyhow, in the book, James explains what he calls his "Daily Practice," something I've mentioned throughout this book. In the Daily Practice he would do something good for himself physically, mentally, emotionally, and spiritually—you guessed it—*daily*. (The thing that he did mentally to sharpen himself every day was—you guessed it again—the Idea List.)

I took this and started running with it. The Idea List in particular led to a renaissance of ideas and excitement for me. I wrote out ideas on better ways to wake up in the morning, new business enterprises, places to volunteer . . . in fact, the book you're reading right now came from one of these original Idea Lists.

This stuff works, and it works like magic.

Now, what is an Idea List? It's taking any topic—just one—and coming up with at least ten ideas about that topic. For instance, you could call your list "Twenty Books I Could Write That Would Change the World." (Which led to this book, by the way.) Or, it could be "Ways to Make My Spouse Feel Extremely Cared For and Special." Or maybe "Simple Ways to Make My Life Better With Very Little to No Brain Damage Done."

The point of the whole thing is that you come up with as many ideas as you can. I always do twenty, but James recommends ten. I wanted to accelerate the progress, and I think I did.

The whole purpose of an Idea List is to get your brain to sweat. You want to use your brain every single day—just like a muscle. It gets tired and it collapses, but it comes back the next day stronger and stronger, until finally you become an Idea Machine. And an Idea Machine is a fantastic person to be.

If you're a true Idea Machine, you'll always have another way to do things if something doesn't work. You have somewhat of a superpower. Any of your family, friends, or loved ones can come to you with problems or for advice, and you'll be able to help them right away. Your brain will be firing on all cylinders, as they say. I've done it, and it's been a huge blessing in my life.

But if you don't exercise your brain, it will stop working as quickly and efficiently. It will start to atrophy—again, just like a muscle. So I encourage you to keep up the practice—*daily*.

Idea Lists can also be used to come up with action plans and execution steps to achieve your goals. If you find an idea you absolutely have to follow—I call that your siren song—if you find an idea like that and you *have to* follow it . . . your next Idea List could be ten quick and easy steps to breathe life into this project TODAY.

But if you don't do this . . . your idea can die before it gets a chance to live.

Mandy, I know you had the idea of sending out monthly "happiness boxes," put together by adults with special needs as a business What are some ways you could implement that idea with very little money, in a short amount of time? This is a *great* Idea List! Some of the ideas might be to find a company where these adults are already working, and see if you can contract out a few hours a week from them. You could put together a list of companies that might want to donate items for such a worthy cause, and plan how you'd approach them. You could brainstorm ways to get Clients, or make a list of people that could help you in the endeavor. The possibilities are nearly endless and really exciting!

I can't say strongly enough how much you need to do this to change your life. And, my children, please know that I don't advise this lightly. *This will help you.* School doesn't tell you how to think. It doesn't give the chance for you to improve your thinking power (other than rote memorization). This, however, actually makes your mind stronger and more fit.

I hope you decide to use it, as I may need to call on your vast ideas, knowledge, and brainpower in the future!

Advice in Practice:

- Commit to making an Idea List for at least two weeks, every single day, with at least ten ideas per day. What you'll find is that, initially, you may not think of *great* ideas. You *may* (you're my children, of course!), but, as you do it day in and day out, you'll find that your ideas get better and better. Mr. Altucher says that within six months of doing this consistently, you can become an Idea Machine. Personally, knowing how smart you are, I think you can do it a lot sooner. But the key is *consistency*. So, right now, promise you'll do it for at least two weeks, and hopefully that will give you enough of a taste to continue doing this longer.

- Next, really *juice* up the titles of each of your Idea Lists. For example: "Twenty Books That Could Revolutionize the World and Cause People to Change Their Opinions for the Better." That gets you excited about *doing* it! It pumps you up, and it would make someone a lot more likely to read it if it had a marketing-type title. It just sells itself, to yourself and others.

- The first list that I want you to write is "Twenty Idea Lists That I Could Write That Would Change My Life for the Better." What's beautiful about this is that whenever you're stuck and you don't know what kind of Idea List to write, you can refer back to *this* Idea List. Or you can write more Ideas Lists of Idea Lists you can write! That sounds very meta, but it's a good thing for you.

- Another list that I would like you to write: "The Top Life-Changing Ideas from *Life Lessons from Dad* to Start Immediately." Go through this, think about some of the things that resonated with you—some of the pieces of advice that stuck with you, that you need to work on, to think about, or perhaps share with other people. Write those out. Again, at least ten.

- Lastly, write an Idea List for a friend, either someone in business or someone who needs help with their personal life. Maybe someone that might just need a helping hand. Write an Idea List that could truly help them out and share it with them—this could bless your life and theirs.

As always, I love you dearly. I pray for you daily, and I want the absolute best for you in life.

Notes, thoughts, and intentions.

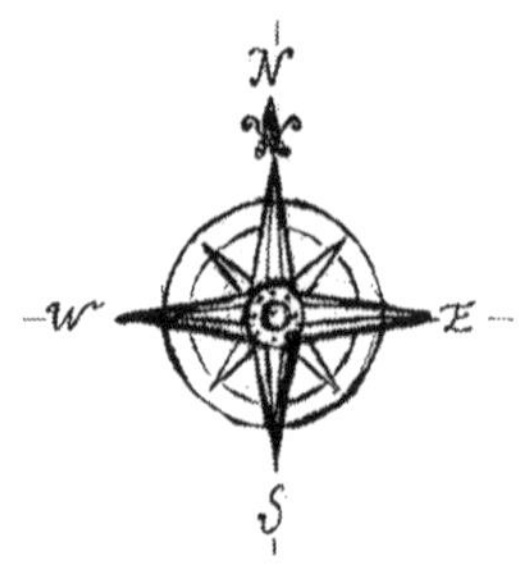

30. Harness the Incredible Power of Goals to Create the Life You Want.

"The greater danger for most of us lies not in setting our aim too high and falling short; but in setting our aim too low, and achieving our mark."
— Michelangelo

Wow.

So, here we are, talking about one of the biggest concepts to help your life—and probably the lives of many of those around you.

Goals. This is one of the most important things that, as your dad, I can ever impart to you. I'm praying now for the wisdom to say the right things. (Literally.) The things that will help you understand how extremely vital this is for your life, and get you to actually use this power of setting clear goals.

Of all of the things that you do, goal-setting is one of the most important.

Why is that?

Let me start by saying that most human beings don't have any goals. Oh, they may have wishes or hopes, some vague dreams of what they'd like in life . . . but my virtual mentor Brian Tracy says that only 3% of adults actually write their goals down. [4]

The sad truth is that the vast majority of mankind are generally wrong. Thoreau said that they "lead lives of quiet desperation," and that they "go to the grave with the song still in them." Beware of this condition! If you don't have goals, this might be you . . . and I don't ever want to let you just waste away your life.

Without goals, your life is like a ship voyage, where you are the ship, and the voyage is your life. Goals are the destination port and the rudder. Without goals, you'll just be sailing, rudderless, in the sea . . . not knowing or seeming to care where you end up . . . which could very well be on the rocks.

My man Seneca had it right all those years ago:

"If a man knows not to which port he sails, no wind is favorable."

It's not usually my nature to start off on the negative and explain what happens if you *don't* do something . . . but the thing is, if you don't have goals, there is a very good chance that you'll be wasting the potential you've been given in life.

---

[4] Brian Tracy, "Success Through Goal Setting, Part 1 of 3" BrianTracy.com (no date given)

I'm starting out negative here because I want to shock you into knowing what life can be like without a clear goal or vision to pull you through it.

You could end up not having a purpose, or a reason to get up and do what you do every single day. You could fall prey to the everyday trance of living—just going through the motions without a clear definable end or reason to your actions.

I sincerely hope that I'm getting through to you the importance of this. Sometimes the fear of pain can be a more powerful motivator than the want of pleasure. Painkillers always outsell vitamins.

But now here's the good news: If you *do* set goals, and let them influence your life, *everything* can change for you.

I got into goal-setting in earnest when I was selling books, door-to-door, for eighty hours a week on my summer internship as a Bookman of Southwestern. They introduced me to reading motivational books, to listening to tapes on self-improvement and how to be better at my job, and it was possibly the greatest learning experience of my life.

(. . . other than being a dad, of course!)

I was just turning nineteen at the time. I was young and impressionable, and eager to start *doing* something with life. It seems that school was all about preparing for something ambiguous down the road, but it was all too ambiguous to form into concrete goals. When I started selling books and making money—and the money that I made solely depended on me—I think that was what started me on the journey of setting meaningful goals.

Setting goals has helped me a lot through life. I've set a lot of them, and have always thought of goals as being somewhat of a "COMING ATTRACTIONS" for my life.

But I'll admit that I haven't always been as good about goal-setting as I should be. Those are the times in life where I feel like I'm wandering with no clear destination. Yet the answer is always there in setting and striving toward meaningful goals.

Here's a quick story to help explain the power of goal setting.

I was in our home office going through a big box of things. I was trying to declutter and get rid of *stuff* so I wouldn't be so distracted by it all around me (see the advice on the magic of the uncluttered, engineered environment) and I came across some old goal lists that I had written about 5 years prior.

Here's what I had written down:

✓ 14. I want a house with 5 BR, an office, a workout area, a playroom for the kids, a media room and a VIEW! 1!!!!!

I know I had actually spent time thinking about this goal. I wanted a view, a lot of bedrooms, and a place for me to plan and execute my big dreams in the office.

What was cool about this is that I was sitting in the very office that I had imagined, in our big five-bedroom home with a workout area, a playroom, a media room, and a view. Yes! I checked that goal off my list.

Now, I had written that at least five years previous to finding this, and I didn't revisit or check on it as often as I should have. Despite that, I firmly believe that getting it in my mind and envisioning it helped make it a reality.

Can you see how powerful this idea can be? Napoleon Hill, in his classic book "*Think and Grow Rich*" says, "Whatever the mind of man can conceive and believe, it can achieve."

That, my beauties . . . is goal setting.

Goals help provide a purpose. They can pull you through hard times. They help direct your actions in meaningful directions.

I'd say that goals can help make you happy, as many of the times I've felt the most fulfilled in life was when I was making meaningful progress towards a worthwhile goal. In fact, that's one of the best definitions of success that I've ever heard.

"Success is the progressive realization of a worthy goal or ideal." — Earl Nightingale.

Here are some of the notes that I took from Jim Rohn on Goals while doing his goal workshop (more on that in the Advice in Practice):

- The greatest pull on your life should be the future. Some live in the past. You can remember that, and use it, but look for the future.

- Happiness is the delicate balance of being happy for all that you have, while striving for more.

- Don't be skimpy on your goals, dreams, and purposes! Goals are like a magnet and, the bigger and more powerful they are, the more they can be used to pull you through the tough times. A bad day can almost overwhelm you unless you have something on the other side to keep you going.

- When the *why* gets bigger, the *how* gets easier, and the price gets easy if the prize gets large.

- Accomplishing goals is the sweetest feeling! The most exhilarating, powerful feeling—is to design an outcome and to live it—to experience it! Ahh, that sweet taste is reserved for but a very few.

- The purpose is stronger than the object. The object can be powerful, but the purpose is even stronger. The million-dollar home is great, but what for? The drama is in the details. Think of the family get-togethers there and the pride the children feel in having their friends over and being the center of activity. Keep describing it in detail and your imagination will attack it, and that's when it will begin to become real; when *nothing* turns into *something*.

- The true value lies where your own spirit compels you to set goals and do it yourself. Self-development, self-esteem. You do it. Not because anyone else told you to do so, but because it was something you wanted.

- Lastly, Mr. Rohn says to include becoming a millionaire on your list. Not for what you get, but for what it makes of you to become one. Challenge yourself and grow. It's the challenge that creates the muscle. It's important to deserve it.

  I hope I've expressed to you some of the things you should know about goals, and that you know how incredibly important they are and how much they can mean to your life.

  No one else sets these goals for you. You set them and make sure they are truly something that you want; where the pursuit, and not necessarily just the achievement of them, will make you happy and fill your soul. When you do that your life will be of such a richer texture. It will have so much more meaning than just running on the job and existence treadmill!

  You're too good for that. By the way, I love you!

Advice in Practice.

- Take some time out each year to plan the year. Jim Rohn talks about this and says to take an hour out to plan the week, an afternoon to plan the quarter, and a day or two to plan the year.
- Really dig in and get some great things planned. Google "Jim Rohn Goal Workshop" and find the video for it on YouTube. It's right there for you. I love technology that brings this wisdom to all of us.

- Take time each quarter to write out what needs to get done, or I shouldn't say "needs," but rather "I choose," and write those out. One of the things that one of my mentors asks, which is a great question, is what would have to happen between now and then to be happy with my progress? I think that quarterly goals are the best timeframe to write goals. It's near enough to have an impact on your immediate behavior, but it's far enough out so that you have time to actually accomplish it. I love 90-day goals. They're just digestible goodness and filled with possibility.

- I like to do this, and the times that I have I've just made incredible progress, but I don't always do it. Keep those goals in front of you on a regular basis. I like to laminate them and put a copy on my bathroom mirror, one in my planner (this is where you should be looking at them on a daily basis), and one in my car. See what works for you, but please make sure that they're in front of you nearly all the time.

- Be careful on who you share these goals with in your life! If you share them with energy vampires they'll make you feel crappy, remind you how you can't accomplish them, and generally act like asses that make you less likely to accomplish those goals. Oftentimes these people will be related to you, too. There are, however, some people that would be great to share the goals with that will encourage you, help you, and be general badasses of goodness, too. I say this humbly, but your daddy is one of those people. It's cool and preferable to share with these people.

- Make these goal sessions regularly! Put it in your calendar and set the reminders to go off a month, a week, a day, and an hour before you're supposed to go over them. Make it an official appointment and don't break it. These are even more important than meetings with other people!
- Lastly, keep these goal lists. It's so much fun to go over when you see an old list and you're like, "Did that, that, that, and that!" WHOO-HOO! Yay, me!!!

Notes, thoughts, and intentions.

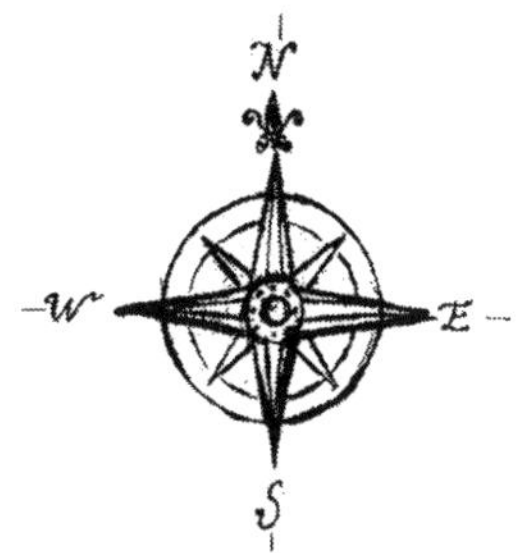

31. Learn What the Heck an OPOA Is, And Start Using It.

Don't underestimate the power of this little piece of advice from your daddy!

This strange little acronym can have a pretty big impact on your life. It helps train you to think critically about what you're doing and accomplishing in your day to day activity, and once again, it's not taught in schools, so it's up to your dear father to teach you how to save a huge chunk of time every day and/or to organize your thoughts.

Simply defined, OPOA is a quick, easy way of *thinking* to get you a desired outcome.

It's an acronym that stands for outcome, purpose, (obstacles) and action. I learned it through Tony Robbins in his excellent course, "Time of Your Life." He did straight OPA, without the "obstacle" part of it, but I've decided to add it to what I do after hearing about a similar thought process called WOOP (Wish, Outcome, Obstacles, and Plan). The obstacles part of the thinking is important, so it's part of what I do now. Tony now calls his system RPM, which stands for Results, Purpose, Massive Action Plan.

But I don't want to drown you with acronyms, so I need to get on with this ASAP (see what I did there?).

The big one you have to remember for this thought process is OPOA. Outcome, Purpose, Obstacles, and Action. Once you do it a few times you won't forget it and it will be part of your everyday process for doing things. It's a way of organizing your time, getting more done, and a way to replace standard "to-do" lists. But more than that, it's a way of thinking.

Let me give you a quick story of how OPOA can be used from my life. I applied for a highly competitive incubator sponsored by 3M Corporation for my company JoeVolunteer. A small percentage of the companies applying actually got the spots offered, but it was an incredible experience. You got access to a mentor, some resources from 3M and their partners, and free office space in downtown Austin if you were selected. But you had to apply and then "pitch" what you wanted to do in front of executives from companies like 3M, Dell, and Microsoft.

I was nervous. I hadn't pitched a company before, I wanted to make a great impression, and I wanted to win the incubator. So, I did an OPOA to help design my speech in front of the people selecting. It helped me focus on the outcome, which was to be selected by making a great impression and leaving them thinking about me in a positive way. It defined my purpose, which was to get resources and get further along the road to potentially helping millions of people in need by helping to get volunteers to them. It helped me see the obstacles. What was I facing as problems for funding and developing the app, and also what could keep me from delivering a fantastic presentation to them. Then, I considered my obstacles, which included the fact that I only had 4 minutes available to make a great impression. I developed an action plan that included giving out miniature video players with a prepared video that showed all the good we were doing in the community how much we wanted to win and that would make them look good for picking us.

This *thought* process made it possible to win this opportunity! Other folks might've just had, "develop great presentation for 3M" on their "to-do" lists. Do you see the gigantic difference? Do you see how it spurs extra thinking and creativity?! That's what the power of OPOA can do for you!

I'll talk about it as a time management system next, but first I want to give you the context for everyday use. It can really make a difference for all that you do. IMPORTANT: there is usually very little critical thought between stimulus and response.

People just hit the next item on the "to-do" list without stopping to think about what they are really going after with this, why they're even doing it, or the best way to go about doing it. That thought process just isn't taught in many places and that's why it is important to me that you learn this. Of course, if you improve on it, or it doesn't serve you like it should, then feel free to change up this process or even disregard it all together. But if you find a better way, you had better let me know!

I try to do an OPOA before any important project, meeting, presentation, speech, phone call, or a big expenditure of time. It may seem overly complicated, but after you do it a time or two it will be intuitive

Before it happens: stop, pause and think. "What is the ideal Outcome? If everything were perfect, what would come of this?" I write it out.

Then, I think about why that's important to me, with the Purpose. If doing a good job is important, how is it helping? Who will it benefit? Is it necessary?

Then think of the Obstacles. I think of the big things that are in the way of that ideal outcome. A little brainstorm here can be good. Solving is for the next step.

Then: the Action part. I try to do a mini idea list. What are the things to think, say, and do to make the ideal outcome happen? I can get creative here and think big. I think of ways to overcome or mitigate the obstacles. Write it ALL out, then pick the few that will make the difference. Idea lists help a lot with this style of thinking.

An example could be a sales meeting where you're trying to get the person you're going to be talking with to purchase what you have for sale. Let's say it's a house selling service you offer as a real estate broker (which I've done for 21 years now). What is the Outcome of your meeting, ideally? You want them to say yes to your offer to help them sell their house. More specifically, you want them to come back to the office to find a price for their home and do the paperwork which officially hires you. That's the ideal outcome. You may even add to the following to that: After the meeting they feel so good about you and what you do that they refer you to their friends and tell them they *must* do business with you! The power of getting very specific with your ideal outcome is important, because now everything that you do and think (consciously or subconsciously) will help towards making that happen.

Then the Purpose, or the why. Why are you making the appointment? Make the why powerful. My mentor (and Tony Robbins' mentor) Jim Rohn said, "the how gets easy when the why gets big enough." Make your reason(s) why important when you write out the Purpose. It's to help them, because you're the best. It's to pay you for your career. It's to help your kids get the best schooling, and food. It could be for you to do your best and make your career a thing of art and beauty. You can do it to perform at your best and live up to your potential. Make it personal to you with this. Get emotional with it, especially if it's something big and important. This can help make it easier to do when the thrill of doing it fades.

Now, the Obstacles to think about. They may not have enough money to hire, they may be considering selling it themselves. They may already have several other real estate brokers coming to give them a presentation. They may have an uncle that is crazy about getting their business instead of letting their business go to you. Think of some of the things that can get in the way. Try to get all of them so you can address them in the next section.

Actions: This is where you start writing out the ideas that can make this special. You can think big and do things that others haven't even thought about because you've got this great system of planning things out with your mind on paper.

Now, OPOA can also be used as a time management tool, too.

Most people just do a 'to-do' list. It's lots of unrelated items thrown out together. Do them, cross them off. Forward things to the next day.

Instead, OPOA! It may seem like a lot to take in first, but it's easy once you do it.

With the OPOA system as a time management system, the first part is that there is a capture, which is like the to-do list. Get everything out of your head and put it on paper or device. Absolutely everything. Be exhaustive.

Take ALL of the items and group several of them together when they are related. Robbins calls this "chunking." Come up with an outcome from the groups of items. We can use a day of paying your mortgage, and house bills as an example.

Outcome:

It sometimes helps to ask this, from Gary Keller and Jay Papasan's book *The ONE Thing*,

> ***"What's the ONE Thing I can do such that by doing it everything else will be easier or unnecessary?"***

Then think about the Outcome. Get the bills paid on time with as little effort as possible, and think about automating the process.

Think about the Purpose.

This is when we ask, "why?" If I can set up a system of paying these bills automatically it will save a fair amount of time every single month. That will give me more time with my child, it will keep me from getting in a dark mood when paying bills, and keep me from losing momentum on other things I'm working on in my life.

Think about the Obstacles. What if I don't have enough money in the account for autopays? Some places don't accept my method of payment.

Think about the Actions. Go to each site and see if they auto payments. Get a credit card where ALL of the bills are paid with. Set up the credit card to automatically debit your bank account for the total (preferred) or minimum, if necessary. Set a reminder to check bank balance every month before credit card bill is paid to check bank balance. Make sure each bill is paid today for certain. Celebrate getting this taken care of for good! Ask others how they do it, see if there's an improvement to how I do it. Set up auto-checks or bill pay from the bank directly to the places that don't accept credit or debit cards.

Do you see how that process for the day is so much different than just having a 'to-do' list of "pay the bills"? Taking just a little bit more thought and effort, this one time can save your time for the next several years, and all because you took this new approach to planning your day.

It may feel a little clunky at first, but I promise that it gets easier. It can and will be such an easy part of your daily routine that you'll feel comfortable writing it out on scratch paper before you make an important phone call, or to help brainstorm fun things to do on vacation. It's an incredible way of thinking, and now you know it!

Advice in Practice:

- Look at and consider purchasing *The Time of Your Life* from Tony Robbins. It's a very detailed course on this type of thinking. You can also Google it to look through some blogs and videos about it.

- Because I mentioned it, check out the WOOP system and see if you prefer that over my version of thinking important things through. You can find info at www.WOOPMyLife.org to get more information on it. It's pretty cool too, but I think the W and first O are a little redundant.

- Let's do a quick OPOA on tomorrow's "to-do" list. Write it all out in your planner, or a journal if you use that. Clear out your head, and put it all down on paper. Notice the similarities between some of the tasks, and group them together. If you're shopping for food and want to have a workout, that could be grouped into "Make Tremendous Progress on My Health," as an Outcome. Then figure out the rest and give this time management approach a shot. If you feel like you need more instruction on this, check out the first piece of the Advice in Practice, as there's a lot of info about this on the good ole' world wide web.

- Try the same process for your weekly planning, and then monthly, or yearly planning. Let me ask you: if you did an OPOA for getting in better shape and to be healthier, and detailed your big "*why*" with consideration to the obstacles in the way of you eating better and exercising, do you think your chances to actually accomplish it go up? You bet they do. That's the beauty of this framework.

- Go through this process with an upcoming appointment and see if the meeting can go better than before when your thought process is on the outcome, and you engage your creativity to make it a more memorable/impactful/friendlier meeting.

- As with any habit, please use this for a while and see what you think. Does it improve things for you? Does it make you more effective? Yes, it does. So, try it!

Oh, I love you.

Notes, thoughts, and intentions.

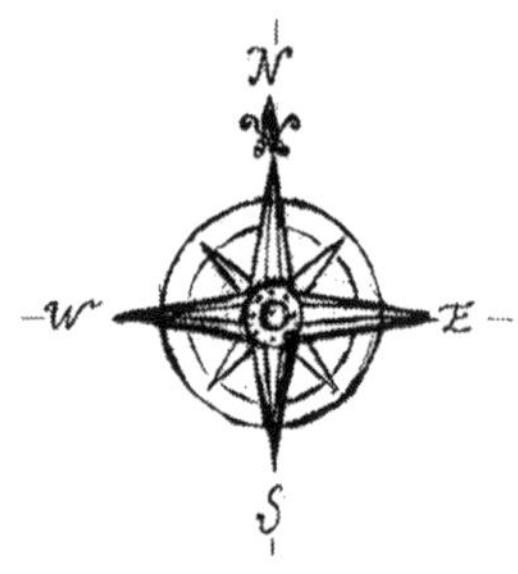

32. Question Everything.

Human beings are silently begging to be led (using terminology from my marketing hero, Jay Abraham). They want a certainty of knowing what they're doing, even if what they're doing is wrong. It's so easy to get on that bandwagon, because EVERYONE else is doing it, too.

It's okay to question how things are done. If there's a better way to do something, then don't be afraid to do it. Sometimes the unconventional is a lot better. Don't do things *just because*. There should be a reason for it, and that reason needs to serve your interests. Doing something *just because*, that's what everyone else does and it is intellectual laziness. Think things through and do what's best for you.

Mark Twain famously said, "When you find yourself on the side of the majority, it is time to pause and reflect." If you just go through life blindly accepting things, and not putting critical thought into it, you'll end up just like everyone else. Instead, there is a moment between stimulus and response where you have a small window of decision. That is where you can stop and exercise free will. Back up and think to yourself if this makes sense. Is there a better way to do this? If there's a better way, try to do that.

Now, some things aren't worth the time and effort of questioning, but *most* things are. Think about the retirement mentality and the career path of most Americans. I know we talk about that in other areas, but is the "Deferred Life Plan," (where you put off what you want to do until some undetermined future date) really the way to go through life? Yet how many of us (me included until the book, *The 4 Hour Workweek*, snapped me out of that thinking) just go blindly through the steps that everyone else does?

The same thing goes for the regular "path," of life—"go to school, get a safe/secure job, marry, raise a family, vacation, repeat each year forty or so times, retire, do what you 'want,' die." Do you think that it would be a good idea to question this?!!

So, I'd like to invite you to a more enlightened way of living. Pause and reflect. Think. Does this make sense? It seems to be the best thing to do. Socrates said that the unexamined life is not worth living. I don't agree fully with that, as all life is sacred, but I get the principle and I ask that you examine where you're going and what you're doing. Question whether or not it's right for you.

One caveat: Just try not to be a butthead about it (I sometimes do that). You don't need to trumpet your "enlightened" thinking from the rooftops unless it's a moral imperative. An example would be militant atheism.

Take the time to examine what you're thinking, saying, and doing. Question whether it's right. Twist it, turn it, pull it apart, deconstruct it, look at the pieces, see if it all makes sense, and then put it back together again.

Also, I won't talk about religion a whole lot here, but here's an area that you can, and I think, *should* question. Don't let anyone or anything tell you how you *have* to think, and that includes your daddy giving you an entire book of advice. YOU, and no one else, get to determine if this is valuable and helpful advice. Your brain is too magnificent to just take things as facts without questioning them.

Advice in Practice:

- Pause when asked a question (including ones that you ask yourself). Consider that moment between stimulus (the question) and response (the answer). That's the moment when reflection will do the most.

- Think about society's assumptions critically. Question them and see if they serve you. Here's a quick rundown of a few things that may need more thinking to see if they're right for you—as-is or with modifications:

- Schooling. Is it best to go Monday through Friday, from 8 to 4 to study the exact same things that have been taught for a century?

- Is the standard American diet, with three meals a day, the best way to keep you energized and in optimal health?

- Is it best to live in one place and to "put down roots"?

- Is it best to have kids??!! I mean, I'm glad your mom and I did, but is that the best thing for you? It very well may be, but do you think that it's a good idea to question that?

- Is college the best way to get the job or start the business? Does it lead to a better life?

- Is the meaning of life to be happy? Is that the best life?

These are just a few to critically think about and see if the "usual" answers serve you.

- One of the best books that I ever read, that truly changed my thinking, was "How I Found Freedom in an Unfree World," by Harry Browne. It will be a little while until you find this interesting, but there are SO many assumptions that are questioned in that book. He says that a lot of people (don't you be one of them) are unaware of the many options and alternatives available to them, and that they accept without ever questioning assumptions that restrict their freedom. Go take a quick run-through the book (it is free online) and read it if/when you are up to the task!
- Last item on this: a friend of mine, Jesse, says that when considering something, the question isn't whether or not it is true, but whether or not it is useful. You can adopt whatever beliefs you want that empower you and make your life better. One of my favorite beliefs is something I heard at a Tony Robbins seminar: "Life is not happening TO you, life is happening FOR you." Or another, "Things always happen for a reason," or "In every

difficulty, there is an opportunity." Are these all true? Maybe not, but they are all *useful*.

Notes, thoughts, and intentions.

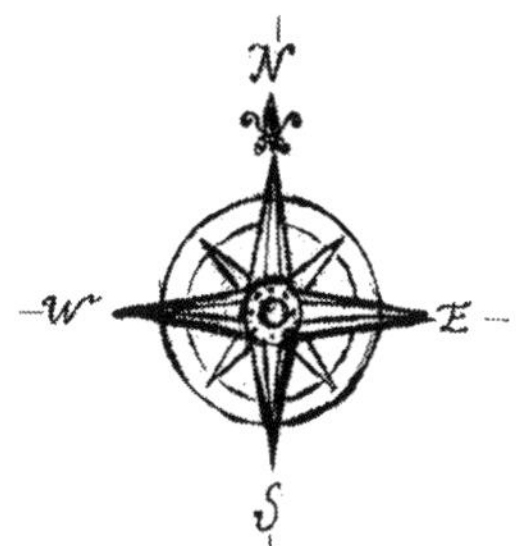

33. Learn the Strangest Secret: You Become What You Think About All of the Time.

Earl Nightingale, another Mentor of mine (via very old recordings) says this: "You become what you think about."

So, think about great things. Think about how grateful you are, think loving thoughts towards your family and friends, and think a lot about your goals (yes, I said that before, but it bears repeating because it's important).

This concept is what's referred to as *The Strangest Secret* coined by Earl Nightingale. I don't know how strange it is, but again, it's pretty magical.

This reminds me of something else Papa Earl said, which is powerful:

"Your world is a reflection of you."

Whether that's good or bad—or more commonly a mix of the two—it's true.

You have seen lots of people with bad attitudes (Mandy, you serve many of them at Starbucks), and it's just like a beacon over their heads. Those people are becoming what they think about, too. They just think about how wronged they are, how they're entitled to things that aren't happening for them, or how the baristas at Starbucks are moving too dang slow . . . etc.

Wow. It's just so easy to fill your mind with much better thoughts. That's one of the reasons I recommend doing a morning ritual, meditating, and/or doing a gratitude journal. All of these things help maintain those good thoughts.

And here it is: the quality of your thoughts dictates the quality of your life. Period.

You become what you think about.

Advice in Practice:

- You need to develop the habit of thinking good thoughts. I know that sounds like the same kind of cliché as "just be happy!" that, when you're feeling rotten and someone says it, makes you want to punch them right in their smiling face. So, you have to develop *rituals* to get you to the place of thinking better thoughts throughout your life.

- As I mentioned previously, some ideas for developing the habit of thinking good thoughts is to research and doing a morning ritual that works for YOU. As you know, I'm a big fan of The Miracle Morning. That'll probably be its own set of advice, but the basic idea is to start off the day the right way each and every morning. This will help to frame your thoughts for the inevitable assault that they will face during your normal day-to-day schedule.

- Set a timer or have a watch that beeps every so often as a trigger to consciously direct your thoughts to something positive and helpful for you. You have seen and heard my "I am blessed" alarm on my iPhone that goes off every day. Well, that helps me stop, take some deep breaths, and think of all the wonderful things in my life. I feel better. As a result, I treat others better . . . it's a virtuous cycle. If you're reading now, and haven't done it, set an alarm on your phone now for the same purpose.

- Put a penny in your shoe. I do this to remind me to be kind and let God's Light show through my actions. Sheesh, I just re-read that, and it sounds like I'm some kind of self-proclaimed Saint. I'm not (obviously YOU know that), but this practice does remind me to be better and directs my thoughts to where they should be.

- The last thing I'll mention on this is to be vigilant in protecting your thoughts. Stand guard at the door of your mind and don't let the negative get into that beautiful noggin of yours. That means, don't do things like watch the news, listen to gossip, or hang out with negative people (even if they're your family). It's not enough to play defense on this and leave when the bad vibes try to make their way into your thoughts. You need to play offense. That means set up your schedule and environment so that you're not even around the bad juju. Got me? Think about your environment and how you can control that. And then do it.

I friggin' love you. I hope this is helping, sweethearts.

Notes, thoughts, and intentions.

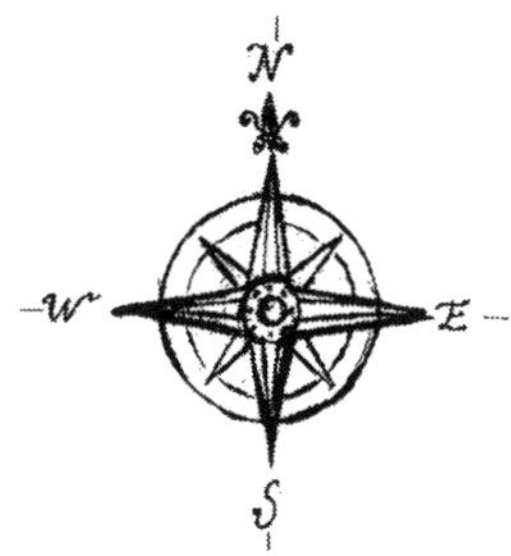

34. But Remember That You are Not Your Thoughts.

This is a hard concept to explain. . . so I'm going to do my best to do this. Then, I'll look back on it and be a little disgusted with my work! But, it's better to try then not to get this to you.

You are not your thoughts.

Children, I love you so much and this is a very, very big thing. If you get this piece of advice right, and this concept right, it's going to help your life tremendously. I forget it sometimes myself, but honestly, if you learn this and you take it to heart and practice it daily, then you're going to have a much better life experience. The big principle is you are not your thoughts. Instead, you are the *observer* of your thoughts and the consciousness that listens to the thoughts going on inside your head. You are not the thoughts. Another useful way to think about your thoughts is to call them your *inner voice* or even your *inner critic*.

Your inner voice is always talking and chattering up a storm all the time. No matter what, it's always going and just doesn't shut up. It comments about everything, and a lot of the times it's not saying good things to you. Now, I got these principles and ideas from two books I read by a gentleman named Michael Singer: *The Untethered Soul and The Surrender Experiment*.

According to Mr. Singer, "There is nothing more important to true growth than realizing that you are not the voice of the mind, you are the one that hears it." That's the concept and the thought process behind it, and you've probably heard it before, but I want you to understand and take this to heart. You are a spiritual being having an earthly existence; and you, your soul, your consciousness, the part of you that makes you *you* (not your physical form or the temple of the body) are actually the soul that inhabits that body. You are spiritual and divine, and the incessant voice inside your head is earthly. Very different things.

This is another quote from Michael Singer. He asks, "How would you feel if someone outside really started talking to you the way that your inner voice does? How would you relate to a person who opened their mouth to say everything your mental voice says?" After a very short period of time, you would tell them to leave and never come back, but when your 'inner friend' continuously speaks up you don't ever tell it to leave. No matter how much trouble it causes, you listen. I'm going to compare your inner voice to, well, it's a little bit like a bitchy friend. The things that it says are things we all know the inner critic, or the voice inside your head, says often. Maybe you're not worthy enough, you don't deserve things, you didn't do that well enough, you're not beautiful, or any of the number of things that it can say that can really hurt you. You are not saying those things, it's the voice in your head.

You don't have to take that, so the best thing you can do is start separating that voice from you. If it says all those really bad things you've got to realize it's not you talking, it's just that alien creature that cohabitates your mind. So often it's mean, selfish, and inconsiderate. You're going to have a lot of problems in life if you let that voice hold sway over you, and if you think it's your voice.

A practice on this, and something to think about, is to learn to lean back from your physical self and realize that you are the spiritual being having the earthly experience. If you can make that change and think about that, then you can actually lean back from a problem you're having or a particularly bad thought, a bad day, or a bad set of circumstances. You can separate yourself from the circumstance and realize that it doesn't have to affect you. You can be an observer to all of these thoughts and fears going on in your head, but you don't have to be an active participant in it once you realize it's not really *you*.

About this internal conflict Michael Singer says:

> ***"Eventually you will see that the real cause of problems is not life itself, it's the commotion the mind makes about life that really causes problems."***

The big thing is we're going to be okay. Our soul, or our spirit, is going to be just fine even if something happens to our earthly vessel. Most of the problems that we create and think about are constructs of our imagination, and it's our inner voice giving credence to these. Singer also says that to attain true inner freedom you must be able to objectively watch your problems instead of being lost in them. Once you know that you are not your thoughts, you can sit back and objectively watch your thoughts go by and consider them without buying into them. That is the mark of intelligence.

Singer also says that if you come to know the one who watches the voice, you will come to know one of the great mysteries of creation. You are divine, the voice inside your head is not. If you keep this principle in mind, that you are not your thoughts, you're going to have a better, easier, happier, and overall a more problem-free experience of life. I hope this wasn't too much to try and explain on just a few pages, but I really think that if you get this concept, it can help you a lot.

Advice in Practice.

- One of the biggest ways of putting this advice into practice is to read, understand, underline, dog-ear, take notes, and refer back to the book, *The Untethered Soul* by Michael Singer.
- The other book by Michael Singer that I would recommend is called *The Surrender Experience*. In fact, this may be the very first book that you read because it's not quite as deep as *The Untethered Soul*. It reads more like a biography than the owner's manual of the mind and spirit that is *The Untethered Soul*. I'd recommend that you read this, take it in, and take some notes from it. I

recommend paying special attention to the moment when Mr. Singer "wakes up" from life, from the incessant chatter, and realizes it's not him that's making all of his thoughts. If you can have that type of epiphany in your own life, it makes everything much easier and much better.

- You should also periodically remind yourself that you are not your thoughts. There are several ways that you can do this. You can put these into your affirmations in the morning if you are doing a miracle morning practice. You can also set timers on your phone to go off once every day or every few days (as often or as little as needed) to remind you, again, that you are not your thoughts, but rather you are divine consciousness. As you get into the habit of doing that, it will become more and more a part of your everyday life.
- As always, I hope this advice has helped you out and will help you out. I ask that if this is important to you, and if it helped you, that you pass it on to others. I love you so, so very much.

Notes, thoughts, and intentions.

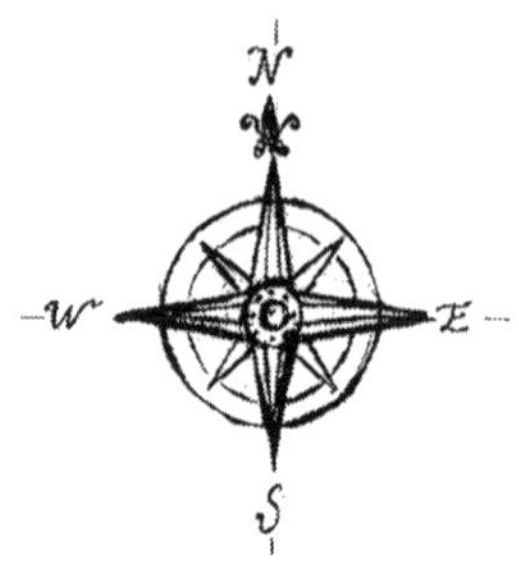

35. Learn "Calmfidence."

Strive to be confident, yet humble. Don't talk about how great you are, even though we all know it's true. Be humble in spirit. Don't be afraid to laugh about yourself. If you're confident enough in who you are as a person, then it will be easy to laugh when you do something silly (and I hope you do something that's silly, or that fails, because if you don't then you're not trying hard enough in life).

There's such a wonderful duality in most everything in life. Give and Receive. Firm yet loving. Bittersweet. The same thing is true of us.

I got reminded yesterday evening of how very small that we are. I got to look out at the stars last night after thinking of this: We are insignificant specks of dust throughout the universe. With literally billions of stars each with the capability to have their own galaxies. The vastness of the world is hard to even contemplate . . . and here we are, just one of 7 billion lives on this planet, with each one being as important in God's eyes as the next. We aren't all that much, really . . .

. . . but the duality is also true.

We are everything. We are our own entire existence, and we're given the God-like power of creation and independent thought! We're also a vital part of the entire human race, and the world would never be the same without us. We're given the ability to help others and to be a large part of their world. We are so very important.

It's good to keep both of these perspectives in mind in how we carry ourselves. Insignificant in the grand scheme, and yet with infinite power.

Keeping these in mind can help with the Calmfidence.

Advice in Practice:

- Make and keep an "Achievement List." This is a list of all of the things that you're proud of; that you can look back and think . . . "Yeah, that was me."
- Divide the list up into personal, professional and community things that you've done.
- Write as many as you can think of out and come back to it later when you've had a chance to mentally reset so you have an entirely new list of things on it.
- I keep mine on Evernote so that I can reference it anytime I want, but honestly, I haven't been doing it as often as I should lately. Right now, while I'm writing this, I'm committing that I'll do it during the affirmation time of my miracle morning practice.

- What's great about this is that 1) You're setting yourself up for 'Calmfidence' throughout the day (awesome!), and 2) You're going to subconsciously want to add to that list every day. It's going to feel so good when you add something you did yesterday, or even today, to that list!

- The next step is to have a "power song." This is a song that gets you pumped up and feeling good! One that causes you to almost burst with powerful energy and confidence. Come on! What's that song for you? I have two, depending on what intention I have for the day. The first song is "Beast," by Rob Bailey and the Hustle Standard featuring Busta Rhymes (whew, that's a lot) from the Southpaw Soundtrack. It's got terrible language in it, so be warned! The other one, when I'm feeling my higher self and I want to exude God's light and love, is "Pride (In the Name of Love)" by U2. I know that you've heard me blast both of these in the morning. Well, come up with your song and add it to your morning routine. Play it before you're doing something that requires some confidence!

- Lastly, something you can do is to create an 'avatar' for yourself. I've recently read about a method where you ask yourself what your future, "better" you would do in a certain situation. Would the best-selling author, doctor version of you get flustered at speaking in front of a room of people? No! Then bring that confidence and that feeling into today, and act as if you've already attained that.

***Special thanks to Dan Martell for the Achievement List concept and calling your song a "power song."

Notes, thoughts, and intentions.

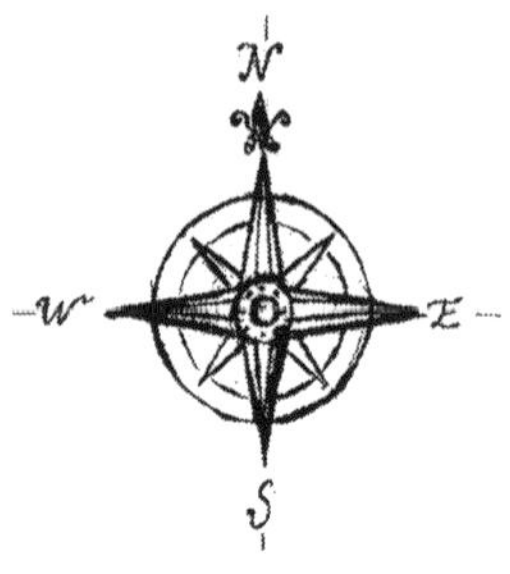

36. Don't Be Afraid to Ask.

Now, here's a big one!

Don't EVER be afraid to ask.

Ask for better out of life. Ask for the upgrade, ask for the better table, ask for a lower price, ask for a favor that you'd really like. Do it with humility, and realize that it's not a zero-sum game—no one else has to lose by you getting more.

You are absolutely worth it, and again people will love to help you.

It's a cool thing that people will feel good about giving you what you want.

Jesus said in the Bible, "Ask, and it shall be given you; seek, and ye shall find; knock, and it shall be opened unto you." Wow! That's so powerful. People live such sheltered lives that they never ask and expect to receive, and yet it's virtually guaranteed!

The kicker here is that you have to ask, seek and knock because it doesn't just happen by itself! So, I expect this of you. The good things are generally reserved for those that ask, seek, and knock.

If you don't ask, the answer will always be, "no," and, Wayne Gretzky said, "You'll miss 100% of the shots you don't take." Please insert other well-known, but cliché truths in on this one.

See, I think that the greatest moments in life are when you are both content and joyful for where you are. Be truly appreciative to God while still striving for more and better. It's okay, and preferable, to love all that you have. An example of this is to think of an airplane seat that allows you to soar over the clouds like an eagle, while asking if you can be moved to a first-class seat on the same flight using the method I use in this book.

It is so easy to do, and yet it's also so easy NOT to do. That's why the "mass of men" (Thoreau, again) don't do it! I think that a lot of it has to do with the perceived self-worth of the asker. If you don't feel like you're worth it, it's more difficult to ask, but I said it above, and throughout this Tome 'o Advice:

YOU ARE WORTH IT.

You are as deserving of God's blessings as anyone.

So, please . . . Ask.

Now, do you know and remember the right way to ask? I've taught it to you, and hope you remember. It's something along these lines of, "Hey, I was wondering if I could get some help with _______. If you can help, that would be wonderful, but if not, that's okay too." There's a whole piece of advice in this about asking the right way.

Just be certain to ask, okay?

Advice In Practice:

- We are generally never as vulnerable as we are when we are reaching out to ask for help. That's another reason that most people don't get the help that they need. I admit, I like to be pretty much self-sufficient, so I may not ask for help from others. My friend Alex calls it, "protection and support." We all need it, and yet we seldom ask for it. So, as you're reading this think of one thing that you could use help with, and go ahead and ask for it. Pull out your phone and just do it. I'll wait.

- Create an Idea List. Here is your topic: "Areas Where I Need Protection and Support." List out a good 20 of those bad boys, and start to think about where you will ask for the help that you need.

- If you ever struggle with the self-worth to ask (I know that I have, and sometimes still do), use affirmations in the morning as part of your miracle morning routine. Some of my affirmations (I used it this morning before I knew that I'd even write this. Yay, me!) are:

  I am worthy.
  I deserve it all.
  I breathe abundance.
  Unconditional love is my birthright.

- Those are the ones that deal with self-worth, and it's been a journey to get some of the negative, "I'm not worthy," inner critic crap out of my head, but it's certainly worth the journey! More on this throughout the book, my sweethearts.

- Imagine you get a phone call now. Someone is able to grant something that you want as you're reading this. Think of that person and what it is that you'd like to ask for . . . and just do it now. Make that phone call, or send a text if it's a weird hour. Don't hesitate. Have the courage to ask.

Notes, thoughts, and intentions.

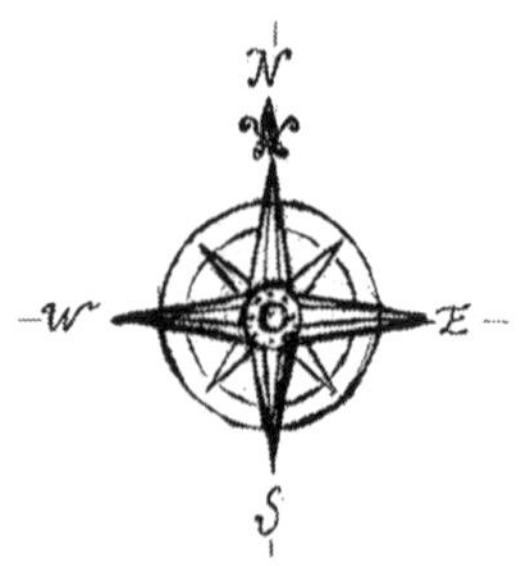

37. Ask the RIGHT Way and Get Everything You've Ever Wanted.

Speaking of words, do you remember the right way to ask for something? I've taught you.

It's cool to have the Jedi-like power to get nearly everything that you want simply by 1) asking, and 2) doing it the right way.

Here's my belief and, whether or not it's true, it's useful:

Everybody wants to help.

There is a spiritual longing in each of our souls that at some level, wants to help other people. It's hardwired into us by God, and that's why we feel so good when we help other people. Seriously, it goes beyond this piece of advice I'm talking about with you now. There have been many moments in life where I've been reduced to tears because I have enjoyed helping people so much, and I wish the same for you. It's one of life's most exquisite feelings.

So, remember that. People want to help you.

We've already covered the courage to ask, and why that is so incredibly important.

Now, it's time to ask the right way. Hopefully you remember this from us practicing on how it's done.

It's something along these lines: "I don't know if you can help me, and if you can't then no big deal, but is it possible to ________________?"

Let's break that down:

"I don't know if you can help me . . ." The word help is important, as we've covered that everyone wants to help. The other part to this is a subtle challenge: "I don't know if you *can* . . ." Maybe that's a little manipulative, but folks tend to rise to a challenge. They're thinking, "Of *course* I can help . . ." This sets up the "ask" as something they want to help you with, and it's a bit of a fun game to see if they can accomplish that. People *want* to help you if you're nice about it.

". . . and if you can't, then no big deal," Really mean the "no big deal," as people know if you're sincere or not. We all have an incredible BS detector built into us as humans, and we perceive body language, eye movement, and breathing patterns automatically with these wonderful senses. So, here's the thing I would say: release the result. That means, be okay with whether you *can* or *can't* get whatever it is that you're asking for. That may take some practice, but if you're living in active appreciation (Advice #1), then you realize that everything is bonus, anyway. We are so very blessed whether or not we get what we are asking for on this.

Sincerely meaning that it is "no big deal" means that, if they're capable of doing it, they're not feeling the pressure to perform.

"But is it possible . . ." Of course it's *possible*. In almost every circumstance, anything is possible. Again, maybe there is a bit of a challenge element to it, but it works.

This should prompt their mind to think something like, "This is a nice person that's asking for help. I can help, and would like to do so, but if I don't (or can't) fulfill their request, that's okay, too. They're asking if it's even possible! Well, I bet it's possible for *me* to help . . ."

The last part: "to __________." This is where your perfect desired outcome is inserted. Make sure it's something that you really want, that it's not too outlandish (although you never know unless you ask), and that you're very specific about what you want. Remember that people are silently begging to be led, and this is where you teach them how to help you.

This is the best way that I've found to do this. And it generally works like magic. I've gotten seat upgrades, free admission to theme parks (with your Mom while we were in college: fun story), admission to a Texas A&M football game (you girls and Alec were with us when that happened), free meals, help with tasks, and folks volunteering. But it goes much deeper than that. I've used it to get classes that I've wanted at Texas A&M, and even your Mom's phone number the first time that we met (I was smitten). Thinking about that last example; perhaps you wouldn't be you if I had not *asked*.

Your Mom says that I can talk anyone into anything, and maybe it's kind of true. It's just practice and positive expectancy. I didn't mention that, but it really helps for you to know that what you're asking for is completely and totally possible, too. Then it works like a Jedi Mind Trick. I mentioned Jedi above . . . y'all know what that means, right? I hope so.

And now you know the magic of how to get nearly everything you ever ask for in life.

You're welcome.

Advice in Practice:

- Go out there and ask. Here's the deal, it's going to take some courage. You have to think of it this way: it's no big deal. Whether they say yes, or no, it's completely fine. What is wonderful and amazing about this, though, is that you'll be exercising that courage muscle. Regular asks will seem effortless, and impossible asks will become merely difficult.

- Let me tell you about the Noah Kagen Coffee Challenge. One of the guys I've listened to on podcasts has this challenge that's designed to get you out of your comfort zone. Simply buy something, and at the register ask if you can have 10% off from your purchase. In the challenge, you're not supposed to frame it with an explanatory statement . . . you're just asking if you can have 10% off. It may sound easy, but it's a little difficult. The whole aim isn't to save you $.50 on your coffee; it's to move you out of your comfort zone. So, if you're reading these words, I challenge you to try this.

- Make an Idea List of all of the things that you can ask for, and expect to receive, using this method. I've recently even used it to get a lower cell phone bill, but you can apply it in almost every area of life.

Have I mentioned that you're loved? Because you are. Very, very much.

Notes, thoughts, and intentions.

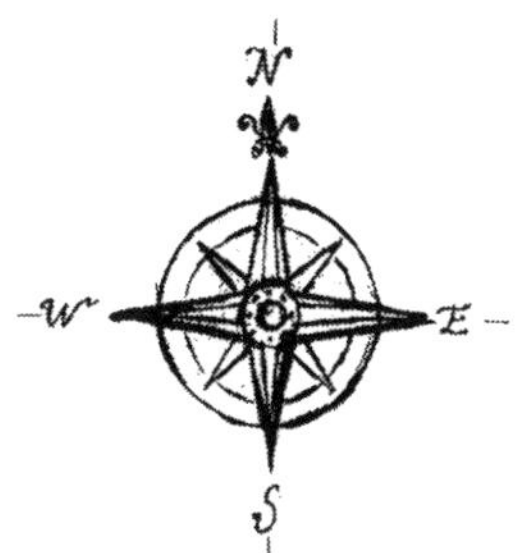

38. Outsource Everything that You Don't Enjoy for Fun and Profit.

My precious treasures!

Now, I get to talk to you about something fun (and kind of cool), and that will save you many hundreds and/or thousands of hours while making your life much more to your liking. It almost feels like cheating in life, but of course it's not.

Imagine writing out a "to-do" list (which I prefer to call Outcomes) at the end of the school or work day. You go home, do your routine, and come back the next morning . . . and BOOM! There is the completed work waiting for you at your computer.

Research, graphic design, a produced video, results of phone calls made on your behalf, finances done, and pretty much any other task you can think to have done. It can be done for you. It's almost magic. Really, due to technology, it is magic.

Here is a quick story. I heard about virtual assistants a while back. In fact, I think that the first time I really remember learning about them was from the book, *The Four Hour Workweek* by Tim Ferriss. The idea intrigued me, but I didn't do anything about it then. Back then, the whole practice was not as good as it is now. It wasn't as easy, and most of the assistants were overseas.

But I heard some more about them from my friend Ari Meisel. I read about it in his book, *Less Doing, More Living*, where he recommended a service there called "Fancy Hands." They are a Virtual Assistant (VA from here on out) company that has a team of people that do general tasks (like making reservations, phone calls) that take less than 20 minutes at a time. What's cool is that you could get started asking them for tasks to be done for you for as little as $25 per month. That allowed me to start to try it to just see what this new world was like.

So, the first task ever that I had them do? I asked them to call all Honda dealerships in all of Central Texas and price shop the exact mini-van that your mom wanted. We had the specifications, and they called to explain what they were doing, and asked for the absolute best price that could be offered for that mini-van. Through doing that we learned that, if we traveled an hour South, we could save nearly $4,000 on that purchase. The total number of calls were accomplished for whopping $20! That was incredible, and it totally hooked me on using VAs. I've done it more often since then and have gotten a lot better at it, because there's a definite skill involved in knowing what to outsource to others, and how to do it.

Since then, some of the cooler things that I've had them do?

- Make real estate calls and set appointments for my team in business.
- Get your (Mandy) homeschooling High School Diploma.
- Research donor possibilities for JoeVolunteer.
- Book the cheapest and best travel options (saved us a few hundred dollars just on one trip).
- Edit and clean up video and add transcriptions and graphic effects to them.
- Had video cards (like a greeting card that you open, and it plays a video, with sound, on a mini LCD screen) ordered.
- They searched for and found someone to cut our lawn regularly, and set it up to be billed to my card as it was performed . . . and I never even met or talked to the person/company doing it. I just typed it out and, like magic, it has been done ever since.
- The VAs are helping me to launch my next company by building a virtual platform for HelpWithAgents.com. They're doing it well, too!
- I had much of this book transcribed from me just "talking" to you and recording it.
- The original front cover design of this book was also designed by VAs.
- I had a recreation of the New York Times Bestseller List with THIS BOOK on it as the #4 Bestseller in its first

week as an April Fool's joke to post on Facebook. It worked too well. . . I'm still getting congratulations messages for it. This was my favorite one of all of these!

To help illustrate how cool they are, and what more they can do, the following is writing from my VA, Nicole Elliott:

~~~~~~~~~~~~~~~~~~~~~~

Chip is exactly right about us VAs. We really can do everything!

Beyond the obvious fact that we can do things, like write this little blurb for your dad's book, we also handle a pretty incredible variety of the coolest, strangest, and most bizarre tasks imaginable.

I reached out to my fellow VAs to hear directly about what some of these tasks have looked like for them.

From the coolest:

"Find something amazing for me to do in London on New Year's Eve"
"Automate a way for me to send brownies to my new patients"

To the strangest:

"Setup Facebook ads to sell firewood"
"Send a life-size Donald Trump cutout to my friend"

To the just plain bizarre:

"Help me buy a 10-ton crane in the U.S. and ship it to Bangladesh"
"Research who I can call to get rid of the dead rats on my property"

Call us wizards, superheroes, or some other impressive sounding word of your choice, and rest assured you're in good hands.
~~~~~~~~~~~~~~~~~~~~~~

(PS: If you ever need a VA copywriter, like myself, or someone to tackle even the most crazy-sounding—though hopefully legal—task, Chip can tell you exactly where to find us!)

~~~~~~~~~~~~~~~~~~~~

See?! It's amazing. They can do almost anything, including finding and hiring local people to do things in person.

Now, I think that this is about to get more and more mainstream in our everyday life. I think that jobs are going to be outsourced to specialty contractors, and businesses won't have to deal with things like payroll taxes, unemployment costs, and the like. What's cool about it is that the VAs doing this can specialize in the work that they're good at; and can do it with just a laptop, Wi-Fi connection, and a phone.

I think the best thing about what they do is to save you time, headaches, and effort on the things you don't enjoy doing so that you can concentrate on what you are great at: your unique genius. That's the beauty of this. Once you're able to make some money and get a little cushion with that, you can literally outsource almost everything that you don't like in life.

It's important to have a "to-do" (or Outcome) list in your life, the things that you want to get accomplished and out of the way. But I'd submit to you that it's important to have a "not-to-do" list as well, and the ability to outsource can help a lot with that.

So, my advice is to get started and try it. My sweet Mandy, I know that you've already experienced a little of this when you had some work outsourced on Fiverr.com. Aly, and others that don't know, that's a website where you can hire people to do almost anything for just $5. Looking at the site, they have people that can promote your Facebook page to hundreds of thousands of people, create an entire "whiteboard," video, design two professional logos (they
~~~~~~~~~~~~~~~~~~~~

look good, too), or one that I've used: leave a voice message as Christopher Walken or Morgan Freeman (and it sounds SO convincing). It's just amazing what can happen with this type of technology and world.

Getting people from other sides of the globe to work for you at cheaper rates is technically called geo-arbitrage. It's still amazing to me all that you can get done for such a low price.

Now, the question is: what do you do now that you know this?

Figure out the things in life that you really don't like doing. Write those down and see how much can be farmed out to someone else. I grew up mowing lawns. I ran my first lawn mowing business at age twelve. I worked at a landscaping/lawn care company when I was a junior in high school, and got the dreaded 'cemetery weed eater' luck of the draw then. They'd drop me off at 8 a.m. with a five-gallon jug of water, a weed eater, and a tank of gas. Then they would pick me up in the late afternoon after I'd trimmed the entire graveyard. Anyway, I don't like mowing our lawn now. So, it's outsourced. I don't feel bad about that as long as I'm doing something more productive with my time, but really that's almost everything else to me, even if I'm just chilling and watching a movie. I deserve it.

What is it that you really don't like doing? Something that would make you smile to know that someone else is doing on your behalf? Are there several things you can think of that you find yourself doing on a daily basis? Well, figure out a way that you can work on your genius, which often pays better than the task you're delegating, while someone else does the thing you hate. The great thing is, usually they enjoy and appreciate the work you're giving them. They're probably better at it than you, too. So, get your "not-to-do" list, and start delegating it!

The next thing you'll need to do is to get really good at writing a great description of what you want from those that will outsource. What I've discovered, and I know I still have a lot to learn, is that you must be extremely clear about the outcome that you're hoping to achieve with them. Let them worry about how it is done, but you get really good at describing what needs to be done. Really, the best way to get great at it is practice and time. You'll get better and better. And don't be afraid to ask for more than what you think you can get. They will often surprise you, especially if they're good at what they do.

One of the biggest things that I think is possible with outsourcing is they can do recurring tasks like clockwork every time it comes due and report it to you when the job is done. Honestly, I haven't set that up as much as I'd like right now, but it's a powerful thing/skill to master. I really need to do more accounting and bookkeeping functions with my VA team, and I'll get to that right away.

Now, a caution. Usually outsourcing is third on the list. My friend Ari, mentioned previously, has a three-word system for making everything in your life better. Before outsourcing something, he says it's best to optimize it first, then automate where you can, and finally outsource the things you can't automate on your own. This is sage advice. I'd say that the optimizing is getting crystal clear on what you want. If you have a fuzzy objective, you'll get a fuzzy result. Automating can be fun, and there are two websites at the time of this writing that make it cool: IFTTT.com (if this, then that), and Zapier.com. They both will stun you at how much you can automate. Ari is a Jedi Knight at the automation. He has his wife notified by text when he's arriving home automatically when he passes a certain point on his route to his home. I'm proud of myself because I get a text sent to me when there's going to be rain the next day. Not that I dress any differently (I wear the same thing every day), but it's still nice to know!

So, now you know. You've been introduced to the wonderful world of outsourcing and remote contract work. The world is moving in this direction, by the way. In the future, you're going to see more and more of this type of work arrangement. That's exciting! That means that the 9-5 existence will be fading. Almost everyone will be able to work when and where they want to work, and the promise of technology will be fulfilled in a big way. We'll also have processes, *thinking* computers, and programs to take over a whole lot of today's production. In my opinion, that's going to be a little weird, but also wonderful. Being as you're my children, I want you to start this and get prepared now, rather than later!

This Advice in Practice is going to be fun, my sweets!

Advice in Practice:

- First, as usual in many of these pieces of advice, pull out a journal or your computer and do an idea list. I want you to dream and put a good 20 things that you could outsource in your life. Really stretch and think. Think about your future, the career you'd like to do, some bucket list items you'd like to accomplish (there's an advice chapter on that in here), and see if there are ways you can be helped by your VA. Go ahead and do it!

- Try out Fiverr.com to do something for you. Just pay the $5 to have something done. Go search their site and get a good idea of the breadth of things that can be done for a mere five-hundred pennies. I bet you'll be amazed. When I show people this site, and they hadn't heard of it, they usually flip out a bit. Just take your time and have something done. If you can't think of anything, have them do a logo for your name, or have someone leave a message as Christopher Walken on your buddy's voice mail (I've done this!). You may end up liking it.

- For more advanced and sizable tasks, some sites that you can check out include Freelancer.com and Upwork.com. *Freelancer* is used more for projects that involve the computer, while *Upwork* is usually more people powered . . . like hiring someone to do sales calls for you. If you check them out, and refer back to your list, there may be something that you can try to hire out to someone else.

- Mentally prepare yourself for the fact that you probably won't be good at delegating to your VAs up front, and that you're going to waste some money when the task goes awry. It's not a waste, and there is never failure if there is learning, but I've seen friends of mine mess up on a task, get discouraged, and conclude that outsourcing doesn't work for them. Just remember this advice when you're doing this!

- As you get better at this, and don't have as much disposable income, try out *Fancy Hands*. Just google them, sign up for a basic package, and have them do some tasks for you. I've had them make reservations at popular Disney restaurants on our vacation by repeatedly calling back on our behalf to get a spot as soon as someone cancels their reservations. That's pretty sweet (and how we were able to eat at the "Be Our Guest," restaurant! Yay, me and *Fancy Hands*)! Get used to having this resource and use it every once in a while, just so it can become a habit for you.

- I mentioned this above, kiddos, but if you're earning less than $20/hr.; consider being a virtual assistant. I mention this often, but who you become at a job is much more important than what you get. Who you become as a VA is a problem solver that can apply your skills to all kinds of situations, and the learning must be off the charts with all of the varied things you're doing in that role.

- Lastly, as you get more income and your time is more valuable; consider using teams of virtual assistants with companies. They can be more expensive, but they're usually really effective at what they do. An example would be them taking 30 minutes to book a flight for me, and saving over $200 on the same ticket that I tried to find. Also, when it really allows you to operate in your genius, and someone takes over everything else, it's really worth it. Just Google some of the options and find the best for you to do this.

You know I love you, right? I'll never outsource that!

Notes, thoughts, and intentions.

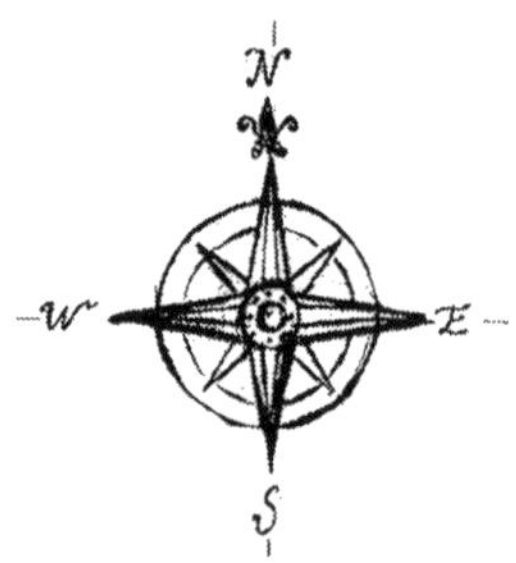

39. Don't Let Money Be a Bully in Your Life.

I heard my friend, Jim, put it like this, and it just makes so much sense.

Girls, you need money to live. I get it. We understand that. However, don't let money determine what you need to do in life. Don't let it dictate to you what you can't do.

In fact, I see this so much throughout life; people that go through the motions every day, working at jobs that don't challenge or fulfill them. They are just treading water, waiting for the weekend, when they can do what they *really* want to do. In fact, I did that for a lot of my life, too.

I've heard Dave Ramsey say something along the lines of, ***"We do what we don't want to do, to earn money to buy things we don't need, to impress people that we don't like."***

It's often a hamster wheel. You make money to earn a lifestyle, and that very lifestyle keeps you on the hamster wheel indefinitely. Then, a year goes by, and two, then a decade, and you realize that you've been having the same year over and over again. That's when money has become your master, pushes you around like it's little plaything, and you've become the part of the trance.

No! My precious children. It doesn't have to be like that.

Even if you have to work at a job that you don't necessarily enjoy, you can have a goal to have a way to get out of it. A way to put it would be to have a vision of a better life for yourself. Then you engage in your Hero's Journey to get to doing what it is that you are meant to do at that time.

You can't just let the money equation keep you down. You can't let it keep you enslaved into an ordinary life. To do this you have to realize what money is and what its purpose is, or should be, in your life.

I believe money is for two things: security and freedom. The security in knowing that you can eat your next meal; and that there's a warm place for you to sleep that night, but freedom, that's what money is really for! My friend Joe calls bills "fun tickets." They let you travel, they let you explore, and they let you give freely with love in your heart to help something. They are able to be traded for experiences; things that make up the rich tapestry of life.

Used correctly, money allows you to do what you want to do with your life. Do you remember when we talked earlier about finding your "magic spot" in your career? One of the questions was, "What would you do if you had a billion dollars in the bank?"

Just having enough to get by and to live, not even that comfortably, can allow you to do something that really means something to you. It can give you a chance to follow your bliss.

Here's the principle that I think can help: when you have enough money to cover just the basic needs, you need to work on finding your bliss in the Hero's Journey.

You need to get to a place where you are doing something that you love, and you can't let money get in the way of that.

Whether that means that you have a "side hustle" while you're working at your day job, or it means you start off following your passion straight out of high school. . . that's the thing that you need to do with life.

And you should not let a temporary need for a paycheck dictate your entire career. You want to make sure that you're doing something you enjoy, otherwise you're letting money be a bully in your life-- doing something you don't want to do every day simply because of the need of money.

I just heard this while re-watching the excellent documentary, *Finding Joe*:

"Don't do what Daddy says," because your daddy generally cares about your security. If you surrender to security early, you'll almost never find your bliss."

That's kind of funny, because this daddy is a lot more concerned about your soul, and your fulfillment, than simple security.

So, here is some of the best advice I've heard on money. It's a lot more easily said than done sometimes, but it's all easily doable, too.

1) "Start thy Purse to Fattening." That's the line from the classic book, *The Richest Man in Babylon*. It means to live a little beneath your means. This does not mean to live in scarcity, and save the $3 cup of coffee every day that you really enjoy just because that $3 compounded every day for thirty years equals to $38 billion, or whatever it is . . . no! The easiest way to do this is to PAY YOURSELF FIRST. From every paycheck or Client check as a business, take a percentage that you never see, and sock it away to create your Living Fund. That's a six-months-of-living-expenses fund that's set aside to give you peace of mind no matter what happens in life. 10% is doable by most anyone. You can get your boss/HR/payroll to do that in most cases. Just send it to an account that's not easily spent, and don't think about it or look at it! Just the thought that this is being done will give you a peace of mind that spending all of your money, and then spending on credit, will never approach.

2) Get that six months of living expenses set aside first thing. Dave Ramsey, in his excellent book, *The Total Money Makeover*, says get an emergency fund of $1,000 and then pay off all of your debt with a debt snowball After that, you can get the six months of living expenses set aside. Well, I like the idea of having the six months first, then paying off everything. That six months is my "sleep at night" fund, and you can get out of survival mode and move on to doing something you'd really like to do in life. That makes a big difference in the quality of life.

3) Don't buy stuff unless you really want it. I think this gets easier as you get older. I just don't like buying "stuff" now. Possessions possess. The things you own end up owning you: in money, time, care, and attention. The less stuff you have, the more freedom you have.

4) When you have the six months of living expenses, then pay off your bills using the debt snowball as explained in the book, *The Total Money Makeover*, to get all debt gone.

5) Then, personally, I like the Jim Rohn 70/10/10/10 plan. That is, live on 70% of your after-tax income, give 10% to charity or a cause/church that you believe in 10% towards saving for retirement, and 10% for active investing for the future. That can include setting aside money for starting your own business, or even self-education and development for you to be able to increase your earning potential.

The thing is, a lot of people write about this kind of thing and say it's a good thing to do, but very few actually do it. I think if it's done early in your life it's a lot easier, and becomes a habit that will make such a huge difference in your life.

I want you to be happy. I want you to be fulfilled. I'd very much like you to be free of worry and anxiety over where the next check is coming from. These ideas can really help you with this. Don't let this advice fall on you without doing something about it! The things you can do to help are in the following Advice in Practice.

Advice in Practice:

- Read *The Richest Man in Babylon*, then you should probably read it again. Honestly, I remember reading it while huffing and puffing away at a long defunct gym in Killeen, Texas while still in my mid-20s, and thinking it made a ton of sense . . . and then proceeding not to do anything with the information! Don't let that be you.

- Also, read and follow *The Total Money Makeover*, by Dave Ramsey. It's a great book. I know that I'm beating this to death, but one of the things that Dave says is that money discipline is almost all behavioral, and that it can be learned. Your behavior dictates what happens. He says do the baby steps in his order, while I like getting the six months of living expenses saved up first (mainly because I had a business with huge fluctuations in income), but I'll leave it to you to do the steps in the order that you like after you read his book. But do this. Take the time to do this. Really. The few hours reading a book like this will make a big difference in your life.

- Go to your boss, HR, or whoever does your payroll, and have them deduct 10% of your paycheck and send it to a savings or money market account that you look at very rarely, and that is tough to spend. At first, don't even worry about the tax implications of this, or do it with a an IRA or some other investment account. Although that's a good way to do things, the thing to remember here is that the behavior is more important than getting this perfect! If you save that 10%, and make it a habit throughout your life, then money won't be a bully to you. Do this until you get to the 6 months' of living expenses.

- Make paying your bills every month as simple as possible and create a system for doing so. Here's the deal: I'm a bit of a hypocrite here, and I feel rotten for telling you this when I'm not doing it like I should. I default to letting your mom take care of the bills. But here is my suggestion, and I will be doing this from here on out as I want to live in integrity; pay everything from a credit card that gives you airline miles, and proactively sends you an email of your monthly expenses. Then, once a month, take the fifteen minutes or so on your calendar, (scheduled) to look over the statement, make sure it's right and that you still need those bills, and then pay off that credit card balance. ALL of it. It's a little like playing with matches when you do this, and if you find yourself starting to rack up a balance then stop paying with a credit card and use a debit card instead with the same principles in mind.

- When you have a spouse, do this with them and get on the same page. I think the biggest fight starters and stressors in a marriage have to do with money and the lack of it. Dave Ramsey has some great advice on that, and how to deal with the "free-spirits" versus the "nerds" in relationships. Done right, it should bring you closer as a couple.

- Set financial goals and look at them each day in your miracle morning practice and/or planning sessions. If it's in front of you, and you're making daily progress, you're going to feel so much better in life.

- Keep up with your Idea Lists! If you devote your idea list time to questions/topics like, "How I Can Double the Amount of Money I Make Each Month in Three Months or Less," then your miraculous brain will provide answers to it. Then follow it up with, "What Can I do to Take Action and Make These Ideas Manifest in My Life?" BOOM! You're going to figure out a way to do it.
- Lastly, remember this advice. Commit it to memory: **Resourcefulness is more important than money**. Continue to improve you and the way you think (becoming an idea machine), and that will serve you better than a giant pile of money. I promise this.

I love you so much!

Notes, thoughts, and intentions.

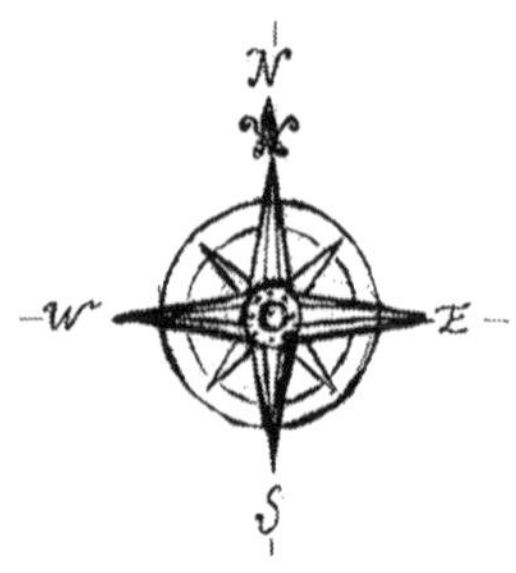

40. Create Your Very Own Ideal Schedule.

Hey, sweethearts! This is a great piece of advice. I know that I'm tooting my own horn about it, but in this case it may be justified.

This one is a little related to the miracle morning advice, but we're going to go deeper. This is all about scheduling your entire day and week to fill it with as much open-mouthed awesomeness as possible.

What's the alternative to you setting an ideal schedule? It's controlled chaos. It makes what you do subject to haphazardness. When you do that, you can end up spending the entire day doing *stuff*, and then wondering where the heck the day went after it's all done. It's the difference between being proactive and reactive. If you wake up and don't have a plan of what to do once your eyes open, then life will intrude. You'll probably do what the majority of the country (maybe world by now) does and look at your phone. You'll see texts, or emails, or things that you need to REACT to, instead of charting your own course for the day and being proactive. And that's just the morning.

During the day, with an ideal schedule, you'll be able to do more. You can have a chance to focus on each individual thing versus all of the things hitting your tired psyche all at once. If you have a set time where you work on projects, you can turn off your phone for that time and get hyper-productive on just doing that. It's better than trying to fit things in after the fact, where the important things often fall away to the trivial. It puts things in their place and gives you time to create.

Here's the idea: a set schedule sets you free. I know that sounds counterintuitive, but hear me out on this. If you don't need to think about what's next, if it's automatic and no brain-power is used, then your mental energy (and actually physical energy) is saved for things that really matter like conversations, innovations at work and creative pursuits like writing. In fact, I'm writing this in the midst of my own Ideal Schedule right now, during my "writing" time.

Now, if the idea of a set schedule gives you the shakes and makes you want to run, this is an important idea: It's only to be used as a guideline. I don't like things forced on me, even if it's a schedule that I've made myself. I know, weird, but my schedule got a whole lot better when I wrote at the top, "only to be used as a guideline." That's funny, but it gives you the freedom whether to follow it or not, and the choice makes all the difference to me.

Optimizing your schedule can be one of the best things you ever do. It's a way to determine what's best in your life. You can decide what's best for you, what habits help you out, and how you'd script your day if everything were perfect. In fact, have you ever had a day when you listened to one of your favorite songs, got all excited and pumped up and as a result, and had a pretty darn good day? I think that we've all had those. Well, how would you like to start every day like that? Of course, you can, and it's actually pretty easy to do, but very few people actually do.

Let's not be like those people. Let's take the time to actually do a little work in designing that Ideal Schedule, to be used as a guideline and subject to constant improvement as you see fit. Then your days will be easier and you can get more done, or if you schedule some YOU time (Friday MY Day, or Monday, Fun Day), you can make sure that you have a good time each and every week. It's just a better way to live—not that I'm biased.

"But, Dad . . ." you say as you're rolling your eyes and arguing that this doesn't apply to you, because you're in school or at a job for eight hours a day.

Well, then I'd say it's even more important, because you have less hours to yourself that are discretionary. You'll start to see this as you get older, but there's a saying (I'll mention it again in this book, because it's profound and true), ***"The days go slow, and the years go fast."***

Your days on a regular job will melt into each other and turn into weeks, months, and years that just seem to pass with a blink of an eye. If you're not careful, you'll end up in a rat race running each day just to make a living and pay the bills, rather than living and doing something extraordinary, or something that you absolutely love and that lights you up like you can't believe.

And the way to get from scraping by to living in freedom and abundance lies in what you do with your time. So, take that seriously, and don't leave it to chance. Create your Ideal Schedule and include the important things on it. Make sure that you have date time with your loved ones (like your dad) on it, or time with your sweet brother. All too often, if you don't make the time for that, these vital blocks of our lives are swept away by the deluge of the daily.

Keep the important things in your routine. Make sure you do what you should and want to do. Create, try, adjust, and then stick to your very own Ideal Schedule.

Have I sold you on the importance of it? I hope so. Now, let's get into how that's actually done.

Advice in Practice:

- Get your journal, or Evernote, and do an Idea List of all of the things that your Ideal Schedule should have in it. Think big rocks first—the really important things in life. Here are some of the things you might want to include:
    - Quality time with your loved ones should go at the top.
    - Rest and rejuvenation time should be included and made a priority.
    - Creative time is so important. Even if you're at a 'regular' job, you should probably have some type of side "hustle" going where you are continuously creating the life you want.

- o Exercise. Hopefully something that you enjoy.
- o Self-development time. Like time to read this book, journal, or meditation. In fact, you can and should do your entire miracle morning and put it into your schedule.
- o Learning/Studying time (I imagine that so few people have this as part of their regular routines).

Then get fun. . .

- o Do you want to take a scheduled nap? Put it in there!
- o Want to listen to your power song every day to get you revved up? Include that into your schedule!
- o Fun times are discretionary. Right now, my latest version of the Ideal Schedule makes Friday, "my day." I only do things on "my day," that give me joy! I'm a movie buff, so that's when I can sneak away to one and enjoy someone spending $200-million just to entertain me (that's a bargain)!
- o Do you want to cultivate friendships? Put that in your schedule, too. Meet for coffee or lunches on Wednesdays. . . whatever! You see how things like that could slip or be left up to chance without building one of these?
- o Times for romance, dates, and surprising your dearest one. If it's in your schedule, guess what? It actually gets done.

- Use your Idea List to get everything that you can think of that you'd like to include. Don't stop with what I've given you here. Use that beautiful noggin of yours to come up with all the building blocks of a perfect week. I don't think that I've mentioned this, but I like to do mine in the form of an ideal week as this usually gives me enough of a canvas with which to paint my masterpiece.

- Now that you have those times you'd like to include—it's time to start organizing them and putting it out on paper or a screen. I've used Microsoft Excel to do the schedule before, but for the latest versions I'm using Google Docs and making up a Google Sheet that can be edited and improved upon.

- When you get it done and ready, remember that it's a work in progress! It's not set in stone unless you decide that it is. I just added swimming to mine today. I'm exercising, but it feels like I'm playing, and I get to go into the hot tub when I'm done. Nice. Now it's a part of the Ideal Weekly Schedule. So, yours can morph throughout the years to better suit you and what you want to do. Just wait until you get kids. Whew! That will set your world on its ears in a very cool, but quite momentous way! You'll need to update your schedule when that happens!

Of course, if you need help be sure to ask your dear ole' dad for that.

You know what I'm going to say, right? I friggin' love you. Write that in your journal.

Notes, thoughts, and intentions.

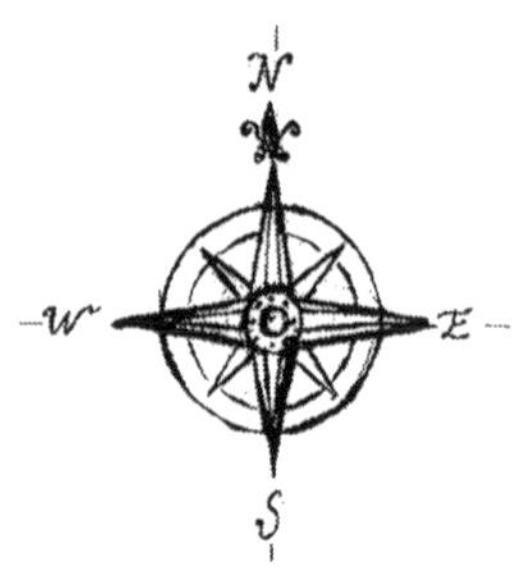

41. Create Your Very Own Reality Distortion Field. Have Fun Doing It, Too.

Hello, my little loves.

This is one of my very favorite pieces of advice. It will be fun to go over it and teach you what I know about how to form and strengthen your personal RDF (Reality Distortion Field). . . and I fully expect you to create it, cultivate it, make it all powerful, and to add to this for others to enjoy.

Yes, this will sound, "woo woo," or you would call it "Hippy Dad Stuff," and maybe it is a little out there. That's okay. If you don't like this, or you don't believe it, it's completely okay to dismiss this as nonsense. It won't work for you, anyway, ye of little faith. But if you do work with it, and you experience some success with it, you too can become a master of the RDF and bend the world in which we live to the fantastic force of your mind.

What is a Reality Distortion Field? I first heard the term while listening to Walter Isaacson's incredible biography of Steve Jobs. From Wikipedia (to whom I just donated some money, so I feel like I can copy that here), here's the definition:

"**Reality distortion field (RDF)** is a term coined by Bud Tribble at Apple Computer in 1981, to describe company co-founder Jobs' charisma and its effects on the developers working on the Macintosh project.[1] Tribble said that the term came from *Star Trek*.[1] In the Menagerie episode, it was used to describe how the aliens created their own new world through mental force." [5]

It was really used to talk about motivating others, like the Apple Macintosh team into thinking that they could do something that had never been done before, but I like the Star Trek explanation better:

"Creating a new world through mental force."

In fact, it's like, "The Force," in Star Wars.

It can be used for things as mundane as getting great parking spots at Wal-Mart, which I do often, to something as grand as launching a movement of kindness to literally change the world. Your mom gets a little angry that I always get the best parking spots. It happens almost without fail, and it's really just residual effect from my unwavering belief that it will happen, so it does. But that's a simplification of things.

---

[5] Various Contributors, "Reality Distortion Field," Wikipedia. https://en.wikipedia.org/wiki/Reality_distortion_field (April 12, 2018).

Some people may even think or confuse this with the concept of, *The Secret* by Rhonda Byrne. But it differs from that in several ways, with the primary difference being that there's actually some action required on your part to bring these things to pass.

Here is my formula for making the Reality Distortion Field happen in your life (this is the first time that I've actually codified it in writing, I'm excited).

1) Get specific on what it is that you want. Really specific. Be clear about it, and think about the ideal outcome of what you want.

2) Think about that exact result happening. Literally visualize it. If it's a big thing, do it often—maybe as part of the miracle morning process. Otherwise, just do it on your own quickly as you need it (like imagining that parking space).

3) Have faith that it will work for you. Believe that it will happen. Know that it will happen for you, even if it doesn't happen for anyone else.

4) Take an action to bring this thought into reality. Something that will work to really make it happen. In the example with the parking space, don't follow another car in the same row because they'll get the first parking spot. Take the other lane. If it's a desired outcome, or "luck," then write it out to happen for real. Prayer works for the believers in this part, too.

5) Release the result. Don't depend on the result actually happening. Don't sweat about it. Don't worry or hold on to

it too tightly mentally. If the result happens, that's awesome. Of course it happened. If it doesn't happen, well, that's okay. It wasn't really meant to happen. What's kind of interesting is that the attitude of the result not having to happen will make it more likely to happen. And sometimes whatever it is not happening turns out to actually be better, anyways.

So, that's the formula that I use. I've gotten free admission to theme parks with it, I've gotten jobs with it, this book is actually a result of this kind of RDF thinking, too. Writing a book was pretty 'out there' from my usual way of thinking, but that thinking changed (thankfully), and I was able to will this into existence in my world. It's a pretty cool tool for the belt when you think about it.

Advice in Practice:

- Let's get the reality distortion working with the example I just used. Getting a parking space. Think about it before you're about to do that. Even if you're not the one driving (Aly, that will be a little while before you're the one driving). Follow the steps above and get the better parking spot. You're going to see this working like magic. The belief when you do something small like this will build up your belief into doing bigger, better things with your RDF.

- Use your RDF to talk someone into doing something for you. This is a lot like the "How to Ask for Something the Right Way," advice, but do it using the steps above. Get a discount, or a perk that others don't get, or something that they, "don't usually do for others." It may take a few times until you get that certain blend of charisma and certainty, but go ahead and do it. You'll get better, my young Jedis.

- Now. . . you've started to use your RDF. You're cultivating it and making your own surround you. That's good. Let's apply it to other areas of your life. Quite honestly, I haven't done this part yet as I'm writing this, but it just hadn't really occurred to me to do it as I'm about to suggest to you. That's about to change, however! I don't want to be hypocritical! Here it is: write out some of the things that you want to change all throughout your life. Use your goal list if necessary. Think on these, follow the advice and steps above and start applying this to areas you'd like. Influence people. Bring about the change you want to see happen. You can do it. I have faith in you, my precious kiddos.

Notes, thoughts, and intentions.

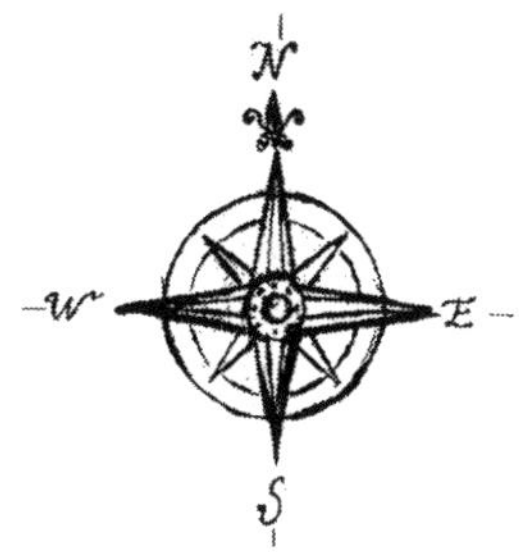

42. Read Several Books At Once.

So, now I get to talk to you about reading several books at one time. I am a big fan of this and have been ever since I started really getting into reading non-fiction books. Now, what's so wonderful about books in general is that someone has spent their life, efforts, and time in learning something that you get to learn about it within a few hours and usually for less than $20. To me, it's one of the best investments that you can make to get the best someone has to offer for just a few dollars.

I have personally loved reading books ever since I was a child. There have been many times where your grandmother, my mom, caught me reading books well past my bedtime with the flashlight underneath the covers. I stayed up late just reading because I enjoyed it so much and it didn't matter if I got tired in the morning. It was just something I wanted to do and enjoyed doing so much. I have carried that love of reading with me my entire life and I am hoping that you always have that love as well. If you don't enjoy reading, then I think you need to find the right material to read and get things that you can and will enjoy reading, because a love of reading will add so much richness to your life. Reading will make your life so much better and can allow you to learn things so quickly.

As far as the advice, I think it's good to have at least two books going at any given time. I prefer to have at least one non-fiction book going, and only one fiction book. The non-fiction book can be read (or listened to) when I'm feeling in the mood for it. I always like to have a book going that helps me solve a problem professionally that I otherwise would not know how to solve. The fiction book is used to wind down at night. . .usually on the kindle.

You should only ever read a book for one of two reasons: you enjoy it or it's useful to you in some way. That's usually to gain knowledge that you don't have.

What I would suggest is to have a plan for each book. Ask yourself specifically, "what do I want out of this book?" Have an outcome for it and what you are hoping to gain.

What's useful and beautiful about this is that there is a book written for nearly anything and any problem that you would ever have. It's easy as downloading something--it takes a few seconds to get the knowledge of the entire cumulative world at your fingertips (which is just amazing).

I am also a big Audible fan and I use that to turn driving time into learning time. It's a great way to learn and get at least another book going in the meantime. So, if you're counting, usually I have a fiction book going, a nonfiction book that I am reading, then also a nonfiction book that I am listening to at any given time to learn something *specific*.

Now the last point I will make about this is that a lot of learning seems to end at graduation, but really that's where it *begins*. In schools, generally you are told what to read and what you should learn. Someone *else* is dictating for you, whereas when you get out of school, *you* get to decide what you want to learn, pursue, and master!

So with that said, I hope you know that you are loved and I encourage you to go out and read.

Advice in Practice:

- Develop a reading list. Ask for some recommendations on good fiction books, ask your friends, put out a post on Facebook to see what others recommend. Ask what books have changed their lives and get some good things to read. You can also see what Amazon recommends for you. Keep a list of these books you'd like to read in an Evernote file, or save them in a "wish list" in Amazon.

- Think about your career and mission and what knowledge will be useful to have. What's something that would make a big difference in what you do every day? Make your professional reading list, and here is the important part—ask what you plan to get out of the book. Set an intention for those books, write it down, and read with a purpose in mind.

- Get a kindle. Right now, I use a kindle paperwhite and it has a backlight on it, so I can read at night. It's been wonderful for me. It has a very low light level, and it doesn't keep me awake at night. Also, with the kindle you can always highlight and take notes on it too...and export them should you want them.

- Order an actual book for your profession/career/mission from Amazon. I am more encouraged to write things out on it and really use the book as my slave of personal knowledge. I would suggest you write out on the inside cover your intention for the book, then keep that question in mind while reading.

- Another piece of advice is getting an Audible account if you can afford it. Right now, it's $15 a month and you get a book a month. Usually, the books cost more than that, but the real value is that it's something that encourages you to keep doing your reading via listening.

- The last piece of advice I have is to think about reading some of the following books that I have loved from non-fiction that are great and those books are:

  The 4-Hour Work Week by Tim Ferriss
  Choose Yourself by James Altucher
  Bold by Steven Kotler and Peter Diamandis
  The War of Art by Steven Pressfield
  How I Found Freedom in an Unfree World by Harry Browne.

Please consider reading those books. As always, you know that I love you tremendously.

Notes, thoughts, and intentions.

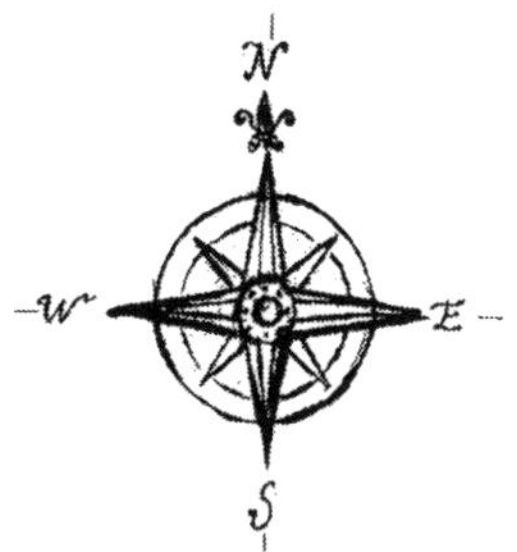

43. Consciously Learn How to Break Bad Habits.

If you have bad habits, they can be very, very hard to break.

"The chains of habit are too weak to be felt until they are too strong to be broken."
— Samuel Johnson

Nip those bad habits in the bud, because soon they'll control you!

***Daddy Disclaimer: I openly admit I've got some bad habits, so please don't invalidate everything I say on this because the worthwhile message is coming from a flawed messenger!

I'm thinking of this right now, as I had a somewhat crippling habit of drinking Coke Zeros/soda in general. It was a very bad habit.

I've read from the book, *Effortless Healing*, by Dr. Joseph Mercola. It said the biggest and easiest way to improve your health is to stop drinking sodas (and other bad drinks) and replace it by drinking pure water. That hit home. I needed to stop drinking soda, for your sake as well as mine. . . I want to be around for you for a very long time. So, I'm working on all of this advice myself while dishing it out to you.

What seems to work for me is to replace your bad habits with other, better habits. Like, in my case with the sodas, I changed to drinking a light (low to no calorie) lemonade or Vitamin Water that I enjoy instead of sodas. Bridge that gap and then switch to the water.

I am also currently drinking between one to two gallons a day of water (you know all about that from the "Come on! Drink your Dang Water!" advice), and I'm certain that helped me break free from the soda habit as well.

One of the things that I got from the *Master Class on Habits 101* at *Optimize* with Brian Johnson was to "avoid kryptonite." That is, don't put yourself in a position to where you're face-to-face with your ugly, bad habit. So, you have to be *proactive* in staying away from the bad stuff, rather than reactive.

Can you imagine how difficult it would be to not eat a beautiful, tasty chocolate cake that sits on your counter, right next to your refrigerator, day after day? We both know that when your willpower is diminished, or if you've had a bad day, or if you haven't eaten . . . and it's right there sitting on the counter, you're going to consume that bad boy. We all know it. So, try to keep it away. Don't buy the bad foods. If you've got family members (ahem, like me) that keep bad food around while you're trying to eat well, then try at the very least try to keep the bad stuff out of view.

There are a lot of books, apps and other information about this, I'd expect you to find them and make it happen.

Advice in Practice:

- Awareness is key. One of the things I'm doing now is using a planner system that asks me every morning where I was uncomfortable yesterday. In it, I put when I failed to eat, drink, or do things that I was supposed to do Just writing it out is cathartic (look it up), and when I write it out too many times, I naturally want to change.

- The same thing goes with journaling. If you feel like you're engaging in some bad habits, write it out. Get it out of your head and onto paper. Just the act of doing that makes it less of an internal struggle somehow. When it's on paper, it loses some of its power over you and helps to bring it to a conscious decision where you can exercise your good judgement, rather than blindly participating in the habit.

- Check out Optimize with Brian Johnson at www.Optimize.me. It's a FANTASTIC resource on almost everything. It costs a bit, $12.50/mo. as of this writing, but it's so good. There is a Master Class on habits that I thoroughly recommend... It's amazing. I like to have the Master Classes on while I'm cooking in the kitchen. It's my happy time and encourages cooking versus going out and eating too much.

- Clear out the bad stuff. Chomping on Cheetos? Throw them away while you're feeling strong and are able to resist eating a few. On this note, always eat a good, healthy meal before going grocery shopping. You won't be as tempted to get as much food, or as bad.

- That goes with your physical surroundings, too. Did you know that clutter saps your willpower? I didn't, even though I've always felt it. You're always behind the 8-ball with clutter. It's tough to concentrate and do new things while the old things that are undone surround you. This is probably going to be its own piece of advice, one that I really need to do myself, but read and apply, *The Life Changing Magic of Tidying Up*, by Marie Kondo. I've done it in doses with my clothes and some books, and it's really helped those areas.

- Save your willpower hit points. Hit points are a term from Dungeons and Dragons. It's how much life you have left. I mentioned this earlier, but your willpower is finite so try your best to conserve it throughout the day, and don't bring your considerable decision-making power to minor things early, while major things later can suffer. This is why, after a hard day at school/work, you're ready to just plop down on a couch and eat a double greasy cheesy (cheeseburger), even though you know it's not good for you, won't contribute to a better life, etc. So, make important decisions early in the day after you get up and moving. Also, try to keep decision-making on the minor things, like what to wear for the day, to a minimum. You know this, but that's why I have a "uniform." It's good enough for Steve Jobs and Mark Zuckerberg. So, it just might be good enough for me.

By the way, all of this advice is good for me, too. I'm learning and trying to get better at these right along with you. That's part of the fun of life—getting better. I LOVE you.

Notes, thoughts, and intentions.

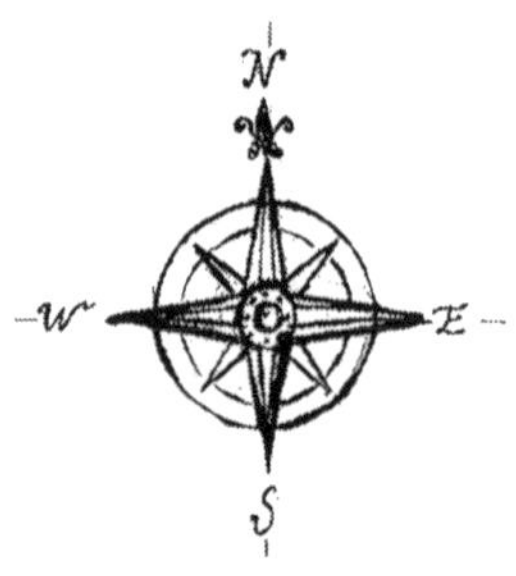

44. Create New, Better, Habits.

Habits. Set up some good ones that support you and make you a better person.

The habit of eating well, of exercising regularly, of planning your days, weeks, months and years. If you start that soon, it will become ingrained in you and it will be easier to do than not to do.

Wow. This sounds so dang general. Again like the advice to "be happy!" (insert unicorn farting a rainbow here). But there is a science to it, even if it needs to be modified to you.

Don't just read past this. It's important to a great life. It's sometimes hard to do that, but life will be so much easier if you're sometimes hard on yourself.

I've read a lot on this, but I'm still not an expert on it. Here's the best information I have on it, and I hope it will help:

Identify some of the habits that will be useful to you. Set aside time for that. Go through your daily routine and ask if what you're doing serves you living a better life or not. If it does, carry on in the next step. If it does not, then go on to the next piece of advice.

When you find the good habits that you want to become a part of your life, set up as much as you can to be done automatically. Don't rely on your willpower, as that is a very finite resource no matter how strong-minded you think you are. To do this, I'm going to mention a process that one of my friends, Ari has pioneered. It's called, Optimize, Automate, and Outsource. It was set up to help with daily business practices, but it can be powerful for habits, too.

Optimize. Really set up a critical thought process: What habits would be good for me to start? What would be good to stop? What truly serves me? Figure out the few that will help the most and concentrate on those. It's the ole' 80/20 rule. 20% of the habits will make 80% of the difference.

> *Eating well >> Moving well >> Sleeping well >> Showing Kindness >> Taking action on the things you should.*

Those habits will cover almost everything in your life. So, to optimize those, let's think about eating well. Optimize. What should you be eating to create the most energy? What should you be eating to sharpen your mind and extend your life? Let's say it's wild-caught fish and some green vegetables for dinner each night. That's great for you. It's optimized.

Next, let's automate that. How can you do this? How about having a grocery delivery service making sure that your food is delivered to you each night? You could always do your grocery shopping at a set time each week, and use a running grocery list on your fridge to make sure you're always stocked. Use your noggin, and do an idea list around all of this.

Lastly, outsource where you can. In this case, it may be expensive, but then again if you're resourceful it may not be. Get someone else to cook for you. Pay them to deliver your cooked food to you each week in pre-portioned, pre-made, healthy and delicious meals. You could find one of your friends that cooks like this, and offer to pay them to make a few extra portions for you.

Admittedly, this is all ideal and may be a little tough to pull off, but how easy would it make eating healthy a habit each night? That's the key. If it's done, and you don't have to think about it, you have a habit that will serve you forever.

And you can do this with most every good habit that you'll want in your life.

You'll find that as you have good habits, they'll reinforce each other, and you'll get an upward spiral effect on them.

i.e. eating right will help you in your exercise endeavors and the like (see Fundies, Movement, and Walking Advice in the "Body" section).

Advice In Practice:

- Pull out the 'ole journal. Think about the few habits that would make the most difference and write down ways that you can optimize, automate, and outsource ways to help make it a habit.

- Try this with exercise. Figure out how to optimize what you'd like to do to keep your body working well. Let's say it's yoga twice a week, "wogging" (walking/jogging) twice a week and lifting weights (you insert what's good for you here). How can you automate this so you don't have to think about it? That to me sounds like a great idea list. Do one on it and start to implement this in your life.

- Get some help! Let your best friend/spouse/dear 'ole daddy know that you're trying to develop this habit and get some leverage in your attempts to do it. Figure out ways to be accountable to that person. Obviously, make sure the person is trying to help you in this endeavor and won't sabotage it.

- The 42-day rule. Some people say that it takes 21 days to make a habit. I think it's tough to know, honestly, but if that's a good number, let's go much further to help ensure that it's a habit.

- Here's some advice on good habits from Hal Elrod, the creator of *The Miracle Morning*. It's knowing the three phases of any habit in advance so that you know what's about to happen. Here are the three phases: Unbearable, Uncomfortable, and Unstoppable! The names pretty much explain it, but just remember that with every time you continue on a habit it gets better and easier for you the next time. Just get past those initial stages and you're going to be fine.

- The MINI-HABIT!!! Strangely enough(or maybe it's God's serendipity), I just heard this piece of advice in the audiobook, *The Miracle Morning for Writers*, by Hal Elrod (listed above, which I wrote before hearing this), Steve Scott and Honoree Carter, to pass on TONIGHT, and it makes so much sense. The idea is mini-habits. That is, set stupid-easy habit goals to reach so you gain momentum, and are able to build on top of, to get better and better. Example: to start an exercise regimen, make it a goal to just do one pushup a day. That's it. One. The idea is that it's so easy to do that you'll probably do more, and from the momentum of doing that you will probably start to do a lot more than that one pushup every day. Another example I heard of this was to floss one tooth a day, which can lead to a powerful self-care habit.

- Lastly—my friend Benjamin Hardy wrote a book on this very subject called, *Willpower Doesn't Work*. Get this book! I'd literally recommend getting it in audio and in physical form. I've highlighted the heck out of it, and it's been very helpful in breaking several bad habits for me.

Notes, thoughts, and intentions.

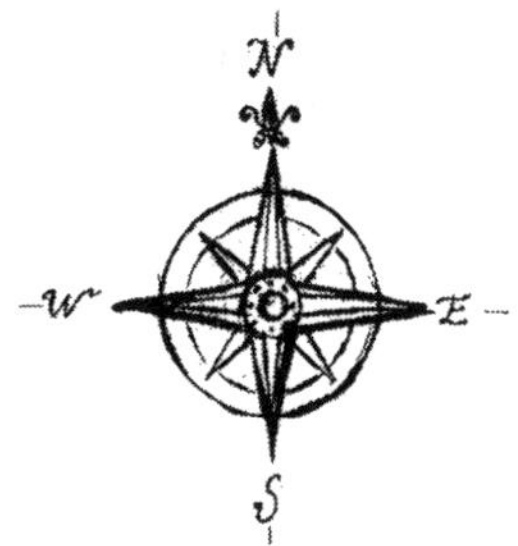

45. Work Harder on Yourself Than You Do on Your Job.

Another gem of Jim Rohn's:

"If you work hard on your job, you'll make a living. If you work hard on yourself, then you'll make a fortune!"

Don't stop learning. Keep growing. Listen to the recordings of the greats. Learn to be better in your career. Learn how to be happy, wealthy and sophisticated. Learn how to be a great parent and spouse.

You see, I think that most of us (I say, "us," meaning human beings) think that we're basically done learning, at least formally, but usually informally, too, when we walk across some stage. That's one of the beefs that I have with formal education and schooling: we offload the responsibility for learning and getting taught to someone else. That's really messed up in a lot of ways.

Take responsibility for your own learning and getting better in general. It's not up to anyone else to make you a better person. It's not your school's responsibility, it's not society's, it's not even your parent's responsibility for you to learn and get better.

It's all up to you. All of it.

Of course, these institutions (especially your parents, yo!) will want to help you and probably will help you (see the book you're holding in your hands now), but you cannot count on any of it.

All of the information you'll ever need is already out there for you to find. Go looking for that, and never stop learning.

So, work hard on your job, and get better at that.

But mainly, work hard on yourself and become the type of person that is always improving on your own. That is so much more valuable than anything that you get out of a job.

Advice in Practice:

- Journal. Do some self-reflection. Hopefully, do it every day. One of my good friends, Jesse, says that journaling is the fastest way to "level up" in life. I believe it. There will be more about journaling in this advice book, but doing this will help in working hard on yourself. In the journaling, write out what you've learned. Write what you'd like to learn and save your progress each day. Like a computer program, but with your real, honest-to-goodness life!

- Figure out how to listen to podcasts and start listening to them during your NET time (NET = No Extra Time,

time) like when you're driving (you'll do that soon), or walking, cleaning, etc. . .

- Remember that learning is done for two reasons, and two reasons only. It's useful towards some end, and/or you enjoy it. If you're forced to learn crap you don't need or want, well, that's formal schooling and we know what I think about that.

- Use the heck out of Google. It's the modern-day Oracle of Delphi (look it up on Google!), and can answer almost anything in the world. I was wondering how to unclog a drain myself this morning. . . and BOOM! There are about 186,000 videos on how to do that right now. What an age that we live in!!!

- Get a great peer group. I bet I'll have more advice on this soon, but Tony Robbins says that one of the biggest indicators of our success in life are the expectations of our peer group.

- Take care of, and actively improve upon, your physical self. Try to increase energy, strength, and thought. Figure out how to do it, and then do it. No one else will do that for you.

- Lastly, as there are really so many things that I can list here, work on your daily practice. Do something good for yourself emotionally, physically, mentally, and spiritually every single day. You will be getting better when you do that.

I love you so much. I hope this message resonates with you, Sweethearts.

Notes, thoughts, and intentions.

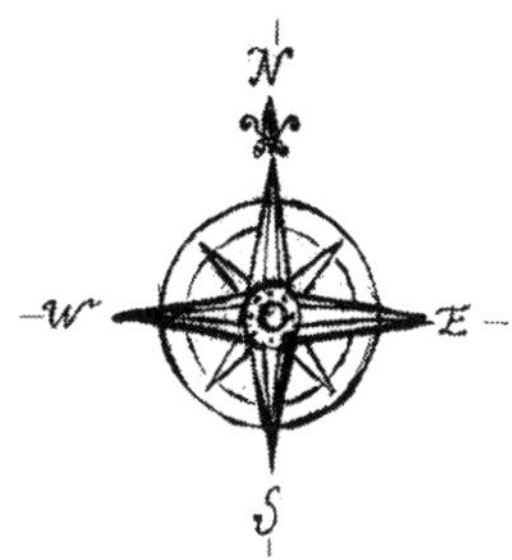

46. Engage in LIFELONG Learning.

I'm kind of cheating with this, as a lot of it was just covered in the "Work Hard on Yourself," advice, but on the subject of learning I have this to say:

Yes, school is important, but do you know what's a lot more important? You learning on your own. If you stop learning when you graduate college, I'll be really disappointed. I'll love you no matter what, but that will upset me.

Instead, establish a lifelong love of learning. Learn about what you love and it will be fun. Love learning, and you'll keep becoming a better and better version of yourself.

The way nature and the universe works is that we're either growing, or dying. That goes with that fantastic, wondrous mind of yours especially.

Some folks develop "bed sores of the mind," because they don't do any critical thinking and keep doing the exact same thing day after day. That will age you quickly (not in a good way, either). I think that's why a lot of people seem to die very soon after retirement. They don't think anymore, and there's just no reason for the brain to go on after that.

Advice in Practice:

- Look at ways to learn new things, like *The Great Courses* (look it up), or MasterClass.com where a master (duh) teaches you the intricacy of their art. Think: Kevin Spacey (you'd recognize him if you saw him) teaches you about acting, or Christina Aguilera (I think you know her, she was on *The Voice*) teaches you how to sing. And do you know how much it is (as of this writing)? $99!!! Their entire professional life's work distilled for you in easily digestible bites, and it costs less than a day's work to get it all! How cool is that?! I'm supposed to get James Patterson's class on writing for my Christmas present this year. I'm already excited!

- Here's a biggie that I don't always do, but it would be good: keep a recurring date in your weekly schedule as learning time. Make sure it shows up on your calendar, and that you get reminded of it often.

- Take notes in Evernote. Often, I'll write it by hand, and then type it into Evernote to remember it better. Or you can take pictures of it and just make sure to label it right if you need to get back to it at some point. I know you know how to do this due to our homeschooling!

- Try this process to remember what you learn:

  Learn >> DO. >> Teach. Teach what you learn to someone else, and it cements it in your brain. I'm proving that right now, because writing this tome of knowledge for you is helping me a tremendous amount.

So, thank you once again for the honor of teaching you, my sweethearts! I love you (but I bet you knew that).

Notes, thoughts, and intentions.

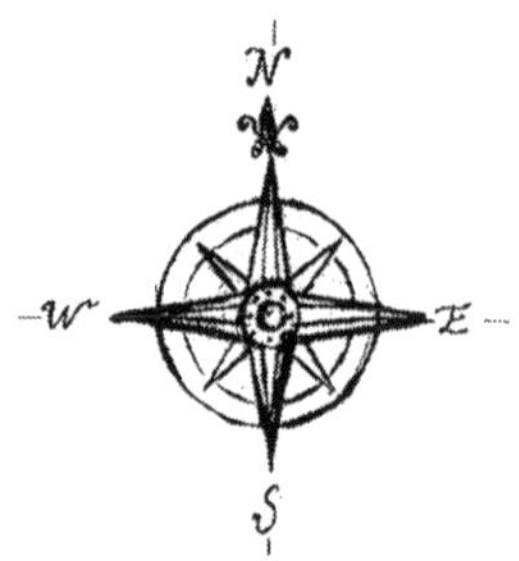

47. Become a Wordsmith of the Highest Order (The Unmitigated Power of Words).

The words you use are so very powerful!

You can get almost anything done in this world if you choose the right words with which to do it.

Ironically, I feel the words for this piece of advice are more difficult for me to come up with, but we'll get through this, because it's so important.

Jim Rohn says that words are almost God-like. You can create anything with them! You can inspire, you can teach, and you can influence with them. But the words you use can also cut others down, hurt them for years to come, and cause folks to despair. In fact, I was thinking this yesterday: you can even say "bigger and vaster than God," and create something even more powerful with the thoughts that are formed around your words.

So, become a wordsmith of the highest order. Learn your language well and practice it. Craft your words with care and use them to make a better life.

First, with others. Your words should be uplifting, humble (unless you're being funny, I try to do that a lot) and should share grace with others.

If you use your words to spread gossip, or just to dump negativity to others, remember that it's like a cancer to the ears of those that hear.

Know your words, study them to give you a vast repertoire (I'm proud of that word) of ways to express yourself to others, and pick those words carefully; especially with children.

Rohn makes the point of saying, "What if you meant to say, 'What's troubling you?' and instead, you said, 'What's wrong with you?'" The difference is vast. It's so important to say the right things to others in the right way using the right words.

I was using this as the importance of being a wordsmith, but I feel the need to advise you on this. As important as it is to say the right words to others, it's more important to use the right words with yourself.

I mean this advice to be on choosing the right words and learning a vast vocabulary, but this is just so important. Consciously choose the words you use with yourself. It's easier said than done, of course, but you can do it and make it a habit through practice. Think of it this way: I know that you (my children) love me. Well, would you let someone constantly berate me and say horrible things to your dear 'ole dad? Of course not, but I can tell you that I think some pretty awful things about myself sometimes. They sneak in even after years of practice in keeping those words out. So, think about this for you. Know that if your dad saw someone telling you that you were ugly, or not smart, or not loved that I would do a serious attitude adjustment with that person. So, don't let yourself say those types of things, either.

Advice in Practice:

- I think you have this down (girls), and hopefully Alec, too, but constantly expand your vocabulary. The best way to do this is to read. Have at least one book going in your life at all times. I prefer to have a few, at least one fiction and one non-fiction. The fiction is to be read after 7 p.m., because if I read the non-fiction book, especially if it's about business, then my mind will start racing and I'll have difficulty going to sleep.

- Try affirmations with a daily practice like *The Miracle Morning*. Those affirmations are words that feel great to say to yourself. If your inner critic is telling you that you're not pretty—then you address those in your affirmations. Try saying, "I am a spectacular creation of God." Because you ARE, and if you say that enough, you'll believe it, and it gets easier and easier to beat down that negative voice inside yourself.

- Write daily. Have a journal going and write in it, even if it's just a little bit, every single day. I've had long stretches when I would do this, and even more stretches when I wouldn't. Any guesses on when I've made the most progress in life and had the most momentum? As I'm writing all this advice to you, I'm getting better at practicing what I preach, too. So thank you for this opportunity!

- Send encouraging words to others often. This can go along with your kind deed for the day. Oftentimes, when it's later during the day or at night and I realize that I haven't done my kind deed, I'll text a friend or family member to let them know something that I admire about them, that I'm thinking of them, and that they're doing well. Really! It's literally just a minute out of your day and think of how someone must feel when they receive something like that!!! It's such a joy to be able to help other people in this way. It's also a great way to use these words that you've worked hard to know.

Notes, thoughts, and intentions.

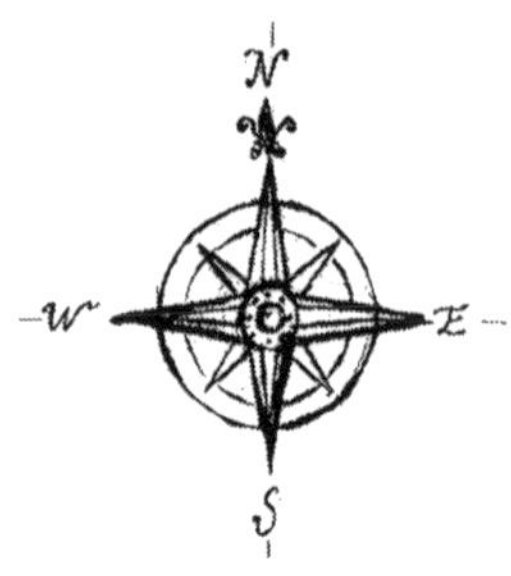

48. Avoid Using Lazy Language.

Don't get lazy with your speaking or writing.

There is a gigantic difference between "you're" and "your."

I know you know that already but put it into practice.

It only takes one mistake like that to make people think you're not as bright as you obviously are. Ooh, I hope that other people get this, too. I'm a bit of a grammar Nazi, and it amazes me how very smart people can get all their language wrong. Most likely because they're not taking the time to edit or proofread what they write, or also say.

YOUR does not equal YOU'RE.

TWO, TO, TOO.

There, Their, They're.

IT'S, ITS.

Know the difference, my loved ones. Please.

Communicate well.

Advice in Practice:

- Listen and read the lyrics to Weird Al Yankovic's song, *Word Crimes*. Aly, I know you love this song, and Weird Al, in general. And oh yes, we will go to a concert of his together at some point, and it shall be glorious.

- Edit each text, Facebook comment, or book that goes out before you send it out. Read it aloud, but be mindful that the phonetics of the sentence will sometimes be very different from how things are spelled correctly.

- Whenever someone makes a grammar or spelling mistake on social media, or in conversation, gently remind them of the correct way to write or say things. If someone writes, "Your going to enjoy that!" on a Facebook post, I find that everyone appreciates when I reply to that comment saying, "***You're." They just appreciate my great, big brain so much when that happens.

Kidding about that last advice, of course. I'm so freaking funny sometimes. Doesn't the fact that your dad is so funny bring you such great joy in the world?!

Notes, thoughts, and intentions.

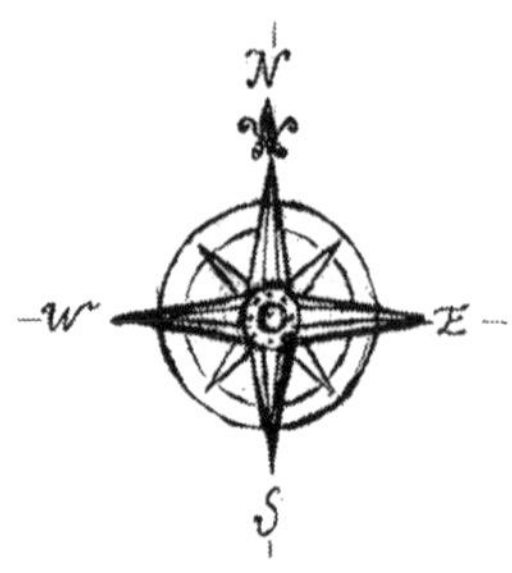

49. Find Your Magic Spot in Your Job or Career.

Find a career that thrills you when you do it. Money is secondary. If you don't enjoy what you're doing, then find a way to get to something you do enjoy that you are passionate about and that is fun for you.

One of my friends, Majeed, calls the overlap between aptitude (good at it), attitude (enjoy it), and market (can you get paid for it), *The Magic Spot.*

Mandy, strangely enough, I talked with you about this today. That's so funny how things work out like that.

Here are what seem to be the American standard ways of picking a career (by the way, I got into my original career of real estate completely by chance, so I'm not judging, I just wish I had this advice about 20+ years ago):

- A guidance counselor tells you what you're good at, or you take a career/aptitude test.
- You see someone on TV doing this profession.
- You know someone in real life doing this and it seems like they enjoy it.

- I've been majoring in this in college (that I picked at eighteen years old), so I had better go into this field.
- I need a job! Who is hiring right now? Will they hire me?

There isn't a real system, or a good way to really explore what you want to do with most of the waking hours of your life. And you'd *think* that there would be a lot of thought that goes into something like that, but there really isn't.

Thoreau (have I mentioned him in this advice book yet?) said, "The mass of men (and women, I'm assuming) lead lives of quiet desperation." I'd say that the "mass of men" put very little, if any, critical thought into their careers.

And what a huge part of life it is! It can determine your happiness, your wealth or lack thereof, your free time, your self-development, your friends, what the world thinks of you, and how many people you can positively impact by what you do.

So, how do you pick the career you want to go into? Read about it. Ask around. Don't limit yourself to dear 'ole dad's advice, but here is some of the best information that I've heard about this. Ask two questions to get some clarity. When you were a child, what did you want to do when you grew up? Personally, I think that God puts that little spark of inspiration in your heart when you're brand new in the world and close to Him.

What would you do every day if you had a billion dollars in the bank? Something that is fun for you, but that also contributes to society and helps people? Something that could make some money, but doesn't necessarily have to?

I'd start with those things and get some direction for . . . (What? That's right, you guessed it . . .) an idea list. This may be one of the most important ones that you'll ever do in your whole life.

What are some things that I'd absolutely love to do as a profession? Temper some of these ideas through the lens of what you're good at, and what you can get paid to do (though you can figure out ways to get paid for doing just about anything if you're resourceful enough).

Then, when you get to a few that really resonate with you, some that strike a chord in your soul and get you excited about the possibility of actually doing, go and find someone who is doing that job in real life.

Ask them nicely (more on exactly how to do that later) if you can take them to lunch and ask them questions about their profession. Find out what the actual schedule looks like day to day. Find out the things they love about the profession, and maybe more importantly, what they hate about the profession. See if you can parlay that into being able to shadow them for a little while to see if you really would enjoy it.

Mandy, I know we did that for you when you were around ten years old and you wanted to be a veterinarian. . . until you worked with them for a day! Think about that. A lot of kids would hold that in their hearts for years, choose a college based on that, study for 6+ years, pay a lot of money towards it, go into debt, move around the country to find a job, start it with bright eyes, and realize that they hate it a week into doing it. Now, that's an extreme example, but it happens a bunch.

I think our way is a better way of doing it, but I may be biased.

Also, remember that there's a very, very high probability that you'll actually have several careers as you go through life, so don't get too caught up in the drama of picking your forever job. I think that it's so absurd for eighteen-year-olds to know what they want to do when they grow up, but that's how colleges are designed (lots more on colleges later, too, of course).

Advice in Practice:

- Follow the plan.
- Use your journal and answer the questions about what you wanted to do as a child when you grew up, and what you'd do now if money were no concern at all. Journal it. Feel it in your heart. Think it through and let God whisper in your ear.
- Then brainstorm an Idea List of things that appeal to you.
- Then, on another day, without looking at the first list, do another one.
- Then, on another day, without looking back on either, go in an entirely different direction and think of the All-

Star life. . . the BIG dreams that, if you were able to do them could be world changing, and flesh out those ideas. I've always thought it would be great to make movies, and I've never done it. It's always been a "what if" for me, but what's really holding me back from putting it down on my list of goals and actually going for it?! You do the same.

- The one that fills your heart and soul with joy, that's the one you start pursuing.
- Next, find and get an appointment with someone that's doing exactly what it is that you think you'd like to do. Pick their brain. Follow them. It's rarely the idealized version of what you're thinking it is. It's best to find out about that now, and not later.
- Rinse and repeat as necessary.

I friggin' love you so much. Please take this advice to heart, my sweethearts!

Notes, thoughts, and intentions.

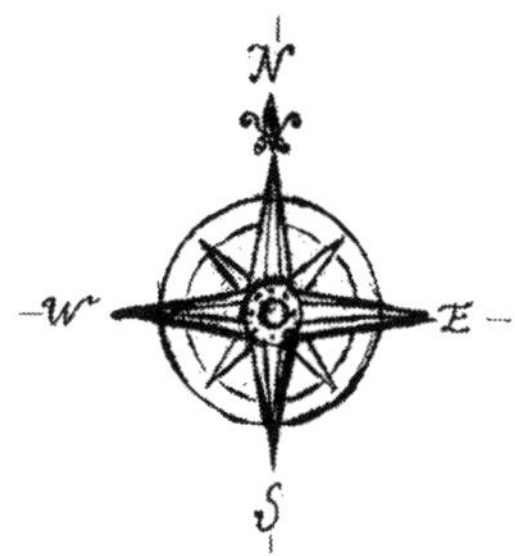

50. Build a Business Doing Something You Love.

Are you ready for more Jim Rohn advice? Huh, huh? Are you?

He says, "Profits are better than wages."

What does that mean?

With all of this talk about finding a profession, and getting a job or career, at least consider the idea of going into business for yourself at some point.

And make it a business that you *love*, okay?

To figure out what business you might want to start, please consider the advice given in *The Magic Spot* that I dispensed earlier. It's all applicable here, too. The only thing that I'd add to it is get advice from those that you trust (hopefully, I'm in that discussion!), to listen to the whispers of God and look for the serendipities that will surely show up along the way.

The joy in this is that the business is whatever you decide to make it. There are no limits, and no set way for you to do things. You get to use your own innovation and creativity to figure out the best ways to serve your clients/customers, and when you do that the world will open up to you.

What's also great is that building a business, whether it succeeds or fails, is one of the best self-improvement programs that you can ever undertake. It will most certainly make a better person of you. And to think that you phenomenal, wondrous human beings can become even better is an incredible thought!!!

Oh, and don't think that you need to sell everything, quit a job that pays everything, with nothing in the bank, and strike off on your own (although that is worlds better than never taking any action). You can, and probably should, start your "side hustle" while working for someone else. Put in some late hours and some early mornings. Get your first clients. Service them well, and when you are able to replace a good chunk of your income with something that you really enjoy, then go full-time into your business.

Just this act will make you a better person.

Advice in Practice:

- Ask the same questions from before. What did you want to do when you were a kid, and what would you do if you had a billion dollars in the bank and didn't have to work for money? (Coincidentally, for me, the answer to both of those is to be a writer! Can you believe that? And I'm literally getting to do that now while undertaking this labor of love for you. Thank you for this opportunity!)

- Brainstorm some businesses that would fit this criterion and do it many times. Create 10+ different lists of business ideas, without cross-referencing them (I think that's important, as the big ideas that are lurking in your soul will probably resurface again and again) and see which one sings its siren song to you. I think that the quality idea(s) can be found in a quantity of them. . . and if you pick the best idea out of 100+ that you've had, well, they're bound to be pretty good!

- Once you have that idea, do an Idea List on the execution of that business. Get advice. Find some folks that are doing something similar. Shadow them. Find out if someone has failed at that business idea and ask them where it went wrong to see if you can navigate around those issues. Find a great course online for someone to do this. I have a great course that I've studied in how to do it that I'll share with you, so please include me on this process.

- But don't fart around too long on the theory of the whole business. Get a customer quickly. Someone that actually pays you, versus someone that *says* they'll pay. There's a big difference in that.

- Reassess and see if you're enjoying doing this periodically. It will probably be a lot different than you expect, and you'll be able to determine if it's not what you want. Don't be afraid to burn it down, or better yet, sell it.

Notes, thoughts, and intentions.

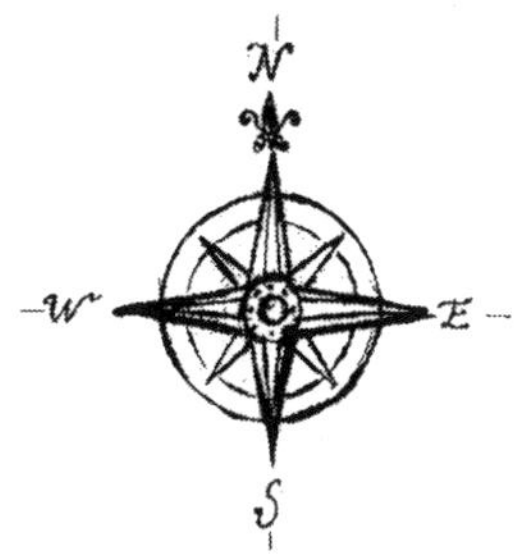

51. Learn How to Get ANY Job You Want.

Okay, my dear wonderful, sweet and perfect-in-all-ways children!

I think I say this about nearly every chapter, but I'm very excited to pass this on to you because it's not something that most schools/parents/people will ever teach you. But this is information that can be invaluable and change the quality of your life tremendously, and that is the incredibly useful skill of getting any job that you might desire.

I feel particularly good about giving you this advice because I have been hired for every job that I've ever applied for with the exception of one where the person was not actually hiring at the time. I've gotten a job at a bookstore using this. I got a job selling computers at college with this method (where I wasn't entirely qualified, but it paid a lot better than the bookstore job). I've gotten into a prestigious incubator sponsored by 3M Corporation. That's just to name a few. But I'm going to make it even better by going further and deeper.

Let's get started by looking at the conventional wisdom of getting a job. How do most people do it? They just look for places that have positions available, that are open right now. They look through the job postings on Craigslist, the job sites and newspaper classifieds to find the places that are hiring for positions right *now*.

They generally find several places that might be attractive, or at least not awful, and then submit a standard resume to those places. That resume goes in a stack of dozens or maybe even hundreds of other applicants that are looking for the same job.

Then, they wait. Maybe they get a call, but more often they don't and then the moaning, wailing, and crying from not getting the position that they'd be perfect for commences.

Conventional wisdom equals conventional results.

The way that I'm about to teach you is different. In fact, it's vastly different than the ways you may have heard about before through more conventional sources. These people all follow the standards set forth by society without knowing that those standards should only apply when they serve you (and don't hurt others). Be warned: you may feel uncomfortable doing this. That's good. Remember that a lot of time discomfort leads to growth.

Some of the excuses for not doing what I tell you:

- It's not my personality!
- Or this is not how I do things!
- What will they THINK?
- What if it doesn't work?

My response to that:

- You want to show them your absolute best.
- You want to secure an interview with them.

To accomplish those, my advice is to do something to stand out and get their attention!

To explain why I advise this, let's get to the psychology of the person that is hiring.

As a business owner myself, I know this thought process very well. I've sat across the table from literally hundreds of job applicants looking to work with our company.

I can tell you without a doubt the thing that employers are looking for the most is the best person for the position. That special someone that can do the job extremely well, earn a lot of money for the enterprise, or that can take problems off of the owner's plate.

If you are working with a Human Resources type person, they are looking for you to make them look good for hiring the right person.

Most résumés aren't designed this way at all. They just show the chronology of the applicant, or where they went to school, and don't delve at all into showing creativity, problem-solving, or even what you're like as a person. They're two-dimensional, outdated forms that don't show the true person at all. They completely fail the mark. The only reason standard résumés exist is the stubborn groupthink that still says, "this is how it's always been done."

Get rid of that ordinary thinking! It is incumbent on you to show them that you're the right person, and to get your foot in the door at least for an interview. I think that this method will pretty much guarantee that. So, suspend some of your doubts long enough for me to show you a much better way to go about getting every job you'd like.

For starters I want you to look for the perfect position for you. Something that you really enjoy and that you could give your heart, time, soul, and passion to each and every day. That position may be something that you think is out of your reach, but the absolute worst thing that can happen is they can say no. Then you'll end up at the same spot that you started: trying to go the conventional route.

This can involve some research, like asking friends what they do. I'd recommend taking a look at the piece of advice on finding the magic spot in your work (in this very section). Find a position you are passionate about, that you're good at, and that can pay you what you'd like to earn for it. When you're able to find a position, or positions, that suit all three of those, then you found the place where you're going to want to apply. Seriously, why not apply for the perfect position? When you do this, you're already doing something a lot different than what most people do.

After finding the perfect position for your unique set of skills: look for the company that can provide it. Find a place where you think you would grow as a person and where your skills will be enhanced. A place that can move you along in life! My mentor, Jim Rohn says, "Who you become is more important than what you get at a particular position." So find a place where you can learn and become better.

The principle we want to use for this is a sniper shot versus a shotgun blast. Most people submit résumés to a lot of different places and just do a typical résumé. The sniper shot I'd suggest means finding one or two places that you'd be *really* interested in, and then go deep on those. Try everything within your power to get one of those positions versus haphazardly trying to get interviews with a whole bunch of places. Rather than going an inch deep and a mile wide, you want to go an inch wide and a mile deep with it.

This is your life! Your career and your job are very important, and time is finite. You don't want to waste it on going to a dead-end job that you don't enjoy. Spending Monday through Friday in misery and waiting for the weekend is no way to live your life.

It all starts with this: finding the right job.

Once you find it, you need to find the right person to talk to; the person that actually does the hiring. You want the one that can say, "yes."

Some people may worry about stepping on toes or going over someone's head, but again, the principle is that you want the person that can say yes to hiring you. That's the person you need to impress. You don't want the gatekeeper to be able to turn you down. Go for the top and impress them. It's much easier to do that than it is to get someone lower on the totem pole to sell you to their boss.

Something else I want to add here is the concept of shadowing. Read the advice on this coming up and you may even be able to get the job you crave without going through all of this. That's usually the next step after finding your magic spot. Go ahead and find that chapter, and dog-ear it to read next. The cool thing about shadowing is that you can even ask the person hiring exactly how they would like to be approached about working with them.

After finding your magic spot, finding the person that can say, "yes," and possibly shadowing; it's time for the "Unrésumé," or the "Shock and Awe Package."

The unrésumé is a way to apply for a job that is completely different than the standard résumé. It's something that stands out, that is memorable, and you'll probably want to make it professional, too.

It's something that arrives in a method that is very memorable. Examples of this could be if you are applying for a position with an airline company to place your résumé on the wings of a to scale model of one of their planes. Or a thing easily done now—a professional video of you, the services you offer, testimonials, people giving you glowing references, and set to music. Make it a video titled, "The Perfect Candidate for _____ ." Something like that takes a little bit of effort, but it's still pretty easy. Despite it being easy, no one is doing it.

One of the ones that I have actually used in the past: a book on why I was the perfect guy to work at Southwest Airlines. It contained my qualifications, my philosophies, why I wanted this particular position, and I made the book look like the actual book of the CEO of Southwest Airlines. The book was called "Nuts!" and my résumé book was called "Nuts, Too!" The cover picture was me doing the exact same pose as the CEO on his book, complete with a fake tattoo.

This is the type of thing that will get your foot in the door!

Some may shake their heads, or you may think that this is not "you," but I guarantee if you do something that's good, that's done professionally like this, then you're going to get an audience with the person that can hire you. That's what the "unrésumé" is all about. We'll talk specifics on it in *Advice in Practice*, but I hope you're getting the idea on this.

The "Shock and Awe Package" is a marketing tactic I learned from a fellow named Dan Kennedy. It's a preponderance of information delivered in a conspicuous fashion to help a decision. In marketing, it's generally sales and marketing material. An example would be something that I used to do in real estate called "Fort Hood-In-a-Box," which I mailed to potential buyers moving to our area. I put real estate magazines, a big buyer package, a local phone book (this was before the internet was really prevalent), local newspapers, information from the chamber of commerce, maps, and glowing reviews of me. It was delivered in a big 5-pound box. It was designed to impress and blow away any insignificant thing that they got from any other Realtor.

For the purposes of your job hunt, it could be to include a regular résumé, a bound portfolio, a video player with a video loaded up that has video testimonials of your former bosses saying wonderful things about you, and a sticky note saying "Play Me." I'd also include research that you've done on the company, and very specifically how you can help them. It's very much like an unrésumé. Its job is to differentiate you from any of the many dozens of people seeking the same position as you. Used well, it can get your foot into any door. So, think about using this when it comes to getting your job.

So, you've decided what position you want, decided who can say yes, and approached them with an *Unrésumé* or *Shock and Awe Package* that gets you in front of them. Next, it's time for the "Mafia Offer." That's a principle I learned from my friends Joe Polish and Dean Jackson from their I Love Marketing podcast. A *Mafia Offer* is an offer that you can't refuse á la the *Godfather* movies.

An example of a mafia offer would be that you work for free for a certain length of time. Maybe two weeks, or a month. Or it could be that you give them a money back guarantee that if they're not completely thrilled with your work, that you will literally pay them back all of the salary that they paid you.

Maybe this sounds kind of crazy, but often you won't have to do it. They are thinking that if you go through this much effort to get the position, then they will want you to work with you. Some laws may actually prevent you from working for free, but you can offer to intern for free in order to get experience.

The idea is to show just how far you'll go to work with them. You just want to make sure it's a place that you really like and you really enjoy. One of the things I've done in the past is to send a fork in a FedEx package after an interview with a note saying, "I want this so much I can taste it!" I got this from another book that I read called *Real World 101*, which is a somewhat obscure book by James Calano and Jeff Salzman. They also introduced me to the concept of the unrésumé. I love this book!

Finally, after doing all of this and it turns out that they're not hiring, you can get a referral to find someone else that might be hiring for the same position. They're probably going to respect your hustle, creativity, and passion. You've made an impression, and chances are that they will want to help you if you've done all of this. They can help you get your foot in the door at other places. Don't discount this idea, as it could change your life.

This is how you do it. You take a different approach, you target the right place, and overwhelm them with evidence that you are the best person for the position. You don't sit around and wait for the traditional approaches to work. In fact, if a company does not appreciate the effort and creativity involved in this method, I'd think seriously about whether or not you'd like to work with them at all.

Go forth and prosper kids. I friggin' love you.

Advice in Practice

- Journal about what you enjoy, what you're good at and what you're passionate about regarding a career and job position. Reread the section on finding the magic spot in this advice book (here in the mind section) and really give that a lot of consideration about the types of places that you would like to work.

- Consider the company and what you become from working there. Do your research on the different places and find out everything that's on the Internet. See if you can interview a few people that work there using the shadowing technique in this book. Make sure that this is a place that you'd really like to work. Narrow those down to just a few places that seem to be the perfect job rather than the many places that are just a place to work.

- Study some folks that have done this the right way. It's amazing to me that this approach is still so rare that when people do it right it's still a really big deal. Here's one that's fantastic: look up www.Nina4AirBnB.com, or if the site is down for some reason, just Google "the perfect résumé for AirBnB" and read the multitude of articles about what she did. Kids, that should be your standard and not something so rare. You can do work like this, or even better than this (she could've put video of herself on it, a highlight reel of testimonials from friends and previous employers, etc.). Learn, adapt, and do it, sweethearts!

- Do your idea lists, make them really out there, and don't be afraid to think big. Make your idea lists of the jobs that you will enjoy. Then I'd suggest doing a second or third that are completely different without referring to your first one. Something that's in your soul will probably repeat itself and come back on the list a few times.

- Trust the siren call of the idea for the job that appeals to you most. The one that strikes a chord in your soul. The one that you have to follow! This is the job that you want. So when you find it, gather as much information as you can. Make the visit, do some reconnaissance, and try to shadow the right person using the advice that I've given you.

- Next do the shock and awe and unrésumé brainstorm in an epic idea list. Do one of at least ten ways that you can approach them to show that you're different. That you are giving them something that's new, innovative, and shows that you are the perfect person to work for them. It's good to do it professionally. Check spelling, get a second pair of eyes on it (as long as they're not energy vampires that "poo poo" what you're doing). Get it right but remember that imperfect action is so much better than never doing it at all. Let's get after it!

- Brainstorm your mafia offer, think about it, and get it ready for your interview when you have the chance to interview with it. Prepare your offer on paper as a marketing piece to leave with them. This is especially important if they are interviewing others.

- The last piece of the advice in practice is to try this! Actually do it. See the results and see what it gets you. If it doesn't work, don't sweat it. You've learned and now you can adapt, iterate, and get better. Your efforts will set you apart from others.

I hope that this is helpful. I love you so much. I appreciate you and I hope that you will take my advice on this. It can mean a very big difference in your life. I love you SO much and can't wait to hear about you doing this.

Notes, thoughts, and intentions.

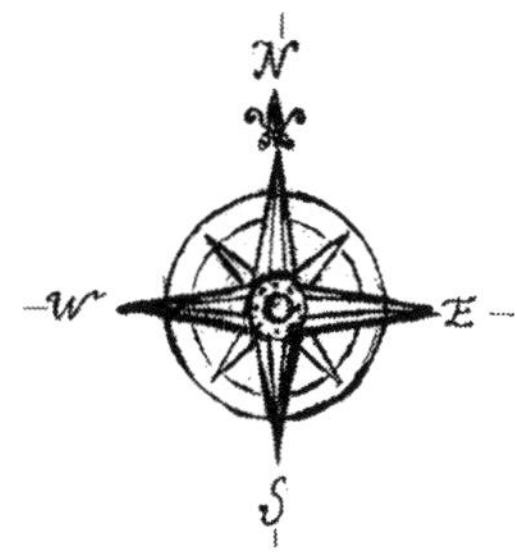

52. Learn the Life Altering Ability of SELLING.

Make sure at least one of your jobs as you go through school involves selling. It's one of the best skills you can ever cultivate. If you become good at selling, you'll always be employable no matter where you live. You don't have to make it a career, just know how to do it.

Selling is one of the most essential skills that you can develop. It's influence. It's persuasion. It's cooperation. It's the ability to get what you want, hopefully in a way that helps others, as well. A lot of people have this horrible notion that selling is something that's disdainful. That it's just annoying, high-pressured badgering. That's obviously not what I'm talking about with this. In fact, here's the definition of selling that I like the most, from my friend Dan Sullivan:

Selling: Getting people intellectually engaged in a future result that's GOOD for THEM and getting them to emotionally commit to take action to achieve that result.

I like that "good for them" part of the definition. That's the difference between good and evil. And also, if you like what you're selling, you'll be happy. If you don't then you'll be miserable, so be careful what you're selling, too.

Now, you know that I owned a real estate company and have been a realtor for over twenty years. I've done a lot of selling, and have been pretty successful at it, but it actually started while I was in college working at the Southwestern Company selling books door-to-door for 80 hours a week. That was extremely hard (I'm pretty sure I mention that elsewhere in the book, as it was pretty formative for me). I'm convinced that getting good at selling changed my life in a really profound way. It's also led to my love of marketing, which is selling to the masses.

Selling is basically getting someone to agree with you. Mandy, you were an excellent debater. It's a little like that, and just adding the actual purchasing decision on top of it. So, if you're trying to get a job, or get someone to join you in the business, or obviously trying to get someone to purchase your product or service. . . it's all selling. Even getting Alec to clean the living room yesterday was a bit of a sales job for me. It's used in every aspect of life.

Here are some of the things that selling has taught me:

1) No one cares about what you're doing or selling until you show them why they should care. Selling taught me how to move someone from total ignorance to desire for what you're doing. It's the use of ideas to persuade.

2) You will never get everyone to buy. It's obvious when I say it like this, but we're all different. We have different motivators, priorities, and resources. One size will never fit all. That's important to keep in mind, because otherwise you can take it personally when people don't buy into what you're doing. Which leads to the next thing to learn . . .

3) Don't take it personally. Some will, some won't. So what? Next. I know that I've mentioned this in this book, but one of my big philosophies that has helped with life is, "release the result." That is, do the best you can and don't worry as much about the outcome (what you can't control) as you do about the effort and thought going into a situation. If you've done your best, you're acting with integrity, and it still doesn't work. . . that's okay.

4) Keep going. Sometimes it's just percentages. There will be people that buy into what you're selling, too. Hopefully, a large percentage. Get to that next person. Don't let the no's keep you from finding the next yes.

Persistence is a grand thing. Persistence with adjustments, improvements, and optimizations is a divine thing. It's a parable for life. You work at getting good. You train and learn, then you get to go out and attempt that thing. You'll get knocked down, you'll get beat up, but you will have triumphs and high points, too. It's being able to get up after you're down that is the real treasure in life. Who you become is more important than what you get, sweethearts.

So, how do you get good at selling? Put yourself in a position to sell. Learn the craft. Get in front of real people and actually do it.

A few things I'll tell you about selling:

It's all about them. If you don't make it about your client/customer, they'll never care about what it is that you do. The word "I" needs to be limited whenever you sell.

Asking questions is so much more important than making statements. Everyone thinks that selling is smoothly saying the right things, when it's much more of a detective-type uncovering process. What are they doing now? What are the problems/challenges with this? If I had a way to eliminate that problem/challenge that made sense to you, would you be interested in that?

Comfortable beats high pressure every time. I think that high pressure selling that forces you to make a quick decision is a bit slimy at best, and kind of evil at worst. One of the things I always like to do (I learned this while selling books) is to give the prospect an out if they're not interested. "Hey, if you like this I'll show you how to get it. If not, that's completely okay, and there won't be any hard feelings." I usually followed that up with rubbing my belly and saying, "obviously, I'm going to eat anyway." That makes it easy for them to say yes, and saves you both some heartache if it is actually a no. When they feel that, and it's genuine, their force field will drop and you'll be able to have an authentic conversation.

Honesty is always best. If you're not honest then you will have a hard time rationalizing what you're doing every day. This is so much more important than whatever it is that you're selling. It goes along with the Biblical principle, "What do you benefit if you gain the world, but lose your own soul?" You're good, I know you are, so I don't need to harp on this, but if you're ever involved in selling something that's not good for the clients, then leave that position. Lastly, people have a built in BS detector, and you won't have success. Unless you're a psychopath, of course.

Finally, I believe that the most important trait of a world-class sales professional is compassion. Here is the definition of compassion (from the Greater Good at Berkeley):

> ***"Compassion literally means "to suffer together." Among emotion researchers, it is defined as the feeling that arises when you are confronted with another's suffering and feel motivated to relieve that suffering."***

If you see your customer, potential client, or someone that you need to bring to your way of thinking as someone who is suffering without what you have. . . and you feel motivated to help them and serve them, then that is the highest form of sales. Having those thoughts and feelings in your heart will help to be successful in sales.

Let me ask you, does that make sense? Can you see the importance of selling? Do you see why the lessons are important? Do the tips and insights into how to do it make sense?

I hope so. Please consider that and learn the art of selling.

Advice in Practice:

- Watch the YouTube video from my good friend, Joe Polish called, Is Selling Evil? Just Google it and it's the first thing that pops up. It's pretty great!

- When getting a job, or starting a business, seek the opportunity to sell. Even if it scares you. In fact, especially if it scares you. If you already have a job, and there is a chance to get more involved in selling, take it! Mandy, I know when you work at Starbucks, you've told me that you'll sometimes sell people on the new drink that you think they'll like. That makes me happy. That experience is wonderful. You don't need to keep the job forever, but take the skills! Absorb them and keep the selling as a tool in your toolbox that you can use at any time. I know that I'll always have a way to make a living, because I can sell. That's a comforting feeling and allows me to have a lot more freedom in the things that I try.

- Read the book, *The Greatest Salesman in the World*, by Og Mandino. Don't you roll your eyes at me! It's a classic. It's also short, so you'll be done quickly, and it can leave you changed. It's a must if you're getting started in the sales field! It is a lot more about the psychology of selling and directing your self-talk (this too shall pass) than about the mechanics of it.

- Another book to read is *Influence*, by Dr. Robert Cialdini. Coincidentally, when searching for great resources for this section, I came across the video, *The Science of Persuasion*, which featured truths from Robert Cialdini and Steve Martin. I started watching (it has more than 8,400,000 views), and then I realized that it WAS Robert Cialdini speaking in the video. He's the foremost psychologist in the world as it pertains to selling, influence, and persuasion. So, read the book (I have a copy if you'd like it), and/or watch this video. It's excellent. I also got to meet and eat lunch with the good doctor last year. I say that for no other reason than to brag.

Notes, thoughts, and intentions.

53. Learn the Sweet Art and Science of MARKETING.

Big piece of advice here; and—surprise, surprise!—it's not taught much in schools, even in business schools, and even in marketing classes.

I think y'all know, but marketing was my major when I went to Texas A&M. I thought I would like it, and I did. However, the real world tactical and practical knowledge on marketing just wasn't taught. I literally graduated without having to write a sales letter, make a sales call, or design an ad that made people want to pick up their phone or directly respond! To me, that's amazing, but having talked with some of my marketing friends, it's the norm rather than the exception.

I don't mean to impugn an entire profession, and actually my favorite professor in school taught marketing, but it was a lot of theory, the five P's (Price, Product, Place, People, and Promotion), and things like benchmarking and focus groups.

But I never got to learn the difference between direct-response marketing and institutional advertising, or to learn the teachings of Jay Abraham or my friend Joe Polish until I was a struggling realtor with a useless degree. I had to learn on my own what makes people buy and how to design a service or product around that decision.

I had a horrible year in real estate in 1999. It was my worst year by far; I sold fifteen homes and was having a real career crisis. Do I continue in this business or try to work in the airline industry for Southwest airlines (a company that I always admired)? I actually applied for Southwest (using the résumé advice I teach you in the book) and was offered a job, but it paid too little to move our soon-to-be family to Dallas for that.

Instead, I came across some audiotapes in the real estate office that my mom was managing. I asked if I could listen to them and was told that I could, as long as I did so at the office and didn't remove them. I did that and spent hours upon hours learning how some of the top guns in real estate plied their trade. They talked about marketing in ways that I'd never even thought about and opened my eyes to a new way of doing things. I took so many notes, and I was excited about business again! I got to try out new ideas, see how they worked, and adjust to do new things.

These tapes introduced me to Jay Abraham, a marketing mastermind that taught real-life usable philosophies like the strategy of preeminence (where you always do what's right for the client, and any decision you face is run through that filter), or the principle that people are silently begging to be led. I learned how to write a real ad, the importance of headlines, and how a difference in copy can make one ad result in one sale, and another result in one hundred times that. It was eye-opening, humbling, and empowering to learn all of this. I fell in love with the art and science of it all, and started implementing it into my business.

The year after the horrible, no good, very bad fifteen transactions I had over eighty sales! That nearly doubled again the next year. I listened in on mastermind tapes of the people that were killing it in the industry and shadowed a top producer in New Mexico (that's detailed in the advice on the power of shadowing).

Learning marketing had a huge and profound impact on my life forever, and I'm encouraging you to learn it, too.

You see, any business has two parts: producing the good or service and getting people to buy the good or service. Ortho offices, veterinarians, mortgage brokers, home builders, book writers. . . whatever it is, they will have to actually sell what they do to others.

That's why marketing is so important. If you can learn marketing, you can write your own ticket in any industry at all. If you can get people to know, like, trust, and buy your product or service, you will always have a usable skill. It's also different than just selling. It's getting the people in front of you to sell to. I was a great salesman even when I sold those fifteen houses that year, but I didn't get in front of enough people to make the sale. That's why this skill is so important.

So, learn marketing. Especially if you take my advice on owning or running a business at some point. Getting and keeping customers is the main function of any business, and you've just got to know how to do it somewhat. It's truly imperative.

By the way, marketing is so much more than just advertising. Ads are a part of marketing, but just a part. The design, the thought, the words that are said, the look and feel of a service, the follow-up after a sale, the planning and structure of a business, and learning what the lifetime value of a client is: all of it is marketing. It's anything and everything involved in making a decision to buy something. It's all so important and can be lots of fun. That's my favorite part of business.

Really learning this science (and not depending on someone else to do it for you) can and will make the difference between you being professionally poor or wildly successful, yet it's rarely ever taught the right way. I'm asking for you to be different and to learn this art. Your life will be richly blessed for doing that, and I'm all for your life being improved. Because I've got love in my heart for you, but I bet you knew that.

Advice in Practice:

- Get out a journal and write out how your life could and would be improved when you learn the art of marketing. Could you have more security or freedom if you were able to earn more money? Would it mean a better life, potentially, for your kids or your family? Could it make you irreplaceable in your job for someone else? Get clear on why it would be good for you to learn these skills.

- Listen to some good marketing material. My favorite? The podcast *I Love Marketing*, with my friends Joe Polish and Dean Jackson. They taught me so much like, "canning and cloning" yourself and your sales efforts, thinking about the lifetime value of a client, the power of recorded messages, free informational products, the Mafia offer, the nine-word email, the principle of more cheese and less whiskers . . . and a lot more. Listening to these guys is light-years better than getting a college degree in marketing. I'm not exaggerating. Go listen to the first several episodes (they're right at 300 as I'm writing this!) and get a feel for how real marketers do things.

- Read a few books on the subject. My favorites are *Joe's Marketing Book*, by Joe Polish which is just about to released (I got an advance copy because I'm cool like that), and *Getting Everything You Can Out of All That You've Got*, by Jay Abraham (who I've met and who helped us out with JoeVolunteer), and *The Ultimate Marketing Plan*, by Dan Kennedy (who also has a series of books called No BS that are excellent). Study them up and down and look for ways that you can apply them to the business that you're doing. Write notes in them, and most importantly take action where you can to improve your business and life through these.

- Shadow someone killing it in your industry. Pay special attention to how they do marketing. Ask them how they're getting results and see if you can emulate them (not blatantly ripping them off, but adding your own flair and personalizing it) in what you're doing in your own marketing. Go read the section in this book on the power of shadowing to get help in this.

- Join a business mastermind of exceptional marketing people. I like to recommend Joe Polish's *Genius Network*, but it's pricey and out of reach for most people (but, oh so worth it--it's worth a Google!). There are also many free Facebook groups, local marketing, and internet marketing groups in cities near you. Check out Meetup.com for business and marketing groups. Just getting around the right people can change your life for the better.

- Scour YouTube for some of the people that I've mentioned above, and really listen to them. They'll also name a lot of resources to explore which I'd highly recommend paying attention to.

- Take some online courses. I like Joe Polish's *Piranha Marketing*" from Nightingale/Conant, and if you're advertising on Facebook I recommend my buddy Nicholas Kusmich's courses without reservation.

- Talk to your dad about marketing. Ask some questions. Bat around some ideas. See what I'm listening to and watching these days! I'll talk marketing all day long with you!

Notes, thoughts, and intentions.

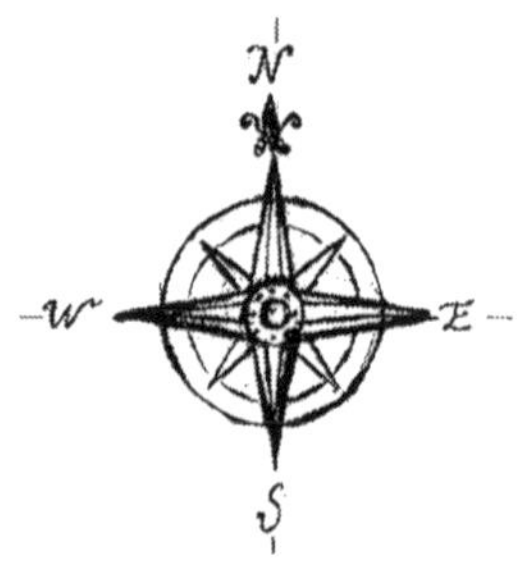

54. Do More Than You're Paid to Do.

This piece of advice seems a little cliché, and it's something that a daddy would say, but it still needs to be said.

When it comes time to work, you'll have a choice: get away with doing as little as possible or going above and beyond while doing more than you are paid to do.

This is a really big deal, and a lot of people choose the easier route thinking that's the best, but it never is. My view on this is maybe a little stark: if you do less than you can or should while you're at work (when someone else is paying you to be "on the clock," anyway) then you're stealing from them. Maybe not in the same sense of actually taking things home that you're not supposed to take, but it's nearly the same in my eyes. You've got an agreement and you should honor it.

The norm of everyday? Most people do just enough not to get fired. Now, it's also probably true that they get paid just enough that they don't leave, but that doesn't make slacking off at the job morally right.

You can slack off, especially when you're not being checked in on often. You will undoubtedly feel that you're not paid enough at times. You will probably do quite a bit more than your coworkers, some of whom may get paid more than you do even if you do slack off, but you'll know if you're doing what you should.

When you make that choice, choose carefully. Doing your best will truly determine the quality of your life. If you do more than you are paid to do, then blessings of all types will come your way. Your bosses or customers will eventually reward you appropriately. Do work that makes you proud.

You can always spot that one person that's just killing it at work. They're smiling. They're encouraging others. They laugh and joke with customers, the boss always counts on them . . . and you know what? Good things will happen to that person, even if it's at a different job. It will always be rewarded even if it takes a while.

[Daddy's Note: I'm writing this while I'm at your work, Mandy, and I'm watching you do exactly what I'm preaching in this advice. Wow. Seeing you serve your customers, and just out-hustling everyone else at the job is just so . . . what's the word? Gratifying? It just makes me so very proud. I love how responsible you are, how seriously you take it, the fact that you're smiling. It's just so wonderful!]

Advice in Action:

- Write an idea list of how you can serve your customers/clients/owners better, and start implementing a few of those ideas. What do they want? How can you over-deliver on your service? If you really want to turbo-charge this, give a copy of this list to the management/owners of the place. That will put you on the map and doing something like this is pretty easy. . . and so uncommon.

- Think about the opportunity that you have to serve other people, and actively appreciate that. You have a chance to make lives better through what you do, even if it's in a small way. You play a part in their life, and that's a wonderful opportunity. Write out why you're grateful for what you do as a profession. Read it when you're not "feeling" it that day.

- Benchmark. That is, look at how others are doing their job, especially if they're doing it better than you think you are. See what they're doing right. Ask them to help you get better and see if you can add to what they're doing to make it even better.

This is a short piece of advice, but truly getting it will add so much to your life. I love you so much, my sweethearts.

Notes, thoughts, and intentions.

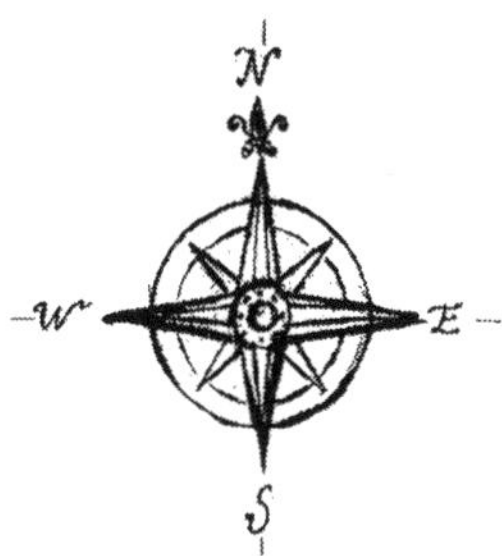

55. Realize That Colleges and Universities Don't Give You What You Need.

We've come to the idea of college and honestly, I have very mixed emotions about it.

The knee-jerk reaction of, "go to school, get good grades, get a nice secure job," is no longer the mantra of anyone looking to do extraordinary things in their life.

Let me explain a few things about college that you've probably heard me say before:

- It does not prepare you for the real world.
- Almost everything you learn there will be worthless; especially if they're still using the 'ole (pretty ridiculous) "memorize facts and regurgitate them for a test" rigmarole. That's pretty much pointless. There is, however, something to be learned from the process of learning how to 'game' the system and showing persistence in getting it done.

- Unless you're getting a degree in law, medicine, or engineering (or something similar), college is not *needed*.

I say this as someone that went to college, understands it, and generally thinks that the classes involved are a waste of time.

HOWEVER...

College can be useful. As of this time, I'm still generally recommending that you go for a few reasons. Namely, it expands your options. I love options for my kids. I want you to have the most options possible. I want you to do absolutely anything that you want to do, and college can still (sometimes) get your foot in the door of a place where you'd want to work. A place where you agree with what they do, feel a duty to serve in their mission, and where you become an even better person by being there.

Also, it's sort of a halfway house. You get to learn about being out on your own for a bit, while not being completely on your own. I don't know if most human beings are really ready to be on their own at eighteen years old. This gives you an enormous taste of freedom while still having a safe support structure. The learning you are doing at college is mainly about how to begin to live on your own, make your decisions sans parents, and interacting with your new friends. Seriously, learning to make friends, develop your daily schedule, and how to approach your studying and classes ("gaming the system" like I mentioned before) is what you learn in college.

Let me be clear on this again, though. College does not prepare you for the vocation that you're trying to attain. Literally a week or two of shadowing someone that's really doing what you want to do can be more effective than years in a classroom.

If you're going to go to college, this is how you maximize your experience:

- Have a side hustle that's "real world." Build a business on the side. Have a part time job in a field that you love; work and learn aside from your classes. Follow the instructions on *Finding the Magic Spot* advice on careers while you're still in college. If you find a professor or teacher that's actually done something outside of the hallowed halls of knowledge, seek their experience and find out what you should really be doing.

- It's the habits that you develop during this time that are more valuable than any classroom knowledge you'll learn. Remember that it's not the facts that you memorize that are important. Instead it's the fact that you memorized, that you had the perseverance to study, to set up your schedule for success, and that you did not party when it was time to buckle down and learn. It's the mental (and physical) fortitude of going to class and paying attention when you're dead tired from working the night before at your job.

- Explore different careers or areas of knowledge you might like! Don't settle on just one focused area of something you might like. No! Do what I mentioned elsewhere about finding some people that are doing something similar to the career or profession you think you like and learn from them! Pick their brains, see if you can shadow them, and get a real taste of that career. I talk about that elsewhere, but always, always keep that in mind.

- Never substitute real learning with classroom learning. Mark Twain (or Grant Allen) famously said, "Don't let school interfere with your education." So many people think they're done when they walk across the stage to graduate. No, no, NO! You need to fall in love with learning, not education. So, taking courses outside of college (many of them free) on areas that you really enjoy is so much more important than cramming for a test in a class you were forced to take. Listen to podcasts. Go to seminars. Read books throughout your life. Listen to Audible. I think all of these are actually more important than the facts you're forced to memorize in school.

- Have fun. Seriously. Don't go off the deep end and start drinking to excess but take the time to truly savor this moment in your life. Soon, you'll have a lot more responsibility and probably a family. While that doesn't *have* to limit your adventures in life, sometimes it will. So, drink deeply from the entire experience. Don't freak out over grades too much, and certainly don't get caught in the trap, as many people do, of thinking that college and grades are real life. If you get a chance to travel as part of your schooling, or to take an internship that gives you school credit? Jump on that.

- Don't go into debt over school. Remember what I said about options above? Debt reduces options. It's a millstone around the neck of freedom. So, work and earn some of your school costs. Get Mom and Dad to pay for a lot of it. Don't even be afraid to take a semester or two off to "earn your learn," where you make sure you can come back, but work for a while to sock away money to pay for your schooling. In fact, that experience would be far more valuable than anything you learn in the classroom.

Here is the major principle of college (and jobs you take, businesses you start, etc.): *Who you become is more important than what you get out of it*. If you decide to go to college, I want you to become a better person when you finish than you were when you first entered school.

So, once you start, think very carefully about quitting. I really don't want giving up to be part of your DNA, unless the options on the other side are so much more valuable. Bill Gates, Mark Zuckerberg, Michael Dell, Steve Jobs . . . all of these people quit college, but they're exceptions and all had other things that they wanted to do, and businesses built on the side that were more valuable than the jobs they could have gotten after going to college. It can still be a choice, but it needs to be a very solid trapeze you're grabbing to let go of the previous one. Oh, and if you leave, don't burn the bridge. See if you can come back if things don't work out. The principle of keeping options open is always important.

The last thing I'll say about this now is to listen to your own guiding voice. You do not have to go to college if it's not in your heart. Thinking about it now, I would've appreciated traveling around the world and starting a business more than school, but I did meet your mom there, so things would've been very different had I done something else. What you think, and your feelings on this are more important than anyone else's. Also, I think your intuition is guided by a much more powerful force and is rarely, if ever, wrong. So, take all of this advice with a grain of salt and do what is in your soul to do.

I promise to love you, regardless!

***One last note: I see a lot of people and friends who go back to school later in life after working many years. This is usually met with a lot of back slapping and people saying, "congratulations," and the like. I usually hate this course of action. The only exceptions are if you have to get an advanced degree to go into a different profession. Some members of our family have done that to go into Speech Pathology, and I can understand that, but to think that going to school is a magic pill that will suddenly lead to increased self-worth, and doors that magically open everywhere is misguided. You can nearly always figure out a way to get what you want without all of the time and added expense of going back to school. Being resourceful is always more important than having book knowledge.

Advice in Practice:

- Read *Unschooling Rules*, which goes over the actual reasons for learning, and is a completely different paradigm than the traditional, "sit down, shut up, and do exactly what we say," model of education. Also, this is a reason you're out of the public schools now.

- Read James Altucher's Report, *50 Alternatives to College*. You can Google it and read it as an e-Book or order it from Amazon for $4.95. (It's actually *40 Alternatives to College* on Amazon). This is required reading for you before going to school. I want you to examine all your choices!

- If you do decide to go to college, treat it as a business decision. Do not go to an expensive private school without good reason. The return on investment for a private school versus a much cheaper state school is generally a whole lot lower, even if it sounds more prestigious. No one will care about your degree after you have your first job/career experience and can show real world results over classroom grades!

- Read *The Miracle Morning for College Students*, by Hal Elrod, Natalie Janje, and Honoree Carter for great tips on what to do if you're in college. Mandy, it made me so happy to see that you're already reading that. You should be proud of yourself!

- Before you go to college, declare a major, or decide what you want to study, really think about what you might want to do and go find people that are doing it. I mentioned it in other pieces of advice in this book, but many people spend a lot of years studying for a career that they end up hating. Do not be one of these people. They do it because they don't have this advice. You do! Use it!

Notes, thoughts, and intentions.

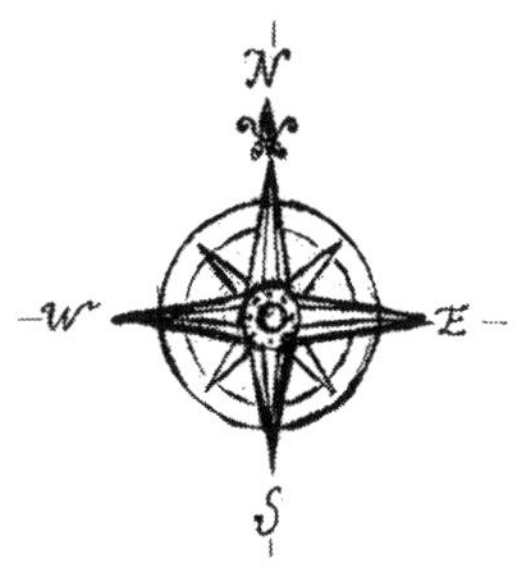

56. Systematize Everything in Your Life.

Systems will set you free: Make your life systematic and automate everything that you can.

"You must methodize your life. God created routine, the Sun shines until dusk and the stars shine until dawn." — Peremahansa Yogananda

Getting into this chapter will be a lot of fun. I will tell you just a little bit about my story and how this can make a difference to you. Typically, I'm pretty haphazard in some of the things that I do. As a kid, and most of my adulthood, I was disorganized with many things and lost a whole lot of other things. I did not systematize things in my life.

But I have since seen the light. I try and make many things in my life the same and systematize them, so that I can improvise and concentrate on the important things. This has made a pretty big difference in my life. Here are some personal examples of how I systematize and automate things in my life:

Right now, I do the same morning routine almost every day. I do the miracle morning routine in the same order. I read something that's inspirational for a good 5-10 minutes (right now it's, *The Daily Stoic* by Ryan Holiday). Then, I meditate for 10-20 minutes. Following that, I will go on a 10-20 minute "primal" walk to include some sprinting. Lastly, I journal for 10 minutes. When I've finished all of that, then I plan my day. Or, as I like to call it, I script my perfect day.

That's the same every morning. So, I don't have to think about it each day. It starts off my day in a great way. Something else I do is wear a "uniform" every day. My uniform is the same exact color shirt, the same shorts, and the same shoes. Like Steve Jobs and Mark Zuckerberg, whom I obviously relate to, hah. It gives me less to think about every day, so that I can spend more time on the important things. It's actually kind of funny how happy this practice makes me.

You have probably noticed this, but I usually eat the same things every day. For the mornings I like to have a green shake, for lunch I've eaten lunch at Chipotle most days for many years now, and then at night, I tend to have a lean protein and vegetable. Now some people hate doing the same thing, but it's just what I do. I think it's made my life a little easier.

I remove myself as a bottleneck and I try to live on an ideal schedule, which I discussed in the introduction of this book. Also, when I write notes, when I listen to things and record things, I keep them all in one place using Evernote. Little systems like this have made a really big difference in my personal life.

Right now, I'm also in the process of automating all of my finances so all of the bills that need to be paid will be paid on one credit card. Then that credit card is paid off every month, so rather than paying 10-20 bills I only pay one. It's automatically billed to a credit card that can be checked. My time spent paying bills every month is less than 10 minutes a month versus having to take more than an hour every month previously.

Now, let's get to you, and why something like this is important.

There is a concept called decision fatigue. I don't remember exactly where I first heard this, but it's an excellent concept that rings true. If you can imagine your willpower every day as a gas tank, and each moment of decision (like deciding what to wear each day, deciding what you're going to eat for lunch, or deciding who the next person is to talk to on your job) will burn some of your gas.

If you have to exercise discipline in a moment, your gas tank will be depleted even more rapidly. So, if you're on a diet and someone puts a big piece of cake in front of you that you really like, turning away that cake and deciding against it will deplete your fuel tank a lot faster. That is why at the end of a really hectic, busy, or tough day it's a lot harder to resist something you should.

You're more likely to pull into the drive-through at a fast food place while you're trying to eat healthy, or you'll skip a workout that you're supposed to do. Your decision-making ability is compromised when your mental gas tank is empty.

That's why making your day as systematic as possible, to eliminate those decisions, can make your days a lot better. You eliminate the decisions you don't need to make daily and save your gas and willpower for the important things.

The other thing is that every minute that you're not making those decisions, paying those bills, or deciding what to wear is time that you can use to do things that are more enjoyable or more useful to you.

Your objection is that you just don't want to do the same thing every day. Maybe you think it's boring or you don't think it's a good use of your time. Well, here's why we say, "*the system will set you free*."

When you systematize something, you take the decisions out of your minor things. It leaves a lot of creative time for your major things (the big rocks!) and allows you to shine in the time that you have available! You can use all that decision making and creativity power to make something truly wonderful, rather than wasting it on the daily mundane.

However, as with everything I've mentioned in the book, if you truly appreciate doing something, enjoy doing it, and/or it's very useful to you, then you can continue doing that. If you really enjoy deciding what to wear every day and going through that whole decision-making process, by all means, do that! Just consider doing this for some of those other things that you don't.

Advice in Practice:

- I want you to think about things that you can systematize in your life. Absolutely everything that doesn't bring enjoyment, systematize it!

  Think about it:

  —What you eat every single day, you can cook one day a week or decide what you're going to eat in advance.

  —When you're traveling, is there a better way to do it? Can you carpool 3 out of 6 days a week? You can get some work done in the car or you can get some interaction with your friends or something like that! At a certain income level maybe hire a driver, or have your assistant do the driving while you're still working in the car. It's a system.

  —What about your clothes? You can either decide to use a uniform like I do, or you can just batch all of your decisions to one time during the week and lay out all of your clothes for each individual day, at one time. Boom. Decision fatigue solved!

  —What about the payments of bills, finances, and taxes? Think about putting all of those on the credit card like I had mentioned before, and just paying the one bill each month. Think of the time you could save!

  —What about your calendar and your schedule? A lot of times you can have things recurring in your schedule. Set up your day or weeks up so you just do certain things on scheduled days. Make sure it pops up in your calendar on a recurring setting so you don't have to think about it.

- So, Mondays might be your planning day and Thursdays might be your day to hit it really hard in the business as a productivity day or a focus/deep work day. Dan Sullivan advocates doing "buffer days," "focus days" (the money-making time), and "free days" where you turn it all off. That clears up so much thought on your part. Think about it.

- And another thing to think about is systematizing the repeated tasks in your profession. If you find yourself doing one thing over and over again, think about making that a system. Optimize it, make it a lot better, see if that there are ways that you can get it done automatically through technology. Then you can actually outsource those things. I wrote a lot more about outsourcing here in the book, so go read that. If you do those things, and systematize it, it will set you free.

- Only things that are in your specific zone of genius that can really make a difference, because it's you doing it, should be done by you.

- Think about this. Consider in your brilliant mind if what I say has some validity. If it does, please consider systematizing at least one thing in your life and see how it feels. If you like that, you can do more.

That's what I ask of you in this *Advice in Practice*. And please let me know if you're doing it, not because I need the ego boost (though, it would be nice), it's because I love you!

Notes, thoughts, and intentions.

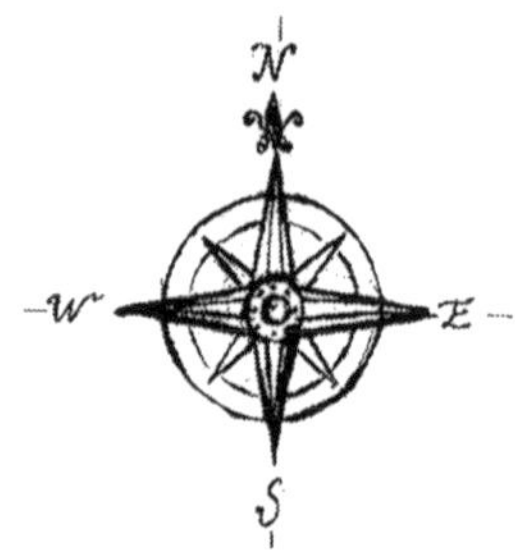

57. "Shadow" Someone That's Doing What You Want to Do at a High Level.

So, now comes the time when I get to talk with you about the immense, awesome, and wonderful power of SHADOWING! It's severely under-used in our society and should be done a lot more often than it is.

Back in the olden days it was common for the people to do apprenticeships to learn the skills of a trade from other people. That has since been replaced with a traditional system of education that we all agree could be done a lot better.

Let me tell you my story about shadowing and its life-changing effects. I have been a real estate broker and salesperson for a long time. Sometime around the time you were born, Mandy (in 1999), I listened to several tips and mastermind calls from top-producing real estate agents all across the country that talk about how to do their business better. These people were mega-agents and they did a ton of business.

On the call there was a gentleman that I listened to, and appreciated, because he was in the market that seemed a little similar to mine--an area with military families. I actually got the idea to look him up online and found his phone number and called him directly. I told them a little bit about myself and some of my aspirations and I asked him if he would be okay for me to actually come out to where he sold real estate in Albuquerque and follow him for a few days, just to get a good idea of what he did (I'm sure I did the "right way of asking" methodology described in this book in the Asking chapter).

This is shadowing.

His name is Ron Campbell and, at that time, he was doing with his team over two million dollars a year of personal commission income back in 1999! He allowed me to check out his office, follow him, and actually check out his systems. I got to interview his people in the office and take a lot of his information with me to better my practice.

Just a few days of following him paid huge dividends in my career, allowed me to make a lot more money, and live a lot more of an enjoyable life while I was in real estate. The month after following him I sold eighteen homes personally, set up listing and buyer packages, and systematized a lot of my business. It was like magic. I was so motivated!

Ron was very gracious. Something I've discovered about successful people is that they are usually very giving people. As long as you are not a complete jerk and a waste of time, they will usually help you. Specifically, if you are in a profession where they are not your direct competitor, then they are very likely to help you. The worst that can happen is they could just say, "no," and then you're no worse off for having asked. You're actually better, because you at least tried and may have learned from it.

One of my biggest realizations is that people have done it before, and there is always someone that has been more successful than you at something. There are people that have done your career and your profession very successfully. You can always learn from that.

Shadowing and spending time with them is a huge shortcut in life.

What I would do is define what it is you really want to learn from shadowing someone. Then, using all of the wondrous power of the internet and your friends, find someone that is doing it at a high level and prepare to approach them.

If you approach them the right way and get to talk to them, there is a very good chance that they are going to accept. But something I have to caution you about it is to approach them the right way. Provide them value first before you ask something of them. Do it genuinely and do it without the expectation of getting something in return.

An example of this might be to purchase their product, buy their seminar, or donate money to a cause that they believe in. Perhaps you can give them some ideas that you think might help them in their business (you are an idea machine after all, right?). Take your time and really do it right and just provide it to them, no strings attached. Hopefully you can help, and if so, great. If not, that's okay too.

People can sense and understand if you're just doing things for your own personal gain. They know if you are genuine.

So, approach them the right way and have the guts and the gumption to actually ask "can I meet with you, talk with you, or ask you a few specific questions about your profession?" Lastly, "can I shadow you?"

When you do that, make sure that they know that you won't be in their way; that you can be a fly on the wall. They can say as little or as much as they would like to or do as much as they are comfortable doing.

Then actually do it.

When you shadow, plan on what you want to get out of it. Do in OPOA for shadowing them. Do you remember OPOA? Outcome, Purpose, Obstacles and Actions! Write it down and plan what you'd like to learn.

People don't do this, but you are much better than that! Just the fact that you are reading this gives me hope that you are going to take heed of this advice and use it.

Advice in Practice:

- Get out the old journal and make a list of the skills you need to learn first. Then brainstorm, or do an idea list, of the people that may be able to help you with that skill. Get several people for each of these skills.

- Ask, "what is the one skill or a piece of knowledge that will help me in my life the most right now?" Let's concentrate on that skill and focus efforts on getting that one first.

- Approach them. Caution: courage needed (read the chapter "Feel the Fear and Do It Anyways" beforehand if needed.

- Know that you could fail but make preparations. Do an OPOA on the call that you are about to make and release the result. That means that you need to be ok whether they say yes or no. You have done what you can and you actually had the courage to ask even though you were probably a little scared, and the rest is with God. If it's meant to happen, it will happen, and if it's not meant to happen, it won't. It will be the best result either way. Repeat these steps as many times as necessary to get a great person that you can shadow.

- Just get a lunch or quick meeting. Asking someone who you don't know if you can follow them is definitely a big ask. It's usually better to ask for small bite-sized chunks of time with a clearly established beginning and end. That would be a lot less threatening to them.

- When you are following, write down an OPOA of what you want to get out of the meeting. Go in with a specific piece of knowledge, skill, or motivation that you want to accomplish with them. Keep that at the forefront of your mind and that's going to help you get what you need out of shadowing them. They'll appreciate that you're specific, too.

- Remember: shadowing is different than just interviewing. It means to watch them in their genius and in their bad times as well. So when you are shadowing, take notes, bring a journal, type away, and record on Evernote. The person you are shadowing will appreciate and respect that you are taking all of this very seriously.

- Implement something that you have learned from them right away. If you do that immediately it's much more likely to have a measurable impact on and in your life.

- Next, tell the person you shadowed what you got out of it and make sure they understand the role that they played in your life. These are some of the sweetest lessons that they could get and will make them happy they allowed you to shadow them. There's a side benefit in that it usually keeps the door open for you to do it again, or for you to have a mentor in that area. When you do this, by the way, I recommend that you actually write a physical letter because that has a lot more impact than a more easily done email, text, or Facebook post.

I hope this has been helpful to you. Mandy, it's interesting because today I was trying to get you to shadow someone in the occupational therapy field. We are very excited for it and I think it's really going to help you out in your life. So, I hope that you are taking this advice and you consider it for the future.

Please know that I love you very much.

Notes, thoughts, and intentions.

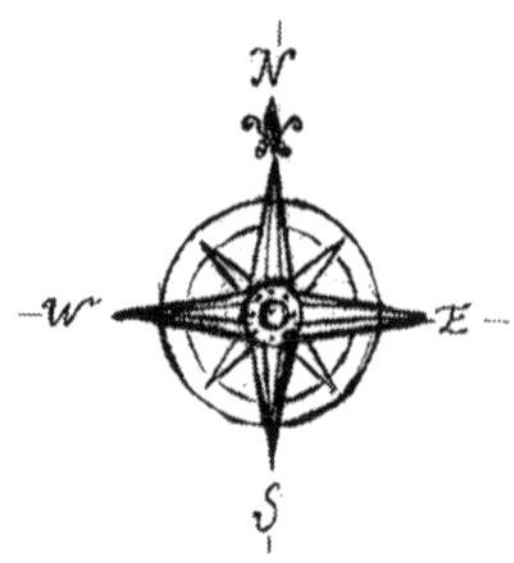

58. Consider the Highest and Best Use of Your Time.

I'm enjoying getting a chance to go over these big life principles with you, and I don't think that they're done every day in normal life, so I'm excited to share this with you once again.

You know, I've been in real estate for many years. In real estate there is a term called HABU, that stands for, "Highest and Best Use." In real estate, it's the best way that a piece of land or a building can be used. It's what creates the most value.

For instance, if a little two-bedroom house is at a busy intersection, it wouldn't have as much value as a commercial place like a lawyer's office or a dentist's office. They could get a lot more money with its highest and best use of that land. It's great to consider your life and the highest and best use of your time.

I got started in real estate just selling on my own and selling houses one by one to each individual family, but as a broker I could have other people showing the houses for me. So, I could use my time to reach out to get more people, and I could have several real estate agents showing houses for me while I was out getting more people with whom to do business .

It was the highest and best use of my time then. I was going to get a lot more business while farming out the time-consuming activities to other people. I figured out that I could teach doing that to a lot of people, so they could sell homes, and I could get a piece of what they earned.

One lesson that I taught an agent could be duplicated many times and pay me several times through my career. That leveraged time became a much better use of my efforts. I created some freedom for myself and learned that I didn't need to do a lot of the activities that had previously been done by me alone.

There is usually always a better way to do things.

Right now, my HABU is to write this book for you. I want to contribute to your life and help you in any way I can. I'm also getting to follow the advice I'm giving you with my own life!

Let's talk about "Highest and Best Use" for economic purposes, physically, and your dollars per hour.

This may not be a real issue for you yet, but it certainly will be at some point in your life:. Don't spend time doing things that aren't worth your time, money-wise, when there are other options.

An example for me in real estate was that whenever I found myself putting out real estate signs, or delivering contracts to different offices, and that kind of thing. That's usually billed out at $10 per hour when time prospecting on the phone in that time could be worth a thousand dollars an hour, or sometimes even more. So, to make highest and best use of time I'd want to make sure that I spend more time prospecting and hiring out, or contracting, the other activities for me.

Your time should be spent in your genius—the thing at which you're truly exceptional. Hopefully, if you've followed the magic spot advice and you're in a career where you're excited, you're good at it, and that pays you. Usually, it's the type of thing that you can "lose yourself" in doing, and when you look up at the clock you can't believe that you've been at it for as long as you have.

Your time should be spent doing things that are enjoyable for you, or things that are very useful for leading a better life.

When I was a kid I mowed lawns. I had a little business with it and did it a lot. I had to cut our own (often massive) lawn, too. I also had a job in high school working at a landscaping company. Because I did it so much, I really learned to dislike mowing lawns.

As I graduated from college and I started working, I realized that I loathed myself a little bit every time I went to mow the lawn. I thought about it and made a conscious decision that I'd pay someone else $40 to mow our lawn. Money was still tight, so I made a deal that whenever someone else was mowing the lawn that I would be doing something that was worth more than the $40.

Now fast forward. I still have someone to mow the lawn, but I just know that my time is going to be better spent whether it's being productive or even taking a rest and enjoying time with my family. Both of those are precious to me, and I find that it's a higher and better use of my time.

Farm out something that's less valuable to your time, so you can do the things that are more valuable. There's always a way to do this. Here are a few principles that can help with this:

The Pareto Principle.

One of the biggest ways to figure out your best use of time is to apply the Pareto Principle to it. You may have heard it called the 80/20 rule. The idea is that 80% of your results are generated by 20% of your efforts.

Going back to real estate for a bit, 80% of the results were generated by the marketing and prospecting for the business. For your school work, it may be studying to take the test. In a relationship, it may be protected time to just talk with each other.

Given this principle, you should spend your time on the important 20% of what drives results, and the other 80% of activities you can either get someone else to do, let it slide, or find a way to systematize and automate it. We'll work on that in a second.

Force Multipliers.

A force multiplier, in military terms, is someone that can get a lot of other people mobilized and working to help win a war or a battle. An example would be a Green Beret that goes behind enemy lines, finds some villages with people sympathetic to their cause, and teaches them how to fight against the enemy.

In deciding the highest and best use of your time, it's useful to think about where you can get force multipliers.

An example I had from my real estate business was working with your grandmother, Amalia. She was spectacular, and literally took the running of the property management company off of my hands, and she ran it much better than I could. She did the hiring, the training, the managing, and even the finances. I can't tell you 1) how grateful I was to have her in the business, and 2) how much time that saved me.

In business, and even in terms of jobs, one of the biggest goals you should have is to get yourself out of the business. That is meaning that you're not necessarily *needed* for the proper running of the day-to-day activities.

You do that to increase the amount of freedom in your life, as I don't really think that we're meant to physically work 40-50 hours per week. That time can be used for your mission or passion, and spending time in relationships that you love.

It's also practical for the business or job. By freeing yourself from the lower level to-dos and having them leveraged to other people by automation or outsourcing, you are freeing yourself to work ON the business rather than IN it. That allows you to take time to think, literally. It gives you the chance to learn, and you can tinker with and iterate the business to make it better. You can actually innovate, which is the highest and best use of your time in a business.

Now we've talked about the economic best use of your time—let's go deeper, and start talking about your soul, what makes you tick, and the reason that you were put on this Earth.

Ask these questions:

- Is what you're doing right now the highest and best use of your time on earth?
- Are you excited about what you're doing every day?
- Are your unique talents being used to serve others in the best way?
- And are you doing what you feel that you were born to do and made to do?

If these questions are answered with a big, fat no, then here's something that I'd suggest:

The highest and best use of your time is to find out what that is for you.

What is the best thing for you to be doing on Earth? This is so important, and that's probably why I've talked about it in the magic spot advice, the deferred life plan section, and in one of the final chapters in the soul about your hero's journey.

My friend Philip McKernan says that the benefit from being so busy in life is that you never have to pause too long to look in the mirror and examine your life, because you might be scared of what you find.

I really feel that a life well-lived is one that you consciously examine. Where you've made sure that you're doing what you really want to do with your life; what's really in your soul to do. I know I've mentioned this before (it's important, dang it!), but the number one regret of the dying[6] is that they did not live a life that's true to themselves.

My sweethearts, it's so important for your heart and soul for you to do that. Please consider that.

Then also consider the fact that you are L-O-V-E-D!

Advice in Practice:

- For the economic part of the highest and best use of your time:

  Go through the daily activities that you do at school, on your job, or at your business. It's useful to literally write them all out and to get literally every bit of it out onto paper. Then examine them and see if you need more or less of that in your schedule. You can even put little up or down arrows on them.

---

[6] Susie Steiner, "Top five regrets of the dying," https://www.theguardian.com/lifeandstyle/2012/feb/01/top-five-regrets-of-the-dying (February 1, 2012).

If you need less time doing certain things (like me putting out real estate signs), then do an idea list of ways that you can optimize that area of your life. For me, it was to get my assistant to do that. I was able to offload nearly all the non-income producing activities to them so that my time was focused on highly profitable parts. What does this look like to you? Spend some time on that list and answer this.

If you need more time doing things, repeat the process with the idea list. How can you get more of this into your daily schedule? In real estate, I could literally double my income by doubling the time spent marketing and prospecting. But what does that look like to you?

- For the soul part of the highest and best use:

  Re-read, and truly answer, the questions above regarding what you do every day, and if you're really doing what you think you're meant to do. I'd suggest writing them out in a journal (yet again) and clarifying those thoughts on paper.

  Take your time and answer the questions posed in the space above. Really dig in and figure a few things out on this. Asking these questions and truly examining your life is some of the best time you can ever spend.

  Read the parts in this book about the magic spot, the deferred life plan, and the hero's journey. Each has some advice to help you find this magic in your life. I'd suggest clearing out an afternoon or evening and going on a soul-searching expedition.

If you're not doing what you are meant to do now, that's okay. At least for a little while. You probably will have some bills to pay and will need to earn a living. What's not okay is to stay like that indefinitely. You can find yourself looking up and realizing that 10 years have gone by, and you've just been on the job/bills/life treadmill.

Create an idea list of how you can incorporate your passion into your life. That's why these idea lists are so powerful. You become your own resource and can answer nearly any question proposed to you.

Of course, you know I'd consider it an honor for you to talk to me about this. So, find me and let's do that. <3

Notes, thoughts, and intentions.

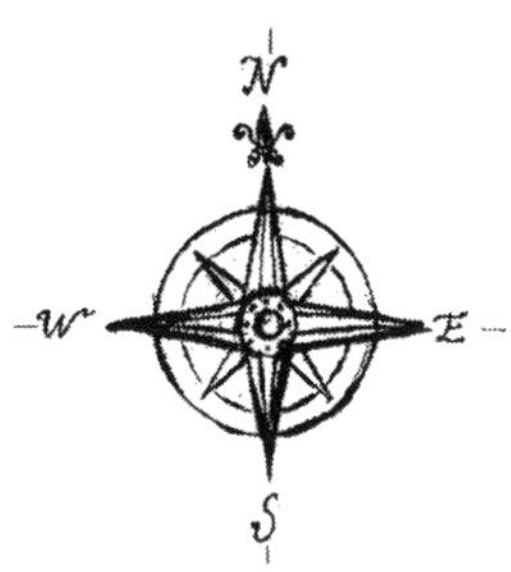

59. Build a Pipeline and Stop Carrying Buckets.

There is a parable that I read in the book, *The Cashflow Quadrant*, by Robert Kiyosaki. It's had a big impact on my life, and I remember it right now without referencing the book. I'm paraphrasing and making it my own, but it goes like this:

A village needed water, so they hired two people to get water for them and they were paid by the amount of water that they delivered.

One of them got busy right away. He got several buckets, and even figured out that he could make the buckets bigger and could carry more with a pole over his back. He started getting the water and was paid for it, but he got tired, and it wasn't a good lifestyle. He even tried to get his children involved in his business, but they refused.

The other did work during the day carrying buckets, but she realized that there must be a better way. She looked at her Zig Ziglar quote, "You can have everything in life you want if you just help enough other people get what they want." And she was determined to get the villagers what they wanted.

So, after hours and on the weekends, and maybe (I'm adding this myself) on a designated day that she set aside for developing the business, of working ON it rather than just IN it. With that time, she decided that a pipeline would serve the village much better. It would bring the water automatically, and in much more abundance to the village.

Now, there were problems with building the pipeline. The soil was extra rocky in places. She needed to take some of her hard-earned money to pay a few people to help when she couldn't get it all done herself. She had hard and rough days, and often didn't feel like working on the pipeline after she'd worked hard carrying buckets.

Nevertheless, she persisted.

And she built the pipeline! There was a great celebration when it worked, and now the villagers had all of the fresh, clean water they wanted. And she was responsible. The other water bucket carrier was out of a job, as he couldn't compete with all the water that the new pipeline brought. The pipeline brought water at all times, day and night, on holidays, and when she was relaxing and spending time with her family (and writing her book). She made a lot of money by serving the people a lot better than anyone else.

And after that, she was able to use some of that money, and the know-how of building pipelines, to help the other villages in the area. Many people were able to live a better life because of her, and as a result she and her family lived a much better life.

So, you kind of get this, right? It's all about creating a system that works for your clients (or the company you work for, or your boss, or your family or just you), rather than doing each thing by themselves.

Some examples would be Henry Ford and the assembly line, the way Apple produced their products that served billions, or even how a bulldozer can do the work of a dozen men in digging a ditch.

When you're at a job, or better yet, at your business, always take time to see if things can be simplified, optimized, and done easier. Constantly think, "How can I deliver more, easier?" There is a very good chance, almost certainly guaranteed, that a process or a way of doing things can be improved. Is there a better way to serve more of your customers ? You can find it, and that is where the value lies. That's where there are riches, freedom, and a better lifestyle awaits. Right behind your own pipeline.

So, if you find yourself carrying buckets, please know that there is a better way, and get to finding out how to build your very own pipeline. It's a better way to live.

Advice in Practice:

- This is a parable for jobs, in general. If you work for a person or a company, and your time is traded for money (say by working 9-5 every weekday and only having the weekends off) then you are carrying buckets. Think about the idea of starting your own business or firing yourself by contracting the work you do for the company. I'm not saying throw caution to the wind, or just blindly doing something. Just think about it, approach it with the idea that you can do better, and hopefully that you will try at one point.

- If you own a business that produces goods or services for people, spend some time and effort on working ON, versus IN your business. That is, think strategically and actively ask, "how can I improve things for my customers?" Do some benchmarking. Is someone else in the field already "building a pipeline?" Is there a better way for them? Can you optimize what you're doing to serve them better?

- Read the book, (I'm sure I will recommend it elsewhere) *The 4 Hour Workweek*, by Tim Ferriss. See if it inspires you to D.E.A.L. in your life (Define, Eliminate, Automate, and Liberate). It had a huge impact on me and because of that, I became kind of obsessive about saving time for myself in business and life.

- Also, check out the book, or CERTAINLY understand the concepts of, "The Cashflow Quadrant," by Robert Kiyosaki. Learning the pros and cons of the E/S/B/I quadrants (Employee, Self-Employed, Business Owner, and Investor), and HOW TO get from one section of the quadrant into another are life-changing principles!

Notes, thoughts, and intentions.

THE BODY.

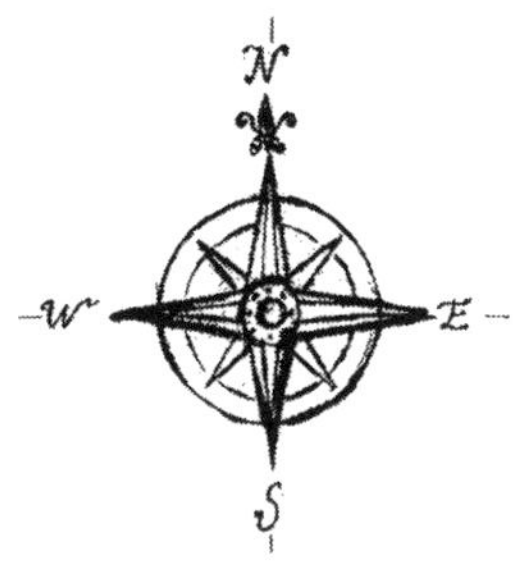

Introduction to The Body.

"A person who is healthy has a thousand dreams. A person who's not healthy, has just one." —Dr. Izabella Wentz.

My sweethearts. As you probably guessed from the title of this section, we're talking about the Body. Honestly, this is the section out of all of these that I was least looking forward to writing. Not because of its importance—how you care for yourself physically is one of the most important decisions of your life, one that you get to make over and over each day.

I somewhat dreaded this, because I don't feel like I've been a great role model on how to take care of your bodies. However, often when there's discomfort like this, we need to lean into it.

As you know, I recently had a stroke . . . at age forty-four. I know you know all about it, but it's important to talk about this. The doctors all said that I shouldn't have had one. My blood pressure was ideal, my blood sugar was optimal. My heart rate and cholesterol—really all of the things that "conventional" medicine looks at—were just great.

But, despite that, while we were on vacation in California, a day after going to Disneyland and California Adventure, I was trying to talk to my dear friend Josh and I found I was unable to say any words. I was completely lucid. I had exactly what I was trying to say in my mind, and the words just wouldn't form at all. I was taken to the ER immediately—as this happened while I was at a conference full of my friends—and thankfully, I got to the hospital in less than 30 minutes after the stroke happened.

I seemed to recover quickly. In fact, the paramedics that arrived didn't think that I'd had a stroke, because I seemed to be back to myself, talking and even joking a little about the spectacle of having all these people surrounding me seeing if I was okay. But my two doctor friends ran an assessment on me immediately afterwards and knew that I'd had a stroke. An MRI the next day confirmed it.

I spent the next three days in the hospital, all alone—you and Mom were room-bound by your own horrible flus. I can say without a doubt that I've never been more scared in my life. Some for me, but even more for you. I don't want to leave you now, or really ever. We all need a Daddy in our lives, and I don't ever want to abandon that duty.

Death of the Body

Well, here's the thing, and we'll get back to the proper care and feeding of the body soon, but as we're talking mortality already:

I will ALWAYS be with you, and no amount of physical distance or even death can change that. You are so very loved, and you will be always—whether or not I happen to be on the same physical plane as you. This feeling of care, of affection, of admiration for you will always exist.

My friend Christina Rasmussen has extensively studied the metaphysics of dying. She's researched, talked to people that have done it (people that have literally been pronounced dead) and is writing her own book about it now. Something that she said stuck with me:

"Death doesn't happen to us, it happens to those in our lives."

So, as I'm writing this, I know that someday my body—which I'm caring for now, taking some of my own advice to you—will stop breathing, grow cold, and "die." But from everything that I feel and know deep down inside, I will not die. It will just be my body. It's just a wrapper for what's inside, it's a bulb for the light of our souls.

Our Bodies as Temples

Bringing it back to what we're talking about in this section. This bulb is of supreme importance. Our physical form is the lens with which we see life, and it colors everything that we experience. It's the temple of the divine.

How we care for it determines how much energy we have to tackle each day, and to even ATTEMPT our Hero's Journey. Vince Lombardi (he's a famous football coach that you don't know) said, "Fatigue makes cowards of us all."

Oh, how true that is. When you're not sleeping well, the next day is just . . . hard. If you are lacking in energy, your courage drops. Your confidence is affected. You just don't want to do the things that you know you SHOULD.

Life is all about moving forward, fulfilling some of your potential and helping others . . . and all of this isn't very possible when you don't take care of yourself.

Now, for the blindingly obvious as I write this: I am overweight. I feel a little like a hypocrite when I'm telling you these things (although I do almost every one of them consistently) when I'm not a great model of how health should look. I've had an up and down battle with weight and health since I've been in college. I've gained and lost sixty-five of the same pounds. I've been extremely strong, and I've been somewhat weak. I've run several half marathons and even a full marathon at altitude in Denver. I have studied nutrition, exercise, and mindfulness . . . but I don't always do what I'm supposed to do. That's not good for me in any way. I regret that, as I think that this would have more weight (no pun intended . . . heh, heh) if I was lean.

But.

I did a walk/sprint session this morning right before writing this. I did my meditation practice. I journaled. I wrote out the things that I actively appreciate today. I am tending the garden of my body and mind—and I feel so good about it. Here's the inescapable fact, said by a mentor of mine Jim Rohn, "Left alone, the weeds will take the garden." I consider exercise, mindfulness, and nutrition tending the garden . . . and when you do that, EVERYTHING is better.

With the stroke—which the neurologist said was a "fluke" caused by extremely high blood platelet levels due to the TERRIBLE flu we were all fighting. The doctors have told me that I'll be much more susceptible to depression and emotions. It's true, and I've already experienced that. I had pneumonia two weeks back, and I allowed that to be an excuse for me NOT to tend the garden. I didn't exercise (that's understandable), I didn't eat well (not as understandable), I didn't meditate, or journal, or write down what I appreciate—and that's not good. When I didn't do that, I could literally feel my heart weighed down by sadness. You'll learn a lot about these practices in the pages to come.

I've gained a new appreciation of taking care of the body through this experience. So, I do feel better about talking to you about it.

You have to love yourself enough to WANT to take care of your body.

We'll talk a lot more about that in other areas of this loving tome. You've got to get that right, and when you do, you'll want to tend to yourself, your mind and body more.

Here's the promise that I make with this section: If you read any of these pieces of advice, and put them into action, it will change your life. The colors will be brighter, the sounds more crisp and joyful. Taking care of your physical form is a gateway to feeling much, much better about yourself. It will allow you to take on the grand challenges. Taking care of yourself will give you the strength and energy to stand back up when you get knocked down—and make no mistake, that's going to happen. When you read and put these practices into your life, you'll be a better role model. Just like I'm wishing I was a better role model for you now.

When you care enough to take care of your body, you'll be more sure of yourself. You'll gain confidence. You'll like who you see in the mirror. Maybe most importantly, you'll be able to go after your dreams.

So, as you get started, know that I'm with you. I love you, and I'm so looking forward to this being able to help with your life. Let's get to the advice.

Notes, thoughts, and intentions.

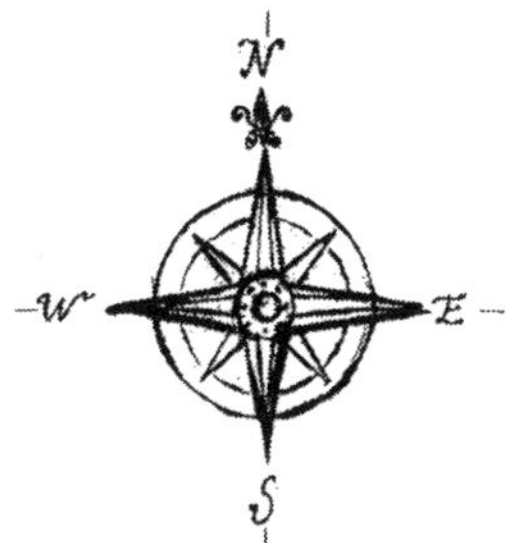

60. Think About Aging and Death, In a Useful Way.

My sweethearts. As I'm writing this, I'm sitting with your Mona (grandmother) in the chemotherapy treatment area of Scott and White Hospital. They just put in her chemo tube, and the chemicals to kill the cancer are dripping into her body.

Now, I expect Mona to be fine. She's strong, has a great attitude, and this is a treatable form of cancer . . . but I don't know if there's a more appropriate place to talk with you about this: the fleeting nature of life.

Here's the thought that I'm having on this, and it's a good lesson for all of us to take away from this circumstance:

Life—at least here, as we know it—is FINITE.

There are a limited number of times that you'll watch a sunrise or sunset.

There are limited number of times that you'll get to actually HOLD your children. Both of you girls are pretty much too big for me to just pick up and hold (it would look a little funny). I'm getting to still hold Alec, and that's lasting longer than his age would dictate, but even that will be finite. I don't know how many more times I'm going to get to hold that precious "baby" boy.

When you're as young as you are, you don't think it's going to end. You're still looking forward to everything that's GOING to happen. When you get your various levels of freedom. When you get to date (Aly), when you're driving your own car and going to college (Mandy) . . . it probably seems like it's taking forever for those things to happen for you.

But here's something to keep in mind:

Time has a way of accelerating. It passes faster and faster as you get older. Every minute and day will be a much smaller percentage of your life than it is now.

You may roll your eyes at this because I sometimes talk about bringing you home from the hospital after you were born, and how you could fit in one of my hands. I could just look at your sweet faces for hours! ***I'm pausing to savor these sweet memories*** But the thing is: I remember it like it was yesterday.

I can still see the outfits and remember that feeling in my heart during that time. And it was EIGHTEEN years ago for you, Mandy and FOURTEEN for you, Aly! Alec's was not so long ago, so it's understandable to remember that.

But that's a loooooong time! And when I think about it, I wonder how much has actually changed since then. A lot of life has gone by, we've raised you, some things have been accomplished—and a lot of things have been left undone, too.

The whole point of this pondering and talking about life passing by is to get to this point:

Steve Jobs said,

> ***"Remembering that you are going to die is the best way I know to avoid the trap of thinking you have something to lose. You are already naked. There is no reason not to follow your heart."***

So.

If you're deciding whether to do it or not.
Do it.
Take the chance, take the opportunity.
Make the call.
Say, "I love you."
Hug FREELY!
Go on that special one-on-one date.
Forgive people *especially your family*.

And . . . go after your dream. Do all of the things that you want to do.

Advice in Practice:

- Get some practice in those moments of decision. When you're thinking of doing something, ask yourself,

"Would I regret NOT doing this?" If that answer is yes, you MUST do it.

- Write out a "bucket" list. You know what that is, right? It's a list of everything that you want to do before you "kick the bucket," aka die. And remember—take EVERY chance you can to actually do it. Whaddya' know? There's a whole chapter of advice on that in the "Soul" section!

- Don't subscribe to the "Deferred Life Plan," which is summarized as working for 40 years so you can "retire" and then, FINALLY do the things that you want to do. NO! Do it as you get the opportunity. That doesn't mean that you don't save money, or that you're unnecessarily reckless, of course.

- But take some time from work to go on THE trip you've wanted to go on. Take a few mini-retirements along the way to explore the things you want to. Don't wait, because tomorrow is not guaranteed. ***Special thanks to Tim Ferriss and The 4 Hour Workweek, for these principles. There is more on this in the "Soul" section, too.

- Take the kids. If you can, wait a while until you have children (even though I want some grandkids to spoil often). Get your financial footing and get to know your spouse before going on that journey. This way, when you DO have the kiddos, you can include them in a life of adventure, of travel, of following your passions WITH them.

Oh man, do I love you. I'm so, so excited about the lives in front of you!

Notes, thoughts, and intentions.

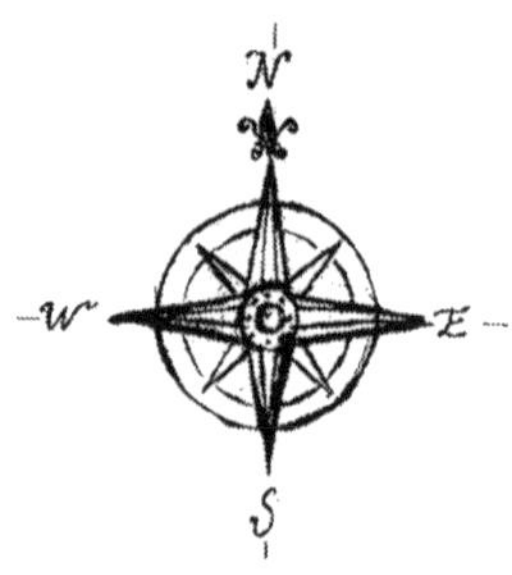

61. Pay Attention to the Fundies.

The fundamentals—or as we like to call them the "Fundies,"—are eating, moving and sleeping.

My precious, wonderful children, , I wouldn't be doing my job as a Dad if I had this chance to talk about all kinds of pieces of life and values and we didn't discuss the fundamentals of your health. These are the big rocks for everything that makes up your physical form, your energy, the mental clarity that you can have, and it's really the base and the fundamentals for a great life. If you don't take care of your fundies, then you'll fall prey to the spirit being willing, but the body being weak.

Something that your Pa-paw (Col. Ron Franks, USMC, retired) said that I thought was neat:

> ***"Being in great shape is something that no one can take away from you. It's something you can do and it's only yours. It's your thing and it makes life so much better."***

You know that he was a Marine and he has been very physically fit his entire life, and his words always stuck with me.

Other things in your life will not matter as much if your health is suffering.

Going back to the quote at the beginning of this, if you don't have your health then usually the ONLY thing on your mind is (or should be) getting that back. It won't leave room in your life for the sweet pursuit of other goals. Your energy will be lacking. You won't be as mentally sharp, and your confidence will be negatively affected.

Maybe you won't notice that as much when you're young, but bad health habits compounded day after day after day will stack up, multiply, and become a burden in your life.

Now, we're going to talk more about each of these-- the eating, the moving, and the sleeping in later chapters--but I want to give you a big piece of advice right now and that is:

You need to love yourself enough to care about doing these things.

You are children of God. You're also in my family and you deserve a life of health, vibrancy, energy and abundance. You deserve to be able to take care of yourself and others with ease, and all that starts with these fundamentals. The fact that you do these and the degree to which you do them will determine how well you can take care of everything else. Having good sleeping habits, good eating habits, and exercising will make everything else possible in this book. I hope that this is hitting home.

Eating, moving and sleeping right are all necessary for a great life. If you don't do even one of them well, you're going to be at a tremendous disadvantage. It's not something you just do every once in a while, practicing these is something you do all the time and there's a running score card for it.

Consistency is so important with this. You're not able to wait a month and THEN work out for twelve hours straight. But twenty minutes every day will make a gigantic difference. The bad news is that the bad habits compound and cause disaster. The great news is that GOOD habits compound and will completely transform your life for the better.

Eating:

Are you eating or drinking for energy and for health, or do you eat whatever feels good in the moment?

Are most of your meals healthy, or is a healthy meal a rare occurrence for you?

If you do what's easy now, you're going to have a hard time later. If you do what's harder now, with a little self-sacrifice and moderation, then things are going to be much easier later.

The big rocks for eating are:

- eat whole food
- avoid processed food (food-like substances)
- very little sugar
- leafy greens
- fewer carbs and no grains

- drink lots and lots of water.

Those are the fundies. A lot of these will have their own chapters of advice because of their importance and how much of a difference they make in your life.

When you're eating cheat meals (I prefer to call them *free meals* because it doesn't sound as bad as *cheat meals*), you just need to make sure those are in moderation. I think it's actually part of a good life to do that every once in a while. You should have your occasional piece of pizza if you love it, go out to the movies while savoring popcorn or eat with your family for a big celebration. It's just that these occasions should be something that's done as a somewhat rare treat, rather than the norm.

Those are the big rocks and the things you need to think about when eating.

Movement:

Do you have a regular, consistent workout routine?

Does that routine make you sweat?

Do you take the time for it and actually schedule it during your week?

Are you working towards a goal, physically?

Are walking and weight training a part of your movement plan?

Now, the big rock on this: you need to move every day, even if it's for a walk.

We start to slow down, age and lose what we don't use. Get out there and at the very least walk. At your best you want to have high intensity interval training (HIIT). HIIT with some walking and wind sprints thrown in for good measure.

Don't run for long distances as that can be bad for your knees and joints and other things. I'm saying this as someone who's run a marathon and a couple of half marathons. See http://alsearsmd.com/2016/06/long-distance-running-effects-your-health/ Running long distances is not the best for you for aging purposes, but you still need to sweat very often.

You also need to lift heavy things. Weight training is so important for males and females. It's so important that it will have its own chapter of advice. Charles Poliquin, a friend of mine who happens to be one of the top strength trainers in the world, told me specifically that muscle mass is the best indicator of aging well, living longer and retaining mental sharpness and acuity later in life. [7]

Make sure that you do have a weight training program as a regular part of your life!

Sleeping.

Are you getting AT LEAST seven to eight hours or more of sleep most every night?

---

[7] Tufts University "Growing Older, Getting Stronger," http://enews.tufts.edu/stories/1090/2002/06/26/NelsonOnStrengthTraining (June 26, 2002).

Do you have a set bedtime routine?

Do you shut everything down at a certain time and perhaps turn off blue screens and blue lights from your smart phones, computers, and TVs before you go to bed?

Do you take naps?

Do you have a room that's dark?

Do you keep it somewhat cool when you go to sleep?

We spend a third of our lives sleeping (hopefully), yet it's something we don't usually talk about in school. It seems strange that we don't have a class on sleeping! It's such a huge part of our lives. That's why this has its own section in the book.

Now the big rocks for sleep:

You need to have a sleep plan. Get a good mattress. Keep your room dark and cool with very little light and have a nighttime routine where you shut everything down so you get a good amount of sleep. There's much more to come on sleep in this book.

Question for you, how did all of these questions make you feel? Are you killing them or are they killing you? Do the questions make you uncomfortable, or do you smile in satisfaction knowing that you're doing pretty good? There's a lot more on this in a few chapters to come soon.

You can be proactive with the fundamentals and go after life and get better, or you can be reactive and take what life gives you. It's easy to just go with the flow and do what you want when you want and hope that things turn out okay. But they won't. Looking after these fundies is going to make such a big deal in your life.

Advice in Practice:

- Create a scorecard, one through ten, one being the worst and ten being the best. How well are you doing in each area? Eating and drinking, moving and exercise, and sleep and recovery. Be honest. Give yourself a number on it and think about how you can use the pieces of advice in this book to get those numbers higher.

- Which is your worst area: eating, moving, or sleeping? The most rapid improvement in your overall life can be made by improving the weakest of these three fundamentals. For your weakest, come up with an idea list of ten to twenty ways to improve that area. Take the best idea from the list and *schedule* it. Put it in your planner, put it some place where you can see it and make it happen because as we learned elsewhere, if you don't schedule it, it does not become real.

- When you do that, make a public declaration on social media or to your. Try to get an accountability buddy, someone who's going to hold you responsible for improving in that area. Get someone that actually checks in on you daily to see if you're doing what you're supposed to do.

- Lastly, let's create a thirty-day challenge for yourself on the new habit. Consciously think how it feels when you start getting better, when you have more energy, when you're able to think with a lot more clarity, and when you're able to leap out of bed in the morning excited about things! Write down all of the good things that happen to you on this journey.

As always, I love you dearly and I hope that this advice has served you well.

Notes, thoughts, and intentions.

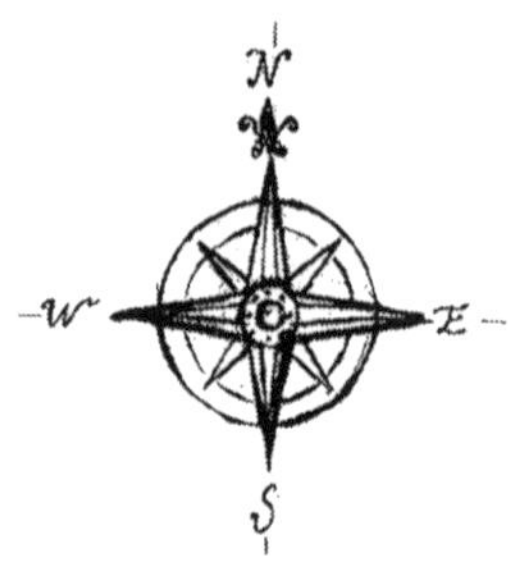

62. Treat Your Body Like a Temple, Love Yourself Enough to Do That.

Are you treating your body like a temple, or like a tent?

Wow. I so hope that I pass this on to you. We've talked a LOT about self-love in this book, but again: if there is ONE thing that I'd wish for you, it would be to love yourself.

I've had some issues with that throughout my life, but I think I've come a long way. . . and I really need to apply this advice to my own life, as well. Love yourself enough to treat your body like a temple, and not a tent (like I've done at times).

The cliché is that youth is wasted on the young. When you're young, you often just don't take care of yourself. Your body will be hurt and age faster because of the poor things that you stuff in your mouth, the lack of exercise (movement), or too much exercise (especially without eating right, or getting enough sleep), not sleeping enough, and all of the stressing out over almost everything (almost everything seems earth-shatteringly important as a teenager and young adult). All of these have a huge effect on you and your body.

This is the only body that you have, and it's going to be with you until you're ready to move on to your next existence. It's tough to have perspective on the whole aging process, but one day, that skin will start to wrinkle, and it will be tougher to move around, to lift and do things that used to be easy . . .When you're young, you just don't think about how life will be when you're older. But it's coming, and it's inevitable. I'm going through a little bit of that realization right now because I'm starting to see a bald spot on the top of my head. NOOOooooo . . .

I've been a lot better about eating well, about exercising, sleeping, meditating, de-stressing (or preventing stress in the first place); I really wish I did it much sooner.

My friend and mentor Joe Polish tells this story:

If you're the owner of a million-dollar race horse, you're going to take the time to make sure it gets fed the right way. You will make certain that the food is on point, that it's the highest quality. You're going to keep it hydrated. Under your watch, it's going to exercise well, and really stretch its legs. It will have the best trainer, and when it's not training you'll make sure it's getting great quality rest. If there is an illness or a problem, you'll make sure that it sees the best specialist for that. This horse is, after all, your meal ticket. You will be taking CARE of it!

It's ironic, then, that you won't do the very same thing for yourself! You are, after all, your OWN meal ticket. You need to fuel properly, feed and rest. You need to keep your mind right and remain in top running shape.

It's truly imperative.

Here is the thing: we are GIFTED this body. It was given to us in all of its glory for our use. It's really just on loan for the time we're here on this planet. But while we are here, it's our entire LENS of the human experience. Everything that we see, hear, smell, touch, and taste is done through the filter of this mortal body.

It just makes sense to treat it RIGHT. And the toughest part of that is making the right decision IN THE MOMENT. When you're about to order that ice cream, or turn off the road to the pizza place, or when you're thinking of pulling the covers back over your head and sleeping rather than getting to your workout.

That's when the magic of *loving yourself* needs to come to your aid. If you're thinking about the future and creating your best self, you'll think twice about it, not do it at all, or maybe just as an *occasional* treat.

If you loved yourself, that's the way you'd think. You would treat what you ate as fuel for performance. You'd eat something to help your build for the future rather than just satisfying a temporary craving.

I know from excruciating experience that this is easier to say than it is to do. But I also know that you are extraordinary, and capable of the very best in life. Oh, and you're loved.

Advice in Practice:

- Pull out the journal, and let's write out what it would mean to be healthy, energetic, and vibrant. How does life feel? What can you do when you're feeling like that? Write it out in glorious detail. The clearer you get, the better this exercise works.

- Now, go back and write out what the consequences of being unhealthy and making bad decisions would be. Think it through carefully and list it all. We're creating a dissonance between the good and the bad. Make sure to put in the effects it can have on your family and loved ones, too.

- Idea lists: List out ten to twenty things you could do to make being healthier a reality in your life. Ways to make it easier to work out; to eat well almost every day; to get better sleep; to de-stress . . . it's all up to you to come up with these and to implement them.

- Swear off sodas. Do it now, and make a HARD BRIGHT LINE against drinking any at all. This has been my kryptonite forever; as I write this, it's been two hundred sixty-five days since I've had a Coke Zero. They are very harmful for your body. I generally eat well, and my inflammation is still extremely high, and I'm pretty sure it's due to the amount of cokes I used to drink.

    a. Dr. Joseph Mercola writes that, "Obesity, diabetes, heart disease, kidney disease, liver damage, osteoporosis, and acid reflux are just some of the health conditions linked to soda consumption."[8]

b. I believe it. It's much, much better to make a hard line cut and never do it again than to taper off and hoping to cut it out someday. I mention all of this because it's already made a difference in my life.

I love you and want the best for you. Please consider this advice.

Notes, thoughts, and intentions.

[8] Dr. Joseph Mercola "Diet Soda Dangers." https://articles.mercola.com/sites/articles/archive/2013/07/24/diet-soda-dangers.aspx (July 24, 2013)

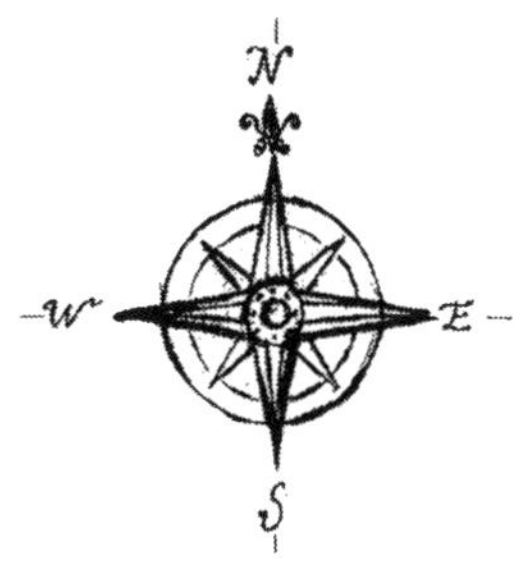

63. Learn The Oxygen Mask Principle

Now we get to talk about the oxygen mask principle and the fact that it is okay to be "selfish."

What is the oxygen mask principle? Maybe you've heard this before or maybe you haven't, but when you fly in an airplane, usually a flight attendant at the front will say something along the lines of, "When pressure is lost in the cabin, oxygen masks will fall out of the ceiling. You need to take an oxygen mask and put one on yourself before you put them on others."

For parents, generally we try to look out for our kids first. However, in a case like this where you might only have seconds before people lose consciousness, it's important to take care of yourself by putting on your own oxygen mask before you try to put on the oxygen mask of your children because otherwise, you *and* your children could potentially be lost.

Now how this applies to life is that you have to take care of yourself before you can take care of others. The proverb is that you cannot pour from an empty cup. So, you need to take care and practice taking care of yourself so that your cup will always be full and you're able to pour for other people.

Now, I think all of us know that there are martyrs out there who will give their last dime financially to someone else and then, of course, not be able to take care of themselves and lean on other people to take care of *them* financially. This is not showing a lot of compassion as you're just transferring the burden to someone else.

Or the people that will spend all of their time and energy taking care of their kids, rushing them different places, and essentially living their entire lives for just their kids. Then perhaps complain, or not complain, that they've given everything to their kids and then their kids somehow owe them for doing that.

What's even worse is when the parent stops all of their dreams in order to just take care of the children. I get it. It sounds like the nice, right thing to do . . . but is it?

Philip McKernan, a friend and mentor of mine says to do this: ask your kids if it's okay to use them as an excuse not to pursue what's in your heart.

No, martyrdom is not the answer. Instead, take time for *yourself*, practice extreme self-care, and look out for yourselves in the different areas. You need to take care of yourself physically, emotionally, spiritually, and financially in life, enough to be able to not only thrive, but to be able to help others in those areas as well.

By doing this, you're not being selfish. In fact, you are making yourself more capable of taking care of others.

So, take time for yourself to get that massage or to go work out. While on the surface, it seems like it may be for you, it's actually for you *and* the loved ones in your life, and it can have wonderful, lasting effects for everyone involved. It's not selfish at all. In fact, something I've heard recently from my friend Giovanni—and I really like this:

"Being selfish is actually the most selfless thing that you can do."

Going back to my example with the parents martyring themselves for the kids—what kind of example are you to them if you're not caring for YOURSELF? You caring for yourself shows them that it will be okay to look out for themselves, too.

So, the advice is: put on your own oxygen mask in life before attempting to put on others' for them. As long as your actions don't harm someone else, you are free to look after yourself in every way.

As your Dad, I expect this of you.

Advice in Practice:

- Something I'd encourage you to do is use your journal to do a self-checkup and think about yourself and your life in the following areas: health, your emotional life, spiritually, and financially. I know we're on the Body section—and we'll start with that—but we need to do an Oxygen Mask check on all areas of your life.

- Go through each one of these, give yourself a number from one to ten. One being awful, horrible, terrible, no good, and ten being the absolute best. Try to be realistic and give yourself a number. The higher the number, the more you're able to take care of others.
- The next piece of advice is to go through each of those areas and brainstorm ways that you can be better. Answer the following questions in your journal. Think them through, get the answers out of your head and out onto paper.
- Being as this is the section on the Body, let's start with Health.

  a. How is your energy level?
  b. How is your strength and your endurance?
  c. How do you feel about yourself?
  d. Are you confident when you look in the mirror? (I think a lot of us would say that the answer is no.)
  e. Of course, these are all things that we need to work on before giving our time and energy to other people.

- Spiritually.
  a. Are you being grateful?
  b. Are you doing acts of kindness for other people?
  c. Do you feel like you have a relationship with God?

d. Those are all questions that you can work on and get better about before trying to help someone else spiritually.

- Your emotional state.
  a. Are you depressed?
  b. Do you regularly do things that give you joy throughout your life?
  c. Are you doing the things that you like to do?
  d. Do you have a fulfilling career or job or purpose or better yet, a mission that drives you? Think of ways that you can improve that.

- Financially.
  a. How are you doing there?
  b. Do you have savings?
  c. Do you have an emergency fund?
  d. Do you have a runway where if you stopped working you could live for at least a while?
  e. Do you have some sound financial habits or are you in a lot of debt?
  f. The answers to those questions determine whether or not you're able to help your loved ones if and when the time of financial need arises, and of course, whether or not you can give to charities and good causes that you believe in as well.

- Lastly, take a look at all your answers, decide on the best idea from each list, and put them in your schedule as an appointment to do. This is so important in actually creating a change.

As always, I love you dearly and appreciate you and want the best in life for all of you.

Notes, thoughts, and intentions.

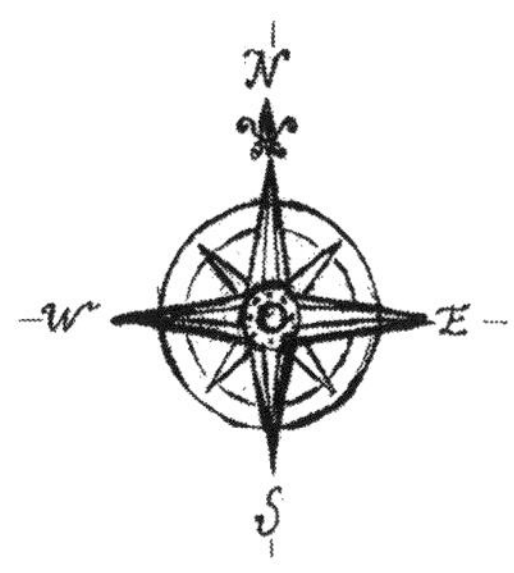

64. Do a Life-Changing, Life-Affirming, Daily Practice.

I feel so blessed to be able to even talk to you about this, because this piece of advice that I'm about to share with you has made such a huge difference in my life. It is the Daily Practice and it's something that I learned from the book *Choose Yourself* by James Altucher.

This book came along at a time in my life when I was pretty down, not feeling good about myself, and feeling very stuck in life. I think the book was something sent divinely because it came at just the right time.

The Daily Practice is something that James, the author, used to get out of several funks in his own life where he was doing very poorly. After he made millions and lost it all, he was physically, relationship-wise and in general just feeling horrible. He used this idea to snap out of it and continues to do the practice to remain well these days.

It worked for me as well to get out of my low points in life. It's called "practice," because it's something that you will always keep doing to get better and better at it. It's something you'll never perfect. But, as you do it daily, you'll get better and better. One percent better each day is the goal.

Now, the Daily Practice is doing something every day that is good for your emotional self, your mental self, your spiritual self, and your physical self. Altucher believes that you have these four parts of you as a person and that every day you have to do something to improve yourself in each of the areas.

For my physical self, I started by doing something very easy but doing it consistently, every single day. In my case, it was taking at least a ten-minute walk. Later that became abstaining from Coke products or any kind of sodas, which are very bad for you. Then later on, as I grew stronger and got in better shape, it turned into weight training and running high intensity interval training as well.

Daily improvement compounds. It stacks up, and you get better and better, and FEEL better as a result. As you overcome the smaller obstacles, you get stronger. That extra strength allows you to do more each day. Of course, that's not just physical—it works on every part of your life.

For my emotional self, one of the things that I did was to avoid emotional vampires. You know, those types of people that come into the room and when they come in, you kind of feel your energy drop like, "Oh gosh, they're here." They leave you feeling a lot wearier when they're done talking with you. So, I avoided people like that. On the positive side, I tried to do something I enjoyed each and every day.

Something that brought me enjoyment and helped me emotionally.

We will cover the mental side of this in another piece of advice in a lot of detail. That is the Daily Practice of writing down at least ten ideas a day. It's something that helped revolutionize my life professionally, because it taught me to be an Idea Machine. The way you do this is to come up with a certain topic. The topic can be anything. I usually tend to use topics that are helpful to me in life, like ten ways that I could get new customers or twenty websites I could start tomorrow that would make money by the end of the week.

But they could also be personal in nature too, like, "twenty ways for me to make my wife feel loved and cherished each and every day." You come up with all of those ideas around that certain topic. The idea is to make your brain sweat, to think hard, and it grows your mind from a weakling to into an idea machine powerhouse. You do that every day, just as if you were in the gym working out every day for your body. I'm such a big fan of this that there's a whole chapter devoted to it, "Revolutionize Your Life with Idea Lists."

The last part is the spiritual body. For me, this was the one that actually pulled me out of the depression more than anything else. I resolved to do a kind act for another human being each and every day. It could even be a very small one like sending an encouraging text to a friend. Or it could be to pull over and help someone on the side of the road if they need help. It could also be volunteering.

Another simple, easy, spiritual practice that I did most everyday was to write down a gratitude list of things that I really appreciated in life. That also helped out tremendously because something that James says, and it rings true, is that, "Fear, anxiety, and depression can't live in the same head as gratitude." So that was part of the Daily Practice that really helped me out.

Something I'd encourage you to do is a Daily Practice of sorts. Generally, I kind of feel that emotional and spiritual are interconnected and can have a lot of the same types of things in them. But I encourage you to make up your own Daily Practice and to write down and accomplish things that are good for you physically, spiritually, emotionally, and physically each and every day.

Advice in Practice:

- Read *Choose Yourself*, by James Altucher. And really everything else he writes. His writing about his experiences really helped to change mine—and without it, this book would never have been written for you.

- Read the advice on the idea lists in this book as well as the part about doing a kind act every day. Those two practices had such a profound impact on me that I wanted to share them in all of their glory with you as separate pieces of advice. Please read those to get a good feeling and a better idea of the types of things that I recommend you do.

- The next thing, I would like you to do some idea lists in your journal or wherever you keep idea lists (personally, I use Evernote). On these idea lists, brainstorm and think about different things you can do for EACH area of the Daily Practice.

- So, come up with ten to twenty things you can do physically. Things that you can do right away to start you on the path to improving your life for your body. You can get some of these ideas from the Body section of this book.

- Write out ten to twenty things you can do for mental juice, and they can be other things aside from idea lists. Again, that's just what I use and what James uses. Examples could be doing Sudoku puzzles. or a daily meditation drawing—my friend Akira does these and they're REALLY good. But whatever's comfortable for you. At least come up with some more ideas of different things that you could do.

- For the Emotional Self, create ten to twenty ideas of ways to make yourself feel better and just to be happier and just to enjoy life more (which is fun to even think about doing). Include the things you can do, and the things you can STOP doing to be happier. You can cheat by reading the chapter on making yourself happy.

- Then last, spiritually. Think of some of the things that could feed your soul and have you feeling good about what you're doing here in the world and how you are showing up to help others, and also to serve God in your own way.

- Next, I would like you to start doing a Daily Practice. It can be little at first. It doesn't have to be a huge ordeal, but I would like you to get started in each of the areas. Something I would recommend at the beginning is to start small and set your bar of accomplishment very low so they will be easy for you to accomplish every day and get into the good habit of doing them. The habit is more important than what you actually do in the beginning.

I promise you is that you will start to feel better every single day that you do these. If you're already feeling good in life and you decide to do these, you'll feel even better. Or if you are like me when I started doing them, it will help to pull you out of the depths of the darkness.

Once again, girls and Mr. Alec, I love you so much and it is such a privilege and such an honor to share this with you.

Notes, thoughts, and intentions.

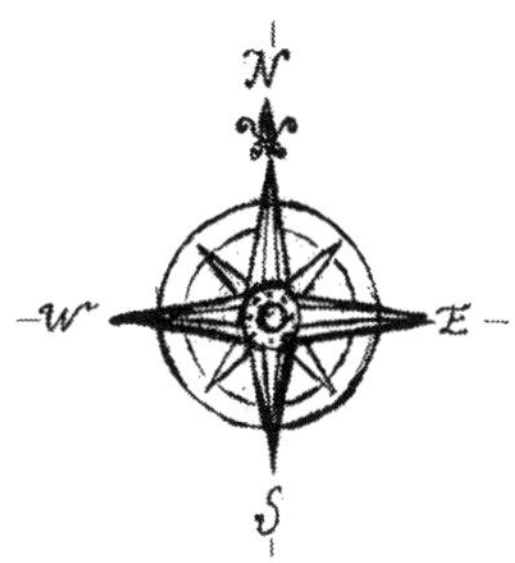

65. Do the Indispensable, Miraculous, Miracle Morning.

Once again, this is something I am so proud and happy to share with you. As my children, you know a little bit about this, but I wanted to make sure that I explained it in detail for you. I think it is something that you can use to enrich your lives so much and help you grow as a human being tremendously, and also to wake up every morning excited and enthusiastic about the future. That is one of the very best gifts that you can ever give yourself as a human being.

Of course, I am talking about the Miracle Morning. I was first introduced to the Miracle Morning by listening to a real estate podcast by my friend Pat Hiban of all things. The episode, if you'd like to look it up, is Pat Hiban's Interviews Real Estate Rockstars #19.

The gentleman that came up with this is named Hal Elrod. I first heard him on my car radio talking about it to real estate agents. The Miracle Morning is a daily routine, something you do first thing in the morning when you wake up, generally for about an hour, although it can be done in as little as six minutes. It is a daily ritual to set yourself up for success each and every day.

Hal is actually a friend of mine now and actually wrote the Foreword to this book, which is really quite something . . . it's funny how life works out like that.

What he recommends is waking up about an hour before you have to start getting ready for school, or work, or whatever. His contention is that most people hit the alarm clock, snooze it several times, and just roll out of bed as late as they can, subconsciously telling themselves that they're not ready to wake up or that they don't want to greet the day.

Of course, that starts the day off in a reactive mode where you have to REACT to everything, versus waking up a little earlier, taking that time for yourself, and being PROACTIVE in setting up your day and making it wonderful.

He recommends doing the life SAVERS routine. SAVERS is an acronym that stands for silence, affirmation, visualization, exercise, reading, and scribing, which is a fancy word for journaling (SAVERJ does not make as much sense as SAVERS). What he recommends is to spend five to ten minutes on each, or sometimes a little more depending on which of these practices you enjoy the most or gives you more of a boost.

Silence would be either meditation, which I do, or prayer, which I also do but not as routinely as the meditation.

Affirmations are where you actively repeat to yourself different affirming sentences that empower you and make you feel better. One of my affirmations is: I am a finisher and I finish the things that I start. Of course, you make up your own affirmations that empower you. This is the time to go through that. It can actually change you, change your personality, and increase your skill level just by the simple act of taking the time to do these affirmations.

Visualization is not necessarily visualizing yourself accomplishing your goals, like standing at the end of a race that's already won, because that can sometimes trick your mind into thinking it's already done and you don't have to do it. Visualization is picturing yourself in the act of eating healthy for instance, if your goal is to lose weight. Or it could be exercising right, actually making phone calls in your business, or having that tough conversation that you need to have. Visualizing it and picturing it as positively as you can in your mind can help you in real life.

Exercise: plenty self-explanatory. Of course, we will talk more about this in the piece of advice about moving your body the right way. I have a more in-depth exercise routine later on in the day that takes about forty minutes to an hour, but as part of Miracle Morning I just do one or two exercises for about five or ten minutes to get the blood flowing, get it pumping, and get me feeling good. Right now, it's Burpees and a long plank. Burpees suck, but they're pretty cool, too.

Reading is usually done with something that's inspiring, that you enjoy, that teaches you something that you can learn from and that sets up your day the right way. This part of the SAVERS routine is actually the one that I begin my Miracle Morning with every morning. Right now, I'm going through The Daily Stoic by Ryan Holiday.

The last one: scribing or journaling. There is another piece of advice strictly on journaling because I think that journaling is literally the best thing you can do for self-development. It is writing down your thoughts onto paper and getting everything out of your head into something that you can look at. It's near the beginning of the MIND section and called, "Partake in the Phenomenal Power of Journaling."

Something that you might do for the scribing part of this morning routine is to go over the things that you're grateful for, or to write out the things that you want to have happen in your life, or record what has happened in your life and perhaps the lessons learned from it. It can also be plans that you have for the future. A lot of times as a part of my Miracle Morning, I do this: I plan the day and write out my intentions for it using a to-do list, or as I call it, an outcome list. That could also be part of scribing. It's definitely good to do some planning for your day as part of a really complete Miracle Morning.

Now my dears, I know the first thing that you think of when you talk about waking up earlier than you do now. Most people don't have a positive view of that. But if you give this a shot and you do the SAVERS that you really *enjoy* personally, I think that you'll find that this is a positive change for your life. I'd love for you to at least give it a shot.

Advice in Practice:

- Pull out your journal and do an idea list for each of the SAVERS, for the silence, for the affirmations, the visualization, exercise, reading and scribing. What I want you to do is write out different ideas that you have to make that individual time better for you and to make it as exciting as possible.

- The next advice in practice is pretty self-explanatory: I'd like you to try a Miracle Morning. If it is too difficult to start to do a complete, total Miracle Morning for an hour or more, I would recommend trying the six-minute version, which is to do each of the SAVERS for a minute. That way you don't have to wake up that much earlier, but you can still start to get the benefits of this practice. Hopefully, when you see that and feel the difference, and you're more excited to wake up each morning, getting up earlier will be easier for you.

- The next thing is to find an accountability buddy and teach this practice to them. Help them learn how to do this, and to keep each other accountable for doing it. Right now, you can do a search for "The Miracle Morning Group," on Facebook. Currently, it has over 100,000 people in it and it's very active. If it's not around—be resourceful and find your own!

- Next, this probably should be first, but I want you to read *The Miracle Morning* by Hal Elrod. Just order it. It's not a very long book but it goes through this in a lot more detail and depth and will heighten and improve your SAVERS practice every day by reading it.

- Go to LifeLessonsBonus.com and sign up for your free course, Design and Execute Your Ideal Week. I go over morning rituals in great detail in that, and you'll get a lot of use out of it.

- The last thing is to do a YouTube search of Hal Elrod and The Miracle Morning, and just watch a few of the videos of him teaching The Miracle Morning practice. He is an incredible speaker and very inspiring and motivating. You can take a couple of minutes to watch what he has to say. I think you'll be inspired to give this piece of advice a go.

I love you, but you knew that, I bet.

Notes, thoughts, and intentions.

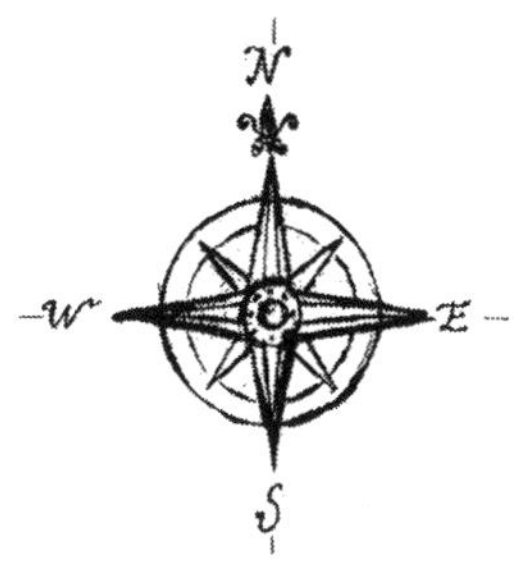

66. Indulge in The Huge, Gigantic, Benefits of Strength Training.

Weight training has such huge benefits, and yes, this refers to females as well! It is such an honor to talk with you about this type of thing, my girls and son! Weight training and getting physically STRONG is so important in life, and I get to talk all about it with you.

Now honestly, where else in life do you get this kind of talk or advice? There is not really a place for it other than a haphazard PE class sometimes in school. Some people may just happen to get into it on their own, but not a huge percentage of the population does weight training. That's something I would like to change, at least for you after reading this.

One of the very cool things that I get a chance to do these days is meet some very interesting, wonderful people. I had a chance to talk with Charles Poliquin about this. He is known as the strength sensei and is one of the world's foremost strength training coaches. He walks his talk like few people I've ever seen and is in incredible shape, he's incredibly strong and he knows the benefits of weight training. I always knew strength training was wonderful, but hearing him speak at a group talk recently really solidified this for me.

I'm hoping that you will listen to or read this with an open mind because it can really change your life. Please know that if you're female, you're not going to end up bulking up like Schwarzenegger. That is a complete myth. If you go to the gym and work out, you'll see some ladies in great shape. They are lean, toned, confident and not at all bulky as popular culture would have you believe. In fact, muscle takes up far less space than fat—the same pound of muscle is a lot smaller than the same pound of fat.

Benefits of Strength Training:

Functional Fitness.

That is the everyday fitness to be able to lift things and do things with confidence that other people can't or won't do.

This is especially important when you have children because you can lift them up, you can help them, you can carry an enormously heavy stroller, get them in and out of cars, and be able to take them with you places. You can hold a baby carrier with a baby in it and have incredible mom-strength as a female. Of course, as a guy, you can do all of this as well, and it's *expected* of you.

Helps prevent aging.

I mentioned this earlier—but I want to make sure this lands with you: In a conversation I had on Facebook with Mr. Poliquin after my stroke, he told me that the best predictor of longevity in people is their muscle mass and how much strength they're able to maintain as they get older. Everything that I've seen verifies this.

If you've seen bodybuilders or people who have been strong their whole life, they tend to age very well. There's a lot of anecdotal proof for it—and even a simple Google search shows a lot of evidence for this.[9]

Folks that train are more functionally capable, they age better—and it seems that they're also mentally sharper with lower rates of dementia.[10]

Strength training will help a lot with higher bone density. One of the biggest causes of people going downhill is that they have brittle bones. The number one cause of nursing home admissions is breaking a hip bone. If you weight train and have a healthy foundation for getting strong, then your bones will remain much denser throughout your lifetime and there will be a lower chance of them breaking or getting brittle in your older age.[11]

Aside from bone density and longevity, with weight training your connective tissue, your ligaments, and (of course) your muscles are bigger and better. When done right and done the correct way (without killing yourself trying to do much

---

[9] Len Kravitz, PhD, "Yes, Resistance Training Can Reverse the Aging Process," http://www.ideafit.com/fitness-library/yes-resistance-training-can-reverse-the-aging-process (August 27, 2008).
[10] Sydney University "Increasing muscle strength can improve brain function: study," http://sydney.edu.au/news-opinion/news/2016/10/25/increasing-muscle-strength-can-improve-brain-function–study.html (October 25, 2016)
[11] Charlie Seltzer, MD "Can Weight Lifting Increase Bone Density?" Medically Reviewed https://www.builtlean.com/2013/12/11/weight-lifting-bone-density/ (February 19, 2016).

more than you're capable of doing), weight training will decrease the chances of you getting injured. That's especially true when you're using correct form, the weight is appropriate, and you do it gradually and get better and better at it.

Improves Mental Clarity.

I know that on the days when I work out, I have this incredible chemical concoction in my system that just allows me to breathe better, feel better, and makes my mind sharper than on the days when I don't.

If you are weight training, you can get into a great meditative state while you're doing it. You regulate your breathing, you learn to focus on getting something done, on getting your sets and your reps finished. Again, that long period of focus or the short burst of activity that you control will help with your mental acuity and just generally help your mind in a ton of ways.

Improves Mood, Emotions, and Feels Good!

Along with the mental clarity, I would say that your emotional state is going to be a lot better. When you're taking care of yourself, you're going to feel better about yourself. There's a higher chance that you'll be happy. When you take the time to care enough about yourself to improve your body, then you're generally going to be a lot happier of a person. Although it *can* be done, it's very difficult to be depressed after a great workout.

The last part that I'll tell you about as far as benefits is extremely important because it actually helps you continue when it's tough at the beginning. Weight training just makes you feel good when you do it. Again, I already mentioned about how I feel better on the days that I lift weights and I'm thinking more clearly. You get a great rush. I like to listen to some incredible music while I'm working out. It gives you a chance to get some aggression out and do something to help with your emotions.

Once you're done, it's just a huge rush of dopamine that you receive when you can check it off and say, "I finished, I DID that!" and you feel better the rest of the day. Go, you!

The Importance of ENJOYING Weight Training.

I heard about a study through Brian Johnson and Optimize.me on people that set New Year's resolutions to lose weight and to get in better shape at the gym. They divided the study into two groups of people. One group of people said that they were doing it for their children and to be around a lot longer for the health benefits that would accrue at a later date, etc.

The other group did their workouts because they said that it *made them feel good* in the moment. They felt a lot better about themselves when they worked out than when they didn't.

Coming back later, the study found that the people that lifted weights and worked out because it made them feel better *were 75 percent more likely to stick with their workout plan* and still be there many months later. On the other hand, the people that were doing it for a far-off abstract goal had often quit long before then. Take care of yourself first—this will allow you to take care of others better.

I would recommend finding a routine that you really enjoy, that makes you feel good, doesn't decimate you, invigorates you and has you feeling great instead of torn down. When you get out of the gym you want to feel better than when you went into it.

My dear wonderful children, I hope you get the importance of this. When you hug me, I want it to be a tight hug!

Advice in Practice:

- Start at home. If you haven't worked out before then do some light body weight exercises rather than going into a place where you pay a whole bunch of money and you may or may not continue. You want to set to the bar of completion a lot lower initially than what you do in the end.

- I'd recommend a home regimen of doing pushups, planks, burpees, air squats and that type of thing even if it's only for five to ten minutes and as a part of your Miracle Morning practice. Do that and start to feel the benefits of feeling better when you do it. I think as you start to feel better, you're going to want to bump up your exercise regimen, start lifting weights and to take the benefits to a higher level.

- The next piece of advice is to find great programs on weight training, especially female weight training. One of the sources I recommend is bodybuilding.com. Don't let the name scare you because there's a lot of great information on it.

- The next thing is to find someone that you know who does this well, who has been weight training for a while, and shadow them on a trip or two to the gym. Tell them what you're trying to do and more than likely they're going to want to help you. If you can tag along with them, see what they do, and maybe get their help in designing a program for you, it will go a long way towards helping you out with this. Also, you'll have someone that knows that you're trying to get better and they'll hold you accountable for what you're trying to do.

- Write out some goals for weight training, fitness or weight loss that you would like to accomplish. Again, don't make this too outlandish. Make it something initially that's going to be fairly easy to accomplish. This can help during the bad times, and you'll be less likely to give up on your goals. You want to be able to accomplish them, get some wind beneath your wings, build some confidence and set higher goals to keep going with this practice.

- Find an accountability buddy. Find someone that's doing it. It could be the person that you shadowed at the gym or it could be someone else that's trying to get into better shape, but just check with them, see what their goals are and hold each other accountable. Check in with them once a day, a few times a week when you're supposed to work out, or maybe once a week, but find someone that can do it consistently and help you out.

- The last part I just want to tell you is to remember that it gets easier! Everything is tough when it starts. You may not feel great about doing it, but as you keep going it's going to become easier and easier. What you'll find is your energy levels will go up, you'll get better at it and it'll be something that you want to continue doing.

Remember that if you stick with it thirty days or sixty days, it really becomes a part of you and it doesn't take a lot of willpower or effort once it becomes part of your everyday life.

So, that is the advice that I have on weight training. I sincerely hope this is one of the pieces of advice that you decide to implement into your life because the benefits from this are going to bleed over into everything else in your life.

As always, I love you, I cherish you and it is an honor to be your daddy.

Notes, thoughts, and intentions.

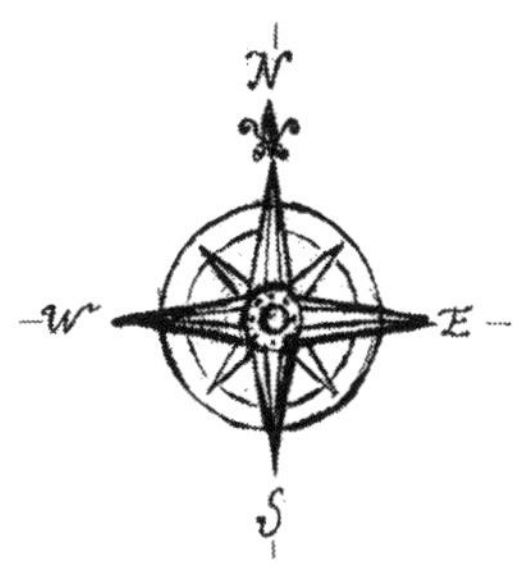

67. Stand Up, Walk Around—We're Made to Move.

You see, I feel GREAT talking to you about this right now. . . because I've been taking my own advice. My muscles are (somewhat) pleasantly sore from lifting weights, I've just finished sprinting/walking on the beautiful trail next to the creek in Georgetown. I feel ALIVE. I'm even firmly convinced that my thoughts are better and clearer because I have the blood pumping through my veins, and oxygen is flowing through me right now.

I've already mentioned this at the top of this piece of advice, but it is SO, SO true:

We are made to move.

The human form is made for motion. But as we have "evolved," we sit a lot more. We stare at glowing screens all day. We wake up from laying down. We sit while we eat. We sit in our cars as we're going to our jobs or school . . . where we SIT. I am certain that we aren't supposed to spend so much time just sitting and being sedentary. But unfortunately, that's how most of our days are designed. Everything is designed for comfort, to make things easier.

As we know, though, too much ease makes us soft and fragile. It's a lot better to make ourselves at least slightly uncomfortable, because otherwise we'll just get used to being coddled all of the time. So, go walking in the rain, and be a little cold or hot. You can take it. Honest.

In fact, our ancestors I'm certain were a lot more "fit" and functionally stronger than we are now. Our older ancestors didn't even have chairs. Maybe a big rock here and there, but to "sit" they often had to squat and could do it for really, really long periods of time—and now, it's tough for all of us.

Have you tried to squat for a while lately? I'm up to doing it for three minutes at a time, and it's hard! They also couldn't lie down too easily. No feather beds or foam mattresses for them. And here we are complaining if we have to sleep on an uncomfortable bed now. I'm getting off topic, but the big thing is that as a race, we used to MOVE a lot more. They walked more, they sprinted to get out of danger (when's the last time you all-out sprinted?!), and they had to lift their own things.

I've also watched as some friends and family members have gotten older, and they move less. As they move less, the aging process seems to accelerate. It is literally a "use it or lose it," function for us. If you stop moving, the moving becomes harder and harder . . . and it's a downward cycle.

But!

The good news is that you can start a new program of moving more at any time, and like anything, we get better as we practice.

So, my advice is this: make a concerted effort to MOVE a lot more in our lives.

Don't necessarily jog or go "running." I don't really think that we were made to run for long periods of time, either. I've done a marathon, and the training for that was super hard for me, and I'll dare say unnatural.[12]

But go walking. A LOT. Make it a part of your daily routine, and increase the distance. And something else I'd add to that is called HIIT: High Intensity Interval Training. That means for short intervals, do something with all of your effort. So that means while walking, throw in some all-out sprints—don't worry about how you look! That's a lot more natural than long periods of sustained jogging (at least that's how it seems to me). Also, sprinters look a lot better than long distance runners. Google those images and see for yourself.

Aside from walking, maybe the most important thing you can do is to take breaks from any desks or sitting that you may be doing. Get up and move at regular intervals. Try to walk around during the day and make it a part of your everyday habits. Set a timer, and every once in a while,

---

[12] Elizabeth Narins "Why Too Much Running Is Bad for Your Health," http://www.active.com/health/articles/why-too-much-running-is-bad-for-your-health? (no date posted).

stand up (if you're not already at a standing desk, which I also recommend), stretch, move, walk, squat, do a few pushups or even burpees. I did that at my real estate office and LOVED the weird looks that I got. I wore them like a badge of honor.

Sure, it looks weird. But I'd much rather be weird and RIGHT than be like the masses of men that go about life doing what everyone else does without some critical thought as to whether or not their behavior makes sense. Does that make sense to you?

Thank you for reading this, my sweethearts. I hope this has helped and put a seed in your mind to have a more active life.

Advice in Practice:

- If you have a chance, get a standing desk where you're going to working a lot. I really dig the new "variable" desks that will raise and lower themselves to allow you to stand and/or sit. I understand that you may have to sit sometimes. Just stand a lot more, k?

- When you find yourself sitting a lot at the job or at school, even while you're eating—set a timer. Maybe using the Pomodoro technique (twenty-five minutes ON, five OFF), to get up and move at regular intervals. Just ask your phone to remind you to set the timer. It's magical. And if you do it for your work, you'll find yourself focusing more during those other twenty-five minutes.

- Put it in your calendar, right now, to WALK. Set a time for it. I LOVE walks. At the beginning and end of the day, even during the middle. They are so awesome. Now, that you set a time in your calendar, put it on REPEAT!!!

- Do a HIIT Walk/Run as a part of your Miracle Morning that we talk about in another piece of advice. Even if it's for a quick ten minutes in the morning. That's plenty to get your blood moving and your brain functioning a lot better. I like doing it right before journaling and planning my day, so my brain has woken up, and I'm in an appreciative state.

- Consider walking on a treadmill while doing work or talking on the phone if you aren't able to get outside—although outside is MUCH, much better. Even if the weather isn't as great. Maybe that's even better as it teaches us to be tougher.

- Squat once a twice a day. Seriously. Just go down on your haunches and hang out there for a while. Yes, it will look a little strange. But do it in honor of dear ol' Dad. If anyone asks, you can say I told you to do it. I think I'll challenge y'all to a squatting contest tonight, hahahaha! I love you. But you knew that, right?

Notes, thoughts, and intentions.

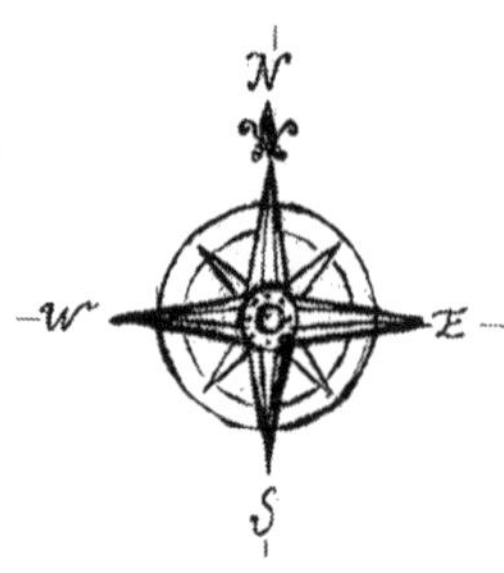

68. Go on Lots of Walks.

I've already told you that I was in a severe funk back in 2014. I just wasn't feeling great about my life, and the potential that I was NOT living up to at the time. Coupled with that, or maybe partially because of that, I was in the worst shape of my life and severely overweight. I lacked energy and motivation and literally didn't want to get out of bed.

I know that a lot of me is in YOU, and if you're ever in that situation this may help you, as it did me. I started the Daily Practice, as outlined in James Altucher's book, *Choose Yourself*, and one of the principles was to do something good for you physically every single day. So, the thing that was the best, low-hanging fruit (the best result from the minimum effort) was to start walking each day. I went out for ten minutes or more—which quickly became twenty minutes, and expanded to some walks that took several hours as I got in better shape and realized that I enjoyed it.

The walks did wonders for me. They were good physically, and also got me back in the gym—see the benefits of lifting weights in this book, yo—but it affected my mind even more.

Here is a list of some of the reasons why it's great to make this a big part of your daily routine:

- It gets blood going, and the processes in your body working better. Robert Cooper, the famous neuroscientist (Google him!), told me that walking immediately after a meal will DOUBLE its energy output for you! Think about that and try it.

- Clears cobwebs from the mind—clear thinking and creativity. I like to do my Idea Lists (much more on these in the Mind section) right after walking and/or exercising. I am a lot sharper right afterwards, and I bet you'll agree with that.

- Sunlight is great for you, and we seldom get it! Vitamin D. Your Mom used to get depressed during the winters in Chicago because it turned to night so quickly, and she didn't get sunlight. It's great and even necessary for you. We're like Superman, and it's the source of our immense power.

- Improves your mood tremendously. It's a combination of the blood going, the cobwebs gone, the Vitamin D—and the fact that you're doing something good for yourself which, in turn, makes you feel great!

- Outdoors gets you closer to our Creator. Appreciation of the wonder of it all is a glorious thing. Sometimes, when I'm walking out in the country where we are, I'll do a mental appreciation list as I'm going. I call these

Gratitude Walks—and it's an INCREDIBLE way to start the day.

- It makes you live longer. What happens when things stop moving? They die! If you do a lot and become "anti-fragile" your functional abilities will thrive long past others your age who are sedentary. We are made to move.

- Walking faster helps your cardio. You can even do the speed walking thing that your Mom does sometimes to our great amusement. Go at a slightly uncomfortable pace after you've developed the habit of walking each day.

- If you walk, you're more likely to SPRINT! YESSSSS! How often do we do an all-out sprint as adult humans in today's lifestyle? Not often, if EVER. This is a great chance to engage in the wonder of what's called HIIT (High Intensity Interval Training), which is a lot better for you than extended periods of cardio like jogging a bunch.

  The idea is to go all out and SPRINT as hard as you can for a bit, walk for a bit, then sprint for a bit, and repeat this many times. I've been running telephone poles out where we live. I'll walk between the first set of poles, sprint the next set, and repeat that a lot. Yes, you'll look funny sprinting, but you'll live longer, reduce body fat, and feel really good about yourself when you're doing or have done it.

- You set an example for your loved ones! We've gone on walks before, right?! I want to do more with you. If you're reading this now, call me up and set a "walking" date, as that would be an absolute pleasure for me!

- It's a GREAT time to connect with friends. Business partners. Family members. Steve Jobs did most of his important business meetings while walking. Make phone calls while walking. The beauty of this is that you get a lot more done while you're walking, and as mentioned above, you're going to be thinking a lot more clearly. It's a joy for me to get a long call while at the office and I get to scamper off to walk while we are talking!

- It gives you something to look forward to during the day. When you really appreciate it, and you feel the incredible benefits of moving like this, you really will look forward to that part of your day. I love my walks, especially if it's with one of my loved ones.

- It's romantic, hold a hand while you do it. Couples don't hold hands enough. It's so infrequent that when we see it, we all go, "Awwwwwwwwww, how CUTE!" Don't be one of those infrequent hand holders! Do it while you're walking, and (more than) double the benefit!

- Time with yourself with NO ELECTRONICS is sacred. Your phone is ever present, and to a certain degree, it runs your life . . . well, break free of those chains at least once a day. Listen to and appreciate the nature sounds. Get back to your roots. My friend Alex goes on "primal walks" every morning; with no electronics and either functional footwear (like Vibram Five Fingers), or even barefoot. It brings us to our roots. If you can, take off your shoes for a while too while you're on the grass. That grounding is supposed to be good for you, and after doing it a lot, I believe it!

- You feel better about yourself. You're walking. That's exercise. You made a goal, and you are DOING it! That is a surefire way to feel a lot better. You friggin' stud(dette)!

- It keeps you generally fit. You can't walk a bunch when you're obese. Your miraculous body will adapt. Of course, that's when you eat like we described earlier and do quite a bit of walking. Even if you are fat, you'll remain able to move a bunch!

- It's functional. It's great to know you can walk many, many miles. You know you're capable and it's possible for you. That just feels good. I like to be dropped off a ways from the house and know that it's an easy thing for me to get back home. If you're ever without a car, this becomes more of a blessing!

- Sometimes, you can meet people while out and about, and it's always serendipitous. You can learn from them and your experiences. So, wave and say, "Howdy." Be friendly, and if they're your neighbors, don't be afraid to talk to them.

- You can see new things you haven't noticed before your walking. Pay attention to what's around you while you're out and about! Like I mentioned above, appreciate the things you see. Personally, I think that God loves an appreciative heart and blesses you more.

- Being in the elements—cold or hot makes you tougher and anti-fragile. Think about this: we live in air that's conditioned for our comfort. We've gotten entitled to a very narrow band of temperature...and THAT is not natural. Increase your comfort by doing the things that don't feel the greatest now, and you'll feel better a lot more in general.

Advice in Practice:

There's not a lot to add to this, is there? Go walk!

- Seriously, though—get a Fitbit, an Oura ring, or use your phone with the app "My Fitness Pal" to measure the steps you take in a day. You can set up a competition with your friends, or your brother and sister . . . don't test me, though, because I'll bury you! Hahahaha!

- Park away from the places you need to go. It's funny how people fight for the good parking spaces outside of a gym! I always found that amusing. Also, if you park away from where you work, you'll have time to get your head in the ballgame going in, and to decompress when you walk away later!

I love you and hope that this once again leads to you doing some walking with your dear ol' Daddy!

Notes, thoughts, and intentions.

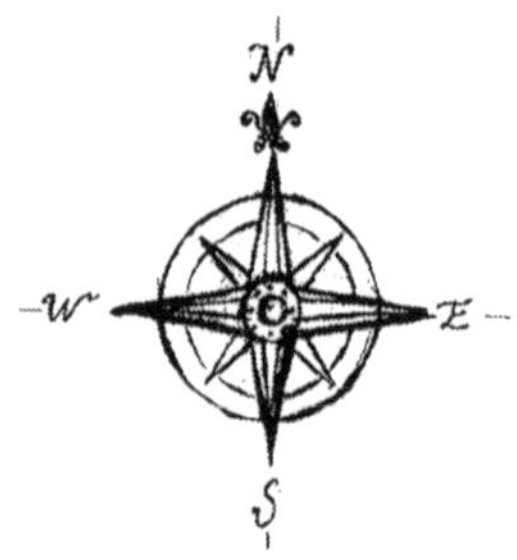

69. Practice the Mechanics of Good Sleep.

I have some great news, and I have some not-so-good news. If you're like Mom, you'll want the not-so-good news first . . . and here it goes:

I haven't been getting a good night's sleep very often. I'm waking up in middle of the night a lot. Sometimes all sweaty and anxious. Alec, at six years old, sleeps with your Mom and I waaaaaaaay too often right now—as much as I love him. The current schedule is him going to sleep with us and after he's asleep, I'll carry the precious boy to his room. The problem is that I usually drift off to sleep before our rambunctious boy and he ends up staying in our bed, moving around and doing the spinning buzz saw of death with his feet often coming into contact with my face.

. . . and even though I can GET to sleep super quickly, literally within a minute or two after hitting the pillow, lately I almost always wake up too soon. Sometimes at 3 or 4 a.m. When that happens, it's often tough to get back to sleep.

So, the bad news is that this advice for you is once again coming from someone that isn't always able to PRACTICE everything that he preaches. That's a bit of a problem. But the good news is that I've been steadily getting better, and after writing this, I'm determined to go back again and do a repeat of my grand sleep "hacking" experiment, where I was able to go from a horrible state of sleeping into the best sleep of my life. [UPDATE: As I'm editing this, my sleep is currently much, much better. Yay, me!]

That's the good news. I know what I'm talking about and have done this before with GREAT success. It all started about the same time that I was in the depression, wondering what the HECK I was doing with my life. I also woke up anxious, sweating, and crazy about what I was doing—or not doing as the case may be—with my life. I wasn't satisfied. I've written about this a lot in other sections of the book, so I won't go into it now, but I experienced a real Renaissance with my life shortly thereafter, and part of that was my sleep hacking experiment. That was me, making an actual *concerted effort* to get better at sleep. To get MORE of it, and to make the sleep a lot higher quality.

I did thc Idca List of ways that I could make sleep better. I researched and studied. I listened to several experts, and most importantly, I experimented to see if it worked. And it did. Big time. I started sleeping a minimum of seven hours, usually eight, even and had one glorious night of eleven hours of uninterrupted, beautifully restorative rest. I still remember that morning . . . ahhhhh.

One of the things I did was actually TRACK my sleep, and it even told me the quality of my sleep, based on movement, heartrate, and breathing . . . and I've achieved a . . . get ready for it . . . 99 percent quality of sleep in those hours.

I want to talk about the importance of sleep first. As newer human beings we are able to maintain some energy even without a good night's sleep. Though now that I think of it, all of you children REALLY love your sleep. Maybe I don't have to talk to you about how vital it is.

Vital. That's a great word. I'm a word-lover. The Latin meaning of vital is "of or manifesting life." And THAT is what sleep is all about—it's making life possible at a higher level, at a more rested level. It's literally energy for you to go out and accomplish what you want to do. I mention this already in another section but it's said and so true—Vince Lombardi said, "Fatigue makes cowards of us all."

When you don't sleep, you're fatigued. You don't have the energy and therefore the FORTITUDE and COURAGE to tackle life. Sleep is so important. It's a background of health. I've even read and heard from health and fitness people that have said out of Eat, Move, and Sleep, that sleep is THE most important. I believe it, because it touches all of the other aspects of life.

That's enough. Are you ready to know HOW to get a better night's sleep, and what worked for me to turn tossing and turning into a blissful, restful, restorative, and rejuvenating experience? YEEEEESSSSSS. Let's get into it.

- Make it a priority. After you consciously think about the importance, make it an experiment to get better. Make it a hacking project. Start to measure it and track it. You've probably heard the adage: what gets measured, gets done. Do some searching for ways to do this. One way I've tracked sleep is by using a device called an Oura ring. It will measure breath and heart rate, and how much you move. It's an excellent way to measure your vitals while trying to get better at sleeping.

- Have bookend rituals for waking and going to sleep. Do the same things methodically when you wake up (I recommend The Miracle Morning, which we talk about in the book) and when you go to sleep. Bookend your day with the times that you can control. For your nighttime ritual, make certain that you include a "digital sunset." That's when you close down all electronic devices a while before you go to sleep (an hour or more is recommended).

- IF you feel you have to have your phone, or are addicted to it (let's be real), then wear blue light-blocking glasses (seriously). At the VERY LEAST turn your phone into night mode which should turn off the blue light and be easier on your eyes than an unfiltered blue screen. But if you can't do without it, that is something that should be addressed, too—and that goes well beyond just your sleeping habits.

- The journaling needs some more explanation. I think it's great to include a form of gratitude (appreciation) practice, and writing down your "wins" for the day (my friend Jesse Elder calls this "saving the progress" for the day), and how you want to wake up in the morning. One of the very best things that I like to do with journaling is to get your anxious thoughts OUT of your head and onto paper where they can face the light of the real world versus letting them fester in the recesses of your mind and causing poor sleep and bouts of anxiety. I need to be more vigilant about that personally.

- Watch what you put in your body, food and drink-wise. Cut any caffeine out of your system, and don't drink anymore after about 3 p.m. Caffeine and stimulants will keep you up longer, and I'd say to avoid eating close to your bedtime—but everyone is different—because I find your stomach working while you try to sleep leads to poor sleep.

- Sleep in total darkness if at all possible. Turn down the displays on electronic clocks, cover the lights on the phone and any TV with tape. Close the blinds as much as you can, and if you're able to get black out blinds or curtains, you may want to think about that.

- Keep the temperature as cold as you're able and that's reasonably comfortable. You'll have deeper sleep. Lastly, something your mom has used that seems to be great is the Chilipad. It's a mattress pad that runs hot or cold water through it to maintain a set temperature.

- Have the phone across the room. There's a few reasons for this. One, is that you won't be so tempted to look at the phone while you're falling asleep. That glowing screen and all of the stimulation of our world, news and social media will keep your brain working and it will mess up your circadian rhythm; your body and brain will think that it's still daylight. More on this in a bit.

Also, when you wake up in the morning (or in middle of the night like I do sometimes) you'll be tempted to reach for the phone first thing. It's not good in any of those circumstances. There's a good chance that there will be a text or email that will keep you up, or the news will engage your mind and make good sleep less likely.

- Buy the best mattress you can comfortably afford. Seriously, you'll be there a good third of your life. If you're going to splurge, do it on something you use ALL OF THE TIME, and where the use of it affects almost everything else.

Some advanced techniques that have worked for me:

A weight training session in the late afternoon or very early evening. Mmmm. That creates some very satisfying sleep. Your body will need the rest to rebuild, too.

Take some magnesium, and/or melatonin, and/or ginseng prior to going to sleep. That will help you go to sleep and stay that way. Please don't take medication if you can help it. I think that it can become a crutch, and it usually has side effects.

A bath or shower before bedtime often makes one feel great when slipping into the sheets. The drawback is that your hair might be crazy the next day . . . but you can deal with that.

I love you. So, so much. Sleep well and sweet dreams, my children.

Advice in Practice:

- I did this section a little differently, a lot of the "Advice in Practice" is listed above. Just do the items above and we're good, hahahaha.

- Seriously, first, set a goal of what you'd like your sleep to be like. How much do you think you need to actually THRIVE? Set that as a goal and WRITE IT DOWN. I'm sure I'll talk about this elsewhere, but there's such power to writing things down, it's like an imprint on your soul when you do it. So, write down "Eight hours of sleep"—or knowing you, even more. Also, let's write out, "How do I feel when I wake up?" And get that out onto paper. I think the rest of these pieces of advice will come more easily when you do that.

- Order the Oura ring, or something that you find that seems to be good, and start tracking your sleep. You don't even need to DO anything just yet. The very act of monitoring will cause you to do better.

- Brainstorm and do an idea list on YOUR perfect nighttime and morning rituals with which to bookend your day. Include all that you want on it. I talk about it on the Miracle Morning piece of advice, and Scheduling Your Day, too. You are the author of your own life. What does an author do? They WRITE. So, write out what you think would be great. What if you found that prayer and gratitude before you closed your eyes at night made for a whole lot better day? Then you'd want to include that in your rituals. **I'm realizing I don't always pray before sleeping, but I'm starting that up again.

- Do a mattress check. Is it good? Does your bed work as a place of restful rejuvenation? If not, and again, if you can afford it, get a better mattress and make that a project.
- If you have a programmable thermostat, spend a good ten to twenty minutes figuring it out, and see if you can lower the temperature close to your bedtime. It shouldn't be too much more expensive if you're not doing it during the relative heat of the day. I bet that temperature variation will make a big difference for you.
- Bring some tape into the room and cover those little lights everywhere. Phone. TV. Clock, etc. Black it out!
- Check out some of the other things listed, and take the time to do them, or at least test them. As with everything I mention and talk about in this entire book—see how you feel about it, and if it makes sense to you, do it. Just do what works.

You are sleeping as I'm writing this, and I hope it's a sweet, restful time for you. Your Daddy loves you dearly.

Notes, thoughts, and intentions.

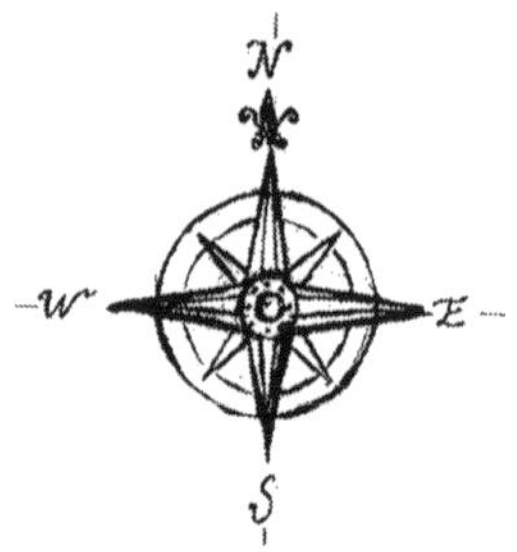

70. Come On! Drink Your Dang Water!

So, this is all about drinking your dang water.

And I say "your dang water" because girls especially, when I tell you all to drink more water, you generally do the teenage thing and roll your eyes at me, and say, "There he goes again." But this is a very important piece of advice and I'd really like you to heed this.

One of the things I want to tell you is I know that you have gotten better since I started nagging you about drinking more water. Although you're heading in the right direction, I'm still pretty certain that my children are dehydrated. In fact, the Medical Daily says that a good 75 percent of Americans may suffer from chronic dehydration. That's not just dehydration, but dehydration all *of the time*.

That doesn't mean the other 25 percent are hydrated regularly. It just means that they're not thirsty all of the time, whereas 75 percent of Americans are.

So this is very, very important for us. Just heeding this piece of advice, this one piece of advice for your body can change your life for the better and make everything easier for you.

Many people just say, "drink when you're thirsty." Let me tell you why this advice is inadequate.

Every time I say, "Drink more water," people say, "No, but I'm not thirsty."

Neural Adaptation.

My friend Alex Charfen talks about this, and he calls what happens in this situation "neural adaptation." And it's not necessarily a good thing. A neural adaptation means you're just used to something, so it doesn't make a big impact on your mind or your brain. You may think about this if you get into really cold water and it's freezing for you, you're frigid. You get in but then after a while, you're just fine. Or if you live next to an airport and you hear the airplanes all the time, but later on it doesn't faze you, you don't think about it, and literally don't hear them unless someone points it out to you. Those are all cases of neural adaptation.

Most of the time it's a pretty good thing, and it's designed to make you function better as a human being so you don't have to think about things so often. But in the case of thirst and needing more water, it can be a very bad thing.

The neural adaptation to thirst means that even though you're thirsty, it doesn't feel like you are because your brain needs to worry about other things. It needs to concentrate on the problems and the issues that it gets moment-to-moment, rather than just thinking, "I'm thirsty, I'm thirsty, I'm thirsty," all the time, so you don't feel thirsty until you get to a critical stage.

We as humans can get used to being thirsty all of the time. Again, that's not a good thing. There is a very good chance that not only are you thirsty, but you're constantly thirsty and you're just missing the natural signal.

The Importance of Water.

Water is so, so critical to your life! The majority of your body is made up of water. Water makes up about two-thirds to sometimes 75 percent of your body! Obviously that is very, very necessary for you.

The *lack* of water causes things like reduced brain function and literally—this is pretty funny—you make yourself more stupid when you don't drink enough water. When that happens, your brain literally shrinks. Information, learning--it all becomes harder to process when you're not drinking enough water.

Lack of water can also lead to things like fatigue, where you just get more tired throughout the day. You don't have as much energy. It can lead to things like joint pain and not having enough water to lubricate the systems. It can lead to weight gain. You eat more if you don't drink enough. Also, things like—how do I put this gently?—your bowel functions aren't as efficient without water.

Dehydration can also lead to ulcers, high blood pressure and kidney disease. Here's one that I talk to you about all the time: I know every time you have one of these, I tell you drink more water. That is headaches. A lot of people get headaches when they're dehydrated. I'm not certain about the percentage on this but I would say that the majority of headaches are actually caused by dehydration. Drink your water instead of taking something that just masks the system like an ibuprofen or aspirin.

Your first line of defense in most physical things is to drink water. Drink your dang water!

The Benefits of Abundant Water.

Now the benefits to having water, is of course NOT having all of the problems that I just mentioned.

When you drink more water, you feel more full. You don't have to eat as much. Of course, that can save a little bit of money, but that is secondary to just maintaining your body, feeling good about yourself and being at a healthy weight.

It also gives you more energy. Because when your body lacks water, you get fatigued a lot easier. So when you have more, that allows you to function at a higher level for a lot longer.

During a meeting I was at, the famed neuroscientist Dr. Robert Cooper said that sipping cold water throughout the day helps you to reduce belly fat. I think it's something about the metabolism, the regulation of temperature in the body and how that works. Of course, less body fat is a very good thing, unless you're into that kind of thing, I guess.

Really, think about it again before I leave this and we get to the specific advice: Seventy-five percent of Americans are chronically dehydrated. That means that if you are reading these words right now, you are more than likely dehydrated. *So drink your dang water.*

Advice in Practice:

- Drink water when you first wake up. I think this is one of the most important things that you can do. If you haven't had anything to drink throughout the night, then you are certainly dehydrated when you wake up. As part of my normal schedule I do a tongue scraping and then brush my teeth. Immediately after that, I drink a lot of water. How much should you drink? I would say drink slightly more than is comfortable for you. Now right now I am drinking at least 60 ounces of water every morning. That's something that you could work up to and get better at it. You get bonus points if you mix in some fresh lemon juice and Himalayan salt to your first glass of the day.

- Carry a water container with you at nearly all times. I like my big, absurdly expensive Yeti cup with my face on it, which I know you've seen. The big, ugly face on it just discourages people from stealing it. You can use whatever you like. It just keeps the water cold for me and makes it comfortable. Of course, I can have water any time I want it. Actually, if you wait until you are thirsty, then you've waited too long and your body is dehydrated. Keep a water container with you and sip it throughout the entire day.

- Google Alex Charfen and his Natural Thirst Challenge. He's my friend, and he got me more involved in drinking a lot more water. He has a challenge for ten days. As of right now, it's free. It will teach you how to recognize your thirst. It gets you to make water drinking a bigger part of your daily practice. It just takes ten days. It can change your life. If you listen to it, he has testimonials where people literally have gotten rid of acne and Type 2 Diabetes (!) just from drinking abundant water.

- If it's "too boring," to drink that much water, add some lemon or lime juice to it. That helps, and it's also good for maintaining a good pH balance in your system.

Again, I hope this advice has been good for you. I love you dearly and I look forward to drinking water with you.

Notes, thoughts, and intentions.

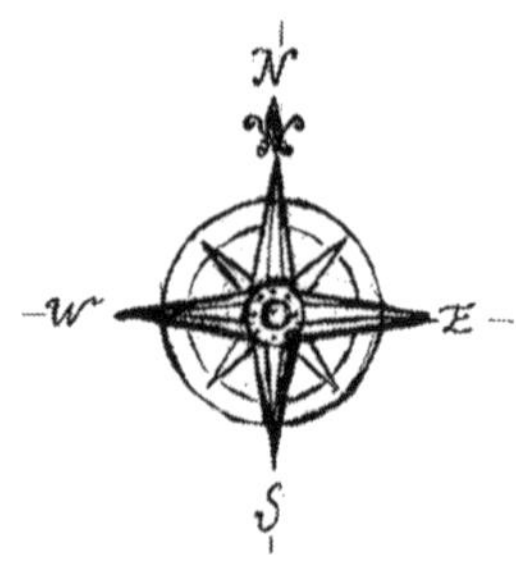

71. Take Some Green Shakes and Vitamins as Nutritional Insurance.

Oh, my precious sweethearts. Judging by the looks on your face every time that I mention these, or have them, I'm guessing you're not going to like this piece of advice. But . . . it's so, so good and important.

I want you to supplement what you eat with green shakes, vitamins, and . . . supplements . . . to be surer you're getting all of the nutrition you should be getting each and every day. I think your long-term health and energy could very well depend on this piece of advice.

Yes. Green shakes look kind of nasty. I'll admit that. And depending on how you make them, what ingredients you use, and your taste buds . . . the taste of them may very well be acquired. Mandy, you made the first one with me in 2009. You thought it was HILARIOUS to watch me drink it while you filmed it for my online health group. They can be a little gross.

BUT.

Since I've been drinking them, I've noticed I have more energy. I feel better about myself when I'm drinking them and practicing this lifestyle. I make sure that I'm getting a lot of good things in my system that I wouldn't have otherwise. Plus, when I'm making and drinking these, it encourages other healthy habits. I exercise more and I binge a lot less often. The good habits tend to stack on each other.

One of the best things? It helps get your vegetables in for the day.

The advice of eat your vegetables is always unwelcome, and always great.

Every single health plan that looks legitimate includes this piece of advice: Eat more veggies.

The Importance of Healthy Fats.

Also, healthy fats can be put in the shake. I like a lot of healthy fats in mine. Currently (as these change over time depending on what seems to be working for me), I'm putting Udo's Oil (a combo of Omega essential fatty acids), MCT oil, (sometimes) Bulletproof brand Brain Octane, and an avocado in the shake.

Some of the benefits of good fats, according to the Poliquin Group are better body composition through improving insulin sensitivity, reducing inflammation, and supporting metabolism. Omega 3 fats can help turn on fat-burning genes and turn off genes that store fat. They can support muscle gain, reduce cravings, keep you feeling "fuller," help hormones, contribute to better brain function (the non-water part of your brain is made of mostly fat and cholesterol), regulate moods, reduce heart disease risk, build a stronger immune system, and give you better skin and eye health. Whew. I didn't even know all of that before I did the research. I just knew that I FELT better when having good, healthy fats in my diet.

Vitamins and Supplements.

Vitamins and supplements also help a lot in maintaining your health. Now, they're not energy in themselves, but they help the body function properly. There's a good chance that you'll have a vitamin deficiency if you don't supplement your diet with them. I've actually heard people argue that you're just paying for expensive urine when you supplement . . . but I disagree completely. Here's my theory, and you're welcome to check up on this with me: your body is very efficient at taking what it needs.

So, with vitamins and supplements, your body will use everything that it can, and will rid itself of excess that it doesn't need. It's like having cops cover every area of the city and watching crime rates decline. If your body needs it, it will have it. That's a better scenario than needing it and not having it. Vitamin deficiency can and will result in some of the following (according to the Mayo Clinic):

- Fatigue
- Shortness of breath
- Dizziness
- Pale or yellowish skin
- Irregular heartbeats

- (Unhealthy) Weight loss
- Numbness or tingling in your hands and feet
- Muscle weakness
- Personality changes
- Unsteady movements
- Mental confusion or forgetfulness

These are pretty serious. And the thing is, you usually can't get ALL of the vitamins you need solely through food. That's why taking good vitamins are so, so important.

Inflammation.

Another piece of information about this is the theory of inflammation that another one of my friends, Dr. Thaddeus Gala speaks about: inflammation is at the root of most every health problem.

Here's what inflammation is according to Wikipedia:

Inflammation (from Latin *inflammatio*) is part of the complex biological response of body tissues to harmful stimuli, such as pathogens, damaged cells, or irritants,[1] and is a protective response involving immune cells, blood vessels, and molecular mediators. The function of inflammation is to eliminate the initial cause of cell injury, clear out necrotic cells and tissues damaged from the original insult and the inflammatory process, and to initiate tissue repair.

The classical signs of inflammation are heat, pain, redness, swelling, and loss of function.

Inflammation is a result of things like poor diet, a sedentary lifestyle, stress, and not sleeping well. The inflammation, in turn, causes all kinds of horrible symptoms in the body. These can include Type 2 diabetes, high blood pressure, heart disease, and stroke. Dr. Thad argues that most doctors treat these SYMPTOMS, but not the underlying cause of them: inflammation.

So, you'll need to eat a lot better and supplement correctly to avoid this. For me, it was swearing off of my crippling habit of diet sodas, which turns out can cause a lot of this inflammation.

So, the advice is this: failing the usual "Eat healthy," use a healthy green shake as part of your diet and take the right vitamins and supplements for you.

You'll need to include it as an everyday habit and make it as systematic and easy as possible in your day-to-day life. There's a chapter of advice in the Mind section here about making things systematic in your life that may help in this regard.

Just do a green shake and take the vitamins and supplements needed each day in one fell swoop, and get the nutrition you need with just the one meal. Just get that meal over and done! Make it a regular part of your life and know that even with that ONE meal you've gone a long way in making and keeping yourself healthy for the day. Make it as simple as possible, because . . .

Execution and actually DOING it beat theory every single time.

So, make your green shake, or your version of it that you like, and try to drink it on a daily or somewhat regular basis, and set a time to take the right vitamins for you.

Advice in Practice:

- Make a pledge that you WILL drink or eat a mega nutrition food once a day for the next ten days. YOUR version of a "green shake." See how it makes you feel. Do it for the ten days that you've pledged. See if you have more energy. See if you feel better about yourself for doing this. See if that helps to do more healthy things as it's a positive spiral.

- Get a blender. This is what I use and LOVE: The Big Nutribullet. I think it was eighty to ninety dollars, but I literally use it every day, and clean-up is SOOoooo easy. Again, you're not going to do it regularly and get in the habit *unless it's easy*. Get it set up. Make your shake, drink it, and rinse it out IMMEDIATELY. Don't let it gunk up and dry or you may lose your sanity trying to clean up dried nastiness afterwards.

- Get together a list of the things that you like, that are unequivocally good for you, that you can put in YOUR shakes. Mine include:

    - Unsweetened coconut milk.
    - Spinach
    - Kale
    - Udo's Oil. The recommended daily dose of it from the bottle

    - Vibrant Health Maximum Vibrance Meal Replacement (plant protein and green powder)
    - Dried goji berries
    - Powdered MCT Oil (Quest Nutrition)
    - Sometimes Brain Octane Oil from Bulletproof
    - Some Stevia for sweetness
    - Moringa powder by Maju
    - Prebiotic by Hyperbotics
    - Ther-Biotic Complete Powder by Klaire Labs (these last two are to help my gut bacteria repopulate—I think the years upon years of diet sodas did some damage there)
    - Sometimes Amazing Grass Green Superfood
    - Sometimes other vegetables or specific fruits (carrots, broccoli, blueberries or blackberries, lemon)

- Make your own! I actually change up the vegetables, and get some carrots, cabbage, and other goodies in it. HEALTHY fats, just a little protein, and lots of great veggies—that's the guideline. Refine your green shake to something that you'll like. Keep that going. I doubt that my shake is in its final form and to me, it just keeps getting better.

- Make your first green shake. Drink it. Don't gag. At least try not to…it gets easier. Also, "chew" it when you can. The saliva activates your digestion system.

- Find and take a great multi-vitamin. The advice given to me by Charles Poliquin includes taking: vitamin D, magnesium, carnitine, and Gamma tocopherol—but this is for making my arteries good and fighting inflammation in my system due to the stroke, BUT—at the very least, take a great multi-vitamin. Read up on it yourself from sources you trust and go ahead and order it. Now. Today.

- Take a good, healthy dose of KRILL oil each day. Failing that, a high-quality fish oil should be next best; but from what I've read now, the Krill Oil is about the best thing you can take. It helps in a lot of ways, and I can say from personal experience that I don't have little aches and pains when I'm taking it versus when I don't!

- What I do often to remind me to take my vitamins is to set my iPhone alarm as a reminder. Especially since your Mom makes me put up the vitamins, and they become out of sight and out of mind. AS SOON as you get the vitamins, set your alarm to remind you.

- Write it out in your journal—what you can expect to GAIN from following this advice; and conversely what you expect if you DON'T take this advice.

Also, remember that your Daddy loves you very much!

Notes, thoughts, and intentions.

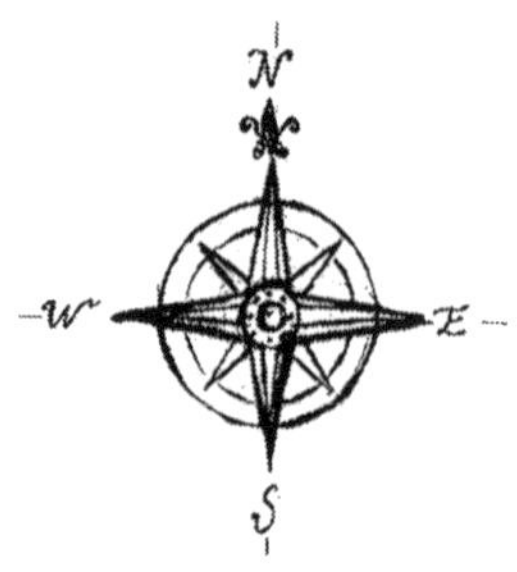

72. Meditate, Baby!

My precious sweethearts, can you guess what I'm about to say?

That's right! I am excited to get this piece of advice to you and I hope that it's going to do a lot of good in your life as it has mine. Please, please, please consider starting a meditation practice. It's such an important subject. You can really get a lot out of this and improve your life a tremendous amount just by taking some of this to heart.

My Story.

Personally, when I used to think about meditation, I always thought it was a little woo woo, kind of mystical and really a little bit silly. I decided to give it a try after people that I respect and admire talked about its benefits and how much it could help. To my surprise it helped my life a tremendous amount.

What has it done in my life? I think you probably are old enough to remember that I used to get really mad while driving. As nice of a person as I thought it was, road rage was a problem—and I wasn't very proud of how I would act when driving.

After working on meditation for a while, I found that my temper had reduced. Even though I will still get somewhat impatient while driving a car, I am very, very rarely ever angry enough to yell or get truly upset about it anymore. I attribute that, and an overall sense of calmness, to the practice of meditation.

What is mediation?

It's a mindfulness practice where you're quiet, still, and calm (usually). It can last for a few seconds of clearing or calming your mind, or it can last days, although the longest I've ever gone is an hour—and it was glorious.

One of the ways I would describe it is to call it mental hygiene. Perhaps even spiritual hygiene. It's like fasting for your brain and it helps clear out negative thoughts. It helps with what could be called the monkey brain, which are a jumble of thoughts coming all the time. Taming that monkey brain has a lot of benefits including being able to calm down and focus.

Why meditate?

Tim Ferriss (he does a very well-known podcast, writes some excellent books and has had a pretty profound impact on my life) says that 80 percent of the top performers and people who are best at what they do in the world have a mindfulness practice. That can be silence, meditation, or prayer. They almost all seem to have that in common. So I think it's at least worth taking a look at in your own life to see if it's something that can help. By the way, I'll give Tim and his podcast credit for getting me started on meditation. Thanks, Tim!

It helps to reduce stress. I think that the world carves out so much of your time and your mental energy and it taxes you so much. When you take a break from that by being quiet, by being contemplative and just allowing your thoughts to happen, it slows the world down and calms you down so much.

I think that it also starts your day in the right way. If you actually do this first thing in the morning, you make your day proactive versus reactive. Many people roll over, look at their phones and start answering emails or texts or messages in the morning. Right away that starts your brain into a fight or flight mode. When you meditate first thing, you begin your day in a mindful state. You are setting the tone for your day and you are being proactive and setting the course versus having that dictated to you.

I'm including this in the Body section as meditation affects in wonderful ways:

- It can help with pain.
- It can lighten the "heavy" areas of stress in your brain.
- It reverses the decline of the prefrontal cortex in your mind due to age.
- It can boost your memory.
- It helps you focus—for me, this is certainly the case and very important!

- It reduces stress-induced inflammation (super important).
- It can lower blood pressure.[13]

Maybe the most important benefit for me is that it seems to slow down time between the stimulus and response. In fact, it can actually help turn a negative *reaction* into a positive *response*.

When someone cuts me off in traffic, my reaction used to be to yell or to get angry or upset. Now that I meditate, I am able to remain calm. Mediation helps your brain to maintain a steadier keel and in doing that, allows you to actually choose your response rather than just having it happen without you thinking.

The last thing I'll mention on the benefits of meditation is that it encourages you to be healthy. If you care enough about yourself that you are seeking to improve through meditation, then you're also going to want to eat better and be productive by following a mission in your life. Every good habit builds on another good habit and it's a positive reinforcement for you to do one good thing and then do another.

How to Meditate.

Now there are a few different ways to meditate. The simplest is complete silence and just thinking about your

---

[13] Meredith Melnick "Meditation Health Benefits: What the Practice Does To Your Body," http://www.huffingtonpost.com/2013/04/30/meditation-health-benefits_n_3178731.html (December 6, 2017).

breath and/or your heart rate and being quiet for a certain amount of time. While I think that there are a lot of benefits to this, especially if you're used to it and good at it, I think guided meditation is superior (at least for me).

Guided meditation is when someone walks you through the exercises, the imaging, what you're thinking about or concentrating on. I think especially at the beginning it's the way to go.

Now before I get into the way I meditate personally, I don't want you to get too caught up in how it's "supposed to be done." You do what works for *you* and that may not be the standard way of doing things.

For instance, I like to actually lay back against the couch while I meditate. A lot of places will tell you the correct way of meditating is sitting up in a yoga position with your back straight and your legs crossed. That has never worked for me and most of the time while I'm doing that I'm just thinking of how uncomfortable I am.

I tend to take at least ten to twenty minutes after I get out of the bathroom in the morning. I usually have a recorded guided meditation on either my phone or my computer, where I can listen and follow along.

I have used the Headspace app before (that's what I used when I started meditating). I also listen to recordings of my friends Jesse Elder and Lisa Berkovitz. I've even recorded a few of my own that I use.

Lately I've been listening to a lot from a lady by the name of Tara Brach and doing her meditations. They are fantastic and are completely free (you can donate though and I've done that) on her website at Tarabrach.com. I'd recommend checking that out. She's also got a useful section on How to Meditate—and she's a LOT more experienced at it than I am.

One of the things I really like to include in my meditation is the fact that we are not our thoughts. There is an entire piece of advice about that in the "Mind" Section of this book. I want you to read that. Every time I meditate I try to remember that we are spiritual beings having an earthly experience, rather than earthly beings having a spiritual experience. For me that's something that's just good to keep in mind and it really keeps my entire day in perspective.

Mindfulness throughout the day.

Another part of meditation that I'd like to bring up is to maintain that sense of mindfulness throughout the day whenever you can.

You've heard my phone alarm go off many times at 7 p.m. It is usually Louis Armstrong singing, "What a Wonderful World," to remind me that I am blessed.

I hear it, and as long as I'm not driving or actually face-to-face talking with someone—I close my eyes and think of how blessed I am. I think of all of the things I actively appreciate, the people in my life (notably YOU), and just this whole MIRACLE of life.

It's such a wonderful time, and it's so easy to set up and do. It's an oasis from the pressure and noise of the day. If you don't do something like this, I'd highly recommend it. It's so easy to do, and so easy NOT to do, as well . . .

I love you, and you're ALWAYS in my list of why I'm so blessed each and every day.

Advice in Practice:

- I would like you to try the 10 for 10 on Headspace. That's what got me into meditating, and it made it very easy to start. Look for it on the App Store or Google Play. The 10-day trial is free. You don't have to continue, but it's relatively inexpensive and getting into the habit of meditating is certainly worth that.
- The next thing I'd ask you to do is to check out Tara Brach's meditations and her websites and try a few of her basic meditations. She has one in particular I like called the RAIN of Self-Compassion. It's excellent if you're feeling down. Her Smile Meditation is also pretty popular. Check it out!
- I also love an app now called, "Insight Timer." It's free, has a lot of pre-loaded meditations, but what I love is the timed meditation function. Get it and check it out to see if you like it, too.
- The next thing is to commit to this for a while, even if it feels weird for you or if you have a real problem taming that monkey mind. I think that the tougher it is for you to do, the more you will actually need it. So, make a promise to yourself that you will do it, then actually put it on your schedule for each day. This habit can and will change your life. So, get after it!

- Come to me for a special meditation that I recorded just for you. <3

I hope that this has been helpful for you. As always, please talk to me and let me know if you're doing this, and how the practice is going for you. I love you so much.

Notes, thoughts, and intentions.

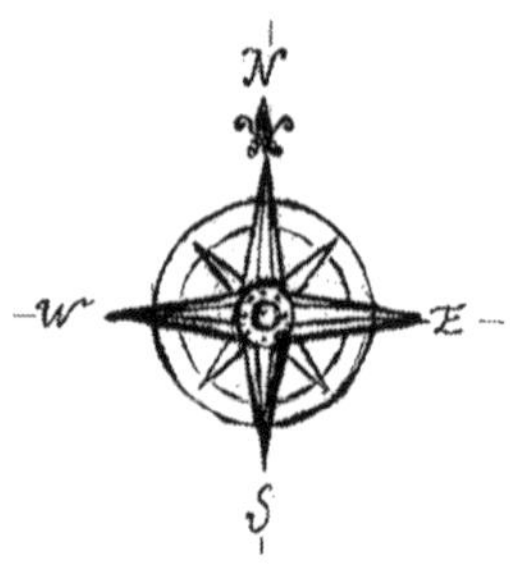

73. Beware and Behold the Tyranny and Triumph of the Mundane.

I'm trying my best to give you some great, actionable advice for a much better life. A healthier, smarter, more loving and spiritual way to live.

I'm including this in the Body section because we'll apply it to your health—but this could belong in any of the sections and it would be one of the most important pieces of advice that I can give . . . and that is to control your simple daily habits so that they become mundane.

Something that my mentor, Jim Rohn, states about things that are easy to do is that they're easy NOT to do, as well. So, I want you to thoroughly consider this advice and apply it in your own life as you see fit. The mastery of it can make your life so much better, and the absence of the thought here can make your life so much more difficult—filled with health problems, a lack of energy, purpose, and probably a bit of self-loathing, as well.

Make sure that your daily habits line up with what you're trying to do in life. For instance, develop the healthy habit of taking vitamins and drinking a green shake every day. That's a fairly simple thing to do—but most will never do it because it's easy not to make happen, too.

It's the same thing with meditation, or a daily session of gratitude and appreciation, or doing a kind act for someone (even if it's small). If you do those things and make it a part of your everyday "mundane" existence, you'll have a fantastic life. But if your "mundane" existence includes cheeseburgers, waking up late, instantly reacting to the day, and neglecting your bigger purpose like the mass of humanity, your life will just be ho-hum and it's doubtful that you'll accomplish something of true significance.

We make our schedule our slave initially; eventually, our schedules will enslave us. I'm hoping that your schedule is filled with good things that add to your life. Almost every habit and activity are either building or tearing down what you're hoping to accomplish, so fill your life with the habits and activities that BUILD rather than tear down.

Now—before we talk more about this, NO ONE advocates only doing things that are good for you all of the time as it's pretty unrealistic. If you think you can only do that, you're set up for some disappointment, as no one—yes, even Dad, hahahahaa—is perfect. The key is to take care of the "big rocks" we talk about in each section of our life.

For the body: exercise regularly preferably including weight training and some HIIT that you enjoy. Also, make good nutrition and vitamins part of the daily routine, as well as meditation or another type of mindfulness practice.

For the mind: Exercise your BRAIN (I prefer idea lists), and make some positive progress towards your hopefully written goals and outcomes daily.

For the heart: Spend time with your loved ones, connecting with them, listening and appreciating them.

For the soul: Do a kind act daily and deeply appreciate the wonder of it all, seeking and finding something that you HAVE to do in your life and following that.

Those are the big things, the big rocks that make up an extraordinary life. Taking care of yourself through these habits make it possible to have the energy, mindset, heart (courage), and soul and passion to go after the grand things in life . . . to serve at a high level because you've taken care of yourself first.

Am I making sense? The cliché way of saying it, which we've probably all heard a hundred times or more is:

You make your habits, and then your habits make you.

The problem is that very few of us take the time to consciously think about what habits are best for us, and then go about making the right habits stick. It's pretty universal. Of course, I've been guilty of that. . .we all have been.

Which of your habits now are serving you? Which are taking you away from your goals? What could you make part of your routine to make your life much better?

Let's take actual time—blocked off, with some heavy duty thought—to think and to do this.

Also, we know it's tough to just start and continue a good habit. It's much easier to pay lip service to it than to actually do it. Otherwise, everyone would be "a billionaire with abs." (I heard that phrase from a very cool guy named Derek Sivers)

So, to actually make these happen, I'd suggest two things to make your "mundane" incredible:

1. Implement one great habit at a time. Doing too much, I think, dilutes your efforts. Once you have one down, look at the next behavior. Then the next, and so on. Constantly upgrade.
2. Consider the OBSTACLES to the attempted habit or behavior. It makes so much sense to do this, but most folks won't do it. Reading and implementing the OPOA section of advice in the Mind section of this book can really help with this.

The warning is this: the days turn into years really, really fast. You are young right now, and everything looks so far in the future. I can tell you, from having been exactly where you are now, and remembering it vividly . . . it all goes by SO, so quickly. I am stunned by how recent memories seem even when they're TEN YEARS OLD now!

Maybe this is something that you won't quite "get," until it happens to you, but please take my advice on this:

Don't wait.

Start improving now.

Start setting up your good habits NOW.

Think about where you want to be, and what you want to accomplish NOW.

Life is fleeting, nothing is guaranteed, and an extraordinary life is on the other side of the thing that you fear.

With that, please know that I love you; and let's get to the practical part of this.

Advice in Practice:

- Please check out the pieces of advice in this book on The Daily Practice, The Miracle Morning, and Creating your Ideal Schedule. Read them, and consider what makes sense for you, habit-wise, and get the wheels turning in your beautiful brain about what habits make the most sense for you.
- Schedule a time away, just for you, to think of what you're wanting to do in life and what habits and skills that you'll need to have to accomplish that.
- Set a time in your calendar NOW to stop and review where your life is, and where it's going about once per quarter. Take a day off and revisit where you are . . . at a job versus a career or MISSION, what you're LEARNING as a person, and whether you're making "progress" in life. This is a lot like the regular "check-in" that I recommend earlier in the book . . . but it's a

deeper, more comprehensive look at the trajectory of your entire life.

- Find someone. A mentor or coach or accomplished friend (perhaps a Daddy ;0) that you can talk to about your life, your goals, and what you're doing now. See if you can set an appointment with them over lunch, or for an hour or so at the office and see what their take is on where you are in life, and give you advice on it.

Notes, thoughts, and intentions.

Go to LifeLessonsBonus.com
for Reports, Resources, and
Your Free ($100 Value) Training,
"*Design and Execute Your Ideal Week.*"

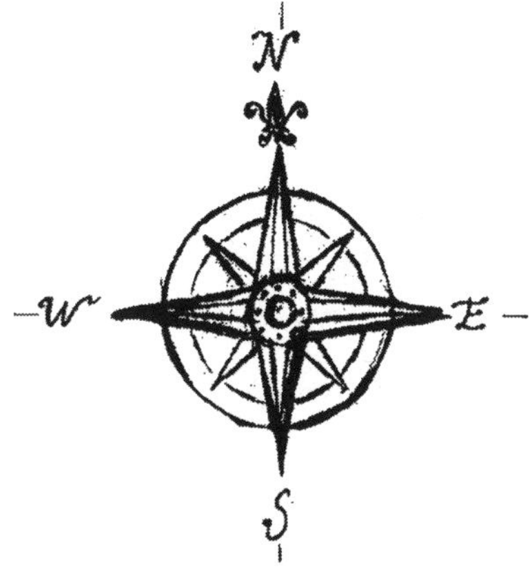

YOUR SOUL.

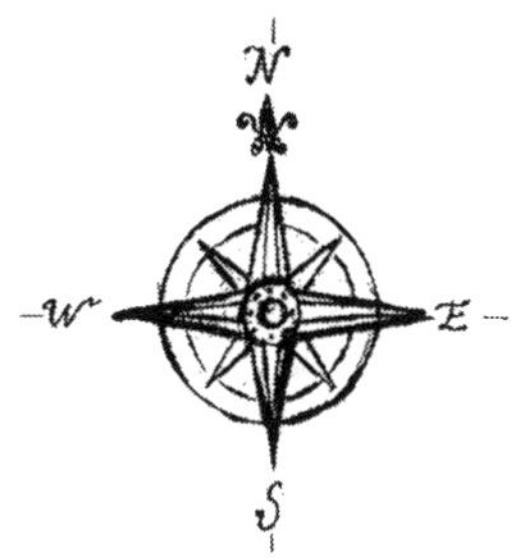

Introduction to Advice on Your Soul

My beauties. Yes, you too, Alec.

The world we live in is more complex than ever. There's more happening, there's more to do, there's more ways to get things done, and there are constant glowing screens vying for your attention all the time. The entire world's cumulative knowledge lays at your fingertips. Geniuses have poured their life work into books and courses for your use and enjoyment.

And yet people are feeling as disconnected and often passionless as ever.

Many people have kind of given up on life—at least truly living it. They're just caught in the whole trance of it. They're just going through the motions and not striving. Not truly living.

"It is not death that a man should fear, but he should fear never beginning to live."
— Marcus Aurelius

As sad as this is to say, I think it's the default for most people. They just aren't as engaged in their soul. They're not REACHING for more, or seeking to truly suck all of the marrow out of life as Thoreau brilliantly put it.

It doesn't have to be that way. I love you so much, and maybe my best mission on this planet is to help YOU (help you as much as is possible that is. You have to commit to helping yourself as well) connect to life and get the most out of it. As your Dad I want to help you with your soul. Your spirit. That feeling that life is magical and worth living.

I've done my best in the pages that follow. I've dug deep and given you the very best life-lessons, examples, tips, insights, and practical things that you can do to help you feel and be more fulfilled in life.

When you read these and truly ponder them, try them on and see if they apply to you. Do some of the things I recommended, because you're going to have a better life. You'll feel more empowered. You'll be even more ready to take life by the throat and drink it down deeply. You'll at the very least be exposed to the ideas, and I've done my best to make all of these ideas tangible.

You know my story. I haven't always been happy and fulfilled. I've had those moments when I've wrestled with darkness. I didn't always win, but I never lost faith or hope. Sometimes the hope was so small and precarious. But I found enough reason to keep going. To get better. To learn and do the things to help feel better about myself. To take action to make my life a better one. I read a lot of books. I took several courses, listened to podcasts, had deep conversations with friends, and went to places where the big rocks of life like this were discussed with intelligent, passionate people.

And I took notes. Lots and lots of them.

I learned. I tried out many things. I created daily practices and rituals. I scheduled times for mindfulness. I was able to stop doing the things that were unfulfilling to me and to start doing the things that satisfied my inner joy.

I'm not perfect, doing all of this over again, I'd do several things differently. However, when you read this advice, you're going to know that it's come from someone that has been in the trenches of life. Trying hard, often failing, but always learning. I can confidently write about this because I've taken some bruises from life, and I've not only lived to tell about them, but I've overcome them and used them as they should be used, which is to make me a better person. These obstacles have made me stronger, and they can do the same for you.

Here are some of the things that you'll find in this Advice on the Soul:

Why active appreciation is better than simple gratitude, and practical ways to get more of that in your life. Anxiety and gratitude cannot live in the same head at the same time after all!

What to do when you're so scared you can't see straight.

The biggest factor in turning around my own depression that can help you in your times of darkness as well.

Why an abundant mindset is one of the very best things that you can have, and how to cultivate it in your life.

Why being happy is the BEST thing you can do for *others*.

How experiences are so much more important than things, and how you can have more experiences now. Anyone can do it, especially you.

All about the magical, life changing concept of what Joseph Campbell called, "The Hero's Journey."

Again, I don't know when life is going to interrupt you. If you're reading these words now, I ACTIVELY appreciate that and feel blessed that my words can help you.

When you take these pieces of loving advice—even one of them—and you make it a part of your daily life, I will personally guarantee that your life will get better. The music will be clearer, the colors you see will be more vibrant, and you'll start to notice the beautiful serendipity of this world and all of the things in it.

IF . . .

If you're bothered to read this now, consider them and apply them to your daily life as you see fit.

OR . . .

You could just go on living your life as you have been. As the famous scene in the "Matrix" says. You can "take the blue pill" and just forget everything you just heard to wake up and live the same way.

I suggest you take this and consider these thoughts and principles. You put your own spin on them. Write about some of the wisdom in your own journal. "Take the red pill!" Dive in and see how far this rabbit hole goes.

Let's turn the page and get started.

(And I love you.)

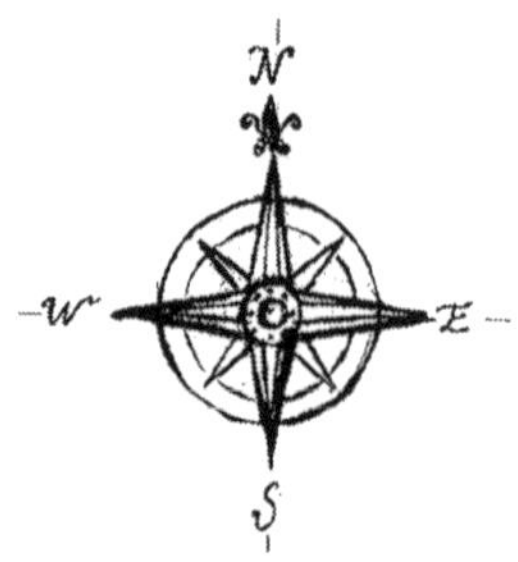

74. Consider More About Who You're BECOMING, Than What You're GETTING.

Let's start this SOUL advice with this little gem. I'm including it here, because what you do can and honestly should be part of who you are.

Money is secondary to you loving your work and growing as a person by doing it. I don't think that you'll be happy if you're not growing as a part of your profession. And if you're just collecting a paycheck and just going through the motions, then your soul will start to die.

Don't worry as much about what you're getting from a job as who you're becoming (advice from the late, great Jim Rohn. I love passing on his wisdom to you).

Are you learning skills? Is what you are doing each day building you into a better person? Is your job or what you're doing in life challenging you at all? Do you need to upgrade yourself constantly and grow to make things happen in your life? If not . . . I would suggest that maybe you're not trying hard enough.

Life is way too short to settle when it comes to work. Doing something that you hate or that doesn't challenge you shouldn't be your point of focus.

Seek to solve the fun problems at your work. Figure out new and improved ways of serving your customers or clients, and don't just settle for repeating the same work day after day. Serving others in some form or fashion is imperative to keeping your soul feeling good. That's true with performing an act of kindness every day, and it's also true with your mission. If you don't feel a soul connection to your profession in some form or fashion, you need to change that. It may not be immediately, but there needs to be a plan to do something that you really feel helps to nourish your soul.

Some people will say that they have twenty years of experience at a job, but what I see more often than not is that they have one year of experience, twenty separate times.

It's true at your job, and it's true in life: If you're not growing, you're dying.

So, choose something that you think will challenge you. And don't settle for anything less. You absolutely CAN have this when you work, and you should strive to do it. I've given you some advice on landing that perfect job as well but keep this in mind when choosing what it is that you want to do.

The Advice in Practice:

- Most jobs are gotten by default. Buck that trend. CONSCIOUSLY CHOOSE where you'd like to work, and let's go after that one. Read, "*Find The Magic Spot in Your Job or Career,*" and "*Learn How to Get ANY Job You Want,*" in the MIND section of this book.

- When you get to choose, look at the skills required to be *exceptional* at your profession. If it takes a lot of skill and will make you a better person to get that position, then really think about making that your job (or your business).

- When you have that job, seek out someone that's really killing it at what you're doing, and learn from them. In the real estate profession, we call that, "shadowing" and it's such an underused strategy in every field. Don't let that be you. Find the best at what you're doing and emulate them and even improve on what they're doing. Once again, I don't mean to brag, but this advice is golden. SO few do it. There's a lesson in this book on this, too . . . of course.

- Seek and write out the outcome of who you'd like to become on your job or in your profession. Think about the best-case scenario and go into your job with that intention in mind. If you do this, and you revisit this from time to time, you WILL grow as a person.

Notes, thoughts, and intentions.

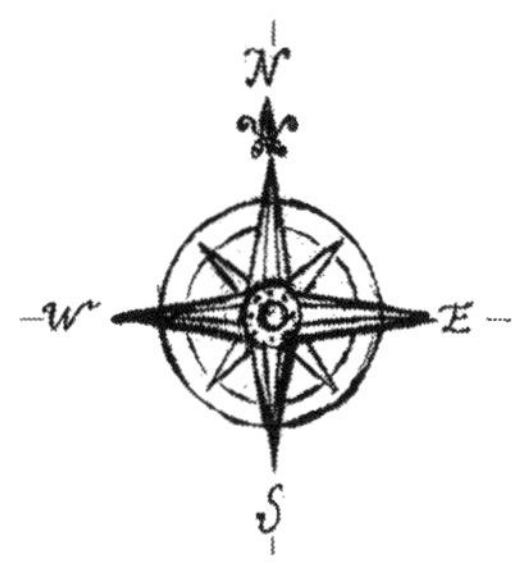

75. Study Stoic Wisdom (Obstacles Make Me Stronger).

Once again, I get to share some wisdom that's passed through me from some of the best minds in history. It's fun for me, and it's an honor to introduce you to this.

So, you should know that I've had some emotional and spiritual times within my life. I was in a rough patch because I wasn't living with purpose. I kept waking up in middle of the night with sweat sticking to the side of my pillow, anxious from thought, not getting rest, not wanting to get out of bed, hating to go into work, not having any enthusiasm (which is derived from *en theos*, or "God within"). There was just a dissonance between what I thought I should be doing and what I was.

I felt horrible and I felt guilty about feeling horrible. These are first world problems after all! I have an incredible family (really, you're amazing), a good business, I have plenty to eat, and a lot of conveniences. I get to take vacations. I have tons of relative freedom. I just wasn't doing anything with it.

I read a few titles that helped me. I read a book that helped my daily habits: *Choose Yourself*, and another that led to this advice: *The Obstacle is The Way*, by Ryan Holiday. Essentially, it's Stoic Philosophy that can be applied to everyday life. This book, and especially one of its chapters, "Amor Fati," truly made a difference in my life. Coincidentally, I got to meet Ryan in person and thank him for that. He was really appreciative to hear it.

"Amor Fati" is Latin for "Love of Fate," or as I choose to think, "Love it ALL." It was my mantra for many months, and I still come back to it when things get tough. Love everything. Appreciate everything. Find joy in the things that hurt. Love the hard times as they make you stronger. Find joy in missing someone—as it means that you love them, and that you got to know them in the first place.

I read the book once and then read it again with a highlighter. I also ordered it on Audible. I tried to internalize the thoughts and make them my own when it mattered the most. It led me to read (and listen) to: *Meditations*, by Marcus Aurelius, and: *Letters from a Stoic*, by Seneca to get a better understanding of this pure gold. I really fell in love with the Stoic philosophy. It feels like being in a brotherhood of badasses for me.

Now, obviously most people think of men sitting down while wrapped in togas and talking about things that don't matter when we talk about philosophy, or college professors that theorize and don't do anything. But real philosophy is so much more than that. It's a way of thinking. It's a way of ACTING. It's a set of tools to use each and every day.

Tim Ferriss and Ryan Holiday call it an operating system for life. I've gotten a lot of my knowledge about them by reading Ryan's books—the one mentioned above, and: The Ego is the Enemy, and: *The Daily Stoic*. I've also listened to a favorite modern-day philosopher named Brian Johnson to get some of the juicy goodness found in this philosophy.

Brian Johnson taught that the teachings of Epictetus were compiled by a student of his, and the title: *Enchiridion*, was translated into: *Handbook*. But what it really meant was: "Ready-at-hand." Like a sword would be kept next to you for use. It's meant to be practical and extremely usable. Now, that's something a lot more valuable than calculating the volume of a cone. And yet it's rarely taught in school.

The granddaddies of Stoic thought are Seneca, Epictetus, and Marcus Aurelius.

What's cool about them is that they were achievers. They were extremely powerful and wealthy, and they got things done. Marcus (I'm on a first name basis) was the Emperor of Rome, which was the richest and most powerful man in the entire world at the time. If you watch the movie: *Gladiator*, with Russell Crowe you'll see Mr. Aurelius. Seneca was a statesman, an author, and a poet—and the second richest man in Rome at the time. Epictetus was a slave that freed himself through his own efforts. These weren't just teachers that theorized. These people lived this and used this philosophy to guide their lives.

Here are some gems for you to consider and contemplate:

- Control what you can control. Accept and even LOVE that which can't be changed. That's a long cry from complaining or bemoaning things that don't seem fair. Remember "Amor Fati."

- Maintain "equanimity," which means balance. Marcus made it a game to see how quickly he could get back to his "center" if good or bad things happened and riled him up. Don't get me wrong though. I think it's okay to really feel joy. It's perfectly fine to get even ridiculously happy. But it's the bad, the dark, the harsh things that happen to shake us. That's when we're really upset. THAT is when it's great to play and win the equanimity game.

- Saying our "OMMS," (that is Obstacles make me stronger). That's the meaning behind the title: *The Obstacle is The Way*. If you can graduate from getting broken and complaining about the everyday occurrences of life, and instead realize that they can serve to make us better, sharper, or more appreciative of the good when that happens, then that's completely different. That is a big turning point in life to appreciate the bad. If you get stuck in freezing rain, then appreciate it for reminding you how much you enjoy warmth when you have it nearly all of the time. You're winning at life.

- I literally just read more this morning in Ryan's piece: *The Daily Stoic*, about not engaging in fights and struggles where nothing is served or changed. Don't argue when it's unnecessary (and it's rarely necessary), because it's an extreme way of saying "pick your battles." That's especially true of this connected world where people are so electronically connected through social media. I used to get into political arguments on Facebook and get worked up about it. Now that seems so ridiculous to me! The Stoics had it right centuries ago!

- Don't feel the need for possessions. Seneca used to go and live as a homeless person for a few days a month. He asked himself constantly, "Is this the condition I feared?" In doing that, he didn't fear much of anything. If your Mom would be on board with it, then I wouldn't mind doing that for myself. It would also give me more compassion for folks as well.

Rather than continuing to paraphrase this wisdom of the ages, let me share some of the thoughts and quotes directly from the masters (via translation, of course):

"Here is your great soul—the man who has given himself over to Fate; on the other hand, that man is a weakling and a degenerate who struggles and maligns the order of the universe and would rather reform the gods than reform himself."
— Seneca

"If you are distressed by anything external, the pain is not due to the thing itself, but to your estimate of it; and this you have the power to revoke at any moment."
— Marcus Aurelius, Meditations

"What really frightens and dismays us is not external events themselves, but the way in which we think about them. It is not things that disturb

us, but our interpretation of their significance." — Epictetus

"If what you have seems insufficient to you, then though you possess the world, you will yet be miserable." — Seneca

"Never let the future disturb you. You will meet it, if you have to, with the same weapons of reason which today arm you against the present." — Marcus Aurelius, Meditations

"It is the power of the mind to be unconquerable." — Seneca, The Stoic Philosophy of Seneca: Essays and Letters

"For what prevents us from saying that the happy life is to have a mind that is free, lofty, fearless and steadfast—a mind that is placed beyond the reach of fear, beyond the reach of desire, that counts virtue the only good, baseness the only evil, and all else but a worthless mass of things, which come and go without increasing or diminishing the highest good, and neither subtract any part from the happy life nor add any part to it?

A man thus grounded must, whether he wills or not, necessarily be attended by constant cheerfulness and a joy that is deep and issues from deep within, since he finds delight in his own resources, and desires no joys greater than his inner joys." — Seneca

"... don't let your desire run ahead of you, be patient until your turn comes. Adopt a similar attitude with regard to children, wife, wealth and status, and in time, you will be entitled to dine with the gods." — Epictetus

"Until we have begun to go without them, we fail to realize how unnecessary many things are. We've been using them not because we needed them but because we had them."
— Seneca, Letters from a Stoic

"Nothing, to my way of thinking, is a better proof of a well-ordered mind than a man's ability to stop just where he is and pass some time in his own company." — Seneca

I know, right? It's great! I love these thoughts! I love it even more when it actually gets implemented into our lives!

As with everything here consider this on your own and use it IF it makes sense to you. I hope that I've sold how this way of thinking and living can help though!

I love the heck out of you, and I'm hoping this helps you in your wonderful lives kiddos.

The Advice In Practice:

- Google some quotes from Seneca, Marcus, and Epictetus. Roll them around in your mind. Consider each one and see if it makes enough sense to you continue some study of this grand wisdom.

- Try an experiment. When something bad happens, ask yourself: "Is this in my control?" Think on that for a bit. The Stoics believe that the only thing in your control is your virtue—your thoughts and actions. All else is to be accepted and even loved. Can you do that for a set number of days? Set a time frame for it, and make it happen.

- Read or listen to some or all of the following:

  The Obstacle is the Way by Ryan Holiday

  Ego is the Enemy by Ryan Holiday

  Meditations by Marcus Aurelius

  Letters from a Stoic by Seneca, in the original Latin (kidding on the last part)

  Enchiridion of Epictetus

  The Daily Stoic (I'm reading it now and taking notes every day; the fact that it takes 2-3 minutes a day, and has me in the right frame of mind almost all the time is magical)

- Sign up for the emails at TheDailyStoic.com, and consider purchasing the "Amor Fati" coin from their site. It's a little pricey, but it's a great reminder to love your fate.

- See if you can get one friend or family member to see the light on this and preach it. Even writing this has helped me some more.

Alrighty then. I love you!

Notes, thoughts, and intentions.

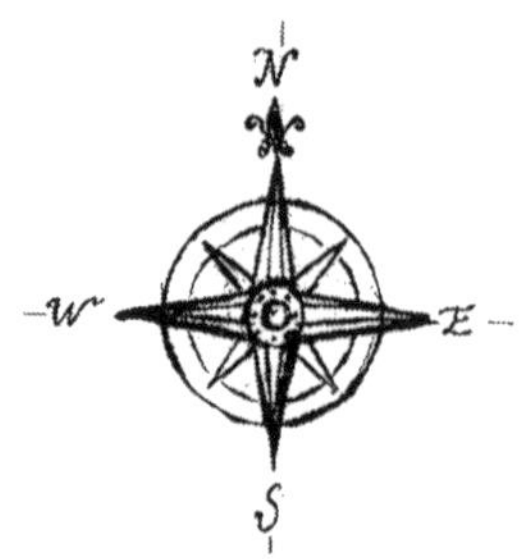

76. Remember That EXPERIENCES Are More Important Than Things (Make Travel a Priority).

I was recently on a flight to Phoenix, and I got to sit next to a delightful lady named Joni who was seventy-six years young and just a happy soul. She was traveling with her husband, a World War II vet that had just celebrated his ninety-second birthday.

I love meeting people like this. They were both happy. They were both just glowing from the inside. I got to talk to Joni quite a bit and she gave me some great advice and "must dos" for your Mom and my trip to Italy.

They had been there twelve times already. They had been vacationing and traveling—and of course many, many other places. She told me stories of traveling the Far East, and their favorite place to visit had been Thailand. She also toured all of the United States and how they went to all of the national parks. She told me about it all with a smile on her face.

It was magical hearing about this. You could tell that they were all fond memories. They had such great times. The two of them were on the plane returning from visiting their grandchildren and were preparing to go on a cruise with their other family in another two weeks or so.

I had already planned on writing this for you, but it was serendipitous to sit next to such a great couple because they shared some important wisdom I'd like you to consider:

Experiences are more important than possessions.

There was no way they would have been speaking with so much affection about a huge TV or car, or even a home. They were experiences that they shared together and with their family. They were enjoying them so much and were planning for more.

So then my advice is this: Make travel a priority. Go and see the marvelous and wonderful things in this world and do it with a sense of open-mouthed wonder that you had as a child.

I got to travel quite a bit while I was in college. That was over twenty years ago now, and I still remember it like yesterday. I traveled with a friend from Cornell who had JUST reached out to me named Chris Murphy. Throughout Europe, we took the train and slept overnight on trains and in the youth hostels, sometimes on cots. I spent less than thirty dollars a day at the time for everything, and those were some of my best and most cherished memories.

Since then we've gone on a vacation nearly every year. We've mainly been to the beach resorts of Mexico and a lot of Disney—sometimes a bit too much! But it's not the same as getting out and staying in a different culture. It's not like being adventurous and completely leaving our way of life behind for a while. That is magic.

I told Mrs. Joni what I was writing for you, and asked her if she had some things to say to you. She had quite a bit to say.

She started by saying that it's important to travel. It's important for you to see that cultures are a lot different. You can see how differently people live, how little many have compared to us, and yet they're still happy.

She said that seeing firsthand how others live and are raised will create a huge level of empathy in you. It will create an understanding of why people think differently. That empathy, she continued, would help you cultivate more awareness and love for others.

She wants you to know and see that not everyone grows up with our comforts. These people have many differences in wealth, religion, and education. She says it will be easier for you to put yourself in another's shoes and see how they think. That will lead to a rare kind of mindset.

This was one of the best conversations I've had in a long time. Joni and her wise-cracking hubby were truly special.

Those are some of the benefits of traveling and making great experiences. But the other thing that I wanted to talk about was about possessions. About "THINGS."

The older I get the more I realize that we really don't need much of anything. There's a bit of a minimalist fad going on where many people are giving up most all of their possessions and going off on the road. I think that trend will continue and get stronger as the years go by. We're a lot more mobile, and more jobs in the future won't require you to be at any given location. If you have Wi-Fi, a computer, and a phone, you'll be able to be work anywhere in the entire world that you want. That's a recipe for a life of adventure. A lot of my friends are doing that now, and that's something that I'd want for you if it interests you at all.

We're in the process now of selling our 4,000 square foot home on acreage in the country. We want to downsize, get closer to the things we do every day and spend less time commuting. We're getting rid of a lot of our things that we just don't need anymore, and I'm really excited about this. Life is about to get much simpler, and the money we're going to save can and will be used to invest in more experiences like the trip together to Italy.

The thing about things is that they hold you down and limit your options. Possessions possess. They need upkeep, and they need to be stored. They require a home to put them in, and that home has a tendency to keep you grounded.

Given the choice between getting a possession or making an experience, I'd encourage you to strongly consider making the experience. It will always be yours, and your life can always be exciting.

The Advice in Practice:

- When you get a job see if you can negotiate more time off to go and travel. When you work look for work that allows you to be location independent. Use the "Proper way to ask," advice in this book for that.

- When you're traveling, keep a journal of what you're doing. Think about what you're learning, notice the differences, and then write them out. Learn from them and allow it to truly affect your soul. As a side note your kids will one day want these journals. They'll bring you some joy in reliving the experiences when you review them.

- Take notice of best practices. Do the folks in different countries have a different diet that you enjoy? Do they treat people differently? Do they have a better attitude towards work/life balance or importance? Do you dig what they wear? Take note of all of it and use it to make yourself a better person.

- See how the cultures are different. Work on your tolerance of things that are a lot different than what you do normally. Seek to understand what they are doing in their differences. Put yourself in their shoes and observe from a place of awareness and love. (This advice is from Joni)

- Use what you see to APPRECIATE how good you really have it! Not everyone grows up with the same socio-economic, religious, or educational backgrounds as you did. Almost everyone on the planet won't have it as good as you do. Use it as a chance to really be grateful. Make a checklist of all the things that make you happier in your mind. Do the traveling before you have kids, before you get married, as a couple, and as a family when that happens. Do NOT let having children become the reason that you don't travel. Don't allow money to bully you into NOT travelling too. Read: *Don't Let Money Be a Bully in Your Life*, and take heed, so that you can turn what you would normally spend on stuff into life-changing experiences.

- Write down your bucket list and schedule some of those experiences now. Don't let it roll around in the back of your mind and taunt you. Then they have a tendency to get away. In fact, as you're reading this, take time to actually book an experience. Go ahead, I'll wait!

Places that I'm visiting, experiencing, and truly savoring in my life are:

1.

2.

3.

4.

5.

6.

7.

8.

9.

10.

11.

12.

13.

14.

15.

The key is, become the person that *MAKES THIS HAPPEN* in your lifetime. The person that creates value for others to pay for it, and the person that takes the time for themselves to actually make traveling a priority.

The entire world is your oyster my loved ones. Understand and appreciate that!

Notes, thoughts, and intentions.

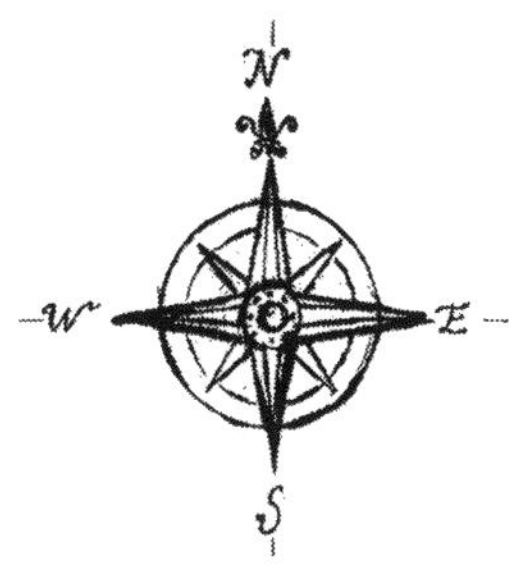

77. Have a Regular Check-In with Yourself.

"The unexamined life is not worth living."
—Socrates.

I hope this is working for you and that you like and appreciate some of what I'm spilling out to you. At least I hope the effort is appreciated even if you don't agree with a lot of it, or you're just kind of sick of the whole, "Success in life is success itself," diatribe!

This practice really can make a big difference in your life. I say that with a lot of these bits, I guess. But I mean it every time.

Please engage in a regular check-in with your life. It's a time where you can objectively look at your life, see how it's going, and make plans to actually improve it.

In business, there is a principle called: "Work ON the business, rather than IN the business." that I've mentioned earlier in this book. The idea is to get things done to improve the overall business rather than getting lost in the weeds of the everyday activities that need to be done to keep things rolling.

I think that it works for your life, too. Actually, that's a lot more important than what you do in business. That's what this check-in is for. It's the time to work ON your life rather than just living IN it every day. You feeling me here?

That's why this is so important. Most people can't or won't take the time to examine their life and how it's going. Some people do it once a year at New Year's and make half-hearted resolutions that peter out after a few weeks.

But this regular check-in is scheduled. It's very important.

You know that I often go off and do my planning on Sundays. I try to get away. I go to where it's quiet and when I'm by myself, I'm usually with a great view of nature like the lake or the creek near our house. I do plan my week out, but it's also where I do my personal check-in. I like to look at the different areas of life and see how I'm doing. I like to pat myself on the back a little by recording "Magic Moments," which is now an Evernote file with a ton of pictures on my hard drive. I write out all of the good stuff that's happened that week. I write out what I choose to take with me.

Then I check in with the different areas of my life. Going by this book, it should be the FUNDIES: eating, moving, and sleeping for the physical part, kindness, self-improvement, and gratitude for my mental portion. That's what I put in the book for the foundation of a successful life. It would make sense to use those as the categories where I check in.

Lately I've been using my mentor Dan Martell's "Seven Pillars": Health, love, mission, friends, finances, hobby (which I'm not good at currently), and spiritual. I do a quick one out of ten assessment, where one is HORRIBLE, or the worst that it could be, and ten is perfection. Then I ask myself what I could do to get myself to the next level in that area. It then goes on my weekly outcome list (like a "to-do" list).

I then plan my week using the OPOA method we talk about in the MIND section. I schedule my week. The weeks that I do this, I feel more connected. I feel more purposeful, and I feel more ALIVE. I have purpose and focus, and I'm constantly in a better mindset because I'm improving. The weeks I don't do it? I probably get less than half done on those weeks. This makes that much of a difference for me.

There are several ways to do it. I mentioned the Martell Framework of the "Seven Pillars" above. The Daddy foundation for a good life was mentioned: Sleeping, eating, moving, active appreciation, self-improvement, and kindness.

My friend Brian Scrone has great criteria for this, and wrote a great book on the subject called, *What Matters Most?*. He calls them his five F's: Family, fitness, friends, finances, and faith. These are outstanding. Faith is a catch-all for spirituality, mission, self-love, etc. I love this.

I've talked about James Altucher and his Daily Practice ad nauseum; but his areas for that are spiritual, mental, emotional, and physical. You can use those pretty effectively for your check-in too.

Tony Robbins calls his system: COI's, or categories of improvement. He suggests that you create a separate area for personal COIs and career. Personal can include "juiced up," titles and areas like: "Wizard of Wealth," or "Energy Automaton." The professional can include categories for improvement, or something like: "Maestro of Marketing." I think you get the idea. The concept is to make these areas fun to spend time with and improve.

We can even go way back to Ben Franklin. He got this concept early on in our nation's history. He worked on his thirteen virtues: Temperance (no gluttony or drunkenness), silence (speak only when it benefits others), order, resolution (Do what you resolve to do!), frugality (waste nothing), industry (no unnecessary actions), sincerity, justice (wrong none), moderation, cleanliness, tranquility, chastity, and humility (he said to imitate people like Jesus and Socrates). These are powerful. Please consider some of these for your personal check-in.

The idea is to reflect on the past, process that information, and assess yourself at that time. How are you doing? Don't be too tough on yourself, but realize that these times are for improving. Look at some of the areas where you'd like to get better. Consciously look at them, measure them in some way, and resolve to get better. Even recognizing these areas will start to work its magic on you, and you'll get better. Making a plan, executing it, adapting it, and persisting will make you even better.

So, go ahead and set an appointment with yourself. Make it sacred. Keep that appointment and take the time with yourself. When you do this, and truly work on your life and getting better it will be some of the very best time that you'll ever spend.

Except maybe time spent chilling with Dad.

The Advice in Practice:

- Pull out the phone and set your next regular appointment. Set the reminder alarms one day before and one hour before. Get your mind thinking about it. DON'T BREAK THE APPOINTMENT. You'll value this time in direct proportion to how serious you are about improving your life.

- Google some of the people listed above and their methods. Think about it and come up with the different areas of life you want to track of and improve. Journal on it. Think about it. Write these out, and truly consider the qualities you'd like to work on during your check-in.

- Create an idea list of different areas and/or qualities you'd like to improve. Maybe you considered some above, but go crazy on this list. Brainstorm that bad boy! Write them all out no matter how out there they may seem. Then cull the list. Curate it. Personalize it. Journal it. Get it ready for your next regular check-in.

- Try to set a goal to do this regularly. Do it for a month and see what you think of it. Is this a valuable process for you? Don't take my word for it. See for yourself! If it is, then keep it going. If it is not, then give it some more time!

- If it's good, then you get value from it. Teach it to at least one other person. Maybe make a video on it, or a social media post encouraging someone else to do this kind of thing. It can help others as well. Precious few people do it. I want my precious people to do it. I love you so, so, freaking much.

Notes, thoughts, and intentions.

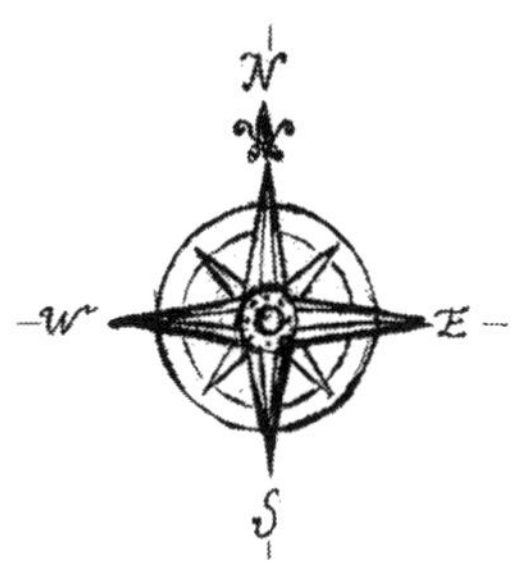

78. Engineer Your Environment to Be Uncluttered, Clean, and . . . Magical.

This may be the toughest chapter of the book to write for me; because I'm an offender of being messy. Yes, I often lead a cluttered life. In a lot of things, my room, our kitchen pantries, often my car too, but strangely not my book bag or planner because I have boundaries. I need to get better about this, and I will. Life isn't about possessions, after all (remember that?).

I've remained a cluttered person for as long as I remember. Your Aunt Laura used to clean up after me as a kid, and she'd complain to your grandmother about it. I wouldn't get in trouble because there was never any evidence that I'd left things a mess. But honestly, your Aunt Laura is ridiculously clean. It's actually kind of frightening! I only joke, but it makes myself feel better if I think of her this way.

We have too much stuff. We bought a big house, and we've had it for over ten years now, and now it's become full of stuff (i.e. "stuff creep"). It's a lot more than when we started too. It's actually lived a full life cycle and started to reproduce! Sometimes I get in one of those moods to throw it ALL away, and I've even thought of hiring someone to come in and do just that, while I keep a handful of things. But, you know, family. Ugh.

Often my desk at work was messy. I remember people saying to me, "A cluttered desk is a sign of a cluttered mind," and then I'd ask them what their empty desk says about them. Pure defense. The fact is that you get more done and just FEEL better in an uncluttered workspace. Your workspace has been self-engineered.

I feel guilty for passing this cluttered lifestyle on to you.

BUT . . .

I'm going to talk to you about this; because I HAVE done some of this. It's been really good for me, and it will lessen my guilt at least a little bit.

When the whole uncluttering process is done it really makes a huge difference.

I'm convinced that we all have a metaphorical "gas tank" for our brains every day, and everything in our day takes uses a little of that energy to evenly process it. If there's a lot of "stuff" around, then it takes up physical space and saps off that energy. Tell me if you feel the same.

There also seems to be a certain amount of guilt about having clutter and being messy. That magnificent brain of yours starts going crazy, saying things like: "I need to clean this up!" in addition to whatever else you're thinking about. It gets tiring using up that mental space, and now your inner critic (who we talk about elsewhere in this book) has all of this ammunition to use against you.

Think about starting the day off strong. Walk into the closet, and if it's a mess, it's kind of screaming at you to get it together and clean up. That's also not good for your confidence each day. It kind of sets the tone for a lot of things in our life but it doesn't have to be that way.

There's a reason we feel good when things are clean. We feel accomplished. We get energy from being in an environment like that. You're just more productive. Your mind (and I'd go so far as to say your soul) are much more at ease, and it's easier to focus. At least that's how I feel.

There's a hugely popular book by a Japanese lady named Marie Kondo called, *The Life Changing Magic of Tidying Up*, and it talks a lot about this. The book made a big impact on me. That may be where the word magic came from in this title. It's just how I felt when talking about this.

Her big principle is about how to get rid of (throw away or donate) everything in your life that doesn't bring you *joy*. She has a system that you can follow, some of which is included in the Advice in Practice section below. She goes through her thinking and methodology about how to tidy up your environment in great detail. She advocates going through your home in a certain order: First all of the clothes, then books, papers, kimono (miscellaneous), then sentimental stuff—which is usually the hardest to get rid of, and that's why it's last.

She advocates committing to do it all at once. That's a big thing. I've started and gotten to books both times and then stalled. The size of our house is just daunting, and it's not just my stuff. It's all of yours too. I think it's best to take a few days off to completely do this. We've done that a few times in our home, but not enough! We have a big home with lots of stuff!

She recommends going through everything in your home. Literally holding something in your hand and asking if it "sparks joy" in you. If not, then thank it for its service and get rid of it. That's it. You'll find that most of your things, if you're being honest, really don't bring joy, and it's just 'stuff' at that point. It's something that you don't need.

This process actually helped with what I was doing. I cleaned *ahem* MY portion of the closet, I got rid of clothes that I didn't wear, and donated nearly everything. Every morning, I can go to my *relatively* clean side of the closet—and feel a little better about myself. I can put on my 'uniform' which I think affects the mind in the same way. I enjoy knowing that what I'm wearing each day without having to devote brain power to it is saving my thinking for the big things later.

So, I recommend doing this. Imagine how good you will feel coming back to your space each day, and having it cleared out.

This is also why I think the minimalist movement has picked up steam and is becoming more mainstream. Keeping only the things that you truly need is important. You can literally carry what you need in a backpack. I've done that for a few weeks at a time in college, and it was a pretty cool way to live.

A few good things about the minimalist lifestyle:

- You appreciate what you have.
- There's just less mental space involved.
- Possessions possess. We talk about that in the, "Experiences are More Important Than Things," section; but it applies here as well, too.

I think all of us need to be vigilant about the clutter that comes into our lives. Don't get too much stuff, because it takes physical *and* mental space. I think it also increases your attachment to things. You don't need it, and if it doesn't give you joy, then stand guard and don't let it into your life. It's easy to say and easy to agree with the philosophy, but sometimes tough to do.

If you do get stuff, then have it replace something. Otherwise a mess happens. You get more and more, and then there's no more space. Google *George Carlin Stuff*, and listen to it. It's pretty hilarious, and it's devastatingly true. (Warning, some language, but you've been to public schools, so . . . you're prepared.)

That's one of the pieces of advice that I can give you: Get rid of the things that don't bring you joy.

The next part is ENGINEERING your environment.

Engineering is defined as: Inventing, innovating, designing, building, maintaining, researching and/or improving tools, systems, components, materials, solutions, and organizations.

That's awesome. I love that definition.

So, the idea is this:

Make your surroundings work for you, rather than you working for your surroundings.

That means putting some real thought into what you do every day, and all of the things you have around you. Think about your routine and your schedule. Give thought to what you have in your car, your office, your kitchen, your bedroom. Support your habits and rituals.

My friend Brett Campbell has an excellent book called: *Right Now!* and in it, there's a great chapter on the environment. He makes the case for setting up your environment according to your senses:

What do you want to see in your daily environment? Motivational quotes or sayings? Pictures of loved ones? Clean and organized furniture? The conspicuous absence of clutter, obviously!

What kind of scents would you like? This one's often overlooked. What would it smell like if everything were ideal? I like me some coconut...but maybe some scents are better for productivity for your work environment.

What do you want your environment to sound like? Music to set whatever mood you'd like, or silence, or ambient sound (turn off the TV in the background). I love to have music for the room and play the same song on repeat, as it seems to put me in "the zone."

What temperature is great for you? During the day, at night; do you like expensive-feeling sheets or blankets, do you prefer leather furniture . . . it's all to be considered.

What are some of the tastes you'd like to experience daily? Do you enjoy a desk that's salty, or slightly sweet? Just kidding. But you can get and keep healthy snacks around you—clear out your pantry of the stuff that's likely to cause you to eat poorly. I blame any extra weight I have on y'all because of the junk food, haha.

Brett also makes the point of getting an excellent mattress and bed. Make that part of your "engineered" environment because you're going to be spending an entire third of your life with it. I touch on that in the BODY section in particular, but you get to hear it again until you get a better mattress.

The thing is that like most of what I mention in this book—is to have INTENTION. Look at where you're spending your time critically, and consciously think of how it can be improved. The mass of men just go through life reactively, and don't put in the thought to really *think* about the best way to do things. I hope, as always, that this helps you consider this, and hopefully change the way you think. If I've even opened your eyes to read *The Life Changing Magic of Tidying Up*, then I've done my duty.

I love you too. I hope that I spark joy so you don't throw me away when I'm older.

The Advice in Practice:

- What's the first thing? *Read The Life Changing Magic of Tidying Up* by Marie Kondo. You can get the ideas in a cool little .pdf, but it's more fantastic to read it and understand the thought process behind it. The thought process is really what's important. She also has a book called, *Spark Joy*, which goes a little more in depth and detail. The ideas also help a lot with the idea of "rebound."

- Get out your trusty, well-used journal, and do the exercise that Kondo suggests: Write out how the uncluttered lifestyle will feel when you're done. Write out your day, and how it feels to have all of that done. Get it out of your head as a dream and prepare to make it real. That's an exciting part of life, isn't it? You get to envision something, and then make it a tangible reality. So, so cool.

- Take the idea of the entire "purge" seriously. Make up your mind and commit to changing your environment. Block off a full day, weekend, or week (depending on the size of the space/purge) in your calendar. Tell friends and family that you're doing it (if that motivates you), and then go through the whole process of "tidying up" or purging your home environment. You're going to feel a difference. You get to experience the *Life Changing Magic!*

- Watch the documentary *The Minimalists*. It is often on Netflix. Think about the lifestyle within the show as a philosophy, and if it makes sense to you. Would it be good for you to adopt some of those principles? If it does, let's set about making it a reality.

- Get the journal again. Think about your entire daily routine, and ALL of the environments in which you live in each day. Think of the perfect day, how things would feel, smell, look, and sound. Get your head around what it would be like to have it all just . . . ideal. Then take up some of the items in it, get the 'big rocks' that could make the most different with the least amount of effort, and begin to change things.

- Create an idea list: *Twenty Things I Can Do to Improve My Environment Nearly Immediately, With Little Effort*. Do the ones on the list. Out of your head and into reality, again. Like magic.

- If you're comfortable with this, or maybe if you're not (then it may be necessary), make a hard and fast rule that when you buy something new, you need to get rid of something. If you adhere to that, clutter becomes an impossibility. And that's cool.

- If you have the means, then do some bed shopping. Go and test a few. I've never done that myself, but I should. Read the reviews of the bed and make the investment. Get a good bed. I know this is in the advice about *Engineering the Perfect Night's Sleep*, but I'll say it again anyways. It's that important. So do it.

- Google: *George Carlin Stuff, listen*, laugh, and be enlightened. I think I have this assigned as advice in practice elsewhere too. So you can clear out two assignments with one action. Gooooo, you!!!

- Make sure there's at least one high-quality, handsome picture of your Daddy around somewhere conspicuous. Please.

Notes, thoughts, and intentions.

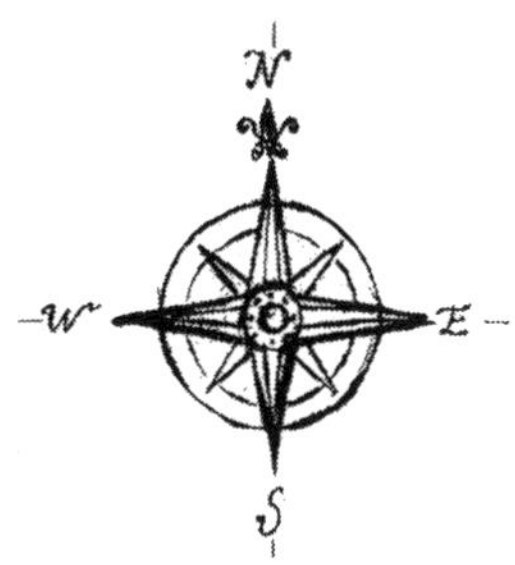

79. Actively Appreciate it All.

This is where it ALL starts.

Always be grateful. I just heard this year from my friend Jesse that instead of being grateful, *it's better to actively appreciate*.

This means that you're going out and finding things that fill your heart with gratitude on days. It's proactive when gratitude seems passive. My friend, Jesse, pointed out that the root of the word, "grateful," is from the Latin "gratis," which means free. If you're receiving something (reactive) free (versus being proactive and APPRECIATING) then you might feel obligated, or that you owe something back to God or the Universe.

When you go out and do the work of appreciating, it's an effort on your part. Just sitting back and allowing gratitude to come to you is much more reactive. It's a thought worth considering. I find truth in it.

An appreciative heart opens the door for more blessings. If you look at any situation, problem or difficulty, there is always, always something good in it. So look for it, and thank God and others for what you are and what you have.

Something that I really enjoy is looking for even the minor things to truly appreciate.

Did you have warm water this morning on a cold day? Many people before your time couldn't have these things. These little things are miraculous to me, and therefore I appreciate them.

Dean Graziosi gave a presentation while I was at Genius Network that talked about this. His advice was: "Lower the bar of gratitude in your life."

"There are only two ways to live your life. One is as though nothing is a miracle. The other is as though everything is a miracle."
— attributed to Albert Einstein

Good Lord! Do you realize how freaking blessed we are? Do you understand that no matter what comes our way in life, we can CHOOSE to appreciate? It's a mindset.

Some people are naturally more appreciative than others. You'll also find that they tend to be better to hang around than those that love to complain. Mandy, you've dealt with those unappreciative people a lot at Starbucks. They live with an entitled mindset. They take things for granted. Honestly, they're unhappy people. They feel entitled, and when they aren't given something naturally, they become easily disappointed.

The good news is this:

The art of APPRECIATION can be learned and cultivated. It's not just something that you 'have' or don't have. You can train in it. You can develop it like a habit and a muscle. Do you get that? It can happen—and it makes SUCH a big difference in your life!

I mention this ad nauseum because it's so profound and struck such a chord in my soul: Appreciation and anxiety can't live in the same head. If you're worried about things, if you're feeling entitled or like things should be set up perfectly for you, it's probably likely that you're not actively appreciating enough in your life. You need to do this.

I tell you to question everything and come up with your own opinions on what I say and write to you. Do that. But honestly, I can't think of any reason to NOT be more appreciative in your life. I think this is an absolute good.

Here are some ways to do it:

Realize the importance of appreciation:

Do you do that already? Can you see the difference between the people that live in this enlightened state versus those that don't? Can you feel the difference it would make in your life? Does it feel better to live in gratitude or entitlement?

You know the answer, but I want YOU to understand and appreciate the importance of being thankful. I want you to appreciate and savor life!

Know that you can change:

If you don't live in appreciation, or do it consistently, or are actually a pretty miserable sonuvabitch (you're not, but if you were . . .), then you've got to know that there IS a better way of living, and that you can tap into that.

It's within your reach, and it's possible to achieve and attain it.

Systematically and relentlessly add appreciation into your life:

To get into the habit of appreciation you need to make it . . . well . . . a habit. It must be a part of your daily schedule. I feel so good telling you this because my appreciation game is completely on point. Man, I love life! Here's some of what I did to get that way:

Start the day off with active appreciation. I write in my five-minute journal each morning within a minute or two of opening my eyes. This is important to get it in that semi-wakeful state where it mystically melds with that subconscious mind. Doing this first thing proactively starts your day with counting your blessings.

It also benefits your soul to have its "Appreciation Antennae," up at all times. The five-minute journal asks: "What are you grateful for?" (We'll forgive them not asking what you actively appreciate.) I love this. It starts the day right.

It has three spaces. I write the first thing that comes to mind with the first space, then I write something that seems relatively minor, but really is a big blessing—like the warm water example from above, or the fact that you get to live in the comfort of freedom. The last one is something that I really like to think on and I reach for it. A friend, an experience that has already happened, and even if it feels weird, an experience that will happen are good points to start from. This process trains the brain. It gets it operating the right way from the start of your morning.

Lately, I've also start writing down something that's 'bad.' It can be an obstacle, or something bad that's happened. It actually forces me to think why this can actually be a blessing. It's a powerful practice. If you get to the point where you can appreciate even the bad things that happen, you're acing this life lesson.

Then, during the early evening my iPhone alarm goes off with, *What a Wonderful World*, by Louis Armstrong. This is probably the perfect song for this by the way. The alarm says, "Remember that you are blessed." I know you're in my presence a lot when it goes off, and I try to stop what I'm doing. I close my eyes, think of all of the things that I appreciate, and what a truly wonderful life it is. I've even had that alarm interrupt me at times when I was feeling bad, and it immediately changed my mood.

Often, I'll also include a coin in my shoe during the day. I got this from my dear friend Dr. Scott Law, and have been using it for years now. It reminds me to be kind, but to also smile and appreciate things in life. Every time I feel that coin move, which is often, it serves as a reminder, or a trigger. It happens a lot.

Finally, at night—in my nightly ritual before bedtime, my daily planner has a space on it for "Active Appreciation," for the day. I fill it in, and often have five or more things that I list out. I put in great things that may have happened that day, or just more things that I appreciate. Sometimes these are even things like my muscles being sore after a workout, because I have muscles, mobility, and a BODY that can do work. Doing this at night creates a nice little bookend to my day. It starts and ends with appreciation.

The frequency of the times of appreciation are important. Mind you, I have three scheduled times for it, and the variable coin routine—and I'm doing great on my appreciation of life. So, if you find yourself struggling with appreciation, set more alarms and times and start sticking to them. The difference it will make in your life is absolutely amazing.

And you deserve absolutely amazing. I love you, my precious babies!

The Advice in Practice:

- This is why we do the practice of what we're grateful for every night with each other, by the way. I love that tradition, and I want you to actively think of all your blessings right before going to sleep every night. I'm hoping that you remember me for that long after I'm gone, and that you get your kids to carry on the tradition.

- Keep a gratitude (or active appreciation) journal by your bed, or even in the bathroom. Just some place where you see it every morning or night. I know you have the five-minute journal, but I need to check on you more often to make sure that you're keeping up with that.

- Set at least one alarm to go off every single day on your phone for the sole purpose of appreciation and counting your blessings. Think of all of the things that you love. Think of the special people in your life. Think of the incredible circumstances and serendipity that has brought you to this very point in life. Savor it. Thank God for it.

- Do the coin trick. Put a coin in your shoe. Lately, I've been putting some Euro coins in my shoe, because, you know, I'm intercontinental and whatnot. Every time it moves and you feel it, think of how much you appreciate things in life.

- When you meditate, pray, or take your moments of silence, add an APPRECIATION practice to it. Add an extra five minutes onto your meditation and use it to think of things that you appreciate. Favorite memories, people that you love and that have helped you, conveniences in life, books you cherish, miraculous sunsets, wonderful serendipities . . . The more you do this, the more you'll find to appreciate. This practice makes you a better person.

- Share this principle. Make a Facebook, Twitter, or blog post about it. See if your friends agree. Start the conversation and see if you can bless others with this message if you agree with it.

- Tell your Dad when you do any or all of these practices, as it would make me very, very happy (and it will appear in my very next Appreciation list).

Notes, thoughts, and intentions.

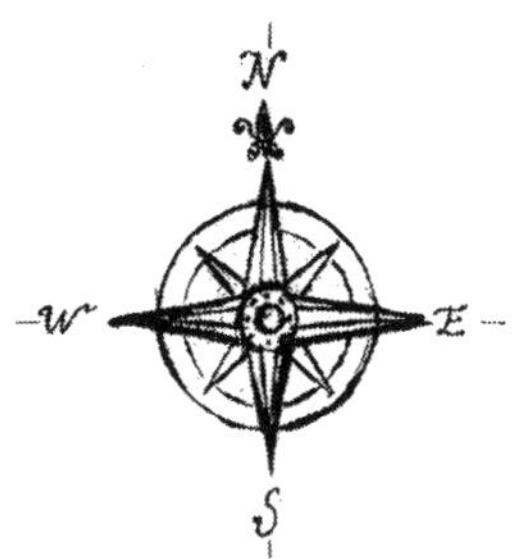

80. Remember That You Are a Spectacular Creation of God.

I was about ready to write out another Advice Chapter . . . and I want you to TRULY and totally get this, because it may be the singularly most important thought for you to adopt and believe in your life.

If you get it and truly make it a part of you, then it can change your life in so many areas. You are completely and totally worth the best. But rather than actually rewriting it and trying my best to convince you of this again, I'm going to post what I wrote about this five years ago.

I sent it out as an email in my series to my real estate clients called Morning Coffee, and I got an overwhelming response to it. Many had been touched by my message, and many of them *needed* this message. So, girls and sweet precious Alec . . . this is for you: You Are a Spectacular Creation of God.

~~~~~~~~~~~~~~~~~~~~~~

A few weeks back, my sweet daughter Aly was having a tough time in school. It seems that some kids were picking on her and calling her "nerd."
~~~~~~~~~~~~~~~~~~~~~~

Full disclosure: Obviously, this is my daughter, and I think the world of her. She is literally brilliant. She's hilarious, witty, fun, and fiercely loving. She is also beautiful in every sense of the word, inside and out. I can barely think about her without a big smile coming to my face. She is truly wonderful.

Now back to the kids at school: Kids can be viciously mean. When I think of them trying to hurt my baby girl, it makes me see red, and I really want a chance to give them an attitude adjustment.

But that wouldn't do too much to help things.

The thing that I realized that would do the most good would be to go directly to my daughter and help her to deal with the inevitable hurts and criticisms that always happen in life (no matter what age we are).

I woke one day during this time and Aly's situation was heavily on my mind. I thought of it immediately when I woke, and I had probably even dreamt about it. There was one overriding thought in my mind about Aly.

"You are a SPECTACULAR creation of God."

I took my girls to school that day, but I didn't really talk to Aly too much about it while her sister and friend were in the car. I planned to keep her in the car with me after the others left, but she didn't give me a chance. She just hopped out and took off through the doors with her big backpack. Yet that thought burned in my mind and I had to tell her. I decided that I needed to take her to lunch that day and have the talk.

So, after working that morning, I drove back to her school and got to take her out of school for a while. We got her favorite meal (junior breakfast burritos from Sonic for some strange reason) and parked overlooking the beautiful creek that runs through my village. There, on that wonderful morning we had the talk. I told her the thought that I had about her. I made her memorize it and say it back to me:

"I am a SPECTACULAR creation of God."

I told her what I think that meant, and why no one, NO ONE should ever make her feel inferior.

If you know the special blood that flows through your veins, and the divine precision with which you were made then you would hold your head high. You were created for great things in this life. You were given potential to do anything!

We both shed a tear, and I could tell that the time I spent with her meant a lot to her. It meant everything to me. There was nothing more important that I could have done with my time that day. I knew it was special, and I took a picture so I could remember it more vividly.

Here's the kicker:

We are ALL spectacular creations of God.

We are all given so much potential and ability.

We are divine in our design and can do so much more than we are led to believe in our everyday lives.

We all have down times in our lives, when we feel inferior, or not up to the task of extraordinary living. In those times, we need to remember that we were all given a wonderful ability. The power of our minds and soul are truly infinite. Keep that in mind when you are feeling weak, or when others make you feel inadequate.

I am a spectacular creation of God.

So are you.

~~~~~~~~~~~~~~~~~~~~

Kids, I know that you understand that I love you so, so very much. You'll get an idea of how much that is when you're blessed with your own child/children. It's incredible just to think of you, and I get a tightness in my chest thinking of you because it nearly hurts.

As much as I love you—I am of the firm belief that God loves you more. Only a loving God could create the feelings that a good parent has for their child.

Your life is precious, and ALL life is precious.

When you think of all of the intricacies of the brain, of the way that blood with just the right amount of oxygen is transmitted, of the delicate chemical balances that keep us moving, breathing, and living . . . it just boggles the mind. It is so overwhelming what an incredibly designed piece of
~~~~~~~~~~~~~~~~~~~~

divine art that we are. Something built so wonderfully is always valuable.

I want you to be able to wake up every day and feel how phenomenal you are. I want you to feel God's love coursing through you and just understand that it's all a miracle. Everything is a miracle, and you are the biggest, best miracle of all in who and how you are designed.

You're never alone, not just from the people that love you like me, but with God. If you close your eyes, and get still, you can feel God. That presence is always with you, and my thought is that you're a part of God and God is a part of you. You're divine. You are a supremely spiritual being.

I know that some people will be cynical about this, and not believe that we're made by anything. Some people will believe that this entire life, and all of the miracles everywhere around us are just some cosmic accident. We were made by a lightning bolt striking some primordial ooze and sparking this grand experience of life.

But it's all too perfect for this to be haphazard or random. It's designed. It's divine, and it's a miracle. So are you.

So, when you're looking in the mirror, and you see an 'imperfection,' or you don't like who is looking back at you, please try to remember this. I think to disparage a creation of God like that is a disservice to his work. See the good, the miraculous, and love the person looking back at you like you'd do your own child. You deserve that, we all do.

I'll finish here—I want you to think about your sweet brother. His almond eyes, and little ears, his precious little nose. He is so cute. So precious. So perfect. I know you feel the same way about him, and yet there are many that would say that he's not, "right." Think of how angry you'd get over someone saying or thinking that. Yet we do that to ourselves almost every day. We are all made in God's image. We are all beautiful, and every one of us is precious.

The Advice in Practice:

- Get out the journal. Write about as many things about yourself that you know are truly amazing. There's nothing wrong with that. It's not arrogant or cocky because you should be able to do this with any human being. Please make that list. I prefer doing it when listening to a power song that fills your spirit.

- Write out, "I am a Spectacular Creation of God," in your affirmations if you're doing a Miracle Morning type of practice. Please repeat it often, and literally hear yourself saying it. I want that to be top of mind for you. It helps for you to know just how wonderful you are; and then when those tough times hit—as they always do—your spirit will be well-armed and prepared for the onslaught that inner critic and the world will throw at you.

- Make a regular practice to tell others that they are a spectacular creation of God too. When you do that, you will lift their spirits and you'll feel good about doing it as well. I think it will reinforce this idea for you every time you share this.

- Teach this concept and idea to others. If you agree with this and fully believe in it, then create your own words that define this idea and do your best to spread it to others.

- You are a spectacular creation of God.
- And I love you, too.

Notes, thoughts, and intentions.

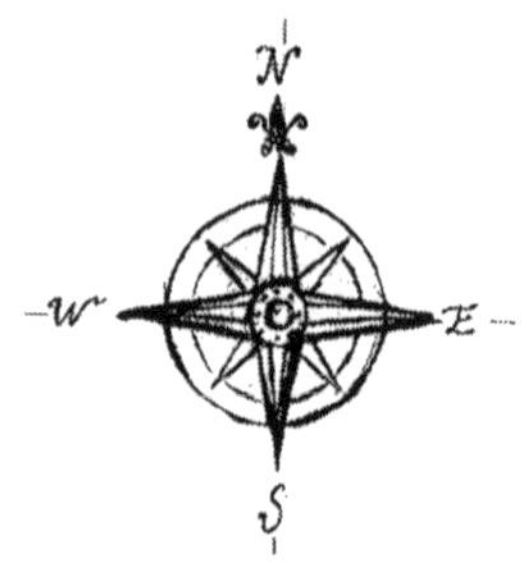

81. Live a Purposeful Life and ALWAYS ASK WHY.

It's not okay to continue along in life without having a bigger vision for it in some fashion. I think that we should always strive to improve in some way. Now, I say "bigger" vision, but really, I just mean an improvement in life for you or the ones you love.

If you're a busy, hard-working executive that gets to spend little time with your kids (my grandchildren), then the "bigger," vision could be a way to take off an extra day a week to spend with them.

If you're working at a dead-end job without any prospect of the job getting better, then the vision could be saving enough money to move to a place where you've always wanted to live.

But the thing is this: if you're not going for SOMETHING better in your life, if you're just treading water without a thought towards a brighter future, then that's not okay. I expect more of you. I expect you to have a vision of a continually better future. Something that you're striving towards, even if it's at a snail's pace, I'd like to see you moving forward and making some progress.

Personally, for many years I lived the same year over and over. I sold houses and continued the same practices in my daily life that didn't really serve me. I lived a lot for the weekend when I could finally do the things I wanted to do, but even then I didn't do the things that I was PASSIONATE about . . . and I don't want that to be you, my children!

The life I was living kind of sucked a lot of my soul away. I had a huge gap between my potential and what I was actually doing each and every day. And that gap, left untended, is going to rob you of life. I have mostly gotten my act together, but I need to keep asking the same questions:

What's my big why?

What is it that gets me up in the morning excited?

What are the big things that I'm looking forward to in the next weeks, months, and years to come?

I started asking those questions, and I didn't like the answers, so I changed them.

I think too often in our lives, we can become complacent and fall into an easy (sometimes not-so-easy) routine. Almost everyone we know, including ourselves, falls into the trance of everyday life. That is to say that we're just existing. We're not trying for anything. I think there's a vague notion of "retirement," or of a time we can stop working to then be able to do what we really want to do, but there isn't a defined future at all.

That retirement is what I've mentioned before called, "The Deferred Life Plan." That's where you put off everything you want to do in order to work, pay the bills, have some security, and do the things of a normal life while having a foggy or nonexistent future.

In fact, thinking about the deferred life plan right now, that's how nearly everyone lives. Every single day! Statistics say that the majority of the people working don't like their jobs. But they continue to do them. Which could be fine, as long as they were working towards the next step. But I imagine that few are. In fact, I lived most of my professional career that way, too. And I'm heavily into self-development, goals, positive mind-set, and the like (I bet you knew that). But I was generally missing the most important point of all: What's NEXT? What am I working toward? How I am making life better for the future?

I think that learning, goal-setting, earning more and refining your skills are all extremely noble. You should always be improving and becoming a better person.

But the question, or more accurately, the thought process that makes it all worthwhile is asking, and answering, "*What for?*"

Why would you want to work harder and longer hours on the job? To get more money? WHAT FOR? What is the purpose of that? Go through that thought process.

Answer the big questions before running faster on a treadmill going nowhere.

Now it could be to save more money to provide security for your children. That's noble and worthwhile, as long as the purpose is truly examined and doing that is deliberate. But, if it just means that you're going to buy more and bigger stuff that won't fulfill you—then maybe the extra hours away from your family aren't worth the effort you put into them. Make sure that the juice is worth the squeeze.

In breaking this down, I think that there are only two reasons to do almost anything: You either enjoy it, or it makes life better for yourself or others. That's why you get a glass of water, and that's also the reason you move across country to follow a lifelong dream. It's the reason that someone picks a life of security. They're plugging away at a job methodically to save money, maybe towards a retirement where they can finally do what they want to do. Or maybe it's to give their kids a better future of doing great things.

Our motivation is to do things that we like, or to make a better life for ourselves or for others. Sometimes we are aware of this and living an awakened life, but I'd venture to say that most people do it by default.

I know I'm getting repetitive. The point is this:

Always, always, always have the next step in mind.

Make certain that the next step is an improvement in some way. Be sure that it makes your life or the lives of others better. Take time out to consciously think, "What am I doing?" and "Why am I doing it?"

I'm starting to think that's what Socrates meant by, "The unexamined life is not worth living."

The life we have is a precious and sacred gift. I think that the best way that we can make the most of the gift is to always strive for that next step to make life even better. It's fulfilling potential by getting better, and to work towards serving ourselves and others more. If we're not, then we are squandering the potential and magic that we've all been given.

You deserve this. Greatness is in you, and it's just waiting on you to tell it what to do next. Please get started on this.

The Advice in Practice:

- Get out your journal. Write out this big question across the top of a brand-new page:
  "WHY AM I HERE ON EARTH?"

- Start writing about it. Write anything. The first things that comes into your mind are often looming on the surface of our hearts. Spend some time on it, because obviously this is important.

- Think about your current position in life. Is this something that you're proud to do? Are you helping others? Are you serving in a great capacity and making life better for yourself and others? It's okay if the answer is, "no," or "not yet." That's fine as long as it doesn't remain your answer for too long.

- If the answer is no, then I'd love for you to start to brainstorm possibilities for your life. There's advice on that here with, "*Find Your Magic Spot in Your Job or Career*," and, "*Embark on Your Own Hero's Journey*," on pages 308 and 650, respectively. Sit still and be quiet for a while. Read things that you enjoy. Spend time alone with yourself. And most importantly, *listen to yourself*. You know that I believe that there's a higher power out there that wants to help with this. Listen carefully for God's whispers on this.

- If the answer is YES, then congratulations! This is wonderful! This makes me so very happy as well! Now, the big question is: What's next for me? What is the next logical step? Think it through consciously. Mull it over and make sure that it aligns with some of the things you've written about in the WHY AM I HERE ON EARTH journaling. Does it feel right? That gut feeling is named because it literally comes from the gut and it's not wrong. Probably not ever, even if it seems like it is.

- Think of the end game. I talk about that in the advice on *Begin with the End in Mind*. Is what you're doing daily moving you towards that end? What would make you satisfied if this were your life's work in the end? Think on it, and again, with a journal in hand, start writing it out. I love this time. Real growth occurs when you really get the words out of your heart and mind and it takes tangible form. Please do this.

- Seek out a friend that you can talk to about this. I'm hoping that you have someone like this in your life. If you don't then you obviously have me. Try to cultivate some friendships like this. When you call them, set a time for lunch or coffee, and tell them you'd really like to talk about their lives and yours. Calm them down, because you may be weirding them out a bit, and make that appointment. Go through some of the things that you've written and thought about. But ask THEM these questions, too. Really listen to their answers and coax them into answering them. Doing this for a friend is one of the best things you could ever do for them.

- If you haven't already, talk to your Dad about it, too. Rumor has it that he loves you!

Notes, thoughts, and intentions.

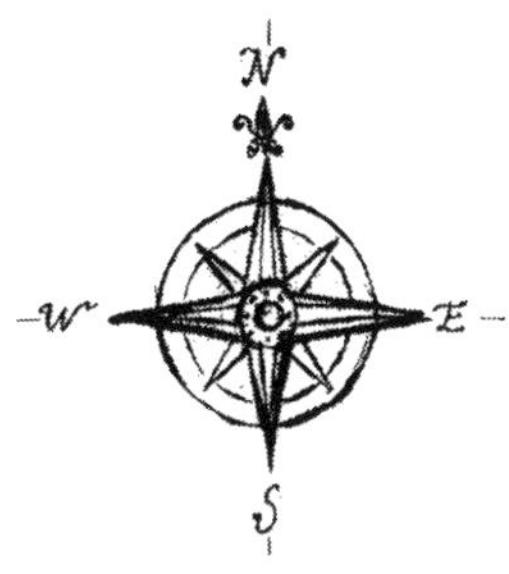

82. Remember That You Are Always Loved.

This is a big, wonderful, and very profound piece of advice.

But first I want to make a confession: I didn't always feel like I was loved and even today, as "enlightened" as I like to think I am, I still have times that I struggle with it or forget it.

When I grew up, I spent a lot of time alone. Your grandmother, during the times when I lived with her, usually worked several jobs just to make ends meet. I didn't see a lot of her. The same thing with your Papaw. When I lived with him, he worked extremely hard as a Marine. I remember him leaving the house at or before six in the morning, and often not getting home until the night had already fallen. He often did that six days a week.

I'm not trying to make a sob story here, but I didn't get to see a lot of them while I was being raised. A lot of the time, I was a "latchkey" kid. I came home to an empty home almost every day and didn't have a lot of adult supervision while I was young. That didn't affect me a whole lot when I was young. I think I became pretty self-reliant and resourceful as a matter of fact. I didn't mind it at all and didn't know that there were other ways of living.

The reason that I mention this is because I didn't really hear my parents tell me that they loved me much while growing up. Now, when I was around them, they told me and showed me in many tangible ways, but sometimes I think if you don't hear it regularly and frequently you can tend to forget it.

Going through my teenage years was probably the worst part. I remember during my sophomore year in high school (between fourteen and fifteen years old) I had the hardest time in life and suffered from very low confidence in myself. This manifested itself in a lot of ways, but I just didn't always feel loved.

But now I know.

I am always loved. I've always been loved. And I always WILL be loved.

The thing is that it's great to hear that from your parents, friends, and other folks that are close to you. That can help reaffirm it.

I know how totally and completely I love you. I would give my life for yours in a second and take nearly every pain from you for myself. The coolest thing about that is that the love from me is unconditional. It doesn't matter what happens in life. It doesn't matter what you do or don't do. I've used this example before, but if you cut off my arms and beat me to death with them, I'd still know I loved you.

I hope that feels good for you to know that, and hopefully believe it.

But the truth is greater and more comforting than that.

God loves you even more than I do.

And that is saying something. I know this because God made this kind of love possible. God granted us this life and all of the beauty in it. God allowed our family to come together and for the unique characteristics of both your Mom and I to show in you. All of your ancestors had to meet and create new life together to create that magical, perfect you. You were given senses, and a marvelous mind that is now contemplating these thoughts.

I mentioned this when talking about The Inner Critic, but one of my main limiting beliefs throughout my life has been that I'm not that "worthy" or, "deserving" of tremendous success. I'd always seem to do pretty well in life up to a certain point, and then I'd do something to sabotage it, or I'd let up before really doing something incredible. I don't think it was something that was really conscious, but it happened many times.

I think that was me not feeling loved enough to think I deserved that. I don't know if you've ever felt that way, or are even experiencing this now, but this is important so please listen up to it, and see if this hits home:

Do you love your brother?

Did you love him when he came into the world? Truly?

I know the answer. I saw you with him. I watched you hold him, I saw the tears when you worried about his future. I saw and still see the concern for him.

Now, let me ask you—did he do or have to do anything to deserve the love that you had for him? Consider that. I know that the answer is no. He didn't need to prove himself. He didn't have to earn it from you.

He was and is loved because it's his birthright.

He deserves it and is worthy because he's living. He is a human. He is imbued with divinity and is touched by God. As we all are.

You deserve love as much as any human on the planet. You are extraordinary. You're living and breathing. Many miracles had to happen to make you the living, breathing, wonderful, perfect creation you are.

Love is your birthright.

And you don't need to depend on others to give that to you because it's always there. The miracles you get to experience in every second of life are all made for you. To me, how much you have been given is proof of how much you are loved.

The proof of that love (if you choose to look) surrounds us. It's there to remind you that you are always loved, no matter what.

All life is precious. It is dear. It is a miracle. And it is loved.

You are loved more than you can ever imagine, and I so want you to know and understand that. Especially in those moments when you're feeling self-doubt. You are loved.

The only question that remains now is: How do you know you are loved? How do we put it into your life? Let's practice it and make it a part of you.

Advice in practice:

- Think about yourself as a child. Try to remember what you looked like, how you acted. If you actually have any videos of you as a child, see if you can go back and watch them. Watch that child or get their image in your mind. Then think of whether that sweet girl or boy deserves love. Do they? You bet.

  Tony Robbins had us do this at one of his seminars. He had us imagine ourselves as a child, like we were watching them, and then played the song, *You Are So Beautiful*, by Joe Cocker while we were doing that we all cried like babies, and it was so profound.

- Now, here's a big thing for you: Know that nothing has changed. You are loved now, and you *always* will be.

- Think about this and then JOURNAL all of the things that have been done for you to show you that you're loved. Did your Daddy wake you up gently and quietly for years to get you ready for school? Has a loved one called to check on you to see how you're doing? Did someone write a book for you? Write down whatever comes to mind, whether they are big or small acts of love for you.

- Now take that list, and truly *feel* them. Internalize them and know that you're loved. There is so much proof of that.

- Look up and read this Bible verse. It was very important to us when your brother was born. It means so much to us and it most definitely applies to him and to you as well: Jeremiah 29:11.

- I think it's more effective if you Google it or grab a Bible yourself to get the message. Please write that message out and realize that it's for YOU.

- I love you so much . . . but I guess I just spent the entire chapter telling you that, eh?

Notes, thoughts, and intentions.

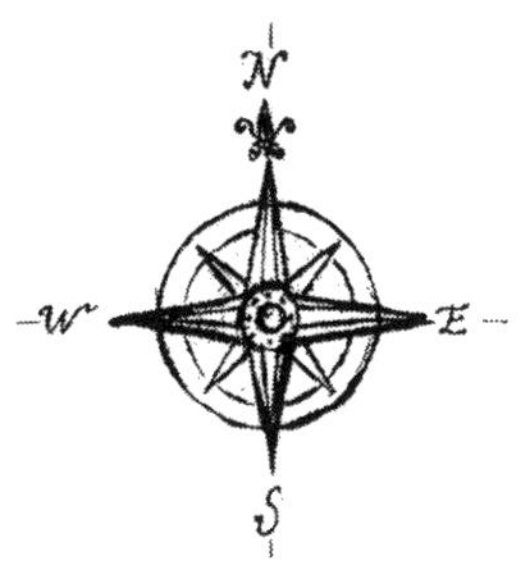

83. Have a Vision . . . Or Perish.

"Without a vision, the people perish."

Now this is actually biblical in nature, and I am a huge believer in the truth of this.

I think that without a vision of a better future, or something to look forward to, nations will suffer. Organizations and businesses will suffer. Certainly families will suffer, and that's something that I am very conscious of right now in leading our family. I also think it's true for each and every one of us.

My precious, wonderful children, I implore you to think about this. I want you to actually have a vision for a better future and have hope that something will make you feel a lot better about your life. My wish is for you to always have that to look forward to in your life.

Here's the thing: Most people just go through life doing their day-to-day routines. They don't stop to actually take a look at the big plan, or where they're going, or the impact that they can have in the world. Usually it's just a struggle to get through the week and get to the weekend. A lot of people are pausing their life while they work, or while they go about their daily routine. They have this vague concept that somehow, sometime in the future, things are going to get better. They think that they'll actually get a chance to live their dream life, to accomplish all of those goals, and fulfill the ambitions that they had when they were kids when they weren't scared of failure.

Something that I'd recommend is to take time out of your yearly schedule, take time out of your monthly schedule, and even take time every week to work on and refine your vision for those periods of time. I don't expect you to know exactly what's going to happen for the rest of your life, but it is good to have an idea of some of the things that you really want to do, have it written down, and to revisit it every once in a while.

Knowledge is worthless if it's unable to be put into practice. Something I would encourage you to do is to actually schedule times to take a look at your future, and to seek the vision for it. I would recommend that you do it as part of your weekly planning process and check in. It's just so important.

When it's time to set goals, (New Years for instance) take time out to look at where you are in life now, where you hope to go, and what your vision for a new, vibrant, and exciting future is.

With that said, please keep this in mind: This is one of the most important pieces of advice.

Whenever you find yourself struggling in life (such as depression) or perhaps just not living up to the extraordinary standards you have for yourself, I think a lot of times it's due to NOT having a vision that's *compelling*. You always need something to work towards, or something to look forward to in life. It's very important and I want that for you.

As always, I love you so much. You mean the entire world to me. It makes me happy to think that these words will be able to help you in your life.

The Advice in Practice:

- Create an idea list of all of the things that you'd like to accomplish in life. Write down some of the things that you thought of as a child. Include what you would do if you had all the money in the world, and what you'd like to see happen. Brainstorm that and get it all out onto paper using the brain mapping technique.

- If you haven't done mind mapping, or it's been a while, look up mind mapping on YouTube and check out some of the better videos on it. Learn exactly how to mind map so you can work on and refine your vision.

- Once you have all of the things that come to mind for your exciting future, make them more concise. Eliminate some of the ones that don't mean as much to you, circle some of the ones that do. Make that list and mind map!

- Now get this into your journal as vision for your life. Don't be crazy about this, or worried that it has to be perfect, because it doesn't. There's a very good chance that your vision will change over time,

- The value of this exercise is that you do have something to look forward to. This vision, what you're writing down now, and what you're thinking about will be like a magnet that can help pull you through tough times. Everyone needs the help through the tough times.

Notes, thoughts, and intentions.

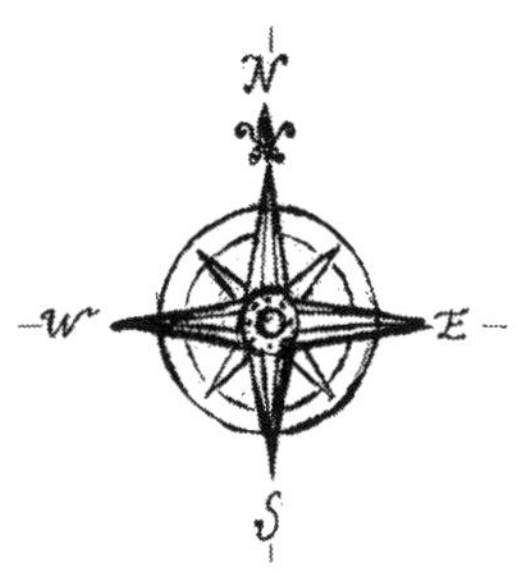

84. Do An Act of Kindness (A-OK) Every Day.

This chapter is dedicated to Skip.

He was a professor at Texas A&M and the father of Daniel, one of my dear friends in high school. I was a senior then and had just moved to town with your grandmother. It was just her and I, a single Mom struggling while raising a teenager by herself. We had one car between us: my Jeep that I bought by working the previous summer with my Uncle Steve.

Every morning I'd wake up, take my mother to her job in the next town over, and then drive back to go to school. When the school day was over, I would drive back to my Mom's work where I worked too. We'd work until the mid-evening and come home to repeat the cycle the next day.

One day, my Jeep didn't start. The problem was that we didn't have money to get it fixed. So, I walked to school for a few days, and your grandmother had to take the bus with many stops and switchovers each day. It was tough, but it didn't last for long.

On a Saturday morning, we heard a knock on our back door where the Jeep was parked. It was Daniel asking for the keys to the Jeep. His father Skip was busy installing a new starter for it, and he needed to make sure that it worked to finish up the job. He heard about our situation, and just helped us.

He didn't ask at all. He just did it. He refused any payment for it, and our entire daily life was changed. I'm convinced that he would have done it completely anonymously if he didn't have to have the keys for it.

I still get choked up thinking about that. It was probably the kindest thing that anyone had ever done for me, an act of kindness that affected me so deeply.

It touched me to my soul, and the thing is that when you do an A-OK, it affects YOUR soul, too.

I don't know that there's a better feeling than just really knowing that you've helped and made a difference to others. In fact, that's probably one of the biggest reasons that I'm writing this to you. I want you to have the benefit. I want you to have a better life—but *subconsciously*, we do things because it feels good for us to do (or it's potentially painful if we don't).

When I was down and going through an existential crisis, I didn't want to get out of bed. I had no energy. I had no desire to do much of anything. I still did things however. I went through the motions and did what I had to do to get through the day. But I was tired. Just tired of it all.

That's no way to live, and *we deserve so much more*.

When I started to get out of this funk, I had a few spiritual practices that I felt helped more than anything else. Doing these, I got to feeling better about myself, and to eventually love myself as a good person with a loving heart.

One of those practices was writing daily (and sometimes multiple times a day) in my journal. I was listing the things that I was grateful for (I've since replaced that with active appreciation). As I've mentioned many times before, my mentor said that: "Anxiety can't live in the same head as gratitude." I believed it and tried to get as much gratitude as I could to fill my head so the other, less kind thoughts wouldn't have room to survive. That worked and made a difference.

But the biggest difference was my other spiritual practice:

I decided to perform an act of kindness each and every day for another human being.

Listing it here for you, I feel like I have some kind of secret. A secret that is powerful. I remember lying in bed, not wanting to get up one day. The inner critic within me was beating the crap out of me, and I was feeling bad about feeling bad. Have you ever experienced that? I thought to myself: *What difference am I going to make today?*

And then that wonderful thought brought about by the commitment to do an A-OK came to mind as my savior: *I know I'm going to make a difference to at least one soul today*.

That moment is still so vivid for me. I get choked up because it saved me that day.

I got up, and it was a great day. I got a big, green trash can that had blown into the middle of a street and picked it up. I rolled it back to the house (where it looked like an elderly couple lived). It wasn't much. It took two minutes honestly, but that little act made *all* of the difference to me that day.

I like to think that I've come a long way since then. I'm physically better. I'm emotionally more stable and secure (with occasional bouts of craziness). My mind is sharper. But more than anything, my spirit is stronger. I know that I'm good, and that I'm a light from God. Does that sound boastful? That's okay with me, because it's true. But the truth is that we are all lights from God, and we have limitless potential to help others. We can all serve with a kind word and acts great or small.

I think that you know this, and it's an incredible thing in the divine design of us as humans:

We can't make someone else feel better without making ourselves feel better.

How cool is that?

So, the question is for you is: do you see value in doing this?

I literally have a line in my daily planner now that has a checkbox (circle, actually) with a blank next it for an act of kindness. It reminds me to do it every day. If I hit the end of the day, and I haven't done something for someone, I try to send a kind text or encouraging word to a friend or family member. It's gotten to be a bit of a habit now.

I hope that I'm not coming across as holier than thou. I'm no better than any human. We're created equal in the sight of God, but I do certainly try to be blessing. Of course, you're doing the act for them—but the happy side effect is that you feel better.

Do a kind act every day. It doesn't have to be huge, or something that takes a lot of time. In fact, it can be as little as praying for someone, and wishing them well. The thing is, you have to have a definable moment where you can say that you did something good for another person. Oh, and the rule is that it's not an act that you would've done anyways. If you make your spouse coffee or do special things for them regularly then that doesn't count. The idea is that you go do something for someone else.

Also, I always gave myself "bonus points," when no one else knew about the act. You feel great when it's just something between you and God. It's your little secret, and rather than bad secrets that eat you up inside, this one fills you with an inner light. It's a great feeling. I remember doing something particularly nice for someone, and when I got to my office and was alone and able to close my door, it felt so good that I just cried some tears of joy. Life is and can be sweet with these moments of pure magic.

But we can all do this. We've got the power, and I'd say the obligation, to spread kindness to others. Serving others, lifting their souls, and giving love is, in my opinion, what life is all about. You don't need a degree to do it. You don't have to have a lot of money, or be good-looking, or have grown up with the right childhood. This divine ability is given to us all.

My advice is to use that ability and make the world a better place because you breathed in it.

The Advice in Practice:

- I'm including an idea list that I did around the time of the renaissance in my life—it's a list of fifty Acts of Kindness that you can do each day. Read it and think of a few that you can do. Get your quiver ready with arrows of kindness ready to be unleashed. Think about what you can do and be prepared.

- Ask someone what the kindest thing anyone has ever done for them. It's amazing how much incredible emotion that brings up when you do it. Listen and feel how much better it makes you feel when you listen to it. It's scientifically proven that we feel many of the same emotions as the givers and receivers of these acts of kindness when we just witness or hear about them.[14]

- Make the commitment to do a kind act for the next ten days. Write them down when you can. Please take note of how you feel when you perform them. Consider this and continue if it feels right for you.

---

[14] Claus Lamm, Jasminka Majdanzic "The role of shared neural activations, mirror neurons, and morality in empathy–a critical comment," https://www.sciencedirect.com/science/article/pii/S0168010214002314 (January 2015).

- Create your own idea list of ways to spread kindness to other people. Make at least twenty ideas and stretch your mind. Create some of the acts on the page and feel it deep in your soul when you do.

- Preach this to others. Get them to agree. We learn better when we teach others to do it too.

- Of course, this wouldn't be complete without mentioning and asking you to help by volunteering your time and skills to others. It's an incredible feeling to do it, and it's wonderful when it's a regular part of your life. Please look for the JoeVolunteer app, download it, and see where you can help others. Spread kindness.

- I'm so proud of your hearts, and the kindness you show. I love you!

Here's the list I wrote back in early 2015 . . . I entitled it "How to Be a Freaking Beacon of Light."

Obviously, there are thousands of ways (tweet them to me @ChipFranks, or comment below because I really want to hear!) to do this, but I'm just listing a few dozen. We'll see how this goes.

1. Pay for the next person's order. This is one of the most common, but it still feels good.
2. Write a heartfelt letter with a pen and paper. Mail the letter as well. Emails and even texts or FB posts count, too. Talk about how grateful you are for someone. Get specific as to why.
3. Donate your clothes. Anything that hasn't been worn in a year. Gone. Homeless shelters are great. Ask churches if

they have something like that. Goodwill is okay in a pinch, but not as good.

4. Send some flowers, just because. You know who you should send them to already, don't you?
5. Offer to babysit for a single parent. They will appreciate it more than you'll ever know. Make sure you're not creepy, though.
6. Give away some of your best ideas to someone if you think it can really help them. If you're an idea machine, and you have some good ones, then this can be very good for both of you.
7. If you're strong, offer to carry or lift something for someone. If you're not strong, or look frail, please skip this one, as it will cause extreme guilt in those you're trying to help!
8. If someone you know is grieving, don't dare let the words, "If you need anything," come out of your mouth or on a glowing screen! Just DO something for them. Make a favorite meal for them. Give them a gift certificate to a night out at the movies. Take something off of their hands that you can help handle while they're not at their best.
9. Tip a great waiter/waitress an extra-large tip for great service. Make sure to write a note on the receipt how much you appreciate them doing such a great job—these feel GREAT on the receiving end.
10. Make certain to go to the management of someone that's done a great job for you and brag on them. Put it down in writing if you can and be specific about how they served you well.

11. Help someone move. Sure, we all hate it, but it makes a big difference in the life of the person you're helping . . . and they won't forget it. There are two types of friends: ones that won't offer to help you move when they know you're doing it, and true friends. Be the latter.
12. Send someone a gift via Amazon. They'll even wrap it for you and put a note on it. You can even do it anonymously. Which I recommend. This is especially cool if you know they really want something. It doesn't even have to be big or expensive . . . The thought really does count in this case.
13. If you have a, "buy one, get one free," coupon, use the free one to give it away. The feeling you get from brightening someone's day is well worth the little bit of extra money you'd save by splitting it.
14. Leave a note on someone's car. Make it encouraging. And then sign it, "Someone who cares."
15. Put together a "Hug," station at a nursing home. Make sure you have kids do it, or it's creepy (see number five), but put up a sign that reads, "Free Hugs!" Offer them to anyone that wants one. Kids love doing this, and it'll be tough to beat the feeling you'll have when you finish.
16. Pay an expired parking meter, but leave a note letting them know someone did it. Don't sign your name but give them a free smile in addition to paying for the parking.
17. Go work at a soup kitchen . . . at a time other than the holidays. I've talked to a lady that ran one, and she says they have plenty of volunteers at Thanksgiving and Christmas, but not as many throughout the year. So, go

work then, and you'll feel just as good. You'll also walk out of there feeling grateful for what YOU have.

18. If you borrow a friend's car, leave it cleaner than you found it, and hopefully with more gas.
19. Write a letter to a soldier that's deployed. Strike up a conversation. Maybe include some goodies as part of a care package. At the very least, tell them how grateful you are for their service, and that you're holding them in your thoughts and/or prayers, and want them to return safely.
20. Write a heartfelt Amazon or iTunes review for a product, or podcast, of something you really love. The authors and artists read those. If it's a bad record, keep your pie hole shut and don't spread the negativity.
21. Pick an address from a phone book. Send them a postcard or quick letter telling them that someone is wishing them well. Put a Thoreau quote on it, and they'll believe it's fate.
22. Here's an easy one: When it's someone's birthday on Facebook, don't just wish them a generic, "Happy Birthday." Instead, list a few things you really admire about that person, THEN wish them a happy birthday.
23. Think now about the couple you know that seems to really have a GREAT relationship. You know, the folks that look really in love after a few decades together. Let them know you appreciate their example.
24. If you've got a spouse/friend that's fighting their weight, cover up the scale number with a sign that says, "You're just right." (I saw a picture of that on the Internet, and blatantly stole it)

25. Leave a bag of food at the door of a family you know is struggling financially. Include a note (disguise your handwriting, or type it) of encouragement, and ask that at some point, if they can that they try to pay it forward for someone else. That little bit can take the sting out of charity for prideful folks AND maybe it multiplies the blessing for more folks down the road.
26. Volunteer at the Special Olympics. Trust me on this one.
27. Give out, "Fonzie," cards. "You're cool, and it has been noticed. Thank you."
28. Set up a High Five Station at a charity race. You'll feel great with every high five you give.
29. When you're in a conversation with a stranger, or a friend you haven't talked with in a while, ask them what the happiest day in their lives was. It's great to see them smile as they relive that magic moment in their minds. You'll both feel great afterward.
30. I borrowed this one from James Altucher (www.JamesAltucher.com): Pick an email you didn't return a few YEARS ago. Respond to it thoroughly, and whenever possible, offer some encouragement along the way.
31. Bring some books you've read and no longer need to a hospital. It can get really, really boring there sometimes.
32. If you do #31, leave some notes of prayer, encouragement, or inspiration throughout the books—or as bookmarks.
33. Get people together to go caroling this Christmas. Visit older folks, or people that live alone. Invite them along afterward, and for crying out loud—don't ask for figgy pudding.

34. If you see a wandering dog or cat, try to see if they have a collar and try to return them to their owner. Especially if they're out in the streets and could get hit a car. This few minutes out of a day could change someone's life!
35. Make up "Homeless Packs." My daughter came up with this idea in our family. Include some snacks, food, water, maybe a book you've read, and a note wishing them well and offering encouragement. My daughter's had a few loving Bible verses in them. Have these packs ready to hand out from your car. This is more satisfying than giving money that may enable some bad habits.
36. Think of a really good time you've had with a friend. Bring back all of the sights, sounds, smells, and experiences of that day. Then call or write and remind them of it.
37. Catch someone doing really great at their job, and let them know they're a tribute to their profession, and that they've made your day more enjoyable. Thank them for it.
38. Send a onetime donation to Save the Children, or if you're really feeling it, sign up for a monthly donation. They're ranked high in the amount of money that actually gets to the kids they're helping.
39. Send an anonymous "Secret Admirer," rose to someone who might need it. Make sure it's really anonymous, yo.
40. Write a real letter to a friend. Use postage. See how nice you can be to them in telling them some of the things you admire about them, and that you'll always be friends, no matter what.
41. Make a very special one-on-one date with a family member. Your child, your parent, your spouse—but this

is important—for no special occasion. Just, "because." Then go all out and really make it spectacular. You'll have fun planning it, and they'll remember it for a while.

42. If you leave a voicemail, tell the person you're calling something that you're grateful for about them when you leave that message, and tell them you're hoping they're having a great day . . . and be sincere about it!
43. Donate your change. Don't spend coins. Put them together in a piggy bank and give it to a worthy cause. You'll never know the difference you're making, and you'll bless them and yourself with the donation.
44. Randomly call your town's fire department and EMS folks. Tell them you're just calling to let them know you really appreciate what they do on a daily basis. Try not to make it weird.
45. When/if you write a gratefulness list, and one of your friends or family makes it on the list, tell them that they did, or send them a copy of it.
46. Buy someone a desert anonymously. Time it right.
47. ALWAYS, ALWAYS, ALWAYS offer your seat to an elderly person, a child, or a lady (if you're a man) if the seats are all taken, you have one and they don't.
48. Send an unsolicited testimonial to a business you enjoy. If you put it in a card, or on a letter and make it nice enough, they can hang it on the wall.
49. Call your Mom. Remind her of something nice she's done for you and thank her for it again.
50. Return someone's trash can from the road. It's simple and easy, and the small effort involved will be swallowed by someone's gratitude for such a simple act.

Notes, thoughts, and intentions.

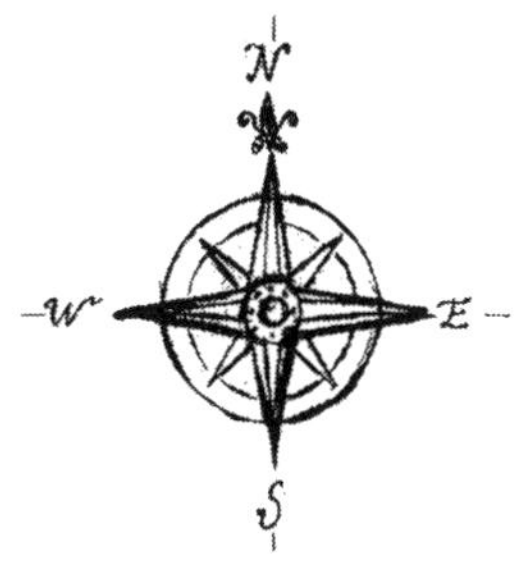

85. Feel The Fear and Do It Anyways.

Choose not to be afraid. Don't make decisions out of fear. It's going to be just fine.

Now, understand that this advice comes from someone that still feels fear on a daily basis. I'm working on it, and I imagine that I always will be. But please don't let the inadequacy of the messenger take away from the message.

I'll start by saying that some fear is necessary, because it has kept us alive for a while. There's a reason that we're born with the fear of falling and loud noises. But you know what? Those are the only fears that we have innately. The rest are learned, and in today's society are largely not needed at all.

What I'm talking about here is the emotional type of fear: Fear of trying new things, fear of standing up for what you believe in, of starting (or ending) a relationship, or of telling the truth. We're talking about the fears that show up in our day-to-day life.

Tony Robbins has said that most of our fears (at least non-physical) come down to two things: fear of not being enough, or fear of not being loved. If it's put that way, and it's true, then these fears are completely unfounded if you take them to their logical outcome.

You are enough. You have the divine running through your blood. We are all God's children and love is our birthright. Just like every baby that comes in the world is worthy of love, so are you. And nothing that you do can change that. Oh, and your Daddy will love you, regardless of anything. (That goes for this realm and anything that happens after this life too.) You can always feel confident in that. Maybe that doesn't help as much when you lose the love of a boyfriend or girlfriend or you are not accepted as a part of the popular crowd. But it should. One of the things I most want to instill in you is confidence in yourself, and absolutely knowing that you are loved and enough. I so hope that you have this, because it's true.

And IF that's true, then fears, as real as they feel, are unfounded.

It's still okay to feel the fear. But the clichéd quote is so true:

"Feel the fear and do it anyways."

You see, the GIFT that fear gives us is the ability to show courage. And the more courage you're able to show, the more confidence you'll have to do it again. That fear loses its hold on you as you conquer it again and again. Courage comes from the Latin "Cour" which means heart. It takes heart to overcome fear and to actually do what it is that fear is keeping you from doing.

Another way to look at fear is that it can point you in the direction of what you need to do or where you need to go.

It's life and God's way of telling you where the chance for the most growth in your life is to be had. You become more of a person of character and moral fortitude every single time you do something that you fear. And honestly, where in this world do we get a chance to actually show courage in the general absence of physical fears? It can be a blessing in that way.

Thinking about this, here's a point that I remember when I was selling books door-to-door in college. I remember being so terrified to knock on someone's door. It was daunting to face that unknown and get started each day. My heart would pound, I would physically sweat, my breathing would get faster, and that act of physically knocking would seem so difficult. I'm hoping you get the mental image of your nineteen-year-old Daddy, skinny, relatively big hair nearly shaking in his shoes at the thought of doing it. And you know what? I DID do it. Several thousand times, in fact.

The principle they taught is one you need to remember: ACTION CURES FEAR.

Performing the action just feels terrific after it's done. It literally feels like a weight has been lifted from your soul. You just feel lighter, and maybe more capable.

The only way that fear is bad is when it causes you to NOT do the things that you're supposed to do. If it's causing you to live a smaller life than you should, or preventing you from talking to that special someone that may be the one for you, or from asking for what you want (see that advice earlier), then it needs to be overcome.

Otherwise it is one of the best personal development tools you can experience.

Here's one of my absolute favorite quotes in the history of mankind. Coincidentally, I learned it while I was selling books. I mentioned it earlier, but I'll leave you with this:

> ***"The credit belongs to the man who is actually in the arena, whose face is marred by dust and sweat and blood ... who knows great enthusiasms, the great devotions; who spends himself in a worthy cause; who at the best knows in the end the triumph of high achievement, and who at the worst, if he fails, at least fails while daring greatly, so that his place shall never be with those cold and timid souls who neither know victory nor defeat." — Teddy Roosevelt. (I'm not a big fan of his populist politics, but he certainly had this right).***

The Advice in Practice:

- I'm trying to put in actual things here that can help in your day-to-day life, versus some flowery sounding generalities . . . and this is one of the biggest practical applications: Run towards your fear. To do this each day, simply do the thing that you fear the most first on your to do list. It's that one that swells up in your throat.
- Make that phone call that you've been putting off for a while. I bet you know the one I'm talking about. Regardless of how it goes, good or bad, you can celebrate that you had the GUTS to do it. Do it now.

- Memorize that Teddy Roosevelt quote above. Use it if you need to. Literally SAY it before you do something that scares you!

- Write out what it is that causes you fear in your journal. Just getting it out, and putting it on paper (I think that it's more effective to actually write it out versus typing it), makes a big difference

- While you're there writing out the fear, it can be a great idea to write out the worst-case scenario. Keep it going until you get to the part where the world explodes, and the entire universe collapses. Because that's usually the worst thing. But I'm betting that it doesn't do that.

- When you feel fear in the moment, in everyday normal circumstances (like I do every time I do burpees, or take a cold shower in the morning), use the "Five Second Rule," from Mel Robbins. Go Google that. You can also read her excellent book on it. It means count down from 5, and then just do the thing that's making you uncomfortable. It short-circuits your brain before it can (skillfully) talk you out of doing it.

Babies, I'm SO, so proud of you. Part of me worries a bit about you getting scared of things, but I know it's good for you to face those fears. I couldn't be more proud of you, because I know that you have that courage inside of you. More importantly than that, you should be proud of yourselves.

Notes, thoughts, and intentions.

86. Do Your Best, Then Release the Result.

This realization in life is a new one for me. I'm a recovering "goal-aholic." Someone that always thought that I could create something in my head and know it could be MADE to happen through creativity, tenacity, and sometimes just plain ole' force of will.

But this past year or so, I've had a rather profound change of mindset on this. I don't know if your experience will be the same as mine, but here's the new principle that guides me:

It's called: "Releasing the result."

In sales I've always had a philosophy of: "Releasing the result." What it means is that I couldn't care too much about the outcome, but just do everything that I should do to get to the right point.

I would (and still do) say, "If it's right for you, great. I'll help you. If not, that's okay, too." Sometimes I'd point to my gut and say, "I'll eat just fine, regardless."

I really mean it, too. I didn't WANT to do business unless it was great for both sides. If it wasn't right for them, it would never be right for me. And I didn't get too worked up if I didn't "make the sale," because I'd still done what I was supposed to do.

This nearly always worked.

Not DEPENDING on an outcome more often than not made it seem like things would always work out for me.

And the opposite also seems to be true.

I'd seen real estate agents that I'd train, that would use the same words as me that would politely ask the clients to buy—and it seemed that they NEVER did from them.

Why?

Because the agent seemed to be so invested in the outcome—they HAD to make a sale—and the clients in question intuitively knew that, and it made them uncomfortable. Desperation is the worst cologne.

There is a gigantic difference between wanting to make a sale, and having to make the sale.

The unfortunate agents were not able to release the result, and they suffered for it. The people that otherwise could have been blessed by the sale went elsewhere too.

There's a point to this.

The older I get and the more in tune I get with God and the beautiful serendipity of the world, the more I realize that, "Releasing the result," is important in EVERY aspect of life, and not just sales.

I don't know exactly how I came to realize this, but it started a little more than a year ago for me: I understand, to the very core of my being, that things truly happen for a reason. Everything unfolds exactly as it's meant to do. Everything.

That doesn't mean that you don't prepare, or try to get better. You still have that responsibility. In fact if you know deep down that you're supposed to be doing something, and you don't, then I think life has a way of correcting you.

The philosophy is do the best with what you can. And then release the preconceived notion of how you think things SHOULD go.

As you do this, you'll notice that your life will start giving you perfect moments. Times of pure serendipity, when the right things just seem to happen magically for you.

You can calm down your mind and spirit, and get present in the moment. That's when God (or the Universe) speaks to you, and you feel that something is right or wrong in your soul.

If something is right, and you're following it, then you know it. You start to feel it in your bones. You feel good about doing it. You can put your heart, effort, and soul into it, and have faith that it's all going to work out good or bad. Just as it's meant to happen. You can release that outcome, and just know that it's meant to be the way it's supposed to be.

Everything will unfold in its own glory. And it's all perfect.

The Advice in Practice:

- See if you can change your self-talk. Whenever you think something is happening to you, choose to think that it's happening FOR you. If you didn't get the result that you wanted, then apply this thinking and think why the result could still be good.

- I mention this in the "learning to sell," advice in the MIND section: But get a job with sales in it. See how you can apply "Releasing the result" to that job.

- Learn the parable of the Sower. Look it up in the Bible in Matthew 13:1-23, Mark 4:1-20, and Luke 8:1-15. The parable is about where the seeds land, and it's such a good story for life. Some will, some won't, so what?

- When you pray, ask that the right outcome happens—regardless of what that may be. Know that whatever happens is *supposed* to happen, and the only way you should ever be mad at yourself is if you didn't put in the right thought and effort to make something happen. Even then, any anger should just be channeled into doing it right the next time.

- Think of something that may have happened in your life that you consider a "bad result." I'd like you to pull out your journal and write about that. Describe it in detail, and then explain how the result was actually good for you.

- Add "I release the result," to your morning affirmations when you do the as part of your Miracle Morning practice. We want this to be top of mind for you, as it makes such a difference in life.

- If you agree with this concept, teach it to others. Post it on Facebook or talk to a friend about it. The best way to really learn something is to teach it.

Notes, thoughts, and intentions.

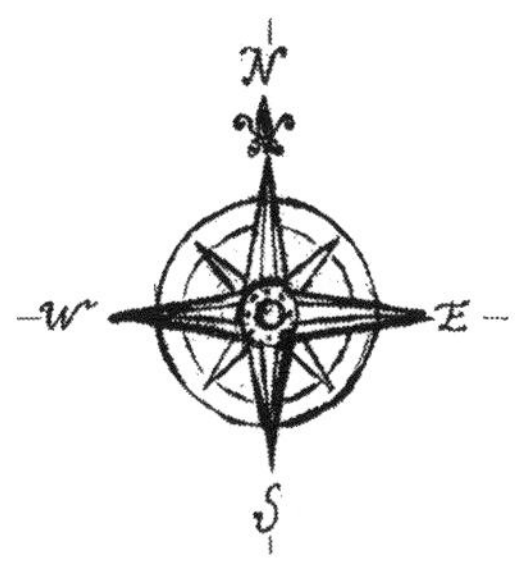

87. Take Extreme Ownership (The Knight on the White Horse Fallacy).

Kids, this is one of the most important pieces of advice that you'll ever get. You have to know this. You have to realize it, and the earlier that you do, the better your life is going to be.

NO ONE ELSE IS GOING TO SAVE YOU.

. . . and that includes Dear Ole' Dad.

This is YOUR life. It's the only one you've been given. If you are coasting through it, just waiting for someone to magically appear to help you improve it, then you'll be waiting forever. It's not going to happen. There is no knight on the white horse . . . (Unless, of course you're talking about yourself.)

I've heard the saying that the best helping hand you'll ever have is the one at the end of your arm.

I've also read somewhere that a majority of Americans think the only way they can get rich is if they win the lottery, and I find that pretty sad.

Here is the cold, hard fact—YOU are the only one that's going to make your life better. No one else is going to do it on your behalf. I think there is always some vague sense we all have that things will change on their own—That we'll all have some kind of bright, shiny future and it's somehow going to happen in our lives without us actually DOING something to actually make that happen.

Here's a quick something to keep in mind, paraphrased from one of my mentors, Jim Rohn:

"Nothing will change, unless YOU change. But if YOU change, everything will change for you."

I was ready for change. I wanted so much better out of this world and life. I didn't want to be on a deathbed wishing that I'd done a lot more with what I've been given. How sad that would've been! I'm trying my very hardest to do what I'm telling you in this advice . . . and the fact that it's here and a material book in your hands is testament to the fact that I did it. I changed what I had been doing for over forty years, and actually got something done. This one is for you.

You've been given so much potential, and what will you have to show for it?

So, here's the challenge. Think about this:

Nothing is going to change unless you change.

Really take some time to think about that. Internalize it. They say that insanity is doing the same thing over and over and expecting a different result. Well, isn't that pretty much what we've been doing our whole lives?

We all want happiness. We all want health. We want people to love us, and we want to love others, and we want *significance* within our lives. We want freedom of our time to do with it what we wish. But when it comes right down to it, what have we really done to make all of this happen? We're just going through the motions, folks. We're doing our everyday habits, not changing a lot, and not even contemplating what that is actually getting us.

Happiness and a great life of significance don't happen by accident. It doesn't happen just by coasting through life. These are things that should be designed and planned in great detail and pursued with all of our fire and energy.

Are you ready to do this?

It's one of the greatest adventures in life for us to be able to do this. To dare to live the life that we all want. But it does take some planning, and courage to actually take the steps to make it happen.

The Advice in Practice:

- Pull out that journal. Take a little time to think about what your life would be like in the future if it were all perfect. (It won't be perfect, but let's suspend that disbelief for this exercise.) Write out what your daily life would be like. What your schedule is. Where you'd be living, and what you're doing as your EPIC mission. Just write it out.

- Read it and think about this: NO ONE but you will make that happen. No one will start it for you, but once you commit, start, and get underway with this, unseen forces will come to your aid. Some seen forces will come to help you, too, like your Dad, but NONE of that will happen unless you set it in motion.

- When I'm hitting my stride, and great things are happening in my life, it's usually because I have these written-down goals, I'm looking at them regularly, and making progress towards making them happen. So read the list of what your future will look like, type it out, make it kind of neat (I don't usually keep stuff around in my own handwriting), laminate it, and put it in a place where you can see it.

- I'd like to see you talk about this with someone that really has your back. Find a close loved one or friend—someone who encourages you and doesn't throw water on the fire of your dream (even if they do so with the best intentions of not wanting you to get 'hurt' by being unrealistic). Talk it over with them, get their ideas for it, and even ask them to help hold you accountable to working towards that big life vision.

- Here's the big one: Add your future vision to some sort of daily practice. Incorporate it into your miracle morning. Look at it often, while knowing that you, and no one else, will be responsible for starting this journey and sticking to it.

I love you so much. I'll help you help yourself during any step along the way. It would be my honor to do so.

Notes, thoughts, and intentions.

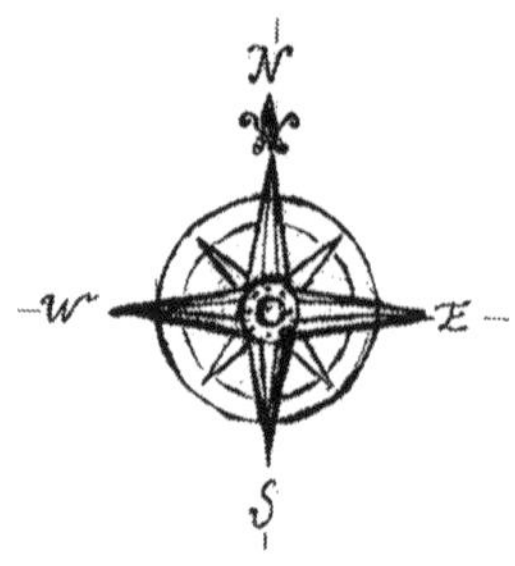

88. Lean Into PAIN, Learn from It.

Improving yourself, and self-development are important.

I think that God wants us to live up to our potential, and that's why we (or at least me, and many of the folks that I talk to) have an uneasiness when we see what we can do, what we're capable of, and what we actually ARE doing.

It feels horrible to know that you're living far below your potential. It feels great to know that you're doing the things that you set out to do. That's why it feels great to check something off of a "To-do," list. That's why we will strive towards something worthwhile. It's why we want to contribute. God formed us perfectly in all of our crazy imperfections.

That general unease that you feel, where you think that something is wrong with you, means that you are functioning completely and totally right. It's God's way of getting you moving, of trying something different.

As humans, we've decided to wear shoes. Some women actually wear what can only be described as fashionable torture devices for their feet (with giant heels, straps, and constraint on the toes). We end up with foot problems . . . and it turns out that God formed our feet, calves, tendons, toes all perfectly. When we add unnatural wedges, padding, and the like, it interferes with their natural functions.

Well, I'm thinking that our spirit and emotions are a lot like that. We never want to feel, down or to go through a hard time. We don't like pain.

But here's the thing, and I think it's profound, so listen up, my loved ones:

Pain causes us to change. Usually in a good way. Being uncomfortable usually means that growth is about to occur, and that we're going to become better versions of ourselves.

That dissatisfaction is a blessed event, because it's the impetus for the change that is about to revolutionize our lives!

So many seek to numb that pain, or shy away from it because it can and does hurt. But here's a new thought on it:

Lean into it. Really feel it and explore all of its exquisite pangs and jagged edges, because that's what's going to cause you to change things going forward.

Now, it takes some courage, because it's scary, but when you decide that this is it (that you've had enough and things are going to change), that kind of spectacular resolve often happens from feeling some not-very-pleasant things.

I am reminded of the teaching of one of friends and mentors, Jesse Elder. He has an acronym for PAIN:

P – Present.
A – Aware.
I – Insight.
N – New (Behavior or Thought)

It's ALL a chance to grow as a person.

And to think of it, I don't know of too many people that have lived lives of significance to others that have NOT gone through some pain and trauma.

I think about the birth of Alec and finding out that he had Down Syndrome (DS). That was the hardest, toughest, DARKEST thing that we've ever experienced. It was so, so difficult to tell people that he had DS. We spent so much time just hurting, crying with deep, wracking sobs over the loss of the life we thought he would have.

But to think of that now, to realize how upset we were is just mind-boggling, because his condition has caused us to become much better as people. I know it's changed me for the better and I see it all over you, as well.

We're able to love more deeply. We are much more compassionate and kind than we would be had our sweet boy been, "normal."

I know that's a big example, but it's so, so true.

The Advice in Practice:

- Get out your journal. I want you to list and brainstorm on several times in life where you were feeling pain. Get them ALL out onto paper. Write it out by hand.

- Now, go through each of these items, and write what the blessing was in the pain you experienced. Think about it. Word it right and take some time to ponder as you're writing this down in your journal. I bet you can always think something good that came of it if you really try. Did it make you stronger? Are you more empathetic now? Are you able to warn other people against it? My depression, and the pain that I was in, helped to lead to a much better life.

- It's good to be uncomfortable. It helps to make you anti-fragile. I think that we're pretty comfortable, temperature-wise almost all of the time. So, do something UNCOMFORTABLE, and maybe even a little painful: Stand in a cold shower. What I'm doing most every day is taking a regular shower, and then turning it to cold and staying under it a minimum of 30 seconds. Sometimes longer if I'm feeling it that day. Experience that cold. Fear it, and DO it. Even something as simple as this gets you feeling better about yourself.

- Play the equanimity game. I learned about it through Brian Johnson at Optimize.Me. It seems Marcus Aurelius had a practice of seeing how fast he could get back to center after something rocked his world. Do that. If something is painful, experience it. Feel it, and then realize that the obstacle makes you stronger, and just get on with it.

- Practice Hal Elrod's principle of: "Can't Change It." What that means is that when something bad happens, you give yourself five minutes to feel bad and sorry for yourself—to get it out of your system—and then you can't complain about it anymore. You saddle up and keep moving. He showed this recently when he went through (and beat) an aggressive form of cancer.

Normally, I don't like the word, "can't," but I'll make an exception for this. Google "Hal Elrod can't change it," and look for the video of him explaining this concept.

Notes, thoughts, and intentions.

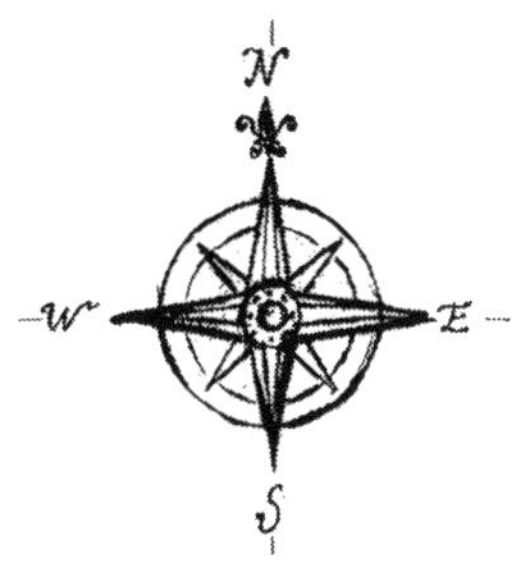

89. Cultivate an Abundant Mentality.

Have an "Abundance Mentality." Easier said than done sometimes, I know.

There is always enough abundance to go around.

No matter how bad things seem, you're going to eat, and you'll always have a place to go.

You can share easily knowing that you'll always have enough. You will.

God will provide for those that work for it.

Something that I'm amazed at is a conversation that I had with you, Aly. Here it is, copied from our "Aly-isms" file:

"Aly-ism: On a Daddy/Daughter + Alec Date Tonight, Aly asks me, "Dad, after I go to college, if I don't have any money, is it still okay to stay with you and Mom?" When I told her of course, she said she's relieved . . . wow. I never knew she'd be worried about that—especially at 10! July 2014"

Ten years old, and you're already worried about making a living!

That floors me, and yet I completely understand and get it.

For the record, you will always have a place to stay with your parents, regardless of your age or circumstance. You'll be welcome to be with us. I've never understood when parents want their children to leave. I understand the preparation for such, and helping you become as self-sufficient as possible, but your Mom and Dad never WANT you to leave.

You'll always have something to eat. You'll have a roof over your head. God will help provide through your parents or someone else.

We are in a world of abundance now. There's a book on this that's aptly called, *Abundance: The Future Is Better Than You Think* by Peter Diamandis and Steven Kotler that goes over all of this. The book was written in 2012, but it all makes sense. To give you a little bit of it here:

> ***"Even allowing for the hundreds of millions who still live in abject poverty, disease and want, this generation of human beings has access to more calories, watts, lumen-hours, square-feet, gigabytes, megahertz, light-years, nanometers, bushels per acre, miles per gallon, food miles, air miles, and, of course, dollars than any that went before."***

The point is THIS:

<u>LIFE IS GETTING BETTER, ALL OF THE TIME.</u>

Just factually, in the last century, infant mortality is down by ninety percent, maternal mortality is down ninety-nine percent, and our average lifespan has doubled. We have easy access to food and water. Even if we're broke, with just a BIT of resourcefulness we literally have the wisdom of the entire world before us available at any time from a glowing screen that will soon be talking to us like our personal, "Jarvis," from the Iron Man movies.

The cool thing is that during your lifetime, it's nearly a certainty that all humans will have adequate food, shelter, and water. It may even happen during mine, as I've heard from Mr. Diamandis at a Genius Network meeting that our current life expectancy is growing by eight hours each day that we live . . . and that number is increasing!

Also, with information becoming free and accessible everywhere, the outdated dictatorships and human oppression will cease to exist at some point.

It's really getting better. I know the news won't have you believe it (don't watch the dang news. It's generally nothing but "bad news" anyways), but we've been getting better as a human race for a long time now and will only continue to get better. That's important to know when having an abundance mentality. If you know and recognize this, then it's easier to be optimistic, and to share, and to know that it's all going to be okay in the end!

At some point, due to technology and the explosion of us using our resources more effectively, money is going to cease to exist and we'll literally all have pretty much everything that we want all of the time. That sounds woo-woo at this point, but it's pretty much a certainty. Think about this: You have access to the same internet, as a poor teenager that the billionaires have. Your quality of life NOW is better than all the kings of old, and that trend will absolutely continue.

So, you can SHARE with others and still know that you have enough. My friend, Joe Polish, frequently says that: "Life gives to the giver and takes from the taker." Know that when you give from that feeling of abundance (or even when you're fearing that things are scarce) that it will all turn out good. Personally, I think that God rewards us tenfold for the things that we give to others both in this life, and in the next existence we'll get to experience!

You can follow your dream and desires and know that you'll be cared for, having at the very least food, water, and shelter.

One of my friends, Mary Agnes, left her high-paying job as an executive assistant earning in the six figures because she knew that she wanted to write. She said that God put that in her heart, and so she made the leap and did it. She said that she'd be happier living under a bridge and writing than doing something that she's not *meant* to do. "And," she smiled as she told me, "I can't imagine God allowing me to live under a bridge if I'm doing what I'm supposed to be doing." She's now an extraordinarily successful writer and copywriter at the head of her own company.

You won't have to live under a bridge while I'm around. That's for sure, but here's something else to consider when having an abundance mentality:

What's the worst that could happen?

Seneca, the Stoic philosopher and one of my favorite historical figures, was the second wealthiest person (to the Emperor) in all of Rome. He had it all: wisdom, kindness and everything available to mankind at the time. As I mentioned earlier, every once in a while, to fight the fear of losing it all, he went into the streets and lived as a homeless person. He lived without any money, and without a title. All the while he would ask, "Is this the condition I feared?" He did this so that he knew that he would be just fine if all of his wealth was taken from him and he was left with nothing.

I think I told you in an earlier chapter that I have daydreams of trying it out myself, but that your Mom would have a cow. Still, I think I'll do it at some point when you're out on your own. It would probably suck, and I don't know how long I'd do it, but a part of me (a sane, rational part) thinks that I would be just fine. I think that I'd have a chance to work on my resourcefulness.

Tony Robbins says at his seminars that, "Resourcefulness is the ultimate resource." So, if you have your mind—hopefully that's been honed to a razor-sharp edge by creating these idea lists--you'll never lack for anything for any extended time in your life.

If you feel resourceful, can use your mind, and ask for what you need (like I've taught you to do here), you'll never be in lack for long.

This is a spiritual thing. If you are constantly worried and filled with anxiety, then it's time to trust God. It's time to pray about things and ask that peace be granted to you. I have some different views on the Bible, but one of the passages that sticks with me when we're not feeling abundance is Matthew 6: 25-33. From Jesus:

25 "Therefore I tell you, do not worry about your life, what you will eat or drink; or about your body, what you will wear. Is not life more than food, and the body more than clothes? 26 Look at the birds of the air; they do not sow or reap or store away in barns, and yet your heavenly Father feeds them. Are you not much more valuable than they? 27 Can any one of you by worrying add a single hour to your life?"

28 "And why do you worry about clothes? See how the flowers of the field grow. They do not labor or spin. 29 Yet I tell you that not even Solomon in all his splendor was dressed like one of these. 30 If that is how God clothes the grass of the field, which is here today and tomorrow is thrown into the fire, will he not much more clothe you—you of little faith? 31 So do not worry, saying, 'What shall we eat?' or 'What shall we drink?' or 'What shall we wear?' 32 For the pagans run after all these things, and your heavenly Father knows that you need them. 33 But seek first his kingdom and his

righteousness, and all these things will be given to you as well."

That's SO POWERFUL! If you keep that promise in mind, that you are cared and provided for, then what could cause such worry for you?

Of course, a cynic will point out that some horrible things have happened to good people (People dying of starvation, the Holocaust, war). I think that it's necessary to talk about and consider the worst possibilities. However, as someone that believes in a loving God, I think that there is reason for everything. I choose to believe that they're in a better place, and that their suffering could be used for a greater good. There was an end to the suffering, and they were comforted in the arms of God as we all will be when this life is over. Remembering that can keep us in the abundant mindset.

Lastly, I know this is a long piece of advice, but this is very important on how you look at life:

The Abundance Mentality is a CHOICE. You can choose to look at life like this, or not.

I hope you choose to do so.

The Advice in Practice:

- Read the book *Abundance: The Future Is Better Than You Think*, by Peter Diamandis and Steven Kotler. Or just the synopsis of it would be okay. Also, something that you might actually do, is watch Peter's TED Talk on the matter: *Abundance is Our Future*. I promise that you'll feel better about things after watching this. I'm listening to it while typing this.

- STOP WATCHING THE NEWS. "If it bleeds, it leads." Think about this: The objective of the news is NOT to inform, it's to get more eyeballs on the screen so they can charge for their advertising. I'm one of the world's biggest proponents of capitalism, but that's pretty messed up. They literally try to scare you into watching. When I gave up watching the news over three years ago, I suddenly felt better—and the abundance mentality comes so much easier.

- Be a GREAT tipper. Not just a good one, but a great one. It will make you feel so good to tip for great service. If you can give an extra few dollars, help someone that probably needs the money more than you do it will make you feel better and more abundant all day long. That's a pretty fine investment.

- On the same note: regularly give some of your money to charity or a good cause that you believe in completely. When you write that check, or more likely, press that 'submit' button, you're going to feel great. Say a little prayer that it will be used well and send it. Even if you don't have much money, sending just a part of it into someone or something that needs it more will make you feel wealthy.

- Work on your resourcefulness. Keep up with your idea lists. Write out twenty or more of the things that you'd do if all of your worldly possessions were gone. Get a good idea of it and feel confident that you'd be alright regardless of what happens.

- Add some abundance affirmations to your list that you go over each morning. Make it more a part of your life every day.
- Write out gratitude and appreciation regularly, as part of your daily schedule. This affects us in so many areas of our lives!
- Lastly, pray for it! There's nothing wrong with wishing for abundance for yourself or your loved ones. Remember the advice about asking? Use that to ask for and receive abundance.

Notes, thoughts, and intentions.

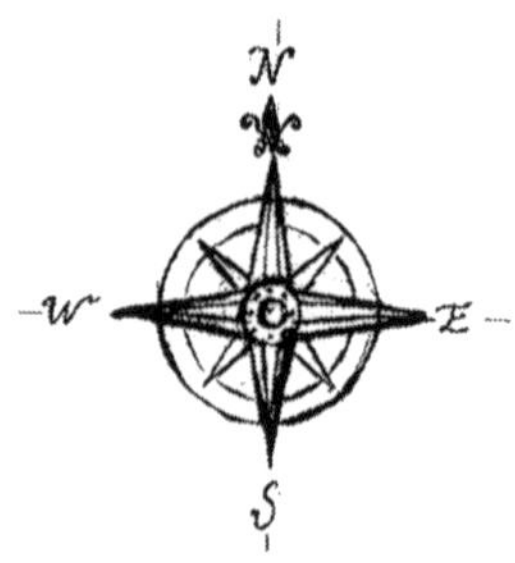

90. Understand That When You Are Looking at the World, It's a Reflection of You.

The world is a reflection of you.

If you're happy and think people are good, then they are.

If you think people are bad, then they are. If you're negative, the world will be.

If you smile and walk with confidence, then the world will respond.

The world is a reflection (sometimes a merciless one) of you.

There's a story that I'll tell you. It sounds a bit cliché, but I find it to be true. I'm paraphrasing, so bear with me. Here it is:

~~~~~~~~~~~~~~~~~~~~~

There was a traveler who was about to enter into a city. He came upon a farmer working the field, and asked:

"Can you tell me what kind of people are in the city?"
~~~~~~~~~~~~~~~~~~~~~

The farmer stops his work, tilts his head to the side and asks: "What kind of people were at the last city?"

The traveler answer, "They are mean, and nasty. They'd cheat you and not think twice about it."

The farmer hangs his head and says, "Well, I'm sorry but you'll find the same kind of people in this city."

The next day, another traveler comes through and asks the same question.

The farmer asks again, "What kind of people were in the last city?"

This traveler says, "Oh, the best. They are good-hearted, and they strive to help others."

The farmer smiles and says, "I'm happy to tell you that you'll find the same kind of people in this city."

~~~~~~~~~~~~~~~~~~~~

If your environment is messy and disorganized, then you are messy and disorganized.

If you are kind and loving, then you'll see it everywhere you go. It happens in everyone. If you're a cynic and think of the world as a place with so many vile and evil people, then that's exactly what you're going to see. You'll also see good when you think of the world as the loving, wonderful miracle that it is too.
~~~~~~~~~~~~~~~~~~~~

The Advice in Practice:

- If you think that people aren't friendly, then there's a good chance that you're not making enough of an effort to be friendly. Be the kind of friend that you want.
- Try to develop the habit of seeing the best in others. Every. Single. Person. Whatever you look for, you'll find. One way of doing this is to make it a part of your daily affirmations in your miracle morning. Tell yourself, with emotion, "I see the best in everyone." Repeat it often!
- Find people giving great service in your everyday life, and let them know it—and more importantly, let their manager know about it. The more you seek that, the more you'll find it. I wrote all about that in the chapter, "Don't Keep Compliments and Gratitude to Yourself."
- Look at yourself in the mirror. Really. Look into the eyes of that person. Do you see a cynic? Do you see someone that's complaining? Or bitter? Or do you see yourself as optimistic? As friendly? As a GOOD-HEARTED PERSON? Be honest. Do you need to work on this?
- Try the ten-day "No-Complaint" diet. For the next ten days, you don't complain. If you do, then the timer starts over, and you go another ten days with no complaints. If you're a complainer, you'll always find things that are wrong with the world. You need to quit that, and rather than complain, practice active appreciation.

I appreciate you, my darlings, and I see some pretty amazing people staring back at me.

Notes, thoughts, and intentions.

91. Make YOURSELF Happy (It's the Best Thing You Can Do for OTHERS).

"People are as happy as they make up their minds to be." Abe Lincoln.

Honestly, I feel a little weird giving you some daddy advice saying something as seemingly simple (yet maybe tough to do) as, "Make Yourself Happy." That's a pretty obvious thing, right? Aren't we all trying to make ourselves happy?

Yes and no.

We often do it when we think about it in the moment. I would submit that very few of us have made a STUDY of this incredibly important aspect in life. Can you rattle off ten things that you enjoy most in the world off the top of your head right now? Most people can't do that. Can you define what happiness means or the know the best way to reach it?

I sound like a broken record saying this—but they don't teach happiness in schools at all. It's one of the most important things to study and understand, and yet, you're on your own for it. It's done pretty haphazardly by almost everyone in life. Luckily, we have this fine book o' advice to remind us.

My own experience with happiness has been up and down (but mostly up), throughout my life. I'm generally a very happy person and have actually thought through it and did some studying on it. I have implemented a lot of things in my life that help with it, but I've also had bouts when I've been extremely unhappy and even depressed.

One of my friends actually pegged this by saying that his happiness is like its own 80/20 rule. He's happy about 80 percent of the time, and the other 20 percent he's a bit tortured, neurotic, and down on himself and the world. He's okay with that as well. I feel the same way. I've come to grips with the fact that I'm emotional, I'm empathetic, and that I have a constant drive to get better and to be better—so I will often not be happy with where I am.

But that little seed of discontent is good for a few reasons. The first being that it makes me better. If we were all too happy all of the time, I think that a lot of growth would stop in our lives. The second reason is that I've had this distinct thought on my own: All genius comes with some madness. After I thought that through, I discovered that Aristotle had said that same thing almost exactly. And that's pretty cool to have had the same original thought as Aristotle!

If being down, depressed, and anxious a fairly small percentage of the time is the price to be paid for the benefits that come with a constantly active mind (and a bias for improvement), then that's something I'm willing to endure. That being said, we can ALL get better.

I think I used to laugh a lot more and had a more joyful outlook on life that was untainted by the world. All of the news, all of the crazy thoughts, and everything else. I think that I don't laugh as much as I used to do, but I also find myself being grateful, appreciative, and full of a quiet joy most of the time these days. That's from doing a lot of the things that I'm about to share with you.

For me, the happiness and fulfillment have a lot less to do with outside circumstances, what I happen to be doing, or my state of mind. It's a lot about how I'm *deciding* how to deal with life and arranging my thoughts around that. It's the mind-operating system that I'm using more and more that makes the difference.

I can't wait to get into this and give you some of the information. When you read this, internalize it. I think it can change your life for the better.

WE (I'll definitely include myself in this) need to keep this advice close by and ready for those times where we forget these principles. I could reread some of these nearly every day and it's would help maintain my mindset and keep the darkness gremlins at bay. I hope it does the same for you, my dears.

Let's get started.

First, what's the definition of happiness?

From Wikipedia: In psychology, *happiness* is a mental or emotional state of well-being which can be defined by, among others, positive or pleasant emotions ranging from contentment to intense joy. Happy mental states may reflect judgments by a person about their overall well-being.

I actually like happiness expert Shawn Achor's definition, better:

Happiness is the joy you feel moving towards your potential.

It's feeling good in the moment, and also in your life.

It's important for the pretty blatantly obvious reasons—everyone wants to live a happy life, regardless of how much of a badass they may pretend to be (not smiling or being too cool to dance, etc.).

But here is a HUGE factor of happiness that I want you to carefully consider, and see if this rings true:

"The best thing you can do for others is to be happy yourself."

My friend Jesse Elder first phrased it to me this way and it struck a chord.

Personally, I think I've held a little guilt over being ridiculously joyful while some of my friends or family may be going through hard or even devastating times in their lives. Who am I to be happy while so many are suffering?

Well. after thinking about this and writing it where it's in the open to examine, that feeling of guilt over being happy is actually pretty silly. Your unhappiness doesn't do anyone any good. Especially you.

I think you know not to be obnoxious and continue laughing like a drunk idiot, but I think about the best demeanor that you can have is just a semi-quiet, deep contentment that others can feel.

In fact, I'll share with you another thought on happiness that I've always enjoyed from my mentor Jim Rohn. He says that the special sweet spot in life is obtained when you get to the point of being grateful (or actively appreciating, as we say) and happy for everything you have now (and I assume everything you ARE now); while simultaneously striving for more.

Enjoy everything now, while still preparing for an *even better* future.

That's the art of exceptional living, and it's the mindset you should strive for.

Now that we know what it is, let's ask the question: Is happiness important? I certainly think so. When we get right down to it, what is the meaning of life, and what makes a great life? I'd say that it's service to the greater good.

But people can do that without necessarily being happy about it, right? That's true—but what's even better is when you're able to do a lot in life while being happy and enjoying the ride along the way.

Happiness makes it so much easier to be effective in your work/your service others. Shawn Achor talks about how happiness can raise our business outcomes, our health outcomes, and educational outcomes (it can make us seemingly smarter).

Here are some more reasons that being happy is important:

It means that you're more likely to earn more money and get promoted, that you will have more friends, and your health will be affected in a good way. You'll even look younger when you're happier.

Well, some might say that they'd be happier if they made more money, had more friends, and looked younger, but the truth is that those things are helped by being happy. It's an *effect* rather than a *cause*. To think that you'd be happy because of those things is the fault of thinking that happiness is caused by something external, outside of us.

The fallacy is that many of us (including me) often think along the lines of, "I'll be happy WHEN _________ happens." Fill in the thing that you're looking for and you have the same exact thing. When I'm financially free, or when I'm married to the person of my dreams, or after I accomplish this goal that I've written down in my journal (that's where I sometimes stumble).

I call it the "*Accomplishment Trap.*" Being happy ONLY when a certain predetermined goal is met. But really, that's a bunch of BS! We can be happy now, if we take the time to study it and cultivate that feeling, that optimism in our lives.

Who says that your happiness needs to be dependent on something like that? We should be able to choose happiness at any given time by changing our focus, our mindset, and maybe most importantly, our habits.

Yes, I know that sometimes when the darkness has overwhelmed us, and it's a chemical thing, that some of this may not work, but we are working on what we CAN control.

Happiness is built on hope, and even faith that things are fundamentally good and that they are getting better. This is personally, in your own life, and in the world in general.

Optimistic people are happier than cynics and pessimists. That is fundamental. If you're the type of person that can find the cloud in every silver lining, you're going to have a tough time being happy, and people won't want to be around you because you're no fun!

However, if you can find the good in ANY situation, and you can focus on that—you'll be a much, much happier person.

You can consciously control what it is you're focused on in any given situation. It takes some time and effort; and even when we're good at it, it's often easy to forget to do this. And that's why each of us need to set up rituals and habits that remind us to look on the bright side.

These rituals can change what we focus on. They improve our attitude and mindset, and they become easier to do over time as they become a part of us. When I'm on the ball and doing these, I find that I'm happiest.

Here are some of the principles and rituals that have worked for me, and I'm hoping they can help you, too.

1. ACTIVE APPRECIATION.

This is first for a reason. If you can train your mind to automatically look for all of the things that we can be thankful for, then happiness will be a lot easier. Our antennae will be up, looking for the good in the world. When this happens, we will find it, every time. If you're appreciating things, then it's a lot harder to be negative and unhappy.

One of my mentors, James Altucher has said, "Anxiety can't live in the same head as gratitude." I know I've quoted this before, but it's so important.

Some of the ways to create this way of thinking include a gratitude (appreciation) journal, scheduled moments of mindfulness (you know about my seven at night "I am blessed," alarm on my phone, where Louis Armstrong sings, "What a Wonderful World), and the automatic habit of asking, "what's the good in this situation?" whenever a challenge comes up. That's what appreciation does for you. Read all about Active Appreciation right here in the Soul section of this book!

2. STRIVING TO BE BETTER IN LIFE.

I think that we're always going to have a pit of dissatisfaction in our lives when we're doing less than we know we can do.

It's the dissonance between our potential and what we're actually doing in our lives to make things better and to serve others. I believe not living up to my potential was the biggest reason for my depression a few years back. I KNEW I wasn't living the life that I should be at the time.

The way to make that better? I have a LOT of advice on that in this book that seems to work for me. Check out the *Hero's Journey* advice, finding the *Magic Spot*, and even the advice on being romantic. If you are actively TRYING to get better, then you're going to feel a lot better about life and be happier.

The joy is found in improving oneself consciously. When I think about the happiest times in my life, it's usually when I'm chasing a goal and making progress on it. The cool thing is that you can do this any time.

3. DOING ACTS OF KINDNESS.

I love this one. It is literally impossible to help people feel better without you feeling better yourself. I know I've told you this before but resolving that I'd do one act of kindness for another human every single day had more to do with me overcoming my depression than anything else. How can you do this in your life?

You can volunteer and help others. I'm reading that the optimal time for that is about 100 hours a year or approximately two hours a week of helping someone else. Can you find a place to do that? A cause that you believe in that you can get behind? Part of my professional life is to make that process easier with JoeVolunteer. I feel pretty strongly about it.

Something else you can do is to wish well for others. Literally, just praying for a friend and/or just consciously holding them in your thoughts and hoping that life is being good to them. Doing that will literally make you feel better.

It's also good to tell them that you're thinking of them. Then they feel good, too, and that makes you a happiness multiplier.

4. TAKING CARE OF YOURSELF.

When you take care of yourself by eating right, avoiding emotional vampires, doing your daily rituals (like the Daily Practice and/or The Miracle Morning)—you're just going to feel better about yourself and about life.

Do you have some daily rituals that help you be happier? If not, you've come to the right book to help you get started! Even taking five minutes a day to yourself to consciously collect your thoughts and be still will have a lot of benefits. You'll feel better that you're taking care of yourself, and that in turn will make you want to do more self-care. It's a virtuous cycle.

Of course, one of the biggest things in taking care of yourself is engaging in exercise. It will literally fill your body with some feel-good endorphins AND you'll feel like a stud(dette) for doing that. I've been reading that exercise is more effective than the mind-altering antidepressants that are too often prescribed by doctors . . . and it has more lasting effects, too.

It also helps with trying to do better in life like we mentioned before. If you're not taking care of your health, then you'll always have a pit in your happiness. So, let's make sure that we're doing something for our health at all times.

The last thing I'll mention about taking care of yourself are the thoughts of a Daily Practice and Miracle Mornings (which I obviously talk about a lot elsewhere). Please consider creating and having your own practice/schedule/routine/rituals that serve your life and help make it better. I find when I'm ON my self-induced schedule, I'm happy. When I'm not, then my happiness is left to chance and can be elusive.

5. GET OUTSIDE, GET SOME SUNSHINE, GET INTO NATURE.

I've read that sunlight helps us with our Vitamin D production, and that in turn improves our mood and makes us more likely to be happy. It helps with our immune system, and has even been shown to decrease chances of diabetes and autoimmune disorders.

Being outside also provides a natural boost to our serotonin levels. That's the natural "feel good" neurotransmitter. How does being in nature do that? I have no idea. I have read that it works, and have experienced that in my own life a lot!

I am just happier when I'm taking my daily walks. Give it a try. I bet the same will be true for you too. I'm kind of excited as I write this—because I'm about to go on a walk as the sun is coming up. That is MAYBE the most magical time we can experience. It's just unreal and wonderful to see the sun rise in all of its majesty. It's a blatant reminder of what a miracle this all is.

6. LOVING AND ACCEPTING YOURSELF.

This may be the one that I've struggled with the most during my life; but I've made a LOT of strides in it over the past few years. When we 'should' all over ourselves, we get into negative thought spirals.

It's way too easy to compare yourself to others these days. It's always been there and a part of life—reading about a celebrity or a successful business person or even someone that gives so much of their time and effort to others (like being jealous of a Mother Teresa figure). But it's way too easy now.

If you're on social media at all, you are generally bombarded with smiley, happy faces of people living the good life and doing great. That's because Facebook is a "highlight" reel of others' lives. The highs are shouted from the rooftops, while the lows are barely whispered.

This gives the impression that everyone is doing better, and we suffer by comparison. My friend Scott calls this, "*compare and despair.*" It's so easy to see these stories of others and then get down on ourselves.

That impulse to self-flagellate is nearly always there and it must be *consciously* fought and countered through your thoughts. Hopefully a ritual helps to counteract this self-induced poisoning.

One way to do that is to have your talk with the Inner Critic (we talk about that elsewhere). Another is to say and FEEL that you love yourself (also in this book) and make a real habit of it.

A lot of that for me is done through journaling and getting my feelings and thoughts out onto paper and out of my head. I know I mention this a lot, but if you don't get it OUT onto paper, then the bad feelings will be left to fester in your head, heart, and soul.

A last way that I use to help with this is through meditation. There is specifically a set of meditations from someone I follow (Tara Brach) that help with this—she calls it the, "RAIN of Self-compassion." RAIN is an acronym.

R: Recognize what is going on.
A: Allow the experience to be there, just as it is.
I: Investigate with kindness. Explore the feeling.
N: Natural loving awareness of it.

She has a great article on it when you Google it. If you go to her page and search on the guided meditations, meditation can be absolutely wonderful

We are all doing the best we can with what we know and have. You'd have some compassion for others that may be struggling. It's time to do that for yourself, too.

7. SURROUND YOURSELF WITH GREAT PEOPLE.

Avoid the emotional vampires. You know the people that I'm talking about when they walk into the room, and immediately your energy level drops and/or your defenses go up. You need to avoid that as much as possible and make conscious choices of who and what you'll be around in your day-to-day life.

It's said that you're the average of the five people that you hang around the most. Well, luckily we get to choose that.

The converse of the energy vampire is the person that you love seeing when they walk into a room. You want to smile and give them a big hug. Your gut knows who your people are. So, make a concerted effort to be around them when you can.

Tony Robbins says in his seminars that the EXPECTATIONS of one's peer group is one of the most powerful forces in our lives. You can use that to help you get and feel better.

8. TAKE TIME TO DO THINGS YOU REALLY ENJOY.

A friend of mine, Gio, has a ritual where he takes off Friday, "Friday MY Day," and he goes to watch a movie in middle of the day all by himself.

I love that. It's just for him. I like to go and see a movie by myself too, but often feel guilty doing it. I COULD be working, getting better, responding to people, etc. . . . and here I am, being still and watching something I enjoy instead.

The movies are awesome. I love them. Someone spent $200 million dollars just to entertain ME for two hours. They tell a story. They use sight and sound to weave an experience just for us, and it costs so little compared to what was spent. They're such a bargain!

Movies don't have to be your thing, obviously—but you should absolutely find some of the things that you enjoy and

SCHEDULE them into your life. It is a wonderful thing to have something to look forward to all of the time.

Do you like to travel, get a massage, or go out with friends? Well, they won't get done until you take the time to make them a part of your life. Do that. Find the things that you really enjoy and make sure that some of your time is spent doing those things.

I promise that you're worth it.

Those are some of the things that have worked to make me happy, and I'm hoping you get some use out of them, too.

But please don't stop with just my list. Happiness is something to be studied and worked on as the fine art it is. You figure out what it is that makes you happy and go after it. It's the best thing you can do for yourself AND others.

I want this so much for you. I can tell you with certainty that you being happy is what's best for everyone. So please spend some time and effort on this and make yourself happy.

As your Dad, there is nothing else that would give me greater pleasure than to see you happy in your lives. I love you so dearly, and I hope you know that.

Advice in Practice:

- If you don't already do it, then find a way to write out things you appreciate each day. When I was down, I pulled out the gratitude journal and filled it with pages upon pages of blessings in my life. It was as simple as things like warm water, or the changing weather. The more down you are, the more gratitude/appreciation you need in your life. Go ahead and pull out your journal and write an entire page (small or regular sized print, don't go cheating!) of things you *actively appreciate*.

- Get the five-minute journal by Intelligent Change. This has been called: "mental flossing" by Tim Ferriss. It's a journal designed to be used for a few minutes in the morning and a few at night. It asks you what three specific things you're grateful for each day, what would make today great, and a daily affirmation ("Today I am . . ."). That gets your day started right. Then at night, it asks you what three AMAZING things happened that day, and what you could have done to make the day even better. It's a great way to think, and an easy barrier to entry of real, heartfelt journaling. Go to IntelligentChange.com to order it, Muchachos!

- Speaking of journaling, pull out your favorite journal and define your own definition of happiness. How do you define it? These are your words after all. They can be anything. Happiness could be sleeping in whenever you feel like it, or knowing beyond a doubt that you helped others in their lives . . . whatever it is, it's your definition.

- Do an Idea List on "The Top Twenty Things that Make Me Giddy With Happiness." That should be fun. Find a way to get one or more of these things in your life. Don't leave the scene of these ideas without first putting one or more of these into your schedule. In fact, it's best if you can make it a recurring date. See Gio's example above in number eight, and see if you have something like that. Use the list and get more of it for you. You need to find a way to do that with your schedule.

- Go and watch Shawn Achor's TED talk on happiness. It's incredible—really inspiring and very useful, too. Google it, and spend that glowing screen time on something very useful in your life.

- You can consider getting into and reading his books, as well. *The Happiness Advantage*, by Mr. Achor, is the one I'd recommend the most. It's maybe more business/life/mission oriented than his others . . . and that's cool by me. Take a look at it.

- You may also bond with Gretchen Rubin. She wrote an excellent book called: *The Happiness Project*, where she detailed her quest to make herself happy. It's a quest I'm recommending to you now, too. Try out the different things that can make it.

- Think about and write out an Idea List entitled, "*Twenty Easy to Do, High Impact Things, Rituals, Things I Can Do, and/or Purchase I Can Make to Take Better Care of Myself.*" Or, something to that effect. Just writing them will help, but take the top item on the list—the biggest impact at the lowest effort, and TAKE ACTION ON IT TODAY, RIGHT NOW. Schedule it. Order it. Resolve on it. Make a declaration to others that support you that you can do it . . . and be like Nike. I did this fairly recently with swearing off of Coke Zero, specifically, and ALL sodas in general. It's been over six months and I know it's had a huge impact on my life already. What's your big thing you can do today?

- This one may be tough, but I want you to think about your crowd. Who are the people that you spend the most time with each day? Who are the people that take your energy? Really think about that (you already know who they are) and think of a few ways that you can limit your time with them. This may be tough if you're related to them, but it's necessary. Remember that you feeling bad does no one any good.

- Now the flip side of that. Who in your circle of friends really makes you feel great? Who is someone that you'd like more of in your life? Think about it and see if there is some way that you can consciously change your schedule and get more of them into your life. Even if it's a scheduled phone call or video chat. Go ahead and do that. Try to see to it that it's someone that can "stretch" you. That means that they inspire you to be even better through the example that they set. Don't wait on this. Do it now.

- Take the daily walk challenge. Even if it's super cold and/or super hot . . . get outside and take a walk for the next ten days. See how it makes you feel. I bet that you'll feel a lot better just by doing that. Google "Brain scans before and after walk." WOW! That's pretty amazing. That's why I like to do a lot of thinking, writing and journaling after getting outside to walk. Can you make it a part of your daily schedule? Try and do it. You can read and get more info on this in the chapter of advice about movement and walking.

- Go and visit TaraBrach.com and look through her guided meditations. Specifically, look up the RAIN meditations. You can click and listen to it without meditating, but I'd recommend that you actually do the meditations. I love her guided meditations because they've added a lot to my life. She also has a book called, *Radical Acceptance*, which I highly recommend. She's a lot more accomplished at walking you through loving yourself than I am, and I urge you to take a look at her work on this. I just pulled it from my bookshelf and realized that I have yet to finish it . . . and I'm going to put it on my nightstand now to take my own advice.

- I know I mention it elsewhere, but one of the simplest yet profound books that I can recommend on loving yourself is called, *Love Yourself Like Your Life Depends On It*, by Kamal Ravikant. It's short, to the point, and for me it was effective. It has several exercises in it that I hope you will do (it's okay, no one's looking).

- The last thing I'll recommend in this long Advice in Practice section is to read and try to implement a Daily Practice and/or a Miracle Morning. Both are absolutely huge in getting your thoughts in the right place. I mentioned it above, but when I'm ON SCHEDULE with my practices, I'm happy. When I'm not on schedule, there's a good chance that I'm NOT happy. Doing one or both of these, I think, is the quickest way to improve your life, and your own happiness.

Please remember that you deserve this, you are worthy of happiness, and that you are loved.

Notes, thoughts, and intentions.

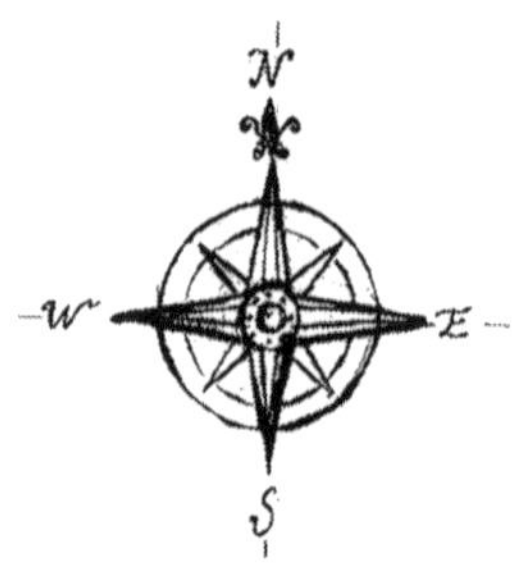

92. Worship in Your Own Way (ANY Way That's Right for You).

As with all of my advice, please take these ideas into consideration. But don't accept without you thinking about them and seeing if they make sense to you. I think all spirituality is personal and unique to each of us. This is between you and God, but I think it's a great idea to explore this thinking for yourself.

I've got to tell you my story about this. You probably know it already, but I was raised spending a lot of time in the church. It was a Southern Baptist church started by and preached to by my granddad, and your great-granddad, Floyd Franks.

I was there every Sunday morning, usually Sunday afternoon for a youth group study, every Wednesday evening for R.A.'s (a sort of Boy Scouts for church), and often Saturday nights for Youth Group, as well. I enjoyed a lot of it, but it really was a lot of time spent in the pews, reading and studying the Bible, and praying.

I think, as with a lot of things in life, if you do too much of something, you can learn to resent it somewhat. That was the case with me and church. I loved God, and I wanted to do the right thing, but I didn't want to be in church a lot. I think that affected me quite a bit when I was out of the home and started college, because I didn't set foot in a church of my own accord for a while. I didn't pray as much, and I lost a lot of what I thought was my closeness with God.

Now, you know that I'm a firm believer in God. Of course, people can debate this, and say that there is NOT a God. At best, they can just say that it's *POSSIBLE* that there's not a God. My reasoning is that something could not have come from nothing. I think that to create something like this, there has to be a higher intelligence.

Personally, I think that God is loving because of all of the wonderful things in life. True love that you feel for another is something that must be divinely created. Any parent looking at their child's face has felt that pull from the other side and understands that there is a deeper power behind it. I am not able to see all of the miracles of life and deny God's hand in it. Also, this is a belief that serves me and my way of thinking.

Believing that God is loving makes life so much better.

We're able to find meaning in everything, even suffering. We can choose to believe that life happens for us, rather than just to us.

The church where I was raised was a Christian church, and believed that Jesus is God's son and also God. We were taught this, we were taught about sin, and that everyone had sinned. We were taught that humanity came short of the glory of God, and therefore deserved to perish. We were told that only through believing in Jesus, and asking him into our heart could we be saved, and not go to the lakes of fire, where there would be a lot of gnashing of teeth.

Even as a boy I had a hard time believing all of this. I remember asking why a man like Gandhi could go to hell, while a man like Hitler could have a death-bed acceptance of Christ and be allowed into heaven. I also wondered about the dinosaurs, and why they weren't mentioned in the Bible. I even asked Pe-paw (your great granddad) about that, and he said that seven days for God could be quite a bit different than seven days in our understanding. I don't know that I believe that, but I do think that much in the Bible is subject to interpretation. It has so many principles that are useful, but also some that I find downright troubling.

Maybe the biggest of all of these is the thought that a loving God would create a hell. It's been my experience that no one ever deserves eternal torment, but many believe that's what the Bible says: Sinners go to hell if they don't believe in Jesus. That's just tough for me to accept. I'd have a hard time worshipping a God that did things that way, because it's just not just in the opinion of this particular human.

So I choose not to believe that.

I believe in God, and his goodness, and that all was created by Him; and that we should worship

Him/It; and thank God daily for this wondrous opportunity and miracle of life.

I also believe that we should be able to worship in our own way. I don't think anyone can be definitive in saying they know *the* correct way to worship, but yet many say only they are doing it the right way. While I won't say they're wrong, I'm also not ready to admit that they are right.

Here's what MY personal view is on what's right for me:

Love God.
Get close to God.
Talk to God.
Pray to God.

Worship God.

Most importantly,

Let God SHOW through my ACTIONS as often as possible.

I've talked about praying already in the book. Personally, I think it's valid. I think it can and actually does affect others.

Now, worship is defined as: The feeling or expression of reverence and adoration for a deity.

I think that worshipping God in its basic form is showing love for God. And I think that there are many ways to show love for God such as prayers of thanks, singing, actively appreciating His creations in the world, and showing thanks for them.

I think that making the most of your potential given to you by God is a wonderful way to worship God. Making more of yourself, and (here's the key), *become better at serving others*.

I also think that being kind and serving others is the most tangible way of worshipping God. Otherwise, why are we here? Is it better to sing in a pew or to go out and help others in the world as they are suffering? I know the answer for me, but I don't presume to say that I'm definitely right.

I think the only true sin is harming others intentionally (legitimate self-defense is exempted, too).

What I would suggest, though, is to figure out how YOU think God should be loved and do that. In fact, I haven't done this as often as I should, but I will make certain to do it regularly.

I would also suggest that ANYONE that tells you that their way is the absolute and total RIGHT way, even though they are completely sincere, *should* be questioned. Any truth, so long as it is the truth, can be subjected to questioning and come out just fine, and even stronger, for the experience. Truth is incontrovertible.

If you choose to worship with others at church or elsewhere, then I applaud that. If you choose to do it quietly on your own, that's certainly wonderful, too. I think God appreciates and loves all forms of worship.

So, do it your own way, but my advice is to actually worship.

Advice in Practice:

- Read a synopsis of the major religions in our world. Approach each with an open mind, and carefully consider them. There is a reason that many millions and sometimes billions of people subscribe to the beliefs of those religions.

- Get your journal and write out what you believe about God, and what you feel are the beliefs that resonate most with you.

- Please consider the opinions and beliefs of others. Personally, I don't want to offend and tell others that they are wrong unless what they do affects others' health and safety. Pick your battles, or don't have battles at all unless absolutely necessary.

- Take time regularly (I think at least daily) to pray to God and offer thanks and ask for guidance. Truly be open and feel God in your heart. Put it in your schedule.

- Always be open to talk about God, religion, atheism, or others' beliefs. Question, learn, probe. Aristotle said, "It is the mark of an educated mind to be able to entertain a thought without accepting it." So, do that.

- Set a time and a place for you to worship. With or without others, with or without rules . . . it's your relationship with God and that's so personal and wonderful for you. Again, if this resonates for you go ahead and schedule that now.

- As always, I love you—the last piece of advice is to talk with me and explain your thoughts. Let's discuss them together.

Notes, thoughts, and intentions.

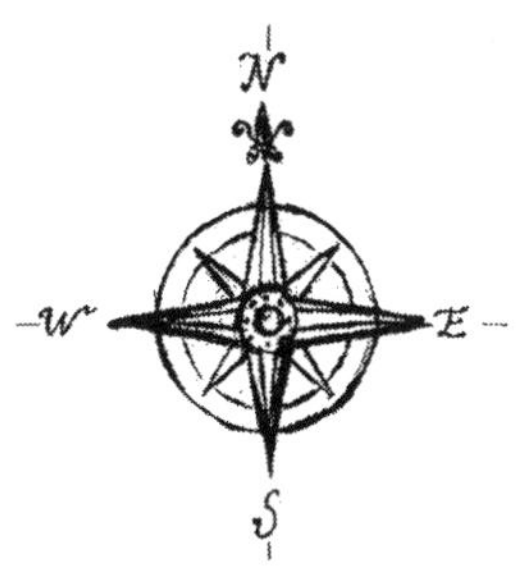

93. Say Your Prayers. For Real, Say Them.

Say prayers at night, before you go to sleep. Make sure to say: "Thank you," a lot to God.

This is such a seemingly simple piece of advice, but I think that it's one of the most important. I know I've told you this before, but as much as I love you (which is a MIND-BLOWING amount that you'll only understand after you have our grandchildren) GOD loves you even more.

Please take what I'm about to say with a grain of salt. Like I've asked of you in previous lessons, question everything. You don't have to believe as I do. You can think all of this is absolute bunk. That's okay. But what I ask of you is to at least explore some of these ideas with an open mind. As I said in the previous advice in practice section, Aristotle said:

"It's the mark of an educated mind to be able to entertain a thought without accepting it."

I firmly and completely believe that God wants the best for us. I think that God would want us to be grateful and appreciate the things in our lives. And I also believe in the power of prayer to help us. I know that many think this is ridiculous, and I'm okay with them thinking that way, but I have many reasons to believe this way. Many of them even fall into the realm of science. In fact, I'm about to get into this, but many believe that spirituality and God are diametrically opposed to science.

You remember the talk between Nacho Libre and his buddy Esceleto talking about being, "A man of science," versus being a man of faith? As if one is one or the other? I don't think anything could be further from the truth. I think that God created science. And the more we learn about how this universe works, and as our capabilities grow, the more we realize that we don't know everything. There is real, tangible proof of Divinity (even if it's not called that).

My belief is that prayer influences. Just a prayer won't mean that things will happen the way you wish of course, and sometimes unanswered prayers are the best. But I think that there is definitely an influencing effect on things when you think hard on something and open yourself to ask for things.

I don't know how well that I will explain this, but I'm going to try. The concepts are the Zero Particle Field, Quantum Entanglement, and the Observer Effect. I'm sure that there are a lot more tangible real things to think about, but this is what I know now from the reading I've done (I'm really interested in this):

The Zero Particle field is the theoretical space between subatomic particles where, "nothing," exists. If you can think and imagine everything that we see is not real. It's all made of space, of electrons, literally made of vibration moving around other vibrations known as nuclei. The "matter," in this is infinitesimal, if it even exists at all. It has no substance, yet it's what makes up everything that we see and experience in our real world. Einstein (more from him in a bit) said it best, "Reality is just an illusion, albeit a persistent one."

It's my personal theory, although I don't know if science will back me up yet, that "God" exists all around us in and throughout all of this space. And at the risk of sounding like Obi-Wan Kenobi, it's the force that binds us together, and connects all of us in one big cosmic family. Using that theory, we are all linked to *everything*. Which makes sense, because science points to a "big bang" where stardust just exploded into what we know as the universe. We're cut from the same cloth as everything.

I know that I'm getting a little in the weeds here, but please hear me out on this. The next concept is Quantum Entanglement, or what Einstein called, "spooky science at a distance." It's where two particles are literally bound together and affect each other—regardless of space (they're not next to each other and could literally be across the universe from the other) and time. It's a real, observable phenomenon. I read about a study where cells from a World War II veteran were removed from his body, and then observed while scenes from the bombing at Pearl Harbor were played . . . and the separated cells physically reacted as the veteran experienced the intense emotions of the scenes. The cells were no longer attached, and yet they reacted! This isn't a science fiction movie, this happened. This, to me, helps show us that we are all connected.

Lastly, and I'll get to my point about praying, is the "observer effect." It's when an experiment is watched, it performs as expected, and when it's not observed, the results are different and random. *The actual observation of particles makes them act differently than if they weren't watched.* I'm going to include a few footnotes on where I saw these, but again, just by adding consciousness and attention to something fundamentally changes something that shouldn't be changed.

These are all unusual phenomena, and to me they just point to the fact that we're all connected. Nothing and no one is in isolation. You are never alone because you are part of us all. If we're going to get really deep, I believe that we're literally all a part of God.

And that's why I think it's a fact that prayers work. Asking for something from the divine is a real and tangible way to help make something happen, and to influence things that would normally remain unaffected.

I was reminded of this today when a friend of mine, Hal Elrod (who wrote The Miracle Morning discussed all over this book), has "miraculously," regrown white blood cells, which had remained dangerously low (nearly fatal) during his bout with leukemia and suddenly jumped to the level of a healthy person overnight. The doctors had not seen anything like it ever before, but you see, Hal has several THOUSAND people praying for him, sending love, and wishing him well. It's a nearly miraculous occurrence, but I think that things like this where the laws of science and medicine seem to be circumvented happen much more often than we think.

For a little more on this, here's a true story I wrote about on Facebook. I get chills even thinking of it, because I felt touched by divinity when it happened. So here it is:

~~~~~~~~~~~~~~~~~~~~

"I just had something really profound happen to me today, and I didn't know if I should post it, because I don't want it to come off as a humble-brag or anything, but I think the message is necessary and maybe it can help to inspire. I just hope my words can do it justice.

I was driving in Harker Heights and it was raining pretty hard. I saw a shirtless man walking along, pushing a shopping cart. I pulled over, and like a movie script it just stopped raining.

I approached him to give him some money, and just to let him know that people he doesn't even know will be praying for him. He looked me in the eyes, just full in the face. I introduced myself and asked his name. He looked to be in his late fifties or so, and was very clear, and spoke extremely well. I could tell he was intelligent.

He thanked me and said something that made an imprint on me. He said that I was an answered prayer. He went on to explain that three times this week, he had specifically asked God for something, and each time it was given to him within three to five hours. He had asked for access to a laptop, and a phone, and then some money—and this was
~~~~~~~~~~~~~~~~~~~~

the third time it had happened for him. He's waiting on Social Security to kick in next week, and his homelessness is about to end.

He hugged me, apologized for talking so much—which is funny in itself as this was one of the best conversations I've ever had. He went on to explain how he does it:

First, he explained that you have to ask specifically for what you want. He said God is great and can grant it.

Then, he said, you have to have faith that it will happen. You need to believe.

Finally, he said that he always got this wrong before and just learned it—he said, "You have to speak it into existence." You need to say it and take action.

It was just so unexpected and so . . . perfect.

He said goodbye, and that he was so grateful for a loving God.

He is so thankful and grateful, even in his circumstances—and here we are with possessions, loving families, and almost unlimited possibilities with what we can do—and we're often not as grateful as we should be.

I sincerely hope I see him again. He touched my life deeply today, and I need to thank him.

~~~~~~~~~~~~~~~~~~~

Prayer works. That's why I'm advising you to do it. Especially if something happens to me, heh, heh.
~~~~~~~~~~~~~~~~~~~

Sweethearts, say your prayers. For real. Say them.

Advice in Practice:

- Think of times in your life where prayer seemed to work. Run them around in your mind, remember as vividly as you can about how something came to pass. Just the thought of it working like this will help cement it in your mind that prayer does indeed work.

- Pray specifically. Think of something or someone that you'd like to help. Get them in your mind. Then pray in the way that makes you feel comfortable. For this one, pray for someone or something else. Come on. No one's watching or listening. You can do this. The prayer can be as simple as, "Please let Mom have a wonderful day." I think this makes a difference—also, it will make YOU feel better for wanting others to do better.

- Now, for the next real prayer, pray for yourself. There is no shame or dishonor in this, provided that your motives are pure and you're not wishing harm on anyone else. There was a book that I read a while back that sold a lot of copies and was a bit of a phenomenon called, *The Prayer of Jabez*. It was all about a man, Jabez, who prayed specifically to increase his lands. If you are a steward, and have noble intentions and pray (and hopefully *take inspired action*) I truly think this helps. So, go ahead and do it, loved ones.

- Now, the big thing. This can literally change your life: Add Prayer to your daily practice/Miracle Morning. Make it an everyday thing for you to do. This is sometimes tough to actually change your daily habits for this, but this one is important. So, please do it!

I love you, and I'm PRAYING for you daily, too.

Notes, thoughts, and intentions.

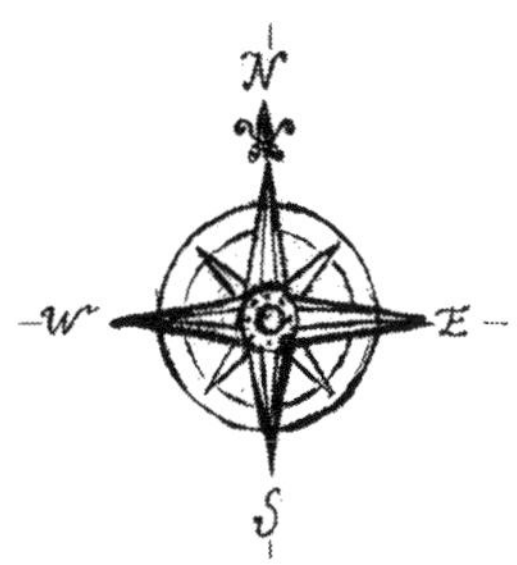

94. Remove the Word "Can't" From Your Vocabulary.

You roll your eyes at me when I say this: Don't say the word "can't." Yes, it's a dad joke: You can't say can't.

It means you're a quitter, that you've given up and shut off that spectacular mind you have.

Instead, what do we say? That's right.

"***How Can I?***"

There you go! Winners think in terms of how, and you, my loved ones, are winners. You're divine in your design and can do pretty much everything you think you can.

This is heard so much that it's turned into a cliché. You hear it all over self-help books and probably see it posted by people all over social media, but it's true.

I think Henry Ford said it.

"Whether you think you can, or you think you can't, you're right."

I've also heard Walt Disney say, "It's kind of fun to do the impossible."

Anthony Robbins, one of my heroes, says, "Impossible is only a state of mind."

I know I'm talking about the big stuff and supposed impossibilities, but it works for the small, mundane things in life, too.

When you say, "I can't find the peanut butter," you're actually shutting your mind off to the possibility of finding it now.

Have you had one of those experiences where you are looking for something like peanut butter, you're searching the pantry through all of the other food (that's a blessing, include that in your Active Appreciation), and you're saying to yourself, "I CAN'T FIND THE PEANUT BUTTER!" And then Mom comes along and BOOM. She pulls the peanut butter off of the shelf right in front of you? Maybe it wasn't peanut butter . . . but you get the idea. It's happened a lot to us all.

I think it's because our mind is so powerful that it makes our reality.

And that's why it's so important to never say the word "can't." Because if you do, you just made your own, now limited world.

Don't say it in my presence. It's like nails on a chalkboard to me. Don't say it when you're not in my presence, either.

You can't say can't.

The Advice in Practice:

- Obviously, try to catch yourself saying it and physically slap yourself across your face every time those words come out of your mouth or run cross your mind. I'm just kidding. About the slapping part. But seriously, be vigilant about that.

- Write out why it's important to you NOT to say the word can't.

- Change these sentences to get the full feeling of this.

  "I can't afford that."

  to . . .

  "How can I afford that?"

  or . . .

  "I can't accomplish that." to "How can I accomplish that?"

- Wow! Can you see and feel the difference? If you catch yourself saying or thinking, "I can't," change the wording to, "How can I?" and unleash that beautiful, incredible, sharp mind of yours on that now possible answer!

- When you ask how—and even if the answer initially is, "I don't know"—what will happen is that your miraculous brain is going to start working on it. Especially if you're using the idea lists and you're an idea machine, magic will be made. Just allow the thoughts to unfold in all of their glory without nipping them in the bud with the negativity of "can't."

I love you, sweethearts. You can't change that.

Notes, thoughts, and intentions.

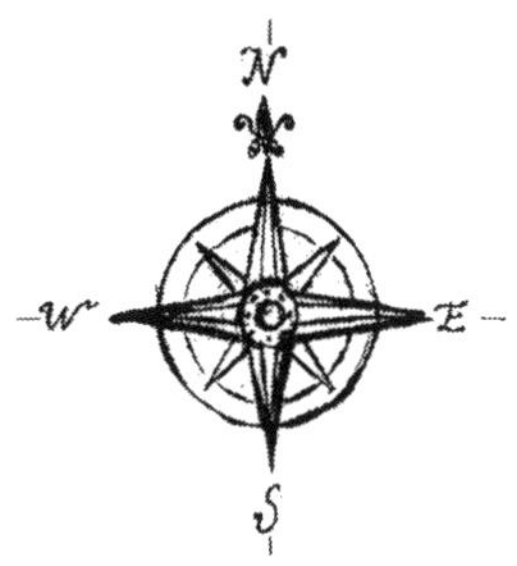

95. Begin with the End in Mind. In Life, And Everywhere.

Robert Herrick, 1591–1674 (Public Domain)

Gather ye rosebuds while ye may,
Old Time is still a-flying;
And this same flower that smiles today
Tomorrow will be dying.

The glorious lamp of heaven, the sun,
The higher he's a-getting,
The sooner will his race be run,
And nearer he's to setting.

That age is best which is the first,
When youth and blood are warmer;
But being spent, the worse, and worst
Times still succeed the former.

Then be not coy, but use your time,
And while ye may, go marry;
For having lost but once your prime,
You may forever tarry.

This is a tough thing to think about, sweethearts, but it may very well be one of the most important.

Our bodies will cease to live at some point. We talked about that at the very beginning of the book, and here it is again. It's a useful thought.

We will stop taking breath, our hearts will cease to beat, and our brains will no longer function. It will happen to us, and everyone else.

Personally, I think that we still will have consciousness. The laws of science say that energy cannot be destroyed, only transformed, and I think that's the same with our spirit which is definitely energy.

However, we won't be of this Earth anymore at that point.

And we can, and I advise *should*, make the most of our experience and what we can do during this life before that happens. I was actually thinking about this concept this morning, and I couldn't wait to share it with you, because I know at some point that this can really help you.

Death isn't the sad part. The part I find depressing—other than the loved ones who are grieving while being left behind—is that most people didn't really and truly LIVE. And that's where I think that death can be an incredible teacher for us.

> ***"Remembering that I'll be dead soon is the most important tool I've ever encountered to help me make the big choices in life ... Remembering that you are going to die is the best way I know to avoid***

the trap of thinking you have something to lose. You are already naked. There is no reason not to follow your heart." — Steve Jobs

Read and then reread this Steve Jobs quote. It is so profound, and the wisdom is timeless. My sweethearts, right now it seems like you have forever. The days spent in your PJs, goofing off and binge-watching Netflix can start to haunt you when you realize that *it all goes so very fast*.

I still feel like a kid. I'm sometimes shocked that I have a child who is technically an adult. I'm amazed that some entity made me a Dad, when I still feel like I've got growing up to do. The years are funny. They accelerate. Each year becomes a smaller percentage of your life, and thus it just seems shorter. The days often go fast that you have a big list of things you want to accomplish, and then you look around and realize that the end of the workday has already arrived.

You have to be vigilant about the passing of time. If you're not careful, it can sneak up on you, and you realize that there isn't any of it left—and you've still got dreams left to accomplish and grand plans you had intended on doing. So, the lesson is this:

TAKE ACTION NOW. Don't you dare wait. Seize the day and make something happen.

You don't know how long you have, and even if you have a while left, I promise it will be shorter than you think.

I found this interesting, and I know that I'll include this in other areas of the book; but some things learned by a nurse at hospice are things from which we can learn. Studying the regrets of death can be very enlightening on the ways in which we can, and probably should live.

The biggest regrets of the dying, according to this nurse, Bronnie Ware?

The number one regret: **Not living a life true to yourself.**

They wished they hadn't worked so hard and missed things. They also wished they'd expressed their feelings and stayed in touch with their friends. The last regret on the list is that they wished that they would've let themselves be happier.

Wow. This is a bit sad to hear, and also such a blessing. We can take what the dying regret and use it as a warning to live our lives differently. I just think that most of us don't think about it often.

Are you proud of what you're doing in life?

Are you living true to yourself?

Are you missing things you shouldn't because you're working too hard?

Do you express your feelings or bottle them up, scared of confrontation, or others' feelings when something deep inside of you needs to speak up?

Are you staying in touch with YOUR friends?

Are you allowing yourself to be happy?

These are the questions of life, and they deserve to be answered. We all owe it to ourselves to answer them.

Remembering that we are mortal and beginning with the end in mind serves to remind us of that.

I love you, dearly.

Advice in Practice:

- Are you doing the weekly check-in yet? If not, take out your phone and set an appointment to do so. An appointment with yourself to just sit down and work on your life. Check in and think about your life on a macro level. Go ahead, please do it now. Get your phone and do it, talk to anyone you need to in order to get a little time to yourself for this. It's very important, and if you don't take action on it now, chances are you won't ever do it.

- Bring your journal and this book to this appointment with yourself. Have a pen and get ready. I like to be in a place that's beautiful for it. Walk around a little bit, stretch out, take some good, deep breaths. Get in a good state for this.

- Next, write out the questions from this advice. I'd suggest a question at the top of each page and leave some space to answer them. "Are you proud of what you're doing in life now?" Put that at the top and just start writing and see what pours out of your soul onto the page.

- Be good to yourself while doing this. Keep breathing well, if you need to get up and walk around, that's okay and recommended. I know I have a tendency to beat myself up when doing something like this because I see a big gap between potential and what I've actually done. Please don't be mean to my treasures. The fact is that you're getting better right now, and that's something you should be proud of yourself for doing.

- Continue to do this with each of the questions above. Take as much time as you need. Feel the answer to each of the questions and get it all out from inside of you to the page. Get some perspective. Take breaks as needed, but finish this deep, soul work.
- Just seeing and really answering these questions are going to make you want to change. But that's not usually enough. The next step is to think of how to get better. You use that brilliant mind of yours, you listen to the sometimes-quiet whispers of your heart, and you set a plan to do it. If you're not spending enough time with loved ones because you're working too hard, for instance, how do we fix that? How can you get everything you want to do at work done and be able to leave it to get to your loved ones? It seems to me to be a perfect time for an idea list for each of these areas where you're dissatisfied.
- Depending on the time you have you can create an idea list now for some or all of them, or you can set a specific time in your schedule to get to each of these. The thing is, we've talked about it so much already. It won't get done if you don't actually make it a part of your life by scheduling. Please do it for your Dad's sake.
- When you work on it, and do your idea lists, think about books you can read, or resources you can research.

Think about people that you can talk to that may be able to help you. Do some great, well-thought out idea lists to help with this. When you see the one or two ideas that will really be game changers for you, then schedule them to become a part of your daily list. I don't want to repeat it, but I will. *Really schedule that.*

- Oh my goodness, I love you. I want you to do this, but I'm not pretending that using the thought of death to motivate you to look at try to solve some of these bigger questions will make everything better overnight. I hope you're not *expecting* that, either. We can put a big dent in it and start to get you on the right path, of course. But this needs to be revisited, and often. Dog-ear this page. When you do your weekly check-in, have these questions out and ready to answer. And now schedule the next time you revisit them.
- I'm not always great at follow up, but something I did in sales that was great was that I never left clients without setting the next appointment. I was disciplined about that. I'm going to ask you to do the same thing for this set of questions. When you revisit them, before you wrap it up—set the next time you will look at them. Please do this, and it's going to help you live a life of fewer regrets.

Sweethearts, I cherish you.

Notes, thoughts, and intentions.

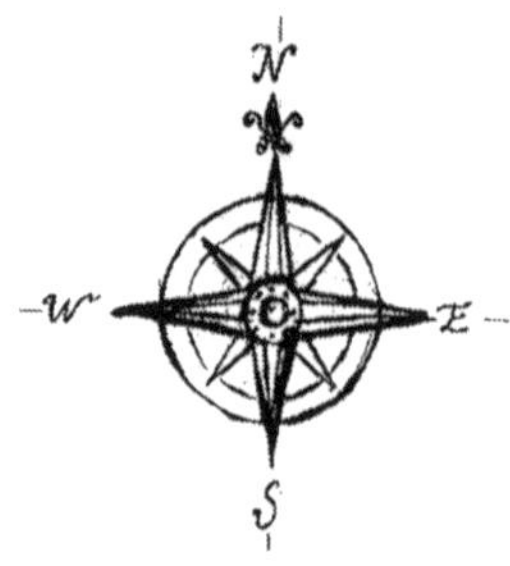

96. Be A LIGHT in This World. It's Your Duty.

"This little light of mine, I'm going to let it shine."

My precious children, here's something to think about: We want everyone on the *light side*.

I've come to realize that there are two types of people in life, and we'll call them the LIGHTS and the DIMS. I woke up thinking about those terms exactly, so I'm hoping it's an original thought and not a repressed memory that's coming to mind. Anyways, I digress.

I think the terms explain the people very well.

The "Lights," are the people that you enjoy when they walk into the room. They radiate happiness. They're funny. They're kind. They have a certain twinkle in their eye, and you just feel good around them. In a metaphysical sense, they GIVE energy. You, and most other people feel better in their presence than without them near. I think you know what I mean, but we'll talk a little more about these people in a bit.

The "Dims,"(I bet you already know intuitively what I'm going to say) drain you. They tend to complain and tell you how something can't be done. They're quick to point out the bad things in life. They'll explain in painful detail how they were unable to sleep well last night, and how the government is screwing us all over (well, they might be right about that one . . . but you don't need to go around telling everyone about it). They tend to be moochers. Asking for more than they give on a regular basis. I just came up with the term, and there's no clinical definition for a Dim . . . but I'm sure that you get the idea.

The terms are nouns that describe what each of the two are. But they're also verbs. Light and dim, to explain what they do.

You're either one or the other.

Now, a Light can have bad days and get down, maybe say some wrong things or have a bad attitude occasionally, but they return to their glorious selves soon.

The Dims can also have good days. But we all know that they'll get back to themselves and the cranky, pessimistic, somewhat cynical nature they exude, as well.

Here's the thing: there is a daily battle over who wins the day. The "good" guys or the "bad." We may not know that there's a battle, and that's the purpose of what I'm writing here. But it IS there. It's always happening whether we choose to admit it, or not.

When your coworker gossips about someone (a clear sign of being a, "Dim"), a shot is fired. The entire energy and the light of a situation is under siege at that very moment, and it is up to the Lights among us to say a kind word, diffuse the situation, or at least leave the temporary darkness caused by the action or they too can be sucked into the negativity, and allow the Dim to take the battle.

Sometimes, unless consciously caught, very good people can unknowingly become a Dim. It can be the default when you're surrounded by a world of negativity.

But, then there are the Lights.

They speak highly of other people. They talk about the things that make them and others happy. They find the GOOD in nearly every situation. They're able to lift everyone with a few well-chosen words, or the easy smile on their faces.

The light of God (or the Universe, if you're particular about that) shines *through* these people. It's an inner light that's allowed to shine, and the mundane and worldly things are inadequate to stop that blessed brightness. Honestly, the light isn't of us, but rather through us, if that makes any sense. We're a conduit from a higher power when we are Lights.

In our highest and best forms, God is shown through our actions.

That is what it means to be a Light. It is my advice, and I will tell you—as a Daddy that LOVES you, and always wants the best for you:

It is your DUTY to be a Light in this world.

Advice in Practice:

- **Be Vigilant**: The knowledge that there is a war is the first step in actually winning this daily struggle. I hope the words you are reading help with that. So be vigilant. KNOW that you are one or the other and allow your light to shine. Stand guard at the door of your mind and keep the negative thoughts from affecting how you act, and how you treat yourself and others. We often beat ourselves up, even as Lights. You wouldn't stand for someone doing that to your friend, so don't put up with it from yourself.

- **Know When to Retreat**: There is a natural tendency for the dark to pull down the light. Especially if the Dims outnumber you. Sometimes it's best to leave a situation than to let them suck you into the negative realm of complaints and cynicism. Retreat to fight again elsewhere. Sometimes people can be helped, and it's actually our duty as a Light to try and help them. However, we need to know when they are sapping our power and winning the match. You're not going to be able to help others if you're in a bad mood and in a poor state of mind. It's the ole' oxygen mask thing: make sure your oxygen mask is on before you try to help someone else with their oxygen mask . . . otherwise you both die. In this case, you'll both be a Dim that day. So, know when it happens.

- **Recruit Help**: Be encouraging to other people. Show kindness in everyday situations. Whenever you interact with ANYONE else, you have a chance to be kind, and to score another victory for the Lights. When you're kind to someone, they will feel that, and it makes them more likely to go out and be a Light themselves. So smile. And maybe more importantly, give that smile to someone else and get help in winning the day. THIS is where the battle is fought and won. It's during your everyday interactions with others . . . and actually, in the way you interact with yourself. Be uplifting. If you have a chance to say something that will make someone feel good, why would you keep that to yourself?

- **Find a way to Serve**: Get out of your own head and sometimes self-sabotaging thoughts, and instead focus on others. It's our highest calling as a human being. You can always help someone else. Sometimes, it's as simple as a caring look to someone else. A hug. A text letting someone know that you're grateful for them. How much time and effort does that take? But, when you do that, it's a strike against the Dims of the world. It helps others and makes the world a better place. Fundamentally, isn't that why we're here, why we exist in the first place?
- I hope this helps. Really observe these human souls and see which side each is playing for by their actions. Then, fully knowing and conscious in the moment, choose to be a Light. I know you are already a light, you just need to let it show through you. It all depends on you.

I love you, and your light.

Notes, thoughts, and intentions.

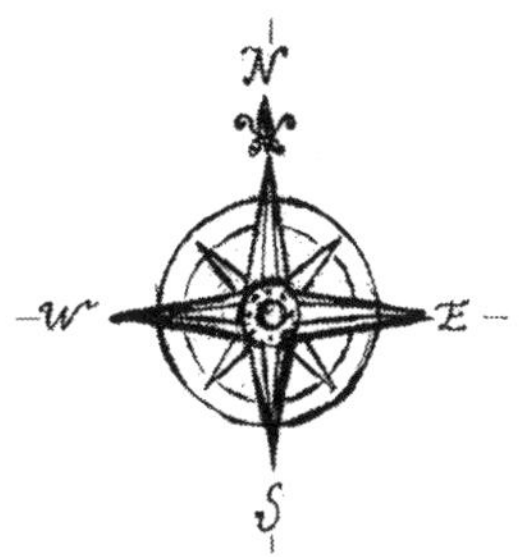

97. Embark on Your Hero's Journey.

"Follow your bliss and don't be afraid, and doors will open where you didn't know they were going to be." — Joseph Campbell

Holy moly. This is such a huge and important piece of advice and taking it to heart WILL absolutely change your life. It's actually the very definition of a life change and journey. I didn't even hear and truly learn about the *Hero's Journey* until I was forty-three years young, and I'm so glad that you get the chance to hear about it at a much younger age and are able to do something about it sooner than I did.

I know you're at least a little familiar with the *Hero's Journey*. Aly, you've studied it at your new school. And Mandy, I've probably talked about it a lot (maybe too much?) in your presence. I know that you have a basic understanding, but we're going to go a little deeper, because this is important.

I mention this elsewhere in these *Lessons o' Love*, but do you remember the number one regret of the dying, according to a hospice worker from Australia that wrote about it? The number one regret is that they (the dying) didn't "Live a life true to themselves." Wow. That's so profound. That's such a big deal, something monumental for each of us to consider.

I think the life that is "true" to us is our own Hero's Journey. It's setting off on our own adventure to do something great, that grand challenge that is awaiting each of us to conquer or give it our all in trying.

The *Hero's Journey* is so important, one of the biggest things we can learn about and yet almost all of us don't learn it. It's not taught in regular schools, at least up through the high school levels, and not in college unless you take some obscure philosophy or mythology classes. Yet studying it, considering, and contemplating it can be the difference between a life unlived or making our own personal mark on the world.

You know about my story. I was living a good life. I have a spectacular family, I had a good business that provided a good living in real estate for the past twenty years. Yet, I became down and depressed with the life I had *because I didn't feel like I was living the life I should be*.

There was just a growing discontent, and an overwhelming feeling that I wasn't living to my potential; or at least *attempting* anything great. Now, I don't think it's a sin to not achieve great things in life; however (and this may sound harsh) I do think that it's a sin to not at least try to do something grand.

My personal hero's journey started with me truly attempting to make my life better when I was down. I read some books, to include: *Choose Yourself*, by James Altucher and, *The Obstacle is the Way*, by Ryan Holiday. I started to do my daily practice. I embarked on *Miracle Mornings*. I started writing about my own journey and the attempt to go from ordinary to extraordinary. I started practicing gratitude and doing kind acts. I volunteered. We did the hug station at the nursing homes, and after hearing one of my mentors, Joe Polish, talking about his experience in a nursing home and the need for, "an Uber for volunteers," on a podcast—I knew I had to pursue it by creating JoeVolunteer.

I helped to raise money for that by speaking on a stage in front of hundreds of highly influential people. After walking off of that stage, a man that has become my friend, Giovanni Marsico, approached me to come to a conference of "Super Heroes," a few months later in California. The group was called Archangel, and the conference theme was, "The Hero's Journey."

I hadn't even heard about the concept of The Hero's Journey before that, even though I'd heard the quote, "Follow your bliss." My eyes were opened when I watched a movie all about it called, "Finding Joe," which I've shared with you. I got to meet Patrick Solomon, the man that made that movie at the conference. I also got to hear about Gio's own Hero's Journey at the conference, where he talked about being in the real estate business, and although being talented at it, he was extremely unhappy. He had anxiety attacks, he suffered depression, and KNEW it wasn't for him. So he started Archangel (Big Hearted Entrepreneurs who want to change the world), and eventually he quit his lucrative real estate practice to follow his dream.

When I was sitting in the audience listening to Gio's story, it punched a hole right in my soul because I felt exactly the same. I didn't plan on selling my business yet, but that seed of dissatisfaction was planted in my heart at that moment; and eventually led me to sell the real estate business and follow my own Hero's Journey. A big part of that is what you're reading right now. I've wanted to be an author since I've been in the third grade, and now I've finally, at long last, done it. I don't know for certain if I'll be successful in my new endeavors, but I can't abide not TRYING.

And that's what I want for you. To try. To attempt to do something great. Something that is in your heart and soul. The thing that makes your heart beat a little faster when you think about it. That grand lure of adventure that we try to keep covered with the trance of everyday life. Working, paying bills, trying to move up, make more money, take more vacations, and be better parents. We oftentimes ignore that pull that's in us when we pause and sit quietly, alone with our thoughts. I think it's a great idea to know more about the Hero's Journey, to understand it, and then apply it in your lives to help on your own path.

There are a lot of stages with it, and you'll recognize them from nearly every story and movie you've ever seen. The formula has been used for thousands of years, and when you know what it is, the similarity of ALL stories becomes apparent. It's always been there, but Joseph Campbell codified and defined it for us in three parts as follows:

The Departure, which includes:

The Ordinary World (which you may be in now in this stage of your journey); the Call to Adventure (maybe the most important part), Reluctance or Refusal of the Call (that inner turmoil of whether to go off on your adventure), Supernatural Aid or Mentor that helps you along the way, Crossing the Threshold (actually embarking), and the Belly of the Whale which is when you've left what you've known and are ready for a metamorphosis.

The Initiation, which has:

The Road of Trials (or the Forest), The Meeting of the Goddess (or Facing the Dragon); Temptations that try to keep you from following the path, Atonement (where you come face to face with yourself and whoever holds the ultimate power in your life), Apotheosis (which is when you attain greater understanding), The Ultimate Boon (actually achieving the ultimate goal of your quest).

And The Return, which is:

Refusal of the return (just wanting to 'bask' in what you've done, rather than finish), The Magic Flight (which is the journey back to where you've started, which may be just as dangerous as any part of the journey), Rescue from Without (where you get help again, maybe after being injured on the way), Crossing the Return Threshold (actually returning), Master of Two Worlds (applying what you've learned/gained along the way), and Freedom to Live (the "Happily Ever After").

That's a lot to take in, but it's great to read into more of these, because when you're on your personal journey, you'll recognize a lot of these stages. It's also helpful to think of movies like Star Wars and The Matrix and their story arcs. They all follow the path of the Hero's Journey very faithfully.

When you study these, and know what's coming, then you can prepare for them in your own life. You can know that so many others have gone through the same kind of trials and tribulations that you are facing, and that there is guidance available for you. Maybe even from your Daddy!

Now, I'm nowhere near the end of my big Hero's Journey, but I have a little wisdom on the process for you that may be of use. Here are a few of my observations:

The Call to Adventure: This is the part that I think most people completely miss.

We're often blind, and just going through the trance of life. The mundane in our faces every day keeps that call from being seen. It's often not something blindingly obvious, so you have to be on the lookout and keep your antennae up for that call. It's important that you find it.

Don't skimp on your hero's journey.

This is your life, and you are completely worthy to attempt something grand. You deserve a big and important Hero's Journey. One that stretches you, that is challenging, and that leaves the world a better place because you took breath in it and attempted to dare greatly.

The Reluctance or Refusal: It is OKAY to be scared and fearful on your journey.

In fact, if you're not scared of it, then you may not be trying hard enough, or setting your sights high enough.

There's no growth in easy. There's no courage without fear.

Feeling scared and doing it anyways is admirable. You are incredible and exceptional, and I expect courage from you.

Watch for Serendipitous moments along your journey.

My friend Gio says that these moments are indicators that you are on the right path in your journey, and it's easy to get off that path when you're in a metaphorical dark forest. So, keep an eye out for those blissful, divine coincidences that are sometimes hard to explain.

You won't be fighting lizards! They are called dragons for a reason.

I heard this from one of my virtual mentors Brian Johnson in his book: *Philosopher's Notes*. If the challenges are too easy, then there isn't any honor in conquering them. The bigger the dragon, the sweeter the victory. If you're attempting something grand, like I argue that you should be, then know it isn't easy. Just understanding this before and during your journey will help you when the time comes. It's great to remember this and keep it top of mind while you are neck-deep in your journey.

One of the most important things about The Hero's Journey is what you gain in undertaking it.

The person you become through this process is important. If you're on a real journey, you're going to be made better through the process. You'll gain new skills, you'll learn persistence, resilience, tenacity, and resourcefulness. You'll become a new and improved creature through the metamorphosis you undergo.

You can and probably will have multiple "Hero's Journeys" in your life.

I think they are continuous, and maybe several are going concurrently. The whole process is completely unique to you. The journey you begin fresh out of school may be completely different than the one you undertake as a grandparent.

It's all about others, too.

A grand Hero's Journey should be about others and helping them. Luke destroyed the Death Star and saved the Galaxy. Your Hero's Journey should seek to serve and make life better for others. When you complete it, the world (or at least your corner of it) should be changed and improved by what you've done.

YOU become the Supernatural Aid/Mentor for others.

You're not just the protagonist for your own story. You're the helper for others, both along the way and when you're done. I think it's imperative for you to take your knowledge and what you've gained along the way and to use that to help others in their Hero's Journey. When you're wise from the process, you become the Yoda to someone else's Luke, the Good Witch to someone else's Dorothy, and etc. You get the idea.

Sweethearts. I truly hope that seeing this and reading about it leaves you changed. That it convinces you to leave your antenna up and receptive for that grand call to adventure. I hope it's something that is large and worthy of someone incredible like you. I know you, I see greatness in you, and I know that you are worthy and deserving enough to attempt to do something great in your Hero's Journey. I love you and know you can do it.

Advice in Practice:

- Watch "Finding Joe" at FindingJoeTheMovie.com. I'd suggest actually buying it and referring back to it often. Have it going in the background as you're working on your personal journey. It helps to remember that you're ON one, and that you are striving for something greater.

- Google Joseph Campbell quotes. I prefer reading them on Goodreads, as I like the format. Get inspired. Print those suckers up and post them conspicuously where you'll see and be motivated by them regularly.

- If you want to go deeper into this subject, look up and order Joseph Campbell's interview with Bill Moyers called *The Power of Myth* on Audible, or in the book form. If you're into this kind of wisdom, it's pretty amazing. Some of his other works get into the weeds a bit, but this one has very regular gems. It's worth reading and/or listening to several times.

- Go to and/or make your quiet place that's a place that's deeply spiritual to you where, as he says, you, "forget about who you owe money to, and who owes you money," and you can be silent, and still—i.e. no cell phones. Get quiet and still. Read a lot of something that inspires you and that brings you joy . . . or bliss. Keep reading and going to the place until something sings you its siren song and you have to follow.

- Journal on your life. See everything around you as your "ordinary world," and start to write on what is your personal call to adventure. What's been lurking in your heart? What's been covered by years, or decades of everyday "trance" that has been keeping you from what you have to do in the world?
- Write an idea list on *The First Steps in My Personal Hero's Journey*. What are some things you can do to find that supernatural aid? What can you do to beat the reluctance and cross the threshold into the adventure of your life?
- Teach this to others. Become Yoda, you must.
- Consult your Daddy early and often on your path. Let's go over this together and see how and what I can do to help you on your path. I love you so much and want you to, "dare greatly so that your place will never be with those cold and timid souls that know neither victory nor defeat."

Notes, thoughts, and intentions.

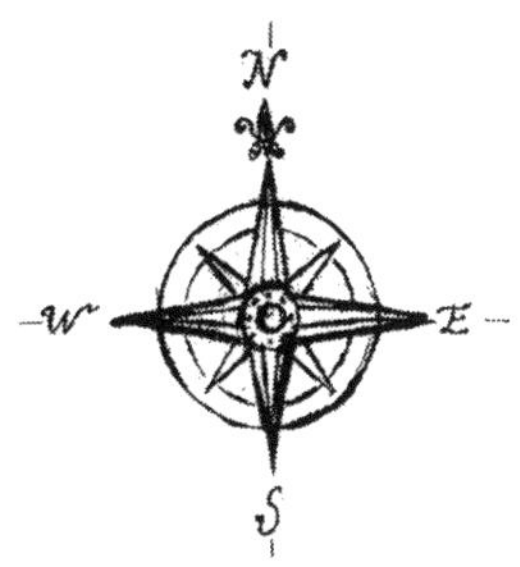

98. Create Your Very Own Bucket List.

Write out a "bucket list," of experiences you want to do while you're in this world. List places you want to experience, things you want to do, people you want to meet. Check them off as you accomplish them.

You know what a bucket list is, right? It was popularized by the movie, *The Bucket List*, with Jack Nicholson and Morgan Freeman. It's the list of things you want to do in life before you, "kick the bucket," (that's a rather curious metaphor for dying).

I just had to know how they got that term, and it seems that when someone got hanged, which happened a lot more when this phrase was created, they "kicked the bucket," away from their feet, which left them hanging. Sorry, that's macabre, but it may add to the whole emotion of this piece of advice and help you remember it. My friend Jim says that EMOTION creates memory. So, this can help you remember and actually do this.

LISTEN UP!!! Lots and lots of people say they have a bucket list, but most do NOT. What they mean to say is that they have a general idea of some of the things that they'd like to do, that they think would make them happy, but I'd say less than one in a 100 actually has a real bucket list. I'll also admit that I don't have one written as I'm writing this (I do have written goals, and a poster of 100 places to visit that I've been checking off though!), but I'm including my personal ones in the back of this book. That way, you'll know that I'm practicing what I'm preaching, which is important, AND you'll get a better insight to who your Daddy is.

Some ideas for a bucket list generally include: Running a marathon, seeing the Eiffel Tower in Paris, taking your children to Disney World (look at their faces when they walk in)! Don't use my list, though. Make your own and make sure they're important to you.

Here is the important thing about the bucket list as it is with goal setting in general: The list and accomplishing of these is not what's really important.

What's really important is what it makes of you to achieve these items.

It's the fact that you are writing them down (the gigantic majority of people out there will never be bothered to do this), and you're living your life in such a way as to do these things.

The more you're able to check off of your list, the more you are doing, the more you're developing yourself as a human being, the more proud of yourself you'll be.

This is an important aspect of the bucket list: You'll always have things to look forward to in life. You can pull out this physical list, look at it, and think of actually doing them and ANTICIPATE how great you'll feel in doing them. That's a great feeling, and it's particularly useful when you're having some bad days.

It's a pretty necessary thing in life to have the feeling that your future will be greater than your past.

Another thing that I'll say about bucket lists is try not to be flippant about them. "Climbing Everest," may sound like a sexy item for your bucket list when you're making it, but that is something that will cost around $100,000 or more, and take over two months to actually do after a year of rigorous training (I Googled it). So, think about what goes on the list, how it would make you feel to accomplish it, and whether or not you'd enjoy the actual process before committing to it.

Here's a quick warning: If there are a lot of items on your bucket list just quietly sitting there for years or decades on end, gathering dust, then I think that actually hurts your confidence. It would be ironic to do a bucket list to enhance your life, make for a richer, fuller experience of your existence on Earth, and then for it to hinder you in life. It's important to have some of the things that are easier to accomplish and take a little less time, and then there are life centerpiece type of bucket list items that take some planning and are major milestones. These are the kind of adventures that are shown on the screen in pictures at your funeral.

I've referred to death a few times already in this advice. I didn't necessarily mean to do that, but it's happening for a reason. You've got a limited time on this planet (at least as of the writing of this tome), and you need to get after it. The bucket list is how you truly live. It's going after a dream. It's the planning, and the anticipation, and the outright JOY of actually DOING it.

In short, it's a microcosm of the good things in life. I think that many folks, including myself, take life too haphazardly. I mean, there is magic and joy to letting loose and allowing serendipity to occur, but NOT planning some of the things that will and need to happen in your life is, I think, a little irresponsible for this incredible gift of life that we've been given.

Actually sitting down, and taking the time to write this out is a *celebration* of life and all of its possibilities! It's creating the script of your life movie. It's taking life by the throat and drinking it down deeply.

And again, most people can't be bothered to do something like this. But you are not most people, my sweethearts! You've got this book of advice, and you're actually reading it, choosing what works for you, and trying it. I love that about you and know that you've got it in you to make the dreams in your beautiful head (and soul), and turn them into a reality.

I love you so dearly. I wish for you a life of fulfillment, of happiness, of joy, and love.

Advice in Practice:

- Google, "How to Write a Bucket List." I have some suggestions and what I'm doing with it, but you can get ideas from a lot of smart minds on the best ways to get this done. Use what works for you. Discard my advice completely if it doesn't ring true, or if someone else has better ideas.

- Start a "Bucket List Project." Do an OPOA for it (read the advice on an "OPOA—Outcome, Purpose, Obstacles, Actions," if you don't remember what an OPOA is!). Determine what the outcome is to do this exercise. Think about the adventures it can start, and the joy it can bring. Think about the stories you can tell your children and grandchildren that you did! Get it all out! Then think about why you are doing one. Get personal. You don't have to share this with anyone. It can be a celebration of life for you, it can prove that you are capable, that you are worthy. It can be to have the feeling of living up to your potential—or anything else you desire. Then, it's time to get to the actions of doing the list.

- Create an idea list and brainstorm where you take a little time and write out everything that comes to mind for you bucket list. If it's even a tingling in your mind, then get it out and put it down on paper. No idea is too crazy, too big, or too small. Just write it all. I don't know about you, but this is exciting for me. The sky and beyond is the limit! Something that really helps when doing something like this, and scripting your life, is to get in a great state while doing it. Your list will be completely different if you're doing it while tired or depressed. So, put on music you love. Jump around a little (unless other people are watching, then jump around a LOT) and get to writing it! Get a TON of them. I'm thinking somewhere around 100 for me. Because quality is often found in quantity.

- You're going to be instantly pulled to many of these ideas. The ones that stand out for you will sing their siren song, and you'll just have to follow them. Circle those. Or put a star on them. Or highlight them. Make them stand out, because they will be helping you do some pretty amazing things! Treat them with respect.

- Formalize the list. After they've been written, I am typing mine into a real, live, breathing list, complete with checkboxes that you can actually check off when they're done. I will be keeping mine in Evernote.

- HAVE A TIME OR A SYSTEM WHERE YOU ACTUALLY LOOK AT THIS AND ARE REMINDED OF IT! It's a strong belief of mine that knowledge is wasted unless it's used. So take a look at these lists. Maybe you can put it in a yearly planning session, or every quarter. Or maybe it's at the front of your planner, laminated, and seen frequently when you're planning your days, weeks, and months. Use this time to cultivate the list, cut what doesn't work and maybe add some items to it, as well. Don't neglect this, or the entire exercise will be futile.

- Talk to others about it—but only those that are supportive and encouraging. You know the right people. I know you can accomplish your dreams, but a lot of people like to gently tear you down (they'll call it 'being realistic') so that they either feel better about themselves for not having done them, or to save you from heartache when you don't accomplish them. Either way, you know those folks, too. Don't tell them, and it may be better to spend less time with them too, by the way.

I love you so, so much. I'm excited and happy for you to do this!

Notes, thoughts, and intentions.

99. Be Your Brother's Keeper.

Here it is: You are your brother's keeper. Take care of him. You are responsible for more than yourself in life.

To be your brother's keeper means to consider your neighbor's needs at all times, whether they are present or not.

It is your job to be your brother's keeper. I mean this literally, with Alec, and in a deeper sense in life towards others as well.

I don't know that I really need to remind you to be Alec's keeper. I'm actually looking at you, girls, while I'm writing this. I see the love of life and joy on your faces. I watch you with your brother often and see how much you love that little man. And *how much* he loves you, too.

I think one of the greatest moments for me as your Dad was to hear you two arguing, kind of half-seriously, half-jokingly over who Alec was going to, "live with," when he got older. I love that, and I really feel that one or both of you truly and honestly plan on having him stay with you when, maybe, he won't be living with your Mom and I, as we are thirty-seven and half and thirty-nine years older than our little man, respectively. The truth is, I think about this a lot; because when he's forty, I'll be eighty. I don't know what life will look like then, but I want to know that we have options. It can be him living with his friends and/or independently; or it can be that he lives with and is looked out for by his loving sisters.

I think you know the most of the story about Alec's birth; but I'm going to take a little time to tell you the details. Mandy, you were twelve at the time and Aly, you were eight. I know your part with Alec was very vivid. I don't know if you know everything that your Mom and I went through at that time.

It was the hardest thing that either of us had ever been through, by far, but it also turned into the most beautiful experience in our lives afterwards. I hope you feel that way, too. I know having a brother with Down Syndrome isn't easy. It's a big responsibility, and it's not necessarily something that you asked for in this life. We're just blessed in that regard, I guess.

Your Mom and I decided that we'd have a third child. Your Mom was a little more reluctant than I was, but my reasoning to her made sense: We'd never regret having another member of the Franks' brood, but there would be a big chance that we would regret not having a third. Both of you brought (and still bring!) much joy into our lives. Of all the things that we've done in the world, bringing our children in it, as the people that you are is our proudest.

After a gut-wrenching miscarriage (which we should talk to you more about), we knew that our baby boy would be coming into our side of the world on your Guela's (grandmother's) birthday: October 25th, 2011. What a day it was! We had an appointment at the hospital, because they were going to induce labor for our new addition to the family. We knew he was a boy, and that everything seemed to be fine and he was healthy. Your Mom and I didn't want to do any advanced testing, as it posed a risk to the baby and it wouldn't have mattered to us if he was born with defects or problems. We'd welcome him, regardless. We knew that he'd have an increased chance for a diagnosis of Down Syndrome, whereas there was usually a one in 700 or more chance for it, Mom's age would mean that it was more like a one in 157 possibility. But we never thought that it would happen. We had a pretty storybook life up until that time in our life.

We were happy and joyful going to the hospital. There is an "official thread of the birth of Alec Cruz Franks," where we promised to keep everyone updated on his entry into the world and joked around quite a bit. It was new and different then for a birth to be shared over social media. Everything went well, which is easy for me to say, as I wasn't giving birth. This was our third time, and we had a comfortable familiarity with the process. The same wonderful doctor that had delivered both of you, our sweet girls, was there to help us usher your brother into the world.

I was in the room when he was born as I was with each of you. They keep a sheet up between the lower half of Mom's body and the upper half, so I was able to be close to her, and hold her hand as Alec was delivered via a C-section. As it happened with both of you, I cried tears of joy when I heard your brother's voice for the first time ever, crying a little (but not too much). They cleaned and handed him to me as they cut the cord, and I was the first person to be in front of him when he opened his eyes for the first time.

And I *knew*.

Right away, I knew that Alec was different, and that he had Down Syndrome, and that our lives were never, ever going to be the same. It was a shocking, numbing experience to know that right away.

Your Mom was having a minor procedure done while they were in there to get her tubes tied, and I was left holding our precious little man, just staring into his face, and those tell-tale almond-shaped eyes for a good forty-five minutes. It seemed like forever, and as light as he was, my arms were getting numb (like my soul at the time) from holding him so long.

I was thinking over and over in my head that this couldn't be. Our life had been pretty picture perfect to that point. No big shocks, surprises, or deaths of someone close in our family. This was the most traumatic thing that had ever happened. I was looking at this sweet, wonderful face, and I'm ashamed (but have since forgiven myself) to say that the first thing on my mind wasn't how much I loved him. It was just shock and a kind of mourning for the child we had planned for. I know I SAID all of the right things to him, but it was more a sense of despair than joy at the time. I don't know if that makes sense to you or not, or to anyone that hasn't gone through something like this.

I remember telling both your Pa-paw and your Uncle Mike (as he was driving you to the hospital). Uncle Mike just asked me, "What's wrong, what is it?" because he knew that something was wrong when I talked to him. I couldn't even speak. I just cried and cried. He kept asking what it was. Wow, I'm getting so emotional right now even writing about it. It's all still so vivid in my mind, and probably will be forever. Your granddad was on a bike ride at the time, and he pulled over and talked to me, and I remember him saying when I said the words, "Down Syndrome," that we were going to love him completely no matter what, and that it would be okay.

But it was still a while before it became "okay" for us. Those first two days after his birth, knowing he had DS and also would require several surgeries in his first few weeks of life were the hardest, toughest, DARKEST days in my life. I know it was for your Mom, too. She had it worse than me, because she wasn't allowed to see Alec due to being confined to her room while he was in the NICU (Neonatal Intensive Care Unit). I had him to look at, to touch and caress in his bed, and your Mom was just left by herself in a dark room with the most horrible scenarios running through her head. I became okay by being with Alec, and getting to know him and his indomitable spirit, even at a few days old. I looked into his face and fell in love with that sweet boy and knew he would have my soul forever then (like you two do).

We made the announcement to the world the day after he was born, and after we told you that he had Down Syndrome. We kept everyone up to date on him and his (and our ordeals) on Facebook, and we were overwhelmed with support. We'd get little notification, "dings," with every comment of love and support and they were like the sound of an angel at the time. You know what happened with the "Hope" hearts—Mandy, when you posted that you'd write a blue heart on your hand with the word "Hope," on it to support your little brother and that was posted on Facebook. We suddenly started getting these hearts sent to us on Facebook from literally all over the world. From our friends and family, but also from Marines, from people in Canada and Australia, and in different languages. It was amazing and humbling, and meant so, so much to us.

We didn't get to bring him home until Thanksgiving Day, a full month after he was born. He went through seven surgical procedures in his first six months of life, and earned the moniker, "The Amazing Alec." He's usually had at least one long hospital visit each year, and that part isn't easy, but having him, and seeing YOU with him is such a joy in life!

I think you'd agree that he's expanded all of our hearts, and that he's made each of us more compassionate. He's also brought so much joy and happiness just by who he is and what he does each day. He is an unfiltered light from God, and the sweetest, most affectionate boy we could ever imagine. I see you with him, and I don't know if any feeling on Earth is better than watching y'all being so sweet and loving towards each other.

So, when I say, "Be your brother's keeper," I mean it in the literal sense. You didn't ask for a brother with Down Syndrome, but he is still your responsibility too. I expect that of you if your Mom and I are somehow unable to watch him, or we've left the physical plane of our existence.

Please promise your Mom and I that you will always have him, and care for him. I'm pretty certain that you do already, but those words would mean the world to us.

Now, here's the other part of this advice: Be your brother's keeper in the larger sense of the word, too. By that, I mean always consider your neighbor as well as yourself at all times, even if they're not with you.

This is Biblical in nature, but I just think that it makes for a better, richer, and deeper life when you're looking out for someone else. That may mean little things like picking up trash that someone else left behind or pausing to talk to someone that looks like they are lonely. It also means big things, like choosing a career that makes a difference to others or trying to fulfill potential given to you by God.

I've written that YOU being happy is the best thing that you can do for others, and I think that some of that happiness is, or probably should be dependent on whether you're being your brother's keeper in the larger sense of the term. Would you truly be happy with yourself if you spent your career pushing gambling, or drinking sodas when you know it's not right for most people? I don't know. Obviously, you make the call on that—but I want you to consider your brother when you do these things. Are you your brothers' keeper?

Answering "yes," to that question is the right way to live, and I humbly suggest it for it you.

I hope you see and understand that I love you.

Advice in Practice:

- Mandy and Aly, talk with your Mom and me about Alec's future, and see what each of us has to say. Are you going to make it a point to be close to him? What will happen to him if something happens to your Mom and me? We will think and talk about it, and you can answer if and how you will be your brother's keeper. This is one of the most important things we can do as a family.

- Write out an idea list in your journal over ways that you can look out for others and have the best interest of all of your neighbors at heart with your daily activities. Little things, big things, include them all. If one or more truly strike you as being important, see how you can implement them into your life.

- Write out your code of conduct and the "rules" you have for yourself in life. If it's doing the kind act every day, or swearing to limit gossip, or only saying things that you'd not be ashamed that someone else heard. Write it out as "Rules of Aly," or "Mandy," or, "Happy Reader of this Book." Consider it, and revisit it. I like to print things out, laminate them and put them in spots I see.

- Evangelize this. It's your actions that make a difference to others and in the world. Can you pass this on to more than one person? Do it. Teach it, and as long as it makes sense to you, try to spread this concept to others.

Notes, thoughts, and intentions.

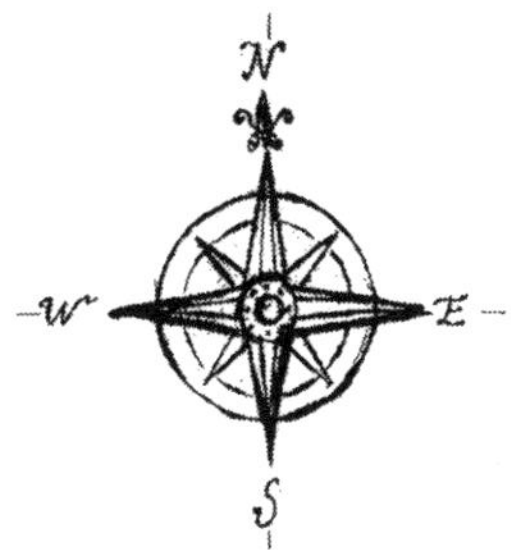

100. Ask Yourself The Important Questions.

It's a very good practice to ask these of yourself, and to answer them. I encourage you to pull out your journal and get to these.

1. Do I truly LOVE myself?
2. Do I have an Epic vision for my life?
3. Am I on a hero's journey?
4. Am I being "True to myself"?
5. What am I doing to help others on this planet?
6. Am I spending enough quality time with my loved ones?
7. Am I experiencing JOY regularly with my life now?
8. Am I living up to my potential—or at least close to it?
9. Do I enjoy what I do as a career?
10. What is my NEXT STEP in life/Something that I'm working towards?

11. What are the things I want to do before I die? "Bucket List"

12. Would my 10-year-old self be proud of me today?

13. What would be said at my funeral if it were held next month?

14. Have I prepared for my family in case of my death?

15. Am I proud of what I do each day?

16. If I could do anything, and be assured of its success—what would that be?

17. Who are the people that I want most in my everyday life?

18. Am I currently making myself a better person? How?

19. What am I looking forward to in life right now? Is there enough?

20. What am I "meant," to do while living?

21. Am I glorifying God (the "Universe," if you prefer) through my life and actions?

Notes, thoughts, and intentions.

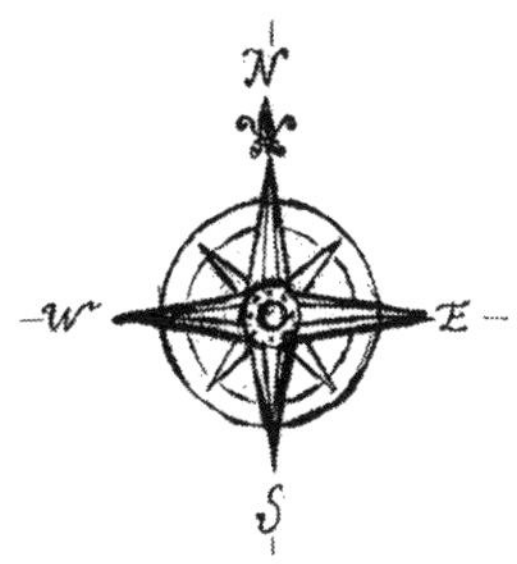

101. Go On With Your Life (The Next Steps).

The end of the book is finally here, and it's over.

I hope you've read this, pondered the ideas, and debated in your mind if each has merit and can be useful in your life. I hope you've questioned them, and honestly that you do disagree with me and can state why. I want you to defend your beliefs, continue to question them, and refine them over time.

The Stoic philosopher Epictetus (you remember him from the lesson on the Stoics, right?) wrote a book called the Enchiridion on Stoic ethical advice. The word 'enchiridion' is Greek for "that which is held in the hand." He meant his book to be at the ready, always ready to help in certain life situations. It's where we get the idea of a handbook.

What I'd like you to do with this book on life lessons is to keep it close when you're going through life. I want it to be ready at hand. I want it to be a comfort and guidance for you. I want it to be my voice to you when you're facing all of the varied situations in life.

Long after I'm gone, I want this book to be a conversation you have with me.

When you're facing fear in the face, break it open and consult the chapter, "Feel the Fear and Do it Anyways."

When you're thinking of getting a new career or job, look up the lesson, "Find the Magic Spot in Your Job or Career," and "Learn How to Get ANY Job You Want." Others like "Shadow Someone That's Doing What You Want to Do at a High Level," and "Do More Than You're Paid to Do," would be helpful, too.

I know I haven't covered everything, but I've touched on a lot. I hope and pray that these lessons will help you in nearly every area of your great, big, fulfilling, and rewarding lives.

Please keep this at hand. Please take the time to write your notes on the different sections. Reason out where you disagree and put in your own reasons. If you give this book to someone else, hoping to help them, please write out the messages you'd like them to know in the lessons. Use it to maintain a dialogue and to discuss important ideas with those you love.

Now, I encourage you to continue this journey. Go on and read the great books, listen to the great lectures, and contemplate—and then put into action the important ideas.

I've put together many courses and ideas for you at LifeLessons.Academy to go much deeper into many of these ideas and more that I'd like you to check out and consider.

Zig Ziglar said,

"People often say that motivation doesn't last. Well, neither does bathing—that's why we recommend it daily."

Well, the thoughts and ideas of these lessons will often make sense, and you'll do them… for a while.

Then the inevitable overwhelm of life can get in the way, and you'll forget some of the concepts you love and appreciate. You'll end up not doing the things you know can improve your life, and make things better for yourself and your loved ones.

That's one of the reasons I wanted to do courses based on this information. I wanted to go deeper on the concepts. I wanted to show you HOW they can be implemented into your life versus simply remaining lifeless and unvisited on paper (or your electronic screen).

So, to keep this from happening, I suggest that you re-read this book and spend some time on each section. Spend a few days or a week on each and work on the ideas and the advice in practice sections earnestly. If you go over one each week, you'll have nearly two years' worth of study and improvement in your life at any given time.

Or, alternately, you can go to LifeLessons.Academy and watch the courses there, take notes, and work on implementing these ideas into your life.

Preferably, you'll do both.

I can promise you that just the pursuit of self-development and getting better will make you a better person. That's even without all of the knowledge and skills you can get from the lessons in each. If you take this suggestion, you'll see that your life will continually improve and become the work of art you deserve.

You can get started on this journey by visiting, LifeLessonsBonus.com to get your free course on "Designing and Executing Your Ideal Week," to get help your time scheduled in the right way.

I invested all of my time and effort into this to help make your life better. When I was on that stretcher in California after my stroke wondering if I had told you everything I needed to tell you—that scared me into doing this.

I hope you understand just how loved you are.

I hope you understand what a SPECTACULAR creation of God you are.

I hope you understand that you are always worthy.

I hope you understand that you are always deserving of the very best in life.

I hope you know that I will always be with you, in life or death looking after you and always wanting the best for you.

You are every hope I've ever had. You are every dream I've ever dreamed. You are the best of me and more.

I. Love. You.

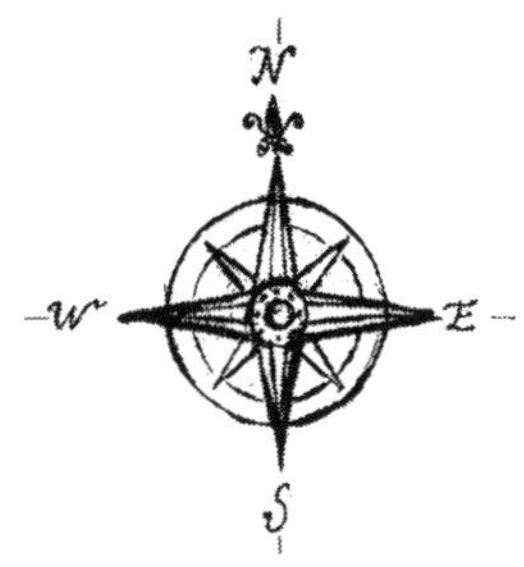

About the Author

First and foremost, Chip Franks is husband to Laura Franks, and father to Mandy, Aly, and Alec Franks.

He was born at the crossroads of the world in Killeen, Texas on June 1st, 1972. A warm day, and not coincidentally the day Picasso finished his last painting.

He was a Marine brat, and as the product of a broken home, he attended a total of 20 schools while growing up in life, to include a stint in college in Brussels, Belgium.

He is an entrepreneur at heart: from selling calendars door-to-door as young boy, selling monster stories to friends in Miss Robinson's class in third grade (his first paid writing gig!), to an illegal nunchakus operation in the 6th grade, selling self-made study guides in 9th grade, a lawn mowing business throughout high school, selling books door-to-door for 80 hours a week while in college for two Summers, and finally by building (and ultimately selling) a real estate and property management company after 20 years as a real estate broker.

He has spoken on the same stages at events with Tony

Robbins, Peter Diamandis, Lewis Howes, Daymond John, and Simon Sinek.

He's read over 1,000 books. He is a podcast junkie, and a consummate student of life with mentors such as Robbins, Jim Rohn, Henry David Thoreau, Seneca and Joseph Campbell.

Most importantly to you reading this--he specializes in providing easily actionable ways to improve life. You can find out much more, and get pretty dang amazing free resources on the ideas in this book at ChipFranks.com. If you'd like to be notified when more books are released, make sure to sign up for his extra-special email list on the page.

Can you help me feed my obviously starving children?

If you enjoyed this book, and even if you didn't, can you leave your honest (5-star haha!) review on Amazon.com for it please?

Reviews from verified purchasers help this get seen by more people looking for something like this. Honestly, it helps to sell more books and hopefully change more lives. You can even consider it your kind act of the day discussed in the book!

Please let me know in the review what you liked specifically, either the particular lesson number or anything else.

I truly appreciate you reading this book, and applying the lessons inside.

To leave a review, you can visit Amazon directly, or to make it even easier and to get access to your bonus material from the book, login to:

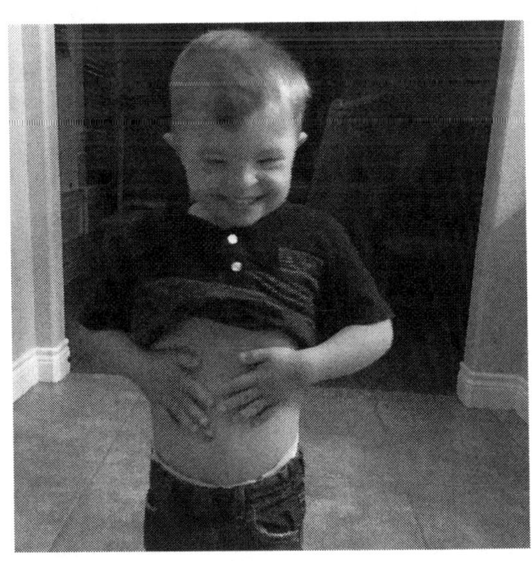

13052597R00418

Made in the USA
Lexington, KY
27 October 2018